Outcomes of Psychoanalytic Treatment

Other titles in the Whurr Series in Psychoanalysis

KLEINIAN THEORY
Edited by Catalina Bronstein

PSYCHOANALYSIS, SCIENCE AND MASCULINITY
Karl Figlio

ORGANISATIONS, ANXIETY AND DEFENCE
Edited by Bob Hinshelwood and Marco Chiesa

A LANGUAGE FOR PSYCHOSIS
Edited by Paul Williams

Outcomes of Psychoanalytic Treatment

Perspectives for Therapists and Researchers

Edited by

MARIANNE LEUZINGER-BOHLEBER PHD,
University of Kassel, Germany

MARY TARGET PHD,
University of London

Routledge
Taylor & Francis Group
New York London

OUTCOMES OF PSYCHOANALYTIC TREATMENT

First published 2002
by BRUNNER-ROUTLEDGE

Published 2017 by Routledge,
711 Third Avenue, New York, NY 10017, USA
2 Park Square, Milton Park, Abingdon, Oxon OX14 4RN

First issued in hardback 2017

Routledge is an imprint of the Taylor & Francis Group, an informa business

A CIP catalog record for this book is available from the British Library.

Library of Congress Cataloging-in-Publication Data

ISBN 13: 978-0-4159-3524-1 (pbk)
ISBN 13: 978-1-1384-6236-6 (hbk)

Contents

Contributors

Cornelia Albani MD, Clinic for Psychotherapy and Psychosomatic Medicine, University Hospital Leipzig.
Folkert Beenen PhD, Research Director, Dutch Psychoanalytic Institute (NPI), Amsterdam.
Manfred E Beutel MD, Dipl-Psych, Justus-Liebig-Universität, Gießen.
Gerd Blaser, Dipl-Psych, Dr rer biol hum, University Hospital Leipzig.
Dieter Bürgin MD, University Hospital for Child and Adolescent Psychiatry, Basel.
Reiner Dilg, Dipl-Psych, Benjamin Franklin Hospital, Berlin.
Anna Ursula Dreher PhD, Frankfurt am Main.
Markus Fäh PhD, Zürich.
Peter Fonagy PhD, FBA, University College London and Menninger Clinic, Kansas. Chair, IPA Research Committee (Empirical Research).
Norbert Freedman, SUNY Downstate Medical Center, Brooklyn, New York.
Tilman Grande PhD, University Hospital, Heidelberg.
Dorothea Huber PhD, MD, Institute for Psychosomatic Medicine, Psychotherapy and Medical Psychology, Munich.
Uwe Jacobs PhD, Wright Institute, Berkeley, San Francisco.
Thorsten Jakobsen Dipl-Psych, University Hospital, Heidelberg University.
Enrico E Jones PhD, University of California, Berkeley.
Horst Kächele MD, University Hospital Ulm.
Wolfram Keller MD, Theodor Wenzel Hospital, Berlin.
Günther Klug MD, City Hospital in Munich-Harlaching.
Otto F Kernberg MD, Weill Cornell Medical College; former President, International Psychoanalytic Association.
Marianne Leuzinger-Bohleber PhD, University of Kassel. Chair, IPA Research Committee (Conceptual Research).
Stavros Mentzos MD, University Hospital, Frankfurt am Main.

Claudia Oberbracht Dipl-Psych, University Hospital, Heidelberg.
Claudia Pauli-Magnus PhD, University Hospital, Heidelberg.
Michael von Rad MD, City Hospital Munich-Harlaching.
Markus Rasting Dipl-Psych, Justus-Liebig-Universität, Gießen.
Robert Rohner PhD, Brandenburg Hospital, Berlin-Wandlitz.
Gerd Rudolf MD, University Hospital, Heidelberg.
Bernhard Rüger, University of Munich.
Rolf Sandell PhD, Linköping University.
Sabine Stehle, Dipl-Psych, Benjamin Franklin Hospital, Berlin.
Hans Henning Studt MD, Benjamin Franklin Hospital, Berlin.
Ulrich Stuhr PhD, Dipl-Psychologe, University Hospital Hamburg-Eppendorf.
Mary Target PhD, University College London. Chair, Research Committee, British Psychoanalytical Society. Member, IPA Research Committee (Conceptual Research).
Helmut Thomä MD, University Hospital Ulm.
Winfrid Trimborn MD, Training analyst and past President of the German Analytic Association.
Robert S Wallerstein MD, University of California School of Medicine, San Francisco.
Gisela Westhoff PhD, Benjamin Franklin Hospital, Berlin.
Stefanie Wilke PhD, University Hospital, Heidelberg.

Series foreword

After the first hundred years of its history, psychoanalysis has matured into a serious, independent intellectual tradition, which has notably retained its capacity to challenge established truths in most areas of our culture. The biological psychiatrist of today is called to task by psychoanalysis, as was the specialist in nervous diseases of Freud's time, in early twentieth century Vienna. Today's cultural commentators, whether for or against psychoanalytic ideas, are forced to pay attention to considerations of unconscious motivation, defences, early childhood experience and the myriad other discoveries which psychoanalysts brought to 20th century culture. Above all, psychoanalytic ideas have spawned an approach to the treatment of mental disorders, psychodynamic psychotherapy, which has become established in most countries, at least in the Western world.

Little wonder that psychoanalytic thinking continues to face detractors, individuals who dispute its epistemology and its conceptual and clinical claims. While disappointing in one way, this is a sign that psychoanalysis may be unique in its capacity to challenge and provoke. Why should this be? Psychoanalysis is unrivalled in the depth of its questioning of human motivation, and whether its answers are right or wrong, the epistemology of psychoanalysis allows it to confront the most difficult problems of human experience. Paradoxically, our new understanding concerning the physical basis of our existence – our genes, nervous systems and endocrine functioning – rather than finally displacing psychoanalysis, has created a pressing need for a complementary discipline which considers the memories, desires and meanings which are beginning to be recognised as influencing human adaptation even at the biological level. How else, other than through the study of subjective experience, will we understand the expression of the individual's biological destiny, within the social environment?

It is not surprising, then, that psychoanalysis continues to attract some of the liveliest intellects in our culture. These individuals are by no means all psychoanalytic clinicians, or psychotherapists. They are distinguished scholars in an almost bewildering range of disciplines, from the study of mental disorders with their biological determinants to the disciplines of literature, art, philosophy and history. There will always be a need to explicate the meaning of experience. Psychoanalysis, with its commitment to understanding subjectivity, is in a premier position to fulfil this intellectual and human task. We are not surprised at the upsurge of interest in psychoanalytic studies in universities in many countries. The books in this series are aimed at addressing the same intellectual curiosity that has made these educational projects so successful.

We are proud that the Whurr Series in Psychoanalysis has been able to attract some of the most interesting and creative minds in the field. Our commitment is to no specific orientation, to no particular professional group, but to the intellectual challenge to explore the questions of meaning and interpretation systematically, and in a scholarly way. Nevertheless, we would be glad if this series particularly spoke to the psychotherapeutic community, to those individuals who use their own minds and humanity to help others in distress.

Our focus in this series is to communicate the intellectual excitement which we feel about the past, present and future of psychoanalytic ideas. We hope that our work with the authors and editors in the series will help to make these ideas accessible to an ever-increasing and worldwide group of students, scholars and practitioners.

Peter Fonagy
Mary Target
University College London

Preface

When Livingstone crossed the Sahara he wondered why his African guides very often used to stop walking and stand still. When he asked them why they did this, they replied 'we want to give our souls a chance to catch up'.

These African guides seem to express a human wisdom well known to psychoanalysts: the soul needs its own time to move, to change and to heal its wounds. This wisdom and our clinical knowledge are in opposition to a *Zeitgeist* assuming that therapeutic changes should take place within short periods of time, as efficiently, straightforwardly and cheaply as possible. Thus, on both sides of the Atlantic Ocean, the pressure has grown to substantiate the clinical experience that stable psychic change is achieved by intensive and long-lasting psychoanalyses and psychoanalytic treatments. Many clinicians and researchers are convinced that - for professional and ethical reasons - it is important to maintain the possibility of offering long-term treatments, particularly to severely ill patients. Thus some of them have taken up the challenge to empirically support their clinical observations.

Of course the methodological and epistemological problems of studying long-term treatments are much more difficult than those of assessing short-term therapies. Nevertheless a number of sophisticated studies have been performed during recent years or are under way, as different European and American research groups will report in this volume. We hope that their findings may contribute to a recognition that saving time and money should not be the only criteria for evaluating psychotherapies, which would risk the loss of a human way to deal with psychic pain in our countries.

We thank all the authors for contributing to this volume and for their engagement and efforts in this difficult area of empirical research. We thank Julian Target for editing the German manuscript with great competence and admirable linguistic skills. Finally, the publication of this volume would not have been possible without the careful and competent work of Ute Ochtendung, mailing the different versions of the manuscripts to the authors all over the world, formatting the texts skilfully and even drawing beautiful graphs. The final stages of preparation were greatly helped by the careful work of Dr Liz Allison.

We are grateful that the Deutsche Forschungsgemeinschaft supported the Conference in Hamburg (October 1999) where most of the chapters in this volume were presented. We also thank the German Psychoanalytical Association (DPV) and the Research Advisory Board of the International Psychoanalytic Association (IPA), which helped to finance the preparation of this book.

Marianne Leuzinger-Bohleber
Mary Target
Frankfurt/London, November 2001

Chapter 1
Introductory remarks

MARIANNE LEUZINGER-BOHLEBER, MARY TARGET

The book is based on a three-day conference held in Hamburg in October 1999. It was sponsored by the Deutsche Forschungsgemeinschaft (DFG), the official foundation for research in Germany. The conference was organized by members of the research committee of the German Psychoanalytical Association (DPV), who also presented a large, representative follow-up study of long-term psychoanalytic treatments at the conference. It was an international meeting, with participants from Scandinavia, Switzerland, the Netherlands, England and the US. The contributors bridged the clinical and the empirical. In this volume, the authors hope to show the (often highly sceptical) wider clinical community that the clinical results of analytic work can indeed be demonstrated through appropriate (extra-clinical) research procedures. Much attention is given not only to findings but also to methodology, epistemological questions and the rules of evidence. Why are these of such importance?

The pressure to demonstrate treatment outcomes

Recent years have seen increasingly informed media commentaries about psychological treatments in the US and in many European countries. New therapeutic approaches (pharmacotherapy, behavioural and cognitive-behavioural treatments) have received considerable exposure, as have critiques of Freud and psychoanalysis. Perhaps as a result, there is increasing disquiet about the time and expense involved in psychoanalytic treatment. Therefore many patients nowadays prefer shorter therapeutic treatment instead of analysis or long-term psychotherapy.

The common-sense view outside psychoanalytic circles is increasingly that psychoanalysis is no more effective than other forms of treatment - some say less - yet it is far lengthier and more expensive than, for instance, medication or cognitive-behaviour therapy. The traditional view on this within psychoanalysis is that analysts know that their form of treatment is effective and in fact unique in its effects and that there is no need to prove this. For those who think beyond this, there is often a further statement that it would, in any case, be impossible to prove the value of psychoanalysis as the important aspects of both process and outcome are (although clear to analyst and patient) impossible to measure (this is discussed below). However, as outcome studies rapidly accumulate that show the potential of many competing forms of therapy (see Roth and Fonagy, 1996), psychoanalysis and psychoanalytic psychotherapy are - at least in the US, England and some other European countries - at an increasing disadvantage in the struggle for credibility and resources. In addition to this consideration of professional survival, we owe it to our patients, their families and those who may be asked to fund this intensive treatment, to show in what ways and in which cases it benefits patients.

Traditional and current approaches

Initially, the preferred method of reporting and assessing the results of treatment was the clinical case study, a description by the analyst of one or more treated cases. This was Freud's technique for conveying both his theoretical ideas and his technique. For many psychoanalysts Freud's epistemology became paradigmatic, but there have always been dissenting voices within the psychoanalytic community (for example, French, 1952; Meyer, 1993; Moser, 1992; Shapiro, 1994; Tuckett, 1994; Widlöcher, 1994). For psychotherapy researchers and critics of psychoanalysis this method is severely limited. They argue that clinicians choose selected highlights of their cases to illustrate their technique, which is legitimate for illustrating a theoretical or technical point but not as the basis for deriving either (see, for example, Grünbaum, 1984; Meyer, 1993). The approach encourages the author to cite more and more confirmatory illustrations, disregarding instances that are inconsistent.

One of the major problems for psychotherapy researchers is the tension between internal and external validity when developing research strategies. A compromise is required between explanatory power and generalizability. Experimental single-case designs have a role to play here because external validity is less of a problem (Leuzinger-Bohleber, 1987, 1989, 1995; Kazdin, 1994; Stuhr and Deneke, 1993). These studies may offer answers to many questions, such as the usefulness of a treatment, the length of treatment required, the relative impact of treatment on particular aspects of the problem, or the contribution of particular components of treatment. However, there also are major problems: the findings are idiosyncratic to a specific therapeutic dyad, hence generalization remains a problem.

There are many other unresolved questions in psychotherapy research that loom large in psychoanalytic outcome studies. First, and fundamentally, which of the currently used theoretical frameworks (Greenberg and Mitchell, 1983; Fonagy, Target, Steele and Gerber, 1995) should be tested, and what of the well-known loose link between psychoanalytic theories and clinical technique (Kurthen, 1998)? Is psychoanalytic technique, as practised by clinicians, relatively pure, or are most practitioners diluting their methods with other techniques (such as suggestion, medication, even frank reinforcing strategies; Garfield, 1991; Goldfried, 1991)? Can measures of outcome appropriate to other therapeutic approaches, such as cognitive-behaviour therapy, ever be applied to psychoanalytic outcome, or should we have our own measures, losing comparability with studies from other traditions?

The epistemological bases of psychoanalytic research

These questions lead to the heart of epistemological debates on research in psychoanalysis, appropriate methodology, the scientific status of psychoanalysis and so on. These debates have a long tradition, especially in France and Germany where an intensive exchange between psychoanalysts and philosophers has taken place (see also the introduction to Part 3). Psychoanalytic research sometimes seems to walk a tightrope between two extremes. On the one hand, promoting exclusively clinical (or hermeneutic) research within the psychoanalytic setting risks withdrawing too much into the psychoanalytic ivory tower and concentrating only on psychoanalytic controversies and discourses. This withdrawal could destroy the relevance of psychoanalysis for medicine and academic psychology, as well as for interdisciplinary dialogue. In the long run it could also reduce creativity and innovation within the discipline. At the other extreme, opening up to empirical and interdisciplinary research creates the danger that quantitative psychoanalytic research applies a methodology unsuitable for the essence of psychoanalysis: unconscious processes, conflicts and fantasies. This might happen because of uncritical identification with an out-of-date 'unified' conceptualization of science and scientific methods (in the German language debate called *Einheitswissenschaft*).

Some leading philosophers of science (such as Hampe, 2000) state that this problem is not unique to psychoanalysis: all contemporary sciences have developed a research methodology specific to their subject and have developed their own criteria of scientific quality and 'truth'. Criteria for one discipline cannot easily, in the spirit of 'unified science', be transferred to others. Criteria for a good experiment in physics are not the same as for an ethological observation, or for 'scientific' analysis of a piece of modern music, although, of course, all sciences do have certain commonalities compared with, for instance, religion or common sense. Different disciplines have their own methodologies, procedures for systematization, while sharing overall, basic aims such as precision, completeness, representativeness, sharp contrasts (*Kontrastschärfe*), transparency of observation and hypothesis testing. Hence, psychoanalytic research has to be a unique way of finding out about unconscious processes, conflicts and fantasies. Submitting to a 'unified' understanding of science would make psychoanalysis just one of many medical disciplines. Its idiosyncrasy (the 'backbone of Freud', as Alfred Lorenzer (1985) described it) is what makes psychoanalysis interesting, and uncomfortable in the best sense of the word, not only for public intellectual discourse but also for our colleagues in other disciplines.

Not only in the English speaking countries but also in Germany and Switzerland, in recent years, the *Zeitgeist* we have described has thrown doubt on psychoanalysis as a science, together with its outcomes and cost effectiveness. However, several substantial papers have argued that some of the critiques in Germany (disputing the objectivity, reliability and validity of clinical research) were less motivated by serious academic concern than by political interests (see, for example, Fäh and Fischer, 1998; Leuzinger-Bohleber, 1995; Rüger, 1994, 1996a, b; Tschuschke, Heckrath and Tress, 1997). When resources in the mental health systems are limited, the claim (far less substantiated than one might think) that quicker and cheaper psychotherapeutic methods of treating psychic illness are more scientific and effective, is of course highly seductive for the mental-health and insurance companies.

Psychoanalysts in these countries therefore feel under strong pressure to produce 'hard, objective', quantitative data. As important as the attempt to respond to this pressure is in our eyes, we nevertheless should not forget that highly plausible arguments against a narrow understanding of measurable, objective truth in a field like psychoanalysis were already advanced during the debate on 'positivism' in the 1950s and, in a different way, again in the 1960s and 1970s. It is therefore curious, at least in the eyes of some contemporary philosophers of science, to find that the debate has resurfaced. These philosophers considered 'unified science', with which these arguments were connected, to have been definitively discredited in the first round of debate. Hampe (2000) writes in the introduction to a book dedicated to these questions 'I do not know any serious contemporary philosopher who still argues for a unified understanding of science' (p. 3). Instead, most of the challenging current debates concentrate on a deeper understanding of the pluralism in different sciences, their specific theoretical and methodological approaches and truth criteria. At the same time all scientific disciplines share the aim of disciplined reasoning and systematic discovery. According to Hampe's well-developed arguments (which unfortunately cannot be reproduced here) it seems wise for psychoanalysis to insist, publicly and scientifically (even in the context of medicine and academic psychology), on the specificity of its form of knowledge and research methodology: the basic research method of psychoanalysis developed within the clinical setting.

The application of this clinical research in an extra-clinical context creates a major challenge, as many research groups in this book will discuss. Some of them relate psychoanalytic research methods to qualitative instruments, which seem to allow psychoanalytic phenomena to be approached from outside the clinical perspective. The tradition of qualitative research instruments is growing across the social sciences worldwide. The aim of the approach has been defined as follows:

> to understand and represent the experiences and actions of people as they encounter, engage, and live through situations. In qualitative research, the researcher attempts to develop understandings of the phenomena under study, based as much as possible on the perspective of those being studied. Qualitative researchers accept that it is impossible to set aside one's own perspective totally (and do not claim to). Nevertheless, they believe that their self-reflective attempts to 'bracket' existing theory and their own values allow them to understand and represent their informants' experiences and actions more adequately than would otherwise be possible.
>
> (Elliott, Fischer and Rennie, 1999: 216)

These authors defined specific criteria for good qualitative research. Among these are owning one's perspective - that is, making clear the personal, intellectual and professional allegiances of the investigators; the grounding of emerging hypotheses in examples; provision of credibility checks, such as triangulation; coherence. Through these processes, the results of several different forms of data and of analysis are drawn together into a net of meaning that has structural strength.

Quantitative and qualitative paradigms tend to be set up as rival methodologies, with attendant academic cultural baggage, which can make the opposition quite fierce. We hope that this volume will go some way towards discouraging such a simplistic polarization. However, we need to remember that neither qualitative nor quantitative methods can actually measure unconscious processes, or the change in these, as psychoanalytic instruments try to do. The issue is what type of description to use for the observable phenomena. Nevertheless, in extra-clinical research qualitative data, framed in terms closer to subjective experience, make it much easier for us to make the inferences about unconscious processes. One may then need procedures, similar to those in quantitative research, for enhancing reliability and validity, such as the use of independent raters and clear definitions. The studies in this book, especially the large DPV study, suggest that these procedures can be introduced without moving us too far from the clinical standpoint, and can be compared critically to results gained by applying psychoanalytic methods themselves to the same clinical material.

One problem that psychologists have in differentiating these methods is that there is generally a vital qualitative stage in quantitative clinical research. To take just one example, Enrico Jones's Q-sort for psychotherapy process (used in some of the studies included in this volume) involves the systematization of qualitative judgements, which then lends itself to either quantitative analysis or clinically rich descriptions of individual themes.

'Field work', in psychoanalysis, centres on intensive clinical work with individual patients in the psychoanalytical situation, because only in this clearly structured setting is it possible for analyst and analysand to observe manifestations of the unconscious in a systematic way and to test hypotheses. The setting and the specific research method (for example, observing and interpreting transference and countertransference reactions, dreams, slips of the tongue and so forth) therefore allow study of the subject of psychoanalysis, unconscious processes, and to tolerate the (often otherwise unbearable) thoughts and feelings that are connected with these. Alternative scientific research methods can, in contrast, be used by the researcher as a defence against the unconscious, complex phenomena to be studied (Devereux, 1967). All psychoanalytic insights, theories and basic concepts, which may later be tested empirically, are originally based in such clinical experience and research (see, for example, Sandler and Dreher, 1996).

But, of course, Peter Fonagy (Fonagy et al., 1999) is right in pointing out that not every clinician is automatically a researcher. Not every surgeon regards himself as a researcher just because he practises surgery. Let us briefly illustrate this point further, using a modified graph by Ulrich Moser (1992), a Swiss analyst and professor of clinical psychology who tried to integrate clinical and extra-clinical research within psychoanalysis (see Figure 1.1).

- The left side of the chart shows that intensive clinical experiences with individual patients are the basis for our clinical and theoretical understanding of unconscious processes within a psychoanalytic framework. The spiralling process of scientific discovery illustrates the critique of the paradigm of logical empiricism: theory and empirical observation cannot be separated; they determine each other.
- Discoveries and hypotheses, collected within the psychoanalytic situation, can afterwards become the subjects of clinical or extra-clinical research. Clinical researchers also have to think systematically and

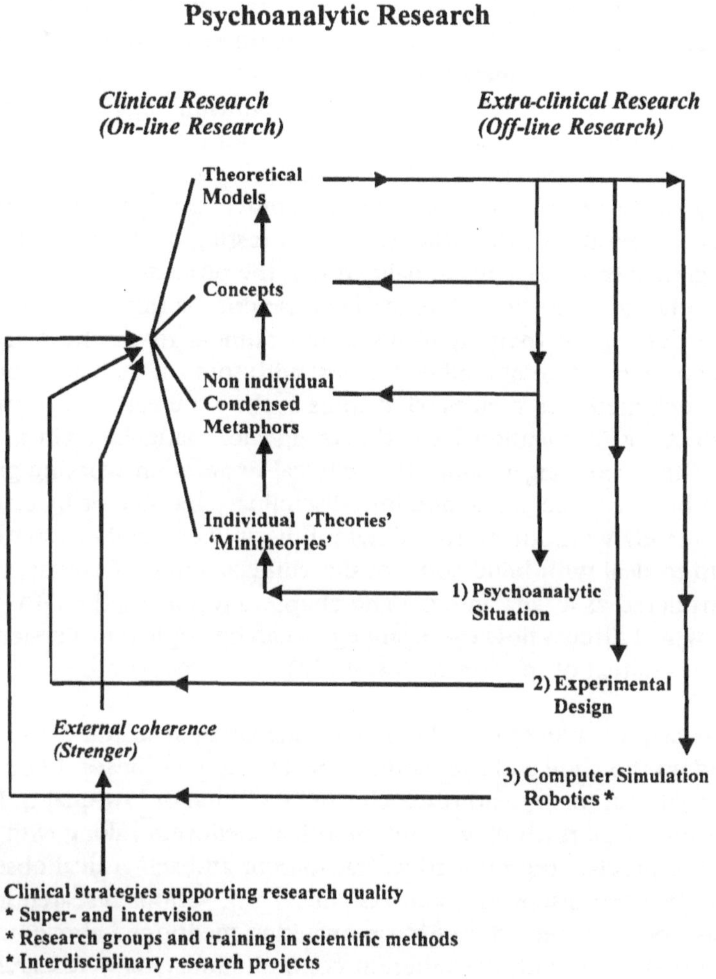

Figure 1.1. Clinical and extra-clinical research in psychoanalysis.

*Note: Moser (1992) mentions a third possibility of systematic, extra-clinical research in psychoanalysis: the application of computer simulation to test the logic, the consistency and the precision of psychoanalytic models (e.g. on defence mechanisms, dreams etc. - see Moser and von Zeppelin, 1991).

self-critically about their observations, testing them again and again in new clinical situations, then comparing them with those described in the psychoanalytical literature, and finally writing them down clearly and strictly. Extra-clinical researchers use material secondary to the clinical situation (for example, reports by the patient or the analyst, tapes, or videos) for their cycles of research, again in a process of critical self-reflection after the analytic sessions.

- The processes of developing a deeper understanding, the successive steps of generalization, are more or less the same for the clinical as well as for the extra-clinical researcher. Both try to discipline their experiences systematically, to be precise, complete, representative, transparent and so forth in their observations, their theorizing and testing of their hypotheses. The difference is not mainly in quality but in the procedure used in testing the hypotheses. Extra-clinical researchers use criteria from empirical research in order to test their hypotheses but clinical researchers also have a spectrum of different methods to deal with some of the limitations of their research methods, such as blind spots in their subjective observations and deductions. To mention a few: the struggle for triangulation in supervision, in critical exchanges with other clinical experts, in working groups but also by a strict scientific and interdisciplinary training or by co-operating intensively with others from different disciplines. All these strategies may help to deal with blind spots of the clinicians but, of course, cannot be considered as a 'guarantee'. (The chapters reporting the DPV follow-up study will discuss how these strategies can be applied in a systematic way in the context of an extra-clinical study.)

In other words: scientific quality in psychoanalytic research does not simply depend on the choice of the method for testing hypotheses. Clinical as well as extra-clinical (empirical) research can be of high or low quality. In clinical and extra-clinical research we find uncritical 'believers', along with scientists collecting precise, representative, transparent and self-critical observations, which offer real discoveries and insights. Thus, serious research in psychoanalysis does not deny the tightrope walking mentioned above but tries to engage rigorously with the inherent contradictions. Many researchers who have contributed to this book have worked in this spirit, although they have found quite different solutions and paths through the labyrinths of clinical and empirical research. All share a common interest: the engagement with psychoanalysis and the hope that psychoanalysis will flourish in the future, not isolated from the public and academic community but contributing to a deeper understanding of central dimensions of human beings: their unconscious fantasies and conflicts. Therefore they take up the challenge connected with the *Zeitgeist* to defend their approach.

This concern for the future of psychoanalysis might be one reason why the authors of this volume chose to dedicate their efforts to studying the heart of psychoanalytic practice: psychoanalyses and psychoanalytic long-term psychotherapies and not (which would have been much easier from a methodological point of view) exclusively psychoanalytic short-term psychotherapies. As, for instance, Wallerstein elaborates in his chapter in this volume, these contemporary researchers carry on a long tradition within psychoanalysis: despite the complex and difficult methodological problems that have been acknowledged, some of the most famous studies in the field of psychotherapy research have been dedicated to long-term therapies and were performed by analysts (see also Fonagy et al., 1999; Leuzinger-Bohleber and Stuhr, 1997). As Wallerstein describes, the research methods and instruments have been much improved during the last hundred years (and particularly the last 25 years), one reason why many very sophisticated studies on psychoanalytical long-term therapies are going on at the moment.

The authors of this volume agree that sophisticated empirical research is of vital concern to all psychoanalytic psychotherapies and psychotherapists, in Europe, the US and Latin America. This concern centres on how long-term psychoanalytic treatment helps shape patients' lives. Does it leave its mark not only during treatment but also after termination? Does it mainly affect symptoms, or also quality of life, object relations and the ability to work creatively? And how does it achieve its results?

This volume also deals with theoretical questions concerning the validity of the analytic model, practical implications for technique and clinical decision making, and economic issues important to the health care community at large. We have been influenced by economic and political developments in Europe, where national health insurance benefits have come under increased scrutiny, and in the US where managed care prevails. These issues affect all practitioners of psychoanalytic therapies, regardless of particular theoretical preference. Finally, the issues posed are relevant to the younger generation of professionals who may consider a career in psychoanalysis. We hope that the demonstration of the results of long-term analytic treatment will draw together the psychoanalytic communities on both sides of the Atlantic.

This volume contains four parts.

Part 1 is entitled 'Long-term treatment in the context of contemporary discussions'. In the first contribution Anna Ursula Dreher (Frankfurt) summarizes a book that she wrote with Joseph Sandler, one of the best-known theoreticians of psychoanalysis: *What do Psychoanalysts Want?* Her chapter was the theoretical introduction to the above-mentioned international conference 'Psychoanalysis and psychoanalytic long-term psychotherapies – a challenge for clinical and empirical researchers' in Hamburg. Her chapter illustrates the state of pluralism in psychoanalysis today and the resulting rich and controversial theoretical discussions. The next chapter by Robert S Wallerstein, one of the former presidents of the International Psychoanalytical Association (IPA) and one of the most experienced psychoanalytic researchers, illustrates this. He gives an excellent overview of psychotherapy research and opens up the horizon for the subsequent contributions. Peter Fonagy (London), co-chair of the Research Committee of the IPA, adds a political perspective in his discussion of the current debate on evidence-based medicine.

In Part 2, 'Long-term psychoanalytic therapies: German studies', we give an overview of the research activities of different groups of psychoanalysts in this country.

The first subsection contains clinical and theoretical studies. Winfrid Trimborn, the former president of the German Psychoanalytical Association (DPV), reports on a psychoanalysis with an adolescent patient struggling for self-healing and identity. He gives a vivid impression of 'what psychoanalysts do' in their everyday clinical practice. These intensive clinical experiences with severely disturbed patients are the 'normal data' of psychoanalysis gained by special 'naturalistic field research' comparable, for instance, to research done by ethnologists living in a foreign culture for a long time in order to study it thoroughly. In his clinical case report he not only illustrates how important for the suffering of this young woman artist the psychoanalysis proved to be but also how much cost for health insurance had been reduced by this treatment. Stavros Mentzos, one of the best-known experts in treating borderline patients in Germany, tries to combine his clinical experiences with theoretical considerations. He differentiates diagnostically two different groups of borderline patients according to his intensive clinical experiences. His classification could be the subject of further systematic empirical research.

The second subsection, 'The psychoanalytic follow-up study (DPV): a representative naturalistic study of long-term psychoanalytic therapies', summarizes a naturalistic study carried out in this field. After a short overview of the aims and the design by Marianne Leuzinger-Bohleber, Ulrich Stuhr describes, in a theoretical chapter, one of the principal methodological aims of this study: to combine psychoanalytical and non-psychoanalytical, qualitative and quantitative methods and instruments. Bernhard Rüger then summarizes the statistical design. Manfred Beutel and Markus Rasting discuss the retrospective views of former patients as studied in the questionnaires. They also summarize first results concerning the economical aspects of psychoanalytic therapies. Finally, Marianne Leuzinger-Bohleber illustrates some of the clinically relevant results of this empirical study.

The third subsection deals with 'Studying mental health costs of long-term psychotherapies', a subject that has already been touched on in the contribution of Beutel and Rasting in the former section. The authors consider current controversies in the US and in Europe, on the effectiveness and cost effectiveness of long-term treatments. Markus Fäh gives a critical overview of the present political situation and questions the direction mental health is taking in Europe and in the US. Wolfram Keller (Berlin) and his group then report on a recent study done in Berlin showing the reduction of mental health costs after long-term Jungian treatments.

Current 'Prospective studies' in Germany are introduced in the fourth subsection. First the research group of Gerd Rudolf summarizes the Heidelberg-Berlin study on Long-term Psychoanalytic Therapies (PAL). They also report on their different instruments, such as the Operationalized Psychoanalytic Diagnostics (OPD), an instrument that has been developed by different psychoanalytic research groups in Germany during recent years. Dorothea Huber, Günter Klug and Michael von Rad compare, in their Munich Psychotherapy Study, the outcomes of low- and high-frequency psychoanalytic therapies with randomly allocated depressed patients.

Part 4 is entitled 'Follow-up and prospective studies and their findings in other international research centres'. Mary Target (London) reports on a programme of research on the outcome of child and adolescent psychoanalysis carried out at the Anna Freud Centre. She shows how research at the Anna Freud Centre tries to respond to the challenge of evidence-based medicine, and reports a variety of empirical studies over the past 15 years. One is an ongoing, medium-scale follow-up study of child analyses and therapies. Rolf Sandell reports an outstanding contemporary study. His methodologically highly sophisticated study was able to show, for instance, that intensive psychoanalyses are superior to low-frequency treatments, and that this gap increases after termination. This research illustrates how interesting a combination of follow-up studies and prospective studies can be. A similar approach is reported in Norbert Freedman's chapter, which summarizes the extensive experiences with empirical research on psychoanalytical long-term psychotherapies done at the Institute for Psychoanalytical Training and Research (IPTAR) in mid-Manhattan. He shows the relevance of both frequency and duration of treatment, observed both during and after psychoanalytic psychotherapy. Enrico Jones has made a highly original contribution using Q-Sort methodology, identifying facilitating and obstructive aspects of the treatment process. As mentioned earlier, his work is an example of how one may combine qualitative and quantitative research because his single case studies are examined by clinical as well as by statistical methods. Cornelia Albani, Horst Kächele and their research group have applied Jones's methodology. In addition, they give an overview on process research and use an example from the rich research tradition of Ulm and Stuttgart (for a long time a centre of officially supported psychoanalytical research).

In Part 4, 'Concluding reflections', the authors open up the horizon of future clinical and empirical research in psychoanalysis. Folkert Beenen, himself a clinical and empirical researcher for several years, ironically characterizes the situation of psychoanalysts carrying out research. He wryly summarizes some of the methodological problems that were discussed at the Hamburg conference from the perspectives of the researchers themselves. Dieter Bürgin (Basel), an experienced psychoanalyst and empirical researcher in Switzerland, gives a theoretical conclusion to the presentations of the book, comparing the 'double life' of psychoanalysts involved in research with birds that again and again turn into fishes (as in an Escher painting). Finally, Otto Kernberg, then president of the International Psychoanalytical Association, outlines his view of future political developments of psychoanalysis as a humanistic and scientific perspective on the twenty-first century.

References

Devereux G (1967) Angst und Methode in den Verhaltenswissenschaften. München: Hanser.

Elliott R, Fischer CT, Rennie DL (1999) Evolving guidelines for publication of qualitative research studies in psychology and related fields. British Journal of Clinical Psychology 38(3): 215–29.

Fäh M, Fischer G (eds) (1998) Sinn und Unsinn in der Psychotherapieforschung. Gießen: Psychosozial-Verlag.

Fonagy P, Kaechele H, Krause R, Jones E, Perron R, Lopez L (1999) An Open Door Review of Outcome Studies in Psychoanalysis. London: International Psychoanalytical Association.

Fonagy P, Target M, Steele M, Gerber A (1995) Psychoanalytic perspectives on developmental psychopathology. In: Cicchetti D, Cohen DJ (eds) Developmental Psychopathology: Theory and Methods. New York: John Wiley & Sons, vol. 1, pp. 504–54.

French TM (1952) The integration of behavior. Vol. II: The Integration Process in Dreams. Chicago: University of Chicago Press.

Garfield SL (1991) Common and specific factors in psychotherapy. Journal of Integrative and Eclectic Psychotherapy 10: 5–13.

Goldfried MR (1991) Research issues in psychotherapy integration. Journal of Psychotherapy Integration 1: 5–25.

Greenberg JR, Mitchell SA (1983) Object Relations in Psychoanalytic Theory. Cambridge, MA: Harvard University Press.

Grünbaum A (1984) The Foundations of Psychoanalysis: A philosophical critique. Berkeley, CA: University of California Press.

Hampe M (2000) Pluralismus der Wissenschaften und die Einheit der Vernunft. In: Hampe M (ed.) 'Die Erfahrungen, die wir machen, widersprechen den Erfahrungen, die wir haben'. Formen der Erfahrung in den Wissenschaften. Berlin: Duncker und Humblot.

Kazdin AE (1994) Psychotherapy for children and adolescents. In: Bergin AE, Garfield SL (eds) Handbook of Psychotherapy and Behaviour Change (4 edn). New York: Wiley, pp. 543–94.

Kurthen M (1998) Intentionalität und Sprachlichkeit in Psychoanalyse und Kognitionswissenschaft. Psyche 52(9/10): 850–83.

Leuzinger-Bohleber M (1987) Veränderung kognitiver Prozesse in Psychoanalysen. Band 1: Eine hypothesengenerierende Einzelfallstudie. Ulm: PSZ Verlag.

Leuzinger-Bohleber M (1989) Veränderung kognitiver Prozesse in Psychoanalysen. Band 2: Fünf aggregierte Einzelfallstudien. Ulm: PSZ Verlag.

Leuzinger-Bohleber M (1995) Die Einzelfallstudie als psychoanalytisches Forschungsinstrument. Psyche 49(5): 434–81.

Leuzinger-Bohleber M, Stuhr U (eds) (1997) Psychoanalysen im Rückblick. Methoden, Ergebnisse und Perspektiven der neueren Katamneseforschung. Gießen: Psychosozial-Verlag.

Lorenzer A (1985) Spuren und Spurensuche bei Freud. Fragmente 17(18): 160-97.

Meyer AE (1993) Nieder mit der Novelle aus Psychoanalysedarstellung. Hoch lebe die Interaktionsgeschichte. In: Stuhr U, Deneke FW (eds) Die Fallgeschichte. Heidelberg: Ansanger.

Moser U (1992) Two butterflies on my head, or, why have a theory in psychoanalysis? In: Leuzinger-Bohleber M, Schneider H, Pfeifer R (eds) 'Two Butterflies on My Head . . .' Psychoanalysis in the Interdisciplinary Dialogue. New York: Springer, pp. 29-47.

Moser U, von Zeppelin I (eds) (1991) Cognitive-Affective Processes: New ways of psychoanalytic modelling. New York: Springer.

Roth A, Fonagy P (1996) What Works for Whom? A critical review of psychotherapy research. New York: Guilford Press.

Rüger B (1994) Kritische Anmerkungen zu den statistischen Methoden in Grawe, Donati und Bernauer. 'Psychotherapie im Wandel. Von der Konfession zur Profession'. Zeitschrift für Psychosomatische Medizin und Psychoanalyse 40: 368-83.

Rüger B (1996a) Eine Erwiderung auf Grawes Artikel 'Psychotherapie und Statistik im Spannungsfeld zwischen Wissenschaft und Konfession'. Zeitschrift für Klinische Psychologie 25: 61-5.

Rüger B (1996b) Fragen und Anmerkungen zu einigen statistischen Methoden in der Psychotherapieforschung. Psychotherapie Forum 4(3): 135-43.

Sandler J, Dreher AU (1996) What Do Psychoanalysts Want? The problem of aims in psychoanalytic therapy. London: Routledge.

Shapiro T (1994) Psychoanalytic facts: From the editor's desk. International Journal of Psycho-Analysis 75: 1225-32.

Stuhr U, Deneke FW (1993) Die Fallgeschichte. Beiträge zu ihrer Bedeutung als Forschungsinstrument. Heidelberg: Asanger.

Tschuschke V, Heckrath C, Tress W (1997) Zwischen Konfusion und Makulatur: Zum Wert der Berner Psychotherapie-Studie von Grawe, Donati und Bernauer. Göttingen: Vandenhoeck & Ruprecht.

Tuckett D (1994) The conceptualisation and communication of clinical facts in psychoanalysis. International Journal of Psycho-Analysis 75(5/6): 865-70.

Widlöcher D (1994) A case is not a fact. International Journal of Psycho-Analysis 75: 1233-44.

PART 1

LONG-TERM TREATMENT IN THE CONTEXT OF CONTEMPORARY DISCUSSIONS

CHAPTER 2

What are the aims of psychoanalysts?

ANNA URSULA DREHER, TRANSLATION BY EVA RISTL

About the problem of the treatment aim

When asked about the aims of psychoanalysts, a spontaneous answer might be that analysts want to earn money and live happily, like others. Although this chapter deals mainly with those specific aims which analysts have when they practise their profession I shall nonetheless devote just a little time to the topics of happiness and money later on.

Whoever defines treatment aims, and then wishes to determine whether these aims have been met, must establish the relevant criteria. Here one always encounters two problems: which criteria to choose and how to grasp them. I shall take up only the first problem, namely the selection. Of course, criteria that are easy to measure are desirable. But, as we know, measuring is a difficult task in psychoanalysis, where the subject matter is too obstinate, the influencing variables are too manifold – and what is more, we are talking about changes of the inner world, with particular emphasis on its unconscious components.

When formulating the criteria for treatment aims reference is, of course, made to psychoanalytic concepts, like transference, or the superego. But for such concepts – as generally for those in the humanities – final or precise definitions do not exist. Among other reasons this is because such concepts are too complex and are constantly changing depending upon theory and practice. Nevertheless, utmost clarity is definitely useful (for a detailed discussion see Sandler, 1983; Dreher, 2000). An appropriate procedure for such clarification consists first of all in the description of concepts in 'elastic meaning-spaces', and in eliciting those relevant aspects which essentially constitute a concept. Joseph Sandler and I tried to do this in a work on the concept of 'aims in psychoanalytic treatment' and for this purpose we chose a historical approach. This is quite common for psychoanalysts: we wanted to reconstruct how the problem had been dealt with in the long history of psychoanalytic theory and find out what suggestions had been made for its solution up until the mid-1990s (Sandler and Dreher, 1996).

We realized very quickly, however, that this concept of treatment aims, in addition to differing definitions and to ordinary semantic vagueness, presented a difficulty that we did not find in other psychoanalytic concepts to the same degree. The influencing factors that co-determine the meaning of the concept come from very different, but interrelated domains:

- first of all from psychoanalysis itself, from the present state of the discussion in theory and practice, as well as from those specific theoretical language games one feels committed to;
- then from the actual individual and social environment of the persons involved, of analyst and patient, but also from the respective institutional context to which both of them belong (private practice or the clinic, for instance), and thus from legislators, insurance companies, and last but not least from therapy researchers;
- finally from the socio-cultural situation, from the *Zeitgeist,* so to speak.

It is this *Zeitgeist,* which, for example, the sociologist Sennett seeks to grasp when he describes the 'flexible character' as the most successful type in modern capitalism. Such a person is asked to 'be open to change at short notice, to take risks continually, to become ever less dependent on regulations and formal procedures' (Sennett, 1998: 9) - subscribing to the motto: 'No[thing] long term' (1998: 24). Life is typically marked by projects, term contracts, by concentration on the current moment. The outstanding characteristic of this 'flexible human being' is the ability to 'let go of the past and dwell in disorder' (1998: 80, 81); there is no longer coherence in real lives; rather, one experiences a 'drifting' in time, from place to place and from job to job.

Sennett asks: 'How can long-term purposes be pursued in a short-term society? How can durable social relations be sustained? How can a human being develop a narrative of identity and life history in a society composed of episodes and fragments?' (1998: 26). These are questions which analysts and patients alike have to deal with in each treatment. If Sennett's description is correct, his 'flexible human beings' do not want to be burdened with such questions at all and it thus would never occur to them to undergo a long and systematic analytic treatment. This might alienate them from their career and social environment; long-term aims and stability might receive a negative rating, or worse, could be judged as failures.

In society distributional conflicts are harsh, and social inequality is increasing. Flexibility is good for some; however, only a few remain on the road to success. Sennett expounds the dilemma that this very flexibility can weaken those qualities of character 'which bind human beings to one another and furnishes each with a sense of sustainable self' (1998: 27). Feelings of fragmentation and of being lost may appear. A growing inability to understand the world may prompt anxiety about losing control over one's own life. We are familiar with such statements from our patients, with their very often diffuse complaints about detachment or ever changing relationships, about their awkwardness 'in personal matters', or about 'a kind of suffering', which they describe as having no feelings, only the feeling that they are not really being alive. In consequence, a strong wish may arise to gain for themselves more than just non-committal recognition through others, and to gain greater self-esteem, the wish not only to discover something useful, but also - to paraphrase Sennett - something valuable within themselves.

Such wishes - in whatever form they may be grasped by the respective socio-cultural context in which they are to be examined - lead us straight into those criteria of aims that retrospective research must define, and as they have been discussed in psychoanalytic literature since Freud founded psychoanalysis. I would now like to undertake a tour through the history of theory, and on the way sketch out the psychoanalytic knowledge, as well as the conceptual field, which one would have to consider in the discussion of the problem of 'treatment aims'. I thereby use 'psychoanalysis', for the time being, as a general term including all of its variants.

About the history of attempted solutions

In the beginning the aim of a treatment seemed unproblematic for Freud. Physician and patient alike were concerned with the 'healing' of the patient, understood as the dissolution of the symptoms. We are also familiar, however, with Freud's rather pessimistic statement that the aim could only be about the transformation of 'hysterical misery into common unhappiness' (Freud, 1895: 305). And this scepticism as to what can be achieved never left him, as we know. Much later, he laconically remarked that the intention that man should be happy is not included in the plan of Creation (1930).

Freud's formulations on treatment aims changed along with the development of his theory. But he always emphasized the dynamic of inner processes: an analytic treatment should essentially make the unconscious conscious, should put the unconscious into words - with the aim of enabling patients, by removing energy-consuming repressions, to be free to enjoy, to work, and to love. In his structural theory Freud (1923) expressed this in the maxim: 'Where id was, there ego shall be.' Unconscious material should be mobilized, understood and interpreted, and integrated into the conscious ego in order to consolidate its adaptive functions. For Freud this was a laborious process - an 'interminable analysis' (Freud, 1937) - which had to take the ego's abilities as well as its limitations into account. The works of Anna Freud (1936) about the mechanisms of defence and of Heinz Hartmann (1939a) about the problem of adaptation gave these ego changes a central place and formed the basis of 'ego psychology', which after the Second World War was to have a great effect on psychoanalysis.

In those early days, it was, above all, interpretations that should explore the depths of unconscious wishes and fears: creating insight was supposed to make a better understanding of one's history possible, and to support healing. But already in the early 1920s the conviction grew that analysis was not so much an intellectual but rather an affective process centring upon new editions of the patient's old conflicts in the relationship with the analyst. And only through this resuscitation of emotional experiences in such a transference was the ego said to have hitherto hidden material at its disposal - the aim of analysis was the working on, and finally the dissolution of, this transference.

Balint (1935, 1950) systematized these first reflections on treatment aims and already in 1934 distinguished between 'classic' and 'romantic' approaches. 'Classics' would emphasize the increase of insight and would comprehend aims in relation to structural changes, while 'romantics' would stress dynamic and emotional factors - as Balint (1932, 1950) himself did when he stressed the 'new beginning' in the analytic relationship. I think today one would prefer an integration of both positions; the results from psychotherapy research also show that not only interpretation and creating insight, but additionally the experience and quality of the analytic relationship are decisive curative factors. The attention paid in the 1930s to this dynamic strongly emphasized the importance of the patient's relationships with sedimented inner objects, as well as with real objects in the outside world. And until today the improvement of these object relations, as the main aim of analysis, has played an important role, above all in the position that has become known as object relations theory.

However, even that approach, which saw the therapeutic process more from the perspective of the ego, considered the treatment aim more systematically, and as directly related to social reality, and not only to the harmonious interaction of all internal agencies, for instance through mitigation of the superego's strength, as elaborated by Strachey at the famous Marienbad symposium in 1936 (Strachey, 1937). Thus treatment aims were discussed in terms of analytic theory, and also in the context of more general questions of mental health or normality. This expansion of the conceptual field was certainly a consequence of the fact that psychoanalysis wanted to establish itself in different countries and cultures. After Freud's death, and the forced emigration of Continental analysts - due to National Socialist persecution - the analytic centres had shifted to the US and to England. These centres also became the most important point of reference for post-war German psychoanalysis.

Without doubt, this hiatus has had a lasting influence on the history of our theory. As regards treatment aims, it is arguable, for instance, whether the emphasis that American ego psychology placed on the ego's capacity for adaptation was perhaps a reflection of the emigrants' preoccupation with their own adaptation to the new culture. In England - or, to be precise, in London, with its dense population of analysts - the so-called Controversial Discussions had to clear the air. The different points of view found unambiguous expression in a Panel about 'the termination of an analysis' at the end of the 1940s: The 'Classical Freudians' emphasized ego-changes as the aim of analysis (Hoffer, 1950), the 'Kleinians' the achievement of the depressive position (Klein, 1950), and the 'Independents' underlined the importance of the 'new beginning' in the relationship (Balint, 1950).

Those analysts who had emigrated to the US were confronted with the requirement of the American medical system to prove the effectiveness of their method (a requirement voiced again strongly in Germany especially since Grawe published his study in 1993). Thus Knight - as long ago as 1942 - made an aims checklist. With it he intended not only to take into consideration internal changes, but also observable behaviour. Knight suggested five criteria for measuring the success of a treatment - all of them criteria that can be operationalized, which is why quite a number of authors took them as a starting point thereafter:

1. symptomatic recovery, taken as the relative freedom of the patient from disabling fears, inhibitions, or dysfunctions;
2. increased productiveness, with improved investment of aggressive energies in work;
3. improved adjustment to and pleasure in sexual life;
4. less ambivalent relationships;
5. sufficient insight to handle ordinary psychological conflicts and reasonable reality stresses.

In the 1950s, following an increased focus on the analytic treatment of severe personality disorders, modifications of the classical technique, for instance for narcissistic or borderline pathologies, were proposed. And, beginning at this time, there have been very different suggestions about how to name and by what criteria to differentiate these modifications from each other. First of all, the variants were compared with 'pure' analysis, (then dominated by ego-psychology), characterized by its 'standard technique' - interpretation: 'pure' analysis was considered as appropriate only for neurotic patients. These patients were understood as repeating a pathogenic infantile neurosis, presenting itself later in treatment in the form of a transference neurosis. The essential aim of analysis was systematically to work through and dissolve that very transference neurosis. The treatment should lead to a higher level of internal functioning and improved reality testing.

Excursion

There have been, however, up to the present time, a multitude of possible criteria for a differentiation between this 'pure' analysis and its variants: in addition to the specific indication, the manner in which transference is dealt with is thought to be decisive; with some analysts stressing the frequency of the sessions, others considering it important whether the patient is sitting or lying down. According to the 'guidelines for psychotherapy' in Germany (Psychotherapie-Richtlinien) one distinguishes - within the procedures that have an analytic foundation - between 'analytic psychotherapy' (*analytische Psychotherapie*) and 'psychodynamically based psychotherapy' (*tiefenpsychologisch fundierte Psychotherapie*). And of course one can look at this distinction also from the perspective of aims. For each change of theory, and each and every change in method, leads to changed ideas about aims. The 'guidelines for psychotherapy', for instance, name both process and outcome goals:

- concerning treatment process, they distinguish whether regressive processes are used to a limited extent, or whether they are explicitly used, and whether there is transference;
- whether countertransference and resistance are merely observed or actively worked with;
- as to outcome, a distinction is made between a defined conflict resolution and structural change.

At times a definitely evaluative distinction is also made between 'pure' or 'true' and 'untrue' psychoanalysis, and there is also the idea that a 'true' psychoanalysis has no aim, that the process is the aim. Followers of this persuasion will certainly have their difficulties with the 'guidelines for psychotherapy', particularly when they write 'just analysing' on the justification forms for therapy from the insurance companies asking them to give details of their therapeutic plan and the aims of treatment. I would doubt, however, whether the initial lack of an explicit and specified treatment aim justifies the claim that 'true' psychoanalysis is generally aimless, for of course there is, implicitly at least, the non-specific aim of healing or helping, otherwise our whole procedure would not be justifiable at all. It remains to be considered whether this position may lead to a loss of the tension built into Freud's 'conjunction between cure and research', to understand psychoanalysis as a therapeutic method and, at the same time, as a research method to investigate unconscious processes - a tension that runs through our clinical work.

I personally am convinced that we should transcend strict categorical differentiations and black-and-white thinking. Studies show that psychoanalysts all over the world are practising variants of the analytic procedure with success in the interests of the most diverse patients. As analysts we do have, after all, the best qualifications for the whole spectrum: we share a common theoretical and clinical background, and a set of ground rules, and on this basis we can justify modifications and carry them out. Only those who know and master the rules can handle exceptions competently; and can pass on the respective knowledge and experience via training and further education.

Returning to our history, to the 1960s

Outside the dominant ego psychology, independent approaches manifested themselves more strongly: let me quote Winnicott as an example, whose ironical formulation of aims puts - for a change - the distressed analyst centre stage: 'In doing psychoanalysis I aim at: keeping alive; keeping well; keeping awake. I aim at being myself and behaving myself. Having begun an analysis I expect to continue with it, to survive it, and to end it' (Winnicott, 1962: 166). In the writings of that period we find, in addition to highly idealistic aims (expressed in the wake of the widening-scope discussions), more and more formulations that emphasize the limitations of what could be achieved: so it would not necessarily be an aim to eradicate a sexual perversion, but rather to enable a patient to live with the perversion without damaging himself or herself and others. Alternatively, patients should be able to accept some degree of serious damage and learn to live with it; they should develop the ability to mourn - that is, learn to accept that others have things which they might never achieve for themselves. Hartmann had already expressed this rather modest understanding in his formulation that a healthy person must have the capacity to suffer and to be depressed (Hartmann, 1939b: 311).

In the 1960s there were attempts to organize the field and find categories or dimensions with which to describe aims: for instance, that analyst and patient may have different treatment aims, conscious and unconscious ones, and that these aims may change during treatment; that there are proximate and ultimate goals. The ultimate goal, for instance, to convey to the patients a general understanding of themselves and others, or the proximate goal - to be achieved directly in the analytic situation - to help patients independently gain a specific new knowledge about their motives. Wallerstein (1965) suggested polarities between which ideas about aims might oscillate, distinguishing, for example, between idealized, ambitious goals, and limited, attainable goals; or between outcome goals and process goals. Ticho's distinction (1971, 1972) between treatment goals and life goals became an important one. Once the treatment goal - the removal of the causes for a pathological development - has been achieved; once, in Winnicottian terms, the true self has been freed, the patient will be able to reach his life goals. At the start of a treatment these life goals can be highly unrealistic, different from the ones that develop in the course of treatment. If patients become aware of the contradiction between unconscious and conscious aims - and this in itself is a treatment goal - they should be able to define their life goals in a rational way.

At around the same time, towards the end of the 1960s, the widespread public debates included basic discussions in psychoanalysis and psychiatry. The questions addressed were, for instance, whether mental illness should be understood merely as a pathological deviation; who should have the 'monopoly to define' the terms 'normal' and 'deviant', and what the socio-political aim of therapy should actually be. Above all, the 'adaptation to the existing conditions', to the 'establishment', attributed to ego psychology, became a focus of discussion. And gradually other theoretical positions gained ground, which have come to represent the by now familiar pluralism in psychoanalysis.

There were, for instance, the object relations and intersubjective approaches, in which - besides the patient's psychodynamics in terms of internal object relationships - the interactive field has received more systematic attention. Treatment aims are now formulated in terms of change within the inner world of representations, as well as in terms of change of the interactive processes in the analytic situation, but also in relationships outside. Attempts to achieve such a change - for instance in the Kleinian orientation - involved working on the processes of splitting and projection, which would previously have caused disturbances in object relations. The integration of these previously split-off parts, however, is said to make one painfully aware that a separation between self and other really exists, and only if the mourning about this is worked through could the aim of analysis be achieved - namely, a strengthening of the ego and a realistic view of the object. A further well-known approach since the 1970s is Kohut's self psychology and his attempt to describe the success of an analysis as the establishment of self-coherence: meaning that patients should be able to organize themselves in a reliable manner. Kohut's emphasis on introspection and empathy has earned him the criticism of being more a counselling therapist rather than an analyst working on inner conflicts. But what he actually did was emphasize systematic working through, and in this he stressed the role of 'transmuting internalization' - a successive internalization that can lead to structural changes via the continuous interaction of the self with an empathic analytic object (Kohut, 1984).

In the psychoanalytic research of the 1980s this interest - to grasp the aims, systematically and quantitatively if possible, in the context of inner and interpersonal micro-processes - developed further. This is also evident in the recent trends in outcome research where the often-criticized systematic investigation into a single case is gaining renewed attention. Particularly in relation to these 'inner' changes, there are also interesting new findings from the field of brain research, which should merit greater attention today. So, especially findings that there are, apparently, different kinds of organic changes in the brain induced by experience, might prove relevant for our concepts of structural change and schema formation. This could perhaps deepen our understanding of those kinds of changes that can be achieved by short-term interventions, and those that can only be achieved by long-term ones.

If one has a holistic view of the human being, as in psychoanalysis, one naturally always has the often laborious integration of steps of change in mind, and the time that this process takes - which may also extend into the post-analytic phase. In the last couple of years there have been a number of studies which seem to prove this 'deferred action' (*Nachträglichkeit*) for therapeutic processes. Especially for psychoanalysis, which - contrary to behaviour-oriented therapies - works, so to speak 'on the inside', on representations and structures, it comes as no surprise that changes in real behaviour and action can only show later.

A framework for thinking about aims

So much for the historical outline. The simple treatment aim obviously does not exist, but we are dealing much more with a richly faceted problem that analysts have tried to solve in ever new ways. How does one handle a concept that has neither a precise nor a consensual definition? Confronted with such conceptual difficulties one might be tempted to look away hoping that the problems will disappear. What alternatives are there? One could endorse a proposal from the theoretical tradition one feels committed to - some do this, for others it is too narrow. One could try a 'do-it-yourself' approach and create a definition from existing ones - but eclecticism does not satisfy everyone. Or, one could try to extract a common denominator from all proposals - but that probably will not lead to a differentiated view. And lastly, one could try to make one's own new proposal - after all a science should always be open to innovation.

Joseph Sandler and I did not conclude our work with a proposal of our own – which some might have found unsatisfactory. Rather, we attempted to provide assistance for structuring the problem, to give a frame of reference, by working out three perspectives that, in our view, should be considered for each proposal of a treatment aim:

- first of all, the historical-conceptual perspective that says that treatment aims must be regarded in relation to the various theoretical traditions (for instance, Freud's structural model, object relations theories, or self psychology);
- then, the clinical and technical perspective that relates to the issue that during the treatment process the ideas about aims can change – as a result of the continuous conscious and unconscious interaction between both analytic parties (an aspect, by the way, highlighted in particular by the contemporary debates on the intersubjective approach in psychoanalysis); underlining that there are proximate and distant goals, intermediate goals, or process and outcome goals; hereby taking into account the particular needs, but also the limited abilities of patients;
- and lastly, the socio-cultural perspective according to which ideas about mental health and illness are to be seen in their respective historical and societal context; ideas that are assimilated into one's own implicit value systems. And this perspective would also encompass the demand of the health insurers, that is of the legislators, for proof of the effectiveness of the analytic method. And finally, our fees also reflect the value that society places on analytic work.

By specifying these perspectives we intended to see the knowledge psychoanalysis already has about aims preserved, but we also wanted to increase awareness as a prelude to necessary changes. We also had in mind communication with those neighbouring disciplines that, similarly, have something to say about aims.

Conclusions

However you see it, there is no simple solution to the problem of treatment aims, and this is not only due to the manifold language games in which we conceptualize aims, but also due to the different perspectives from which aims can be seen. I had initially remarked that doing conceptual research on aims and recording aims by measuring are two very different activities. One presupposes the other, of course – one cannot attempt to grasp something empirically without at least having a rough idea initially.

But as regards empirical accessibility, something else should be kept in mind: the problem of aims does not only involve descriptive, but also normative questions. Each answer to a question about aims will, explicitly or implicitly, contain a statement about mental health - a concept as complex as that of treatment aim. What health and normality mean in the individual case and what they mean in general is embedded in a far more essential question in our Western culture, namely in that of 'a good life'. And this is also a question about happiness, not only for patients. After all, ancient philosophy actually began with the question about the truth of knowledge but was also concerned with the question of how one should live as a human being. There seems to be no simple answer - Freud has only highlighted another essential facet with his indication of the importance of unconscious factors. The definition of a treatment aim always remains linked with this question about the good life, it therefore always has an evaluative aspect, to which the answer cannot only be descriptive. Last, but not least, this insight triggers methodically more complex procedures as evident, for instance, in the recent follow-up study of the German Psychoanalytic Association (DPV) (this volume).

Sennett's 'flexible character' also wants to live well, but 'well' means above all economically successfully. Sennett draws a pessimistic conclusion when he thinks that the very flexibility, which brings this economic success, 'corrodes' the character in a way for which there is no simple remedy. It would certainly be too shallow to see psychoanalysis as a tested and quick working remedy for the everyday career obstacles of the 'flexible character'; for psychoanalysis has never been suitable for helping people become well-adjusted employees or clever business people. This would be more easily achieved through good coaching. Psychoanalysis is, rather, a procedure that perceives the sufferings and the despair of those people who cannot keep up with this culture of flexibility any more, who wear themselves out between the demand for flexibility and their need for stability. The question remains whether people are actually helped by a technology that keeps them fit and functioning for the next task or whether they would perhaps get more help from what psychoanalysis can truly offer: no reduction to functionality, but a closer listening to the nuances, in order to recognize the 'neurotic misery within common unhappiness' - with the aim to achieve long-term inner change and stability, so that people may experience their lives not as patchwork, but as a coherent story. As said earlier: the implications of this formulation of aims must, of course, also be examined from different perspectives.

It may be that self-reflection and dialogue are old-fashioned, but also possibly modern: Sennett at any rate also sees - in the case of suffering - self-criticism and narration as the only tested remedies, a healing that is achieved by creating meaning and structure. 'The healing of narrative comes from precisely that engagement with difficulty' (Sennett, 1998: 135) - that is from a systematic working through of the conflictual - as performed in a psychoanalytic treatment. Individuals should no longer be forced to use all of their energy for self-presentation; they should no longer be forced to go from pathological conflict to conflict, plunging into illness after illness, but should gradually feel empowered to decide, for example, for or against flexibility, thus actively to self-determine their life story. This, finally, is the prerequisite for finding one's way in the world on a permanent rather than a short-term basis - an aspect that also stands up to a cost/benefit calculation. Psychoanalysis will have to exist in this tension, perhaps it should take a more active role in determining what else is to be included in this calculation and in the criteria of effectiveness and economic viability.

Maybe what psychoanalysis has already thought about treatment aims appears to be too much, possibly too complex, but people and their inner worlds are complicated. And the very strength of psychoanalysis is to take this into account. In fact, our knowledge should make us optimistic for dialogue and competition with others who are also trying to understand and help people and have similarly something to say about treatment aims. Our body of knowledge gives us the richest possible framework for doing psychotherapy research, at the same time keeping it as close to reality as possible.

References

Balint M (1932) Character analysis and new beginning. In: Balint M (1932) Primary Love and Psychoanalytic Technique. London: Hogarth Press, 1950.

Balint M (1935) The final goal of psychoanalytic treatment. In: Balint M (1935) Primary Love and Psychoanalytic Technique. London: Hogarth Press, 1950.

Balint M (1950) On the termination of analysis. International Journal of Psychoanalysis 31: 196-9.

Dreher AU (2000) Conceptual Research in Psychoanalysis: An introduction. London: Karnac Books.

Freud A (1936) The Ego and the Mechanisms of Defence. London: Hogarth Press.

Freud S (1895) The psychotherapy of hysteria. In: Breuer J, Freud S (1893-5) Studies on Hysteria. The Standard Edition of the Complete Psychological Works of Sigmund Freud, ed. James Strachey, 24 volumes. London: Hogarth Press, 1953-73, vol. 2.

Freud S (1923) The Ego and the Id. Standard Edition, 19.

Freud S (1930) Civilization and its discontents. Standard Edition, 21.

Freud S (1937) Analysis terminable and interminable. Standard Edition, 23.

Grawe K, Donati R, Bernauer F (1993) Psychotherapie im Wandel. Von der Konfession zur Profession. Göttingen: Hogrefe.

Hartmann H (1939a) Ego Psychology and the Problem of Adaptation. New York: International Universities Press, 1958.

Hartmann H (1939b) Psychoanalysis and the concept of health. International Journal of Psychoanalysis 20: 308-321.

Hoffer W (1950) Three psychological criteria for the termination of treatment. International Journal of Psychoanalysis 31: 194-5.

Klein M (1950) On the criteria for the termination of an analysis. International Journal of Psychoanalysis 31: 204.
Knight RP (1942) Evaluation of the results of psychoanalytic therapy. American Journal of Psychiatry 98: 434-46.
Kohut H (1984) How Does Analysis Cure? Chicago: University of Chicago Press.
Sandler J (1983) Reflections on some relations between psychoanalytic concepts and psychoanalytic practice. International Journal of Psycho-Analysis 64: 35-45.
Sandler J, Dreher AU (1996) What Do Psychoanalysts Want? The problem of aims in psychoanalytic therapy. London/New York: Routledge.
Sennett R (1998) The Corrosion of Character. New York: WW Norton.
Strachey J (1937) Symposium on the theory of the therapeutic results of psychoanalysis. International Journal of Psychoanalysis 18: 139-45.
Ticho EA (1971) Probleme des Abschlusses der psychoanalytischen Therapie. Psyche 25: 44-56.
Ticho EA (1972) Termination of psychoanalysis: treatment goals, life goals. Psychoanalytic Quarterly 41: 315-33.
Wallerstein RS (1965) The goals of psychoanalysis: A survey of analytic viewpoints. Journal of the American Psychoanalytic Association 13: 748-70.
Winnicott DW (1962) The aims of psychoanalytic treatment. In: (1976) The Maturational Processes and the Facilitating Environment: Studies in the theory of emotional development. London: Hogarth Press.

CHAPTER 3

The generations of psychotherapy research: an overview

ROBERT S WALLERSTEIN

The following chapter is designed to provide an historical overview of what I call the successive generations of psychotherapy research, as background context for all the many investigators of psychoanalytic treatment processes and outcomes who have contributed chapters to this book.

I have chosen to offer an historical perspective upon the entire field of psychoanalytic therapy research, tracing its history and its development from origins as close to the start of the twentieth century as 1917, up through its current exponential burgeoning and worldwide geographic spreading, as portrayed in an article by Peter Fonagy and myself published in the *International Journal of Psychoanalysis* early in 1999 – all of this exposition within an organizing framework of successive 'generations' of psychotherapy research, each new generation marked by increasing methodological sophistication and technological enhancement. I should insert here the caveat – and the apology – that my chapter will be unduly weighted towards contributions within the American scene, partly because of my own career development within the American clinical and research ambience, but also because of the priority and the primacy of this research development, fostered within the scientific pragmatic empiricism of our Anglo-American intellectual tradition. But of course this has never been an exclusively American enterprise. Across the span of my own research career, starting in the early 1950s, there have been parallel developments in both Great Britain and Germany, and in the recently published *Open Door Review of Outcome Studies in Psychoanalysis* (1999), Fonagy and his collaborators discuss and categorize some 50 established and currently ongoing psychotherapy research projects around the world, only 19 of them in the US, and the second largest number, by far, in Germany.

The central research questions in psychoanalysis and in the expressive and supportive psychoanalytic therapies qua therapies are, of course, 1) *what* changes take place during and as a consequence of therapy (the *outcome* question), and 2) *how* do those changes come about, or how are they brought about, that is through the interaction of what factors in the patient, in the therapist and the therapy, and in the patient's evolving life situation (the process question). In theory, process and outcome are necessarily interlocked. Any study of outcome, even if it counts only the percentage of cases 'improved' must establish some criteria for 'improvement', and these criteria, in turn, must derive from some conception of the nature of the illness and the process of change, whether or not such a conceptualization is explicitly formulated. Similarly, any study of process, in delineating patterns of change among variables, makes cross-sectional assessments at varying points in time, which, if compared with one another, provide measures of short- or longer-term outcome.

On practical grounds, however, outcome studies and process studies are usually separated. Although process is conceptually not separable from outcome, methods that yield the best judgements in the one area are often operationally opposed to those that yield the best judgements in the other. For example, judgements of outcome will be scientifically most convincing if bias is minimized and freedom from contamination maintained by keeping those who make the 'after' judgements unaware of the 'before' judgements and predictions. From the point of view of process judgements about the *same therapy,* such care to minimize contamination would be unnecessary. Indeed, it would be counter to the whole spirit of inquiry into process, in which maximum knowledge of all the known determinants, as these have varied over time, is essential, in order best to understand the changes that occur. Given this situation, I will group the studies I review under either the outcome or the process heading, indicating as well those that have endeavoured to pursue both outcome and process aims.

But first, I need to mention some of the considerations related to the topic of process and outcome research in psychoanalytic therapies - issues that, although beyond the scope of this presentation, are nonetheless indeed germane to its central argument, and are of course significant determinants of the complexity of therapy research. These include:

1. The goals of these treatment modalities, both ideal and practical (realizable).
2. The issues of suitability or *treatability* as against *analysability,* which is not the same thing, although the two are easily confounded.
3. The *indications* and *contra-indications* for this array of treatments, as these have evolved over time with increasing experience and expanding theoretical and technical knowledge.

4. The role of the initial *diagnostic* and *evaluation* procedures in differential treatment planning (as against the view that only a trial of treatment can lead to proper case formulation and prognostication).
5. The place of *prediction* (and predictability) in relation to issues of change, realistic goals and their limitations.
6. The *theory of technique* (how treatment works and achieves its goals - that is, the relationship of means to ends).
7. The *similarities* and *differences* between psychoanalysis and the dynamic psychotherapies, as compared from the perspective of different goals projected for different kinds of patients, determining through these differences the specifically appropriate technical approaches from within the available spectrum.
8. The *criteria* for satisfactory treatment termination.
9. The *evaluation of results* (process and outcome changes, therapeutic benefit, and analytic completeness).
10. The conception of the *ideal state of mental health* and the unavoidable impingement upon its empirical assessment by value judgements as well as by the vantage point and partisan interests of the judge.
11. The place of *follow-up study* as a desirable, feasible, and appropriate activity (or not) in relation to psychoanalytic work, for research and/or for clinical purposes. And
12. The place of the continuing accretion of knowledge in relation to all these areas, by the traditional *case study method* innovated by Freud as against the desirability or necessity for more *formal systematic* clinical research into these issues, by methods that are responsive of course to the subtlety and the complexity of the subjective clinical phenomena, while simultaneously remaining loyal to the canons of empirical science.

So now to what I call the *generations* of psychotherapy research, beginning with the early statistical studies that comprise the first-generation outcome research. As early as 1917, within the first decade of the introduction of psychoanalysis in America, Coriat reported on the therapeutic results achieved in 93 cases, of which 73% were declared either recovered or much improved; these rates were nearly equal across all his diagnostic categories. As with all the early statistical studies to be reported here, the judgements of improvement were made by the treating clinician, according to (usually) unspecified criteria, and without individual clinical detail or supporting evidence.

In the decade of the 1930s, several comparable but larger scale reports emerged from the collective experiences of the psychoanalytic treatment centres of some of the pioneering psychoanalytic training institutes. In 1930, Fenichel reported results from the initial decade of the Berlin Institute, the first formally organized psychoanalytic institute in the world. Of 1955 consultations conducted, 721 patients were accepted for analysis; 60% of the neurotic patients were judged to have received substantial benefit, but only 23% of those who were labelled psychotic. Jones, in 1936, reported on 738 applicants to the London Psychoanalytic Clinic, of whom 74 were taken into analysis; 28 of the 59 neurotic patients were judged to have benefited substantially, but only one of the 15 so-called psychotic patients. And a year later, in 1937, Alexander reported on 157 cases from the Chicago Psychoanalytic Clinic, with 63% of the neurotic patients, 40% of the psychotic patients, and 77% of those designated psychosomatic, judged to have received substantial benefit from their treatment. During this same period, Kessel and Hyman (1933), two internists who followed up on 29 patients referred for psychoanalysis, reported almost all the neurotic patients to have benefited from the treatment, and all the psychotic ones to be either unchanged or worse.

In a 1941 review article evaluating the overall results of psychoanalysis, Knight combined the findings of all of these studies (except the first one by Coriat) and added 100 patients treated at the Menninger Clinic, where the results were judged to be completely comparable to those of the other studies in the observed outcomes with neurotic and psychotic patients. The overall composite tabulation comprised 952 patients, with the therapeutic benefit rate approximately 60% for the neurotic, close to 80% for the psychosomatic, and only 25% for the psychotic patients. Knight made particular reference to the pitfalls of these simple statistical summaries; the absence of agreed definitions and criteria, the crudeness of nomenclature and diagnostic classification, and the failure to address issues of therapeutic skill in relation to cases of varying severity.

The most ambitious study of this first-generation genre was the report of the Central Fact-Gathering Committee of the American Psychoanalytic Association (Hamburg et al., 1967).[1] Data were collected over a five-year period, beginning in 1952; altogether there were 10,000 initial responses to questionnaires submitted by 800 analysts and candidates, with some 3000 termination questionnaires submitted upon treatment completion. As with the other studies cited thus far, criteria for diagnosis and improvement were unspecified, and these and other flaws and ambiguities resulted ultimately in a report that was declared to be simply an 'experience survey' consisting of 1) facts about the demographics of analysts' practices, 2) analysts' *opinions* on their patients' diagnoses, and 3) analysts' *opinions* on the therapeutic results achieved. Not unexpectedly, the great majority of patients were declared to be substantially improved.

Finally, in the very next year, Feldman (1968) reported on the results of psychoanalysis in 120 patients (selected from 960 evaluations) treated at the

Clinic of the Southern California Psychoanalytic Institute over its 11-year history. Again, the reported improvement rates were completely comparable to those of all the preceding studies, with two thirds of the outcomes being in the 'good' or 'very good' categories; and once more, difficulties were experienced due to lack of clear and agreed-upon criteria, concepts, and language for diagnostic assessment, analysability, and analytic results.

Altogether, this sequence of so-called first-generation outcome studies of psychoanalysis, spanning a half-century, from 1917 to 1968, was scientifically simplistic and failed to command much interest in the psychoanalytic clinical world. Most practitioners agreed with Glover (1954) in his dour assessment: 'Like most psycho-therapists, the psycho-analyst is a reluctant and inexpert statistician' (p. 393) - and, we could add, researcher. It was such conclusions that spurred what I call the second-generation studies - the efforts at more formal and systematic outcome research geared toward overcoming the glaring methodological simplicity that marked each of the studies described to this point.

These methodological flaws in the first-generation statistical enumeration of psychoanalytic outcomes have already been indicated. In addition to the lack of agreed criteria at almost every step - from initial assessments to outcome judgements of therapeutic benefit and analytic results - and the use of these judgements (derived from unspecified, and even unformulated, criteria) by the (necessarily biased) therapist, as the (usually) sole evidential primary data base, there was also the methodological difficulty that these studies were all retrospective, with all the potential therein for bias, confounding and contamination of judgements, *post hoc ergo propter hoc* reasoning, and the like. Efforts to address these issues, including the introduction of prospective inquiry and even the fashioning of predictions to be validated or refuted by subsequent assessment, began in earnest in the 1950s and 1960s in America, and have spread world-wide in subsequent decades.

I will very briefly describe six major American projects from this second-generation research approach, three based on group-aggregated studies of clinic cases from the Boston, the Columbia, and the New York Psychoanalytic Institutes, and three based on individually focused studies in New York, San Francisco, and Chicago. I will also mention here, out of the many currently ongoing elsewhere in the world, three major programmes, though not all three live up to all the second-generation criteria here specified, because one is retrospective, albeit with outcome judgements made more objectively, not by the therapists with unspecified criteria, but by independent researchers with carefully worked out outcome criteria. The three quite large European projects of this kind that I want to mention are 1) the Anna Freud Centre chart review of 763 cases treated over a four-decade span with psychoanalysis or psychotherapy (Fonagy and Target, 1994, 1996; Target and

Fonagy, 1994a, b); 2) The German Psychoanalytical Association (DPV) Study of the long-term effects of psychoanalysis and the psychoanalytic psychotherapies involving the study by the researchers of 190 patients (120 in analysis, 70 in psychotherapy) drawn from co-operating DPV members (Leuzinger-Bohleber and Stuhr, 1997); and 3) the European multi-centre collaborative study of long-term intensive psychoanalytic treatment involving analysts from Holland, Finland, Norway, Sweden, and Italy (Szecsody et al., 1997).

Now to the better-known and earlier American second-generation studies. In 1960, Knapp et al. reported on 100 supervised psychoanalytic patients from the Boston Institute Clinic, rated initially for suitability for analysis, of whom 27 were followed up a year later with questionnaires addressed to the treating analysts to ascertain just how suitable the patients had indeed turned out to be. The evaluation procedures (i.e. the initial judgements and the subsequent questionnaire responses) were 'blind'. There turned out to be fair but limited success in this assessment of suitability for analysis from the initial evaluation. However, two significant limitations of this study should be mentioned. First, the testing of the predictions took place only at the one-year mark rather than more suitably upon treatment termination; clearly much can change in this regard - in both directions - at later points in analysis. Second, and this is a problem with all research on this model, the patients selected by psychoanalytic clinic committees are already carefully screened, with obviously unsuitable cases previously rejected. The range of variability in the accepted cases is thus considerably narrowed, making differential prediction within that group inherently less reliable.

Sashin et al. (1975), inspired by this work, subsequently studied 183 patients treated at the same clinic from 1959 to 1966. Final data were collected on 130 (72%) of these patients after an average of 675 treatment hours and at a point averaging six years after treatment termination. Predictor variables were assessed with a 103-item evaluation questionnaire and via six major outcome criteria: 1) restriction of functioning by symptoms, 2) subjective discomfort, 3) work productivity, 4) sexual adjustment, 5) interpersonal relations, and 6) availability of insight. Only 10 of the 103 predictor items demonstrated some predictive value in relation to assessed outcomes and that only with modest (albeit statistically significant) correlations. As a group, however, these predictor variables 'made little clinical sense'. Overall, the Boston Institute studies yielded only fair prediction to judgements of analysability as assessed at the one-year mark in treatment, and no effective prediction at all to treatment outcomes from the patient's characteristics as judged at initial evaluation.

The Columbia Psychoanalytic Center project, contemporaneous with the Boston studies, was written up in final accounting in a sequence of published reports in 1985 (Bachrach et al., 1985; Weber et al., 1985a, b, c). This project consisted of prospective studies of a large number of patients (1348 in sample 1 and 237 in the later sample 2), all treated by the same body of therapists. Data were collected from multiple perspectives over time (initially and at termination), with opportunities to compare findings in psychoanalysis (about 40% of the total) with those in psychoanalytic psychotherapy (the other 60%). The authors stated that all previous studies had been limited in at least one of the following ways: small sample size, inadequate range of information about outcomes, not based on terminated cases, or restricted to retrospective data. Further, no other studies had permitted comparison between large numbers of terminated analyses and psychotherapies conducted by the same therapists. And in addition, criteria for therapeutic benefit were established, distinct from separate criteria for the evolution of a psychoanalytic process.

The most striking finding from this project was that, across every category of patient, the therapeutic benefit measures always substantially exceeded the measures of an evolved analytic process. For example, only 40% of those who completed analyses with good therapeutic benefit were characterized as having been 'analysed' by the project criteria. An equally striking finding was that the outcomes of these treatments, in terms of both therapeutic benefit and analysability, were only marginally predictable from the perspective of the initial evaluation. This finding was, of course, in keeping with those of the Boston studies just cited - and for the same reasons. As noted by the authors (Weber et al., 1985a), 'the prudent conclusion . . . is *not* that therapeutic benefit or analysability are *per se* unpredictable, but that once a case has been carefully selected as suitable for analysis by a candidate, its eventual fate remains relatively indeterminate' (p. 135).

As would be expected, those selected for psychoanalysis were assessed initially as functioning at higher levels than those selected for psychotherapy, and those in psychoanalysis achieved greater therapeutic benefits than those in psychotherapy. In conclusion, the authors stated that sample 1 was three times larger than that in any previously published study, and that the project was the first to have a psychotherapy comparison group and one of the first to make the conceptual distinction between analysability and therapeutic benefit. Sample 2 was a smaller number, assembled a decade later with some refinements in methods of data collection and some differences in observational vantage points, but in almost every particular, all the findings of sample 1 were replicated. From the two studies, the authors concluded 'that a substantially greater proportion of analysands derive therapeutic benefit than develop an analytic process, and that the development of an analytic process is associated with the highest levels of therapeutic benefit. Yet, what we do not yet know precisely is the nature and quality of benefit associated with the development of an analytic process and without its development' (Weber et al., 1985b: 261).

The final article in this series (Bachrach et al., 1985) was devoted to a review of clinical and methodological considerations. The authors stressed the advantages of their project over other comparable studies: 1) the *n* was very large; 2) it was a prospective study with predictive evaluations performed before outcomes were known; 3) they used (mainly) clinically meaningful scales; 4) aside from evaluations by patients and therapists, they used independent judges; and 5) psychoanalysis and psychotherapy were comparatively assessed.

The third of these group-aggregated studies, the New York Psychoanalytic Institutes studies (Erle, 1979; Erle and Goldberg, 1979, 1984), was similarly constituted, although with more of a focus on the study of treatments carried out by more experienced analysts. There were two samples. The first (Erle, 1979) consisted of 40 supervised analytic patients selected from 870 applicants to the Treatment Center of the New York Psychoanalytic Institute. The results were completely comparable to those at the Boston and Columbia centres. Twenty-five of the patients terminated satisfactorily, but only 11 of these were considered to have completed treatment; 24 of the patients were judged to have benefited substantially, but only 17 were judged to have been involved in a proper psychoanalytic process. A group of 42 *private* patients from seven analyst colleagues of the author, who had begun their treatments in the same period and were assessed in the same manner as the Treatment Center patients, showed substantially comparable results. The second sample (Erle and Goldberg, 1984) extended the work to a group of 160 private patients gathered over a subsequent five-year span from 16 co-operating experienced analysts. The outcomes from these experienced analysts were completely comparable to the results of their own (and of all other) earlier studies of clinic patients treated by candidates.

To turn now to the individually focused American studies. Over a time span parallel to that of these relatively large-scale outcome studies of psychoanalytic clinic patient populations (as well as some comparison private patients) assessed by pre- and post-treatment rating scales and grouped statistically, Pfeffer, at the same New York Psychoanalytic Institute Treatment Center, initiated a wholly other kind of outcome and follow-up study of terminated psychoanalyses by intensive *individual* case studies of a research-procured population (Pfeffer, 1959, 1961, 1963). He first reported on nine patients who had completed analyses under Treatment Center auspices and had agreed to a series of follow-up interviews by a 'follow-up analyst' who had not conducted the treatment. The interviews were open-ended, once a week, 'analytic' in character, and ranged from two to seven in number before the participants agreed upon a natural close. The chief finding, that occurred in *all* instances, consisted of the rapid reactivation of characteristic analytic transferences, including even transitory symptom flare-ups, as if in relation to the original treating analyst, with subsequent rapid subsidence, at times aided by pertinent interpretations, and in a manner that indicated the new ways of neurotic conflict management that had been achieved in the analysis.

In the last of this sequence of three reports (1963), Pfeffer attempted a metapsychological explanation of these 'follow-up study transference phenomena' (p. 230). His overall conclusion was that 'The recurrence in the follow-up study of the major pre-analytic symptomatology in the context of a revived transference neurosis as well as the quick subsidence of symptoms appear to support the idea that conflicts underlying symptoms are not actually shattered or obliterated by analysis but rather are only better mastered with new and more adequate solutions' (p. 234). The neurotic conflicts thus 'lose their poignancy' (p. 237).

Two other research groups, one in San Francisco (Norman et al., 1976; Oremland et al., 1975) and one in Chicago (Schlessinger and Robbins, 1974, 1975, 1983), replicated the Pfeffer studies, with some slight alterations in method, and in both instances confirmed what has come to be called 'the Pfeffer phenomenon'. The San Francisco group concluded that, 'the infantile neurosis had not disappeared. What had changed was the degree to which it affected [the patient's] everyday life' (Norman et al., 1976: 492). The Chicago group concluded that, 'psychic conflicts were not eliminated in the analytic process . . . the more significant outcome of the analysis appeared to be the development of a preconsciously active self-analytic function, in identification with the analysing function of the analyst, as a learned mode of coping with conflicts' (Schlessinger and Robbins, 1983: 9). This overall finding from all three groups - that even in analyses considered highly successful, neurotic conflicts are not obliterated or shattered, as was once felt, but rather are tamed, muted, or lose their poignancy - is echoed in the well-known analytic quip that we all still recognize our good friends after their analyses.

I note one final consideration: a shared characteristic of these second-generation studies - whether the group-aggregated broad statistical accounting (the Boston, the Columbia, Erle and Goldberg in New York) or the individually focused in-depth research studies (Pfeffer in New York, the San Francisco, the Chicago) - was the failure to segregate outcome results discerned at treatment termination from the issue of the stability (or not) of these results as revealed at some established follow-up point subsequent to termination, with all the different possibilities: for consolidation and further enhancement of treatment gains, for the simple maintenance of treatment achievements, or for actual regression back towards the pre-treatment state.

Conceptually, this was a failure to accord specific theoretical status to what Rangell (1966/1990) has called the 'post-analytic phase'. Rangell described a variety of possible courses that can characterize this phase and concluded that, 'the desired goal should be a transition to a normal interchange in which the analyst can be seen and reacted to as a normal figure and no longer as an object for continued transference displacement' (1990: 722). In the third-generation studies, next to be described, the distinction between results at the termination study point and those at a subsequent prearranged follow-up study point (anywhere from two to five years later) becomes a clearly demarcated research focus - among the advances over the second-generation studies.

What I am calling the third-generation studies of the outcomes of psychoanalysis have actually been contemporaneous in time with the second-generation studies just described. These third-generation studies are systematic and formal psychoanalytic therapy research projects that have attempted both to assess analytic outcomes across a significant array of cases *and* to examine the processes through which these outcomes have been reached via the intensive longitudinal study of each of the individual cases. In this, these projects have combined the methodological approaches of the group-aggregated studies with those of the individually focused studies. Like the best of the second-generation studies, they have carefully defined their terms, constructed rating scales, and tried to operationalize their criteria at each assessment point. These third-generation studies have been constructed prospectively, starting with pre-treatment assessment of patients. Unlike the second-generation studies, they have carefully separated outcomes at termination from functioning at a specified subsequent follow-up point and have attempted to account for the further changes, in either direction, that took place during this 'post-analytic phase', Bachrach et al., in their comprehensive 1991 survey of research on the efficacy of psychoanalysis, singled out the newer Boston Psychoanalytic Institute studies (Kantrowitz, 1986; Kantrowitz et al., 1986, 1987a, b, 1989, 1990a, b, c) and our Psychotherapy Research Project (PRP) of the Menninger Foundation (Wallerstein, 1986, 1988) as the only ones to fully meet their array of state-of-the-art specifications for outcomes studies. It will be these two that I will review here as exemplars of this third generation.

The Boston studies were undertaken in the 1970s and came to publication in the following decade. Twenty-two supervised analytic cases at the Boston Institute Clinic were selected for prospective study, with the initial assessment based on a projective psychological test battery used to yield measures of 1) affect availability and modulation, 2) quality of object relations, 3) adequacy of reality testing, and 4) motivation for change. Approximately a year after treatment termination, the initial test battery was repeated, and both the patient and the treating analyst were interviewed.

A series of three papers (Kantrowitz et al., 1986, 1987a, b) described the results. Nine of the 22 patients were felt to have had a successful analytic outcome, five to have had a limited outcome, and eight to be unanalysed. Nonetheless, the greater number achieved therapeutic benefits along each of the change and outcome dimensions, and along each dimension the therapeutic benefit *exceeded* the analytic result in terms of the degree of successfully completed analytic work. That is, a consistent and important finding was that therapeutic benefit was achieved by the majority of the patients, and was regularly in excess of what could be accounted for by the evocation and the interpretative resolution (as far as possible) of the transference neurosis. However, although most patients derived significant therapeutic benefit from their analytic experience, successful outcome could not be predicted from any of the predictor variables.

This finding led these investigators to speculate that 'a particularly important omission (from the predictor variables) might have been consideration of the effect of the [therapist–patient] match in shaping the two-person psychoanalytic interaction' (Kantrowitz et al., 1989: 899). By 'match' they meant, 'an interactional concept; it refers to a spectrum of compatibility and incompatibility of the patient and analyst which is relevant to the analytic work' (p. 894). They further noted that although, 'this mesh of the analyst's personal qualities with those of the patient has rarely been a special focus of [research] attention . . . most analysts when making referrals do consider it; few assume that equally well-trained analysts are completely interchangeable' (Kantrowitz, 1986: 273).

This same team then returned for follow-up interviews with the same patient cohort in 1987, now 5 to 10 years after the treatment terminations, this time including the retrospective assessment of the 'goodness' of the analyst–patient match as one of the variables contributing to the patient outcomes (Kantrowitz et al., 1990a, b, c). Nineteen of the original 22 patients could be located and of these, 18 agreed to be interviewed. Again, a variety of change measures were used: global improvement ratings, affect management, quality of object relations, adequacy of reality testing, work accomplishment, and overall self-esteem. Overall results at the follow-up point showed three of the 18 further improved; four were stable, six deteriorated but were restored with additional treatment, four deteriorated despite additional treatment, and one returned to the original analyst and was still in treatment and was therefore not counted.

The most striking finding, however, was that, again, the stability of the achieved gains in the follow-up period could not be predicted from the assessments at termination – that is, according to Kantrowitz and colleagues (1990a), 'psychological changes were no more stable over time for the group of patients assessed as having achieved a successful analytic outcome concomitant with considerable therapeutic benefit than for the other group of patients assessed as having achieved therapeutic benefit alone' (p. 493). In focusing on the assessment of analyst-patient match (Kantrowitz et al., 1990c), the authors concluded that with 12 of the 17 patients, the kind of match (impeding or facilitating) did play a role in the outcome achieved. They gave examples of facilitating matches with good outcomes, impeding matches with poor outcomes, and more complex situations in which the kind of match was at first facilitating to the unfolding of the analytic process but later seemed to have an influence in preventing the completion of the analytic work.

The other so-called third-generation psychoanalytic therapy research study to be described here is the Psychotherapy Research Project (PRP) of the Menninger Foundation. Of this project Bachrach et al. said in 1991: 'Systematic, methodologically informed research about psychoanalytic outcomes began with The Menninger Foundation Psychotherapy Research Project.... [It] is by far the most comprehensive formal study of psychoanalysis yet undertaken and remains the only study of outcomes that spans almost the entire life cycle of many of its patients' (p. 878). . . . [It] stands in a class by itself among psychoanalytic research efforts' (p. 884). Certainly PRP was the most ambitious such research programme ever carried out (Wallerstein, 1986, 1988; Wallerstein et al., 1956). Its intent was to follow the treatment careers and the subsequent life careers of a cohort of patients (ultimately 42 in number), half in psychoanalysis, and half in other psychoanalytic psychotherapies - and each in the treatment deemed *clinically* indicated - to follow them from the initial pre-treatment comprehensive psychiatric evaluation, through the entire natural span of their treatments (for however many years that entailed), and then into formal follow-up inquiries at several years after the treatment terminations, and with as much of an open-ended follow-up thereafter as circumstance might make possible and as the span of interested observation might last. The patients entered into their treatments over the span of the mid-1950s (contemporaneous with the bulk of the second-generations studies); their periods of treatment ranged from 6 months to a full 12 years; all were reached - 100% - for formal follow-up study at the two-to-three-year mark; and more than one third could be followed for periods ranging from 12 to 24 years beyond their treatment terminations (with four still in ongoing treatment when my book *Forty-two Lives in Treatment*, the overall clinical accounting of this project, was published at the 30-year mark in 1986).

The aim of PRP was to learn as much as possible about 1) *what* changes actually take place in psychoanalysis and other psychoanalytic psychotherapies (the outcome question), and 2) *how* those changes come about - through the interactions over time of which variables in the patient, in the therapy and the therapist, or in the patient's evolving life situation, as they together co-determine those changes (the process question). Three overall treatment groups were set up - psychoanalysis, expressive psychoanalytic psychotherapy, and supportive psychoanalytic psychotherapy - in accord with the then consensus in the psychoanalytic literature regarding the defining characteristics of these three therapeutic modes, together with differential indications for their deployment derived from the dynamic formulations of the nature of the patients' lives, history, character, and illness structure.

The project goals within this framework were to specify in detail the particular reach and limitation of the therapeutic outcome for each kind of patient appropriately treated within each of the proffered therapeutic approaches. There was a special interest in the more empirical elaboration of the psychological change mechanisms operative within both the uncovering (expressive) and the 'ego-strengthening' (supportive) therapeutic modes. My 784-page book *Forty-two Lives in Treatment* represents the full statement of the project's findings and conclusions (Wallerstein, 1986). For an overall capsule summarization of the main highlights here, I can best report by paraphrasing (and sharply condensing) a several-page segment from the concluding part of a summarizing paper about the project (Wallerstein, 1988: 144-9).

The overall project conclusions, as of 1986, can be brought together as a series of sequential propositions regarding the appropriateness, efficacy, reach, and limitations of psychoanalysis and of psychoanalytic psychotherapies (variously expressive and supportive) - always, of course, with the caveat that this segment of the overall patient population (those usually sicker individuals who are brought to or who seek their intensive analytic treatment within a psychoanalytic sanatorium setting) are not necessarily representative of the usual outpatient psychoanalytic therapy population.

1. The first proposition concerns the distinction so regularly made between true 'structural change', presumably based on the interpretative resolution, within the transference/counter-transference matrix, of unconscious intrapsychic conflicts, as against 'behavioural change', based on 'just altered techniques of adjustment', and presumably all that can come out of the other, non-interpretive, non-insight-aiming, change mechanisms. Intrinsic to this way of dichotomizing change has always been the easy assumption that only structural change, as brought about through conflict resolution marked by appropriately achieved insight, can have some guarantee of inherent stability, durability, and capacity to weather at least ordinary future environmental vicissitudes. The PRP experience clearly questioned the continued usefulness of this effort to make so tight a link between the *kind* of changes achieved with the intervention mode - expressive or supportive - by which they are brought

about. The changes reached in the more supportive therapies often seemed enough to represent just as much structural change, in the terms indicated, as the changes reached in the most expressive analytic cases.

2. The second proposition concerns the conventional proportionality argument - that therapeutic change will be *at least* proportional to the degree of achieved conflict resolution. This proposition is, of course, almost unexceptionable, because it is clear that there can be significantly more change than there is true conflict resolution, on all the varying supportive bases through which change can be brought about, as well as properly proportionate change in which the change is on the basis of conflict resolution with accompanying insight - if such an ideal type ever actually exists in practice. Conversely, it would be hard to imagine real conflict resolution (and accompanying insight) without an at least proportional concomitant change in behaviours, dispositions, and symptoms.
3. The third proposition, often linked to the proportionality argument but much more debatable and clearly separate from it, concerns the necessity argument - that effective conflict resolution is a necessary condition for at least certain kinds of change. It is clear that an overall PRP finding - and almost an overriding one - has been the repeated demonstration that a substantial range of changes - in symptoms, in personality functioning, and in life-style - has been brought about via the more supportive therapeutic modes, cutting across the gamut of declared supportive *and* expressive (even analytic) therapies, and that in terms of the usual criteria, these changes can be (in many instances) quite indistinguishable from the changes brought about by typically expressive analytic means.
4. A counterpart has arisen to the proposition based on the tendency to overestimate the necessity of the expressive (analytic) treatment mode's operation via conflict resolution in order to effect therapeutically desired change. This is the other proposition, based on the happy finding that supportive therapeutic approaches so often achieved far more than was expected of them - and, indeed, often enough reached the kinds of changes expected to depend on more expressive and insightful conflict resolutions - and did so in ways that seemed indistinguishable from those seen in 'structural' change. In fact, proportionately, each within its own category, the designated psychotherapy cases did as well as the designated psychoanalytic ones. More to the point, the good results in the one modality were not overall less stable or less enduring or less proof against subsequent environmental vicissitude than in the other. And, more important still, within both the psychotherapy and the psychoanalysis groups, the changes predicted, although more often predicated on the more expressive techniques, in fact were achieved to a greater than expected degree on the basis of the more supportive techniques.

5. Considering these PRP treatments from the point of view of psychoanalysis as a treatment modality, just as more was accomplished than expected with psychotherapy, especially in its more supportive modes, so psychoanalysis, as the quintessentially expressive therapeutic mode, achieved less - at least with these patients - than had been anticipated or predicted. This more limited success in part reflected the ethos of the psychoanalytic sanatorium and the psychoanalytic treatment opportunities this setting is intended to make possible - that is, the protection and life management of those temporarily disorganized individuals who cannot be helped sufficiently with any other or lesser treatment approach than psychoanalysis, but who cannot tolerate the rigours of psychoanalytic treatment within the usual outpatient setting.

   This is the concept of so-called heroic indications for psychoanalysis, and in the PRP experience these particular patients did poorly with the psychoanalytic treatment method, however modified by parameters or buttressed by concomitant hospitalization. And there were certainly enough instances of very good outcomes with these 'sicker' patients in an appropriately modulated supportive expressive psychotherapy, especially when we could ensure adequate concomitant life management. The shift is in the departure from the effort at psychoanalysis per se (even modified analysis) as the treatment of choice for these 'sicker' patients in that setting. On this basis, we can speak of the failing of the so-called heroic indications for *psychoanalysis* and can invite a repositioning of the pendulum in its swings over time around this issue, more in the direction of 'narrowing indications' for (proper) psychoanalysis.
6. The predictions made for prospective courses and outcomes tended to be for more substantial and more enduring change (more 'structural change') where the treatment was to be more expressive analytic; *pari passu,* the more supportive the treatment was intended to be (had to be), the more limited and inherently unstable the anticipated changes were expected to be. All of this presumption was consistently tempered and altered in the actual implementation in the treatment courses. Psychoanalysis and the expressive psychotherapies as a whole were systematically modified to introduce more supportive components, and they by and large accomplished less than anticipated, with a varying but often substantial amount of their achieved outcomes obtained by supportive means. The supportive psychotherapies, on the other hand, often accomplished a fair amount more - and sometimes a great deal more - than initially expected, again, with much of the change on the basis of more supportive techniques than originally specified.

In conclusion, these overall results can be generalized as follows: 1) the treatment results in psychoanalysis and in varying mixes of expressive supportive psychotherapies tend to converge, rather than diverge, in outcome; 2) across the whole spectrum of treatment courses, from the most analytic expressive to the most single-mindedly supportive, the treatments carried more supportive elements than originally projected, and these elements accounted for substantially more of the changes achieved than had been originally anticipated; 3) the supportive aspects of psychotherapy, as conceptualized within a psychoanalytic theoretical framework, deserve far more respectful specification than they have usually been accorded in the psychoanalytic literature; and 4) from the study of the kinds of changes achieved by this patient cohort, partly on an uncovering insight-aiming basis, and partly on the basis of the opposed covering-up varieties of supportive techniques, the changes themselves - divorced from how they were brought about - often seemed quite indistinguishable from each other in terms of being so-called real or structural changes in personality functioning.

In their article's overall summation, Bachrach et al. stated of PRP: 'The prospective design, clinical focus, scope, duration, extensive collection of case histories spanning decades, painstaking accumulation of follow-up information, quantitative sophistication, careful definition of terms, and systematic review of treatment processes and outcomes from multiple points of view, are all admirable features of the study' (1991: 884).

Because of inherently greater conceptual and methodological complexity, counterpart research into the nature of the *processes* by which change comes about or is brought about in psychoanalytic therapies - the answer to the *how* question - has been more recent in origin and has not yet undergone generational transformations.[2] Also, because it necessarily (or at least usually) entails more detailed focus on moment-to-moment therapeutic interactions, process research has only been rendered feasible on a significant scale by the more recent - meaning basically since the 1970s - development and deployment of suitable technology - namely, the possibilities for audio and video recording, and of computerization and high-speed computer word or situation searches.

Audio recording was actually introduced into psychoanalytic research as early as 1933, when Earl Zinn was known to have made dictaphone recordings of psychoanalytic sessions with a patient at Worcester State Hospital (Carmichael, 1956). Since then, recordings have been advocated and used by a widening array of analytic investigators. In a major overview in 1971 of 'issues in research in the psychoanalytic process', a colleague and I (Wallerstein and Sampson, 1971) reviewed the literature to that date on the use of audio recording in therapy sessions and discussed the various arguments for and against such use. The major arguments *pro* were the greater completeness, verbatim accuracy, permanence, and public character of the database, as well as the facilitation of the separation of the therapeutic from the research responsibility, with the possibility of thus bypassing the inevitable biases of the analyst as a contaminant of the data filter. The major arguments *contra* were the indeterminate impact of this (research) intrusion upon the 'naturalness' of the therapeutic process (including the compromise of full confidentiality and the insertion into the treatment of goals other than therapeutic) and the sheer enormity, complexity, and cost of the database thus made available (cost being not just for recording but for faithful transcription, including prosodic elements as much as possible, in addition to lexical accuracy).

It is only within the past two, or perhaps three, decades that an adequate consensus has emerged that analytic therapy *can* go on under these observed circumstances - that is, that a properly therapeutic process can nonetheless evolve - and that computer technology has advanced to where the enormous database generated can be feasibly managed. This has led to the recent almost explosive proliferation of psychoanalytic therapy process research, mainly in the US and Germany (centred there initially at Ulm University), but also in Great Britain and elsewhere. The elaboration of modern-day empirical psychoanalytic process studies is exemplified in the contents of a 1988 book, *Psychoanalytic Process Research Strategies*, edited by Dahl, Kächele, and Thomä - a close American-German research collaboration - the proceedings, actually, of a major workshop of American and German researchers on 'Empirical Research in Psychoanalysis', held in Ulm just prior to the 1985 International Psycho-Analytical Association Congress in Hamburg, Germany.

The Ulm workshop brought together many of the most significant research groups in America and in Germany that had been engaged in the microscopic study of moment-to-moment psychoanalytic interaction processes, in single hours, or in small segments of hours, using audio-taped and transcribed psychoanalytic treatment sessions. Each of the participating groups had developed its own concepts of the basic units of the psychoanalytic situation and of psychoanalytic process, and its own instruments to measure these, and had utilized its measures in relation to its own available database, though there had been some significant sharing of sample hours from a particular psychoanalytic patient (Mrs C) across a number of these groups. The book edited by Dahl and his colleagues was an effort to compare findings from these disparate studies in a search for elements of convergence. In the introduction to that book, Dahl expressed the hope that this convergence could be found in the principle enunciated by Strupp, Schacht, and Henry in the initial chapter: 'that the description and representation, theoretically *and* operationally, of a *patient's conflicts*, of the *patient's treatment*, and of the *assessment of the outcome* must be congruent, which is to say, must be represented in comparable, if not identical, terms' (Dahl et al., 1988, ix). This fundamental integrative principle - proposed to subsume conceptually the entire array of process and outcome researches, however seemingly disparate their concepts and their instruments – is termed the Principle of Problem–Treatment–Outcome Congruence ('PTO congruence' for short) (Strupp et al., 1988: 7).

A major effort in this direction is the still continuing Collaborative Analytic Multi-Site Program (CAMP) which I was asked to organize under the auspices of the American Psychoanalytic Association, now a decade ago (Wallerstein, 1991). The effort was for an ingathering of the known psychoanalytic therapy research groups, process and outcome, including all of the US groups represented in the book edited by Dahl et al., and the ongoing outcome groups from the third-generation outcome studies (including the group headed by Kantrowitz in Boston and my own current successor group to the Menninger Foundation studies, in San Francisco), and including as well some participation from outside the US, the child therapy outcome studies at the Anna Freud Centre in London represented by Fonagy and Target, and the Ulm Textbank group in Germany represented by Mergenthaler and Kächele. The initial participating CAMP groups were 16 in number, 12 of them clearly process research groups, and the numbers have fluctuated slightly over the decade of, first, two whole days of meetings each year, in conjunction with the spring and autumn meetings of the American Psychoanalytic Association, and, most recently, just one day, during the American's December (fall) meeting time.

This CAMP programme is designed to accommodate all of the participating groups' own concepts and instruments in relation to a *common* agreed-upon database of available audio-taped and transcribed psychoanalytic sessions from already completed psychoanalytic treatments, as well as hours from new psychoanalytic cases, so that appropriate before-and-after studies (as well as planned follow-ups) can be prospectively built in. The comparing and contrasting of findings in relation to the same database by all of these process and outcome groups would finally make it possible to determine the degrees of convergence of the concepts and instruments elaborated to this point by the different groups, and also to determine the degree and the nature of the imbrication of process and outcome studies – that is, the degree to which the Principle of PTO Congruence can be realized.

This is a major direction that what I call fourth-generation studies are taking – one that, if successful, promises not only to integrate the various psychoanalytic process studies carried out more or less independently over the past two decades, but also to integrate process studies with outcome studies in a more complete fulfilment of the aim articulated at the very start of this presentation.

Unhappily, the fulfilment of this fourth-generation aim is still music for the future. The cost of implementing the CAMP programme would be high, with each of up to 16 collaborating groups requiring up to $25,000 per year, plus the very significant costs of central co-ordination and administration, as well as at least one (better two) two-day meetings each year to present the work and findings of each of the participating groups, working on the shared database, for comparison and contrast. Thus far, efforts to obtain such funding from governmental and private foundation funding sources have been unsuccessful, but working within the limitation of the very small grants that have been secured, collaborative work has taken place within small groups of the CAMP colleagues, and all are continuing their own research activities, with or without external financial support.

Space constraints preclude even identifying the collaborating CAMP groups, let alone any statement of their conceptual base, their instruments, or their mode of operation. In the Fonagy et al. (1999) *Open Door Review* of 50 projects listed, only nine are placed by them in the pure process category - with another six called process-outcome - and of the nine listed as process studies, four are regular members of CAMP (Dahl's studies of FRAMES, which are Fundamental Repetitive and Maladaptive Emotion Structures, built upon a classification system of emotional expression, Luborsky's CCRT, or Core Conflictual Relationship Themes, based on a categorization of transference expressions, Bucci's Multiple Code Theory (MCT) and Referential Cycle, based on the activity of the referential connections between the non-verbal systems and the communicative verbal code, and Jones' Psychotherapy Process Q-Sort (PPQS), a Q-sort providing a language for the description and classification of treatment processes in a form suitable for quantitative analysis). Of the other five designated as process studies by Fonagy et al., the three in the US have participated occasionally in CAMP activities; these are the Weiss and Sampson Control Mastery Theory (CMT) and Plan Formulation Method, based on the disconforming of debilitating 'pathogenic beliefs' within the therapeutic situation, the M Horowitz Configurational Analysis and Role-Relationship Model (CARR) based on the interacting of mental schemas, or structures of meaning, as they affect thought and action concerning the self and others, and the L Horwitz Menninger Treatment Interventions Project (TRIP), exploring the evolving relationship between the state of the therapeutic alliance and the interpretation of the transference.

Clearly, the fourth-generation studies so sketchily outlined here are very much today just in *statu nascendi*, but evidently, psychoanalytic therapy research, which has already yielded significant knowledge about the nature of treatment outcomes and efficacy through the first three generations of studies from 1917 to the present, is now poised at a new level. This new level holds the potential for truly accelerating breakthroughs, not only methodological, but also substantive, as the currently conceived fourth-generation studies actually do get carried out through their natural cycle. It is indeed a hopeful and promising note on which to end this overview of these generations of psychotherapy research.

Notes

1. Although the span from Coriat (1917) to this study (1967) is a half-century, I call all of these studies 'first generation' in terms of their degree of conceptual and methodological sophistication, rather than in temporal terms - although, of course, each 'generation' started at a later point in time than its predecessor, or spanned a later period of time.
2. On the basis of my statement at the beginning of this chapter that in theory process and outcome are necessarily interlocked, the Menninger Foundation Psychotherapy Research Project was itself conceived as an inquiry into both the outcomes *and* the processes of psychoanalytic therapies. However, as also stated there, operationally the methods appropriate to the two realms of inquiry are often in opposition to each other, and, as it turned out, PRP was indeed much more an outcome study; the light thrown there on the treatment process was more inferential, and based primarily on clinical, not research-specifiable judgements.

References

Alexander F (1937) Five-Year Report of the Chicago Institute for Psychoanalysis: 1932-1937. Chicago, IL: Chicago Institute for Psychoanalysis.

Bachrach H, Galatzer-Levy R, Skolnikoff AZ, Waldron S Jr (1991) On the efficacy of psychoanalysis. Journal of the American Psychoanalytic Association 39: 871-916.

Bachrach HM, Weber JJ, Solomon M (1985) Factors associated with the outcome of psychoanalysis (clinical and methodological considerations): Report of the Columbia Psychoanalytic Center Research Project (IV). International Review of Psycho-Analysis 12: 379-88.

Carmichael HT (1956) Sound film recording of psychoanalytic therapy: A therapist's experiences and reactions. In: Gottschalk LA, Auerbach AH (eds) (1966) Methods of Research in Psychotherapy. New York: Appleton-Century-Crofts: pp. 50-9.

Coriat I (1917) Some statistical results of the psychoanalytical treatment of the psychoneuroses. Psychoanalytic Review 4: 209-16.

Dahl H, Kächele H, Thomä H (1988) Psychoanalytic Process Research Strategies. Berlin/New York: Springer.

Erle JB (1979) An approach to the study of analyzability and analysis: The course of forty consecutive cases selected for supervised analysis. Psychoanalytic Quarterly 48: 198-228.

Erle JB, Goldberg D (1979) Problems in the assessment of analyzability. Psychoanalytic Quarterly 48: 48-84.

Erle JB, Goldberg D (1984) Observations on assessment of analyzability by experienced analysts. Journal of the American Psychoanalytic Association 32: 715-37.

Feldman F (1968) Results of psychoanalysis in clinic case assignments. Journal of the American Psychoanalytic Association 16: 274–300.
Fenichel O (1930) Statistischer Bericht über die therapeutische Tätigkeit 1920–1930. In: Zehn Jahre Berliner Psychoanalytisches Institut. Internationaler Psychoanalytischer Verlag: 13–19.
Fonagy P, Kächele H, Krause R, Jones E, Perron R (1999) An Open Door Review of Outcome Studies in Psychoanalysis: Report prepared by the Research Committee of the IPA at the request of the President. London: University College London.
Fonagy P, Target M (1994) The efficacy of psychoanalyses for children with disruptive disorders. Journal of the American Academy of Child and Adolescent Psychiatry 33: 45–55.
Fonagy P, Target M (1996) Predictors of outcome in child psychoanalysis: A retrospective study of 763 cases at the Anna Freud Centre. Journal of the American Psychoanalytic Association 44 (1): 27–77.
Glover E (1954) The indications for psycho-analysis. Journal of Mental Science 100: 393–401.
Hamburg DA, Bibring GL, Fisher CS, Alfred H, Wallerstein RS, Weinstock HI, Haggard E (1967) Report of ad hoc committee on Central Fact-Gathering Data of the American Psychoanalytic Association. Journal of the American Psychoanalytic Association 15: 841–61.
Jones E (1936) Decannual Report of the London Clinic of Psychoanalysis, 1926–1937. London: London Clinic of Psychoanalysis.
Kantrowitz JL (1986) The role of the patient-analyst 'match' in the outcome of psychoanalysis. Annual of Psychoanalysis 14: 273–97.
Kantrowitz JL, Katz AL, Greenman DA, Humphrey M, Paolitto F, Sashin J, Solomon L (1989) The patient-analyst match and the outcome of psychoanalysis: A pilot study. Journal of the American Psychoanalytic Association 37: 893–919.
Kantrowitz JL, Katz AL, Paolitto F (1990a) Followup of psychoanalysis five to ten years after termination (I): Stability of change. Journal of the American Psychoanalytic Association 38: 471–96.
Kantrowitz JL, Katz AL, Paolitto F (1990b) Followup of psychoanalysis five to ten years after termination (II): Development of the self-analytic function. Journal of the American Psychoanalytic Association 38: 637–54.
Kantrowitz JL, Katz AL, Paolitto F (1990c) Followup of psychoanalysis five to ten years after termination (III): The relation between the resolution of the transference and the patient-analyst match. Journal of the American Psychoanalytic Association 38: 655–78.
Kantrowitz JL, Katz AL, Paolitto F, Sashin J, Solomon L (1987a) Changes in the level and quality of object relations in psychoanalysis: Followup of a longitudinal prospective study. Journal of the American Psychoanalytic Association 35: 23–46.
Kantrowitz JL, Katz AL, Paolitto F, Sashin J, Solomon L (1987b) The role of reality testing in psychoanalysis: Followup of 22 cases. Journal of the American Psychoanalytic Association 35: 367–85.
Kantrowitz JL, Paolitto F, Sashin J, Solomon L, Katz AL (1986) Affect availability, tolerance, complexity, and modulation in psychoanalysis: Followup of a longitudinal prospective study. Journal of the American Psychoanalytic Association 34: 529–59.
Kessel L, Hyman H (1933) The value of psychoanalysis as a therapeutic procedure. Journal of the American Medical Association 101: 1612–15.

Knapp PH, Levin S, McCarter RH, Wermer H, Zetzel E (1960) Suitability for psychoanalysis: A review of one hundred supervised analytic cases. Psychoanalytica Quarterly 29: 459-77.

Knight RP (1941) Evaluation of the results of psychoanalytic therapy. American Journal of Psychiatry 98: 434-46.

Leuzinger-Bohleber M, Stuhr U (1997) '... die Fähigkeit zu lieben, zu arbeiten und das Leben zu genießen.' Zur psychoanalytischen Katamneseforschung. In: Leuzinger-Bohleber M, Stuhr U (eds): Psychoanalysen im Rückblick. Gießen: Psychosozial Verlag: 12-32.

Norman HF, Blacker KH, Oremland JD, Barrett WG (1976) The fate of the transference neurosis after termination of a satisfactory analysis. Journal of the American Psychoanalytic Association 24: 471-98.

Oremland JD, Blacker KH, Norman HF (1975) Incompleteness in 'successful' psychoanalyses: A follow-up study. Journal of the American Psychoanalytic Association 23: 819-44.

Pfeffer AZ (1959) A procedure for evaluating the results of psychoanalysis: A preliminary report. Journal of the American Psychoanalytic Association 7: 418-44.

Pfeffer AZ (1961) Follow-up study of a satisfactory analysis. Journal of the American Psychoanalytic Association 9: 698-718.

Pfeffer AZ (1963) The meaning of the analyst after analysis: A contribution to the theory of therapeutic results. Journal of the American Psychoanalytic Association 11: 229-44.

Rangell L (1966) An overview of the ending of an analysis. In: Litman RE (ed.) Psychoanalysis in the Americas. New York: International University Press, pp. 141-65. Reprinted in: Rangell L (1990) The Human Core: The intrapsychic base of behavior, Vol. 2. Madison, CT: International University Press, pp. 703-25.

Sashin JI, Eldred SH, Van Amerongen ST (1975) A search for predictive factors in institute supervised cases: a retrospective study of 183 cases from 1959 to 1966 at the Boston Psychoanalytic Society and Institute. International Journal of Psycho-Analysis 56: 343-59.

Schlessinger N, Robbins FP (1974) Assessment and follow-up in psychoanalysis. Journal of the American Psychoanalytic Association 22: 542-67.

Schlessinger N, Robbins FP (1975) The psychoanalytic process: Recurrent patterns of conflict and changes in ego functions. Journal of the American Psychoanalytic Association 23: 761-82.

Schlessinger N, Robbins FP (1983) A Developmental View of the Psychoanalytic Process: Follow-up studies and their consequences. New York: International University Press, p. 228.

Strupp HH, Schacht TE, Henry WP (1988) Problem-treatment-outcome congruence: A principle whose time has come. In: Dahl H, Kächele H, Thomä H (eds) Psychoanalytic Process Research Strategies. Berlin/New York, Springer-Verlag, pp. 1-14.

Szecsody I, Varvin S, Amadei G, Stoker J, Beenen F, Klockars L (1997) The European Multi-Site Collaborative Study of Psychoanalysis (Sweden, Finland, Norway, Holland and Italy). Paper presented at the Symposium on Outcome Research, International Psychoanalytical Association Congress, Barcelona, August 1997.

Target M, Fonagy P (1994a) The efficacy of psychoanalysis for children with emotional disorders. Journal of the American Academy of Child and Adolescent Psychiatry 33: 361-71.

Target M, Fonagy P (1994b) The efficacy of psychoanalysis for children: Prediction of outcome in a developmental context. Journal of the American Academy of Child and Adolescent Psychiatry 33: 1134–44.

Wallerstein RS (1986) Forty-two Lives in Treatment: A study of psychoanalysis and psychotherapy. New York: Guilford Press, p. 784.

Wallerstein RS (1988) Psychoanalysis and psychotherapy: Relative roles reconsidered. Annual of Psychoanalysis 16: 129–51.

Wallerstein RS (1991) Proposal to the Ludwig Foundation for a Collaborative Multi-Site Program of Psychoanalytic Therapy Research. Unpublished report.

Wallerstein RS, Sampson H (1971) Issues in research in the psychoanalytic process. International Journal of Psychoanalysis 52: 11–50.

Wallerstein RS, Fonagy P (1999) Psychoanalytic research and the IPA: History, present status and future potential. International Journal of Psycho-Analysis 80: 91–109.

Wallerstein RS, Robbins LL, Sargent HD, Luborsky L (1956) The Psychotherapy Research Project of the Menninger Foundation. Bulletin of the Menninger Clinic 20: 221–78.

Weber JJ, Bachrach HM, Solomon M (1985a) Factors associated with the outcome of psychoanalysis: Report of the Columbia Psychoanalytic Center Research Project (II). International Review of Psycho-Analysis 12: 127–41.

Weber JJ, Bachrach HM, Solomon M (1985b) Factors associated with the outcome of psychoanalysis: Report of the Columbia Psychoanalytic Center Research Project (III). International Review of Psycho-Analysis 12: 251–62.

Weber JJ, Solomon M, Bachrach HM (1985c) Characteristics of psychoanalytic clinic patients: Report of the Columbia Psychoanalytic Center Research Project (I). International Review of Psycho-Analysis 12: 13–26.

CHAPTER 4
Evidence-based medicine and its justifications

PETER FONAGY

Reasons behind the insistence on evidence

Psychoanalysis is a clinical treatment. Its aims and ambitions, at least from the point of view of most patients, are clearly associated with those of other healing arts such as surgery, physiotherapy or osteopathy. Admittedly, this is just one aspect of the psychoanalytic enterprise, but one that is crucial to its standing within most of the cultures where it is practised.

Over the last 10 years, all aspects of medicine have come under scrutiny, where increasingly both commissioners and funders of medical intervention, as well as those managing and directing clinical services, have embraced the values of 'evidence-based medicine' (Sackett, Rosenberg, Gray, Haynes and Richardson, 1996). Clinical judgement is no longer accepted as sufficient grounds for offering medical treatment. Recommendations at national policy level, and at local health care provider level are now expected to be based upon evidence of effectiveness. What factors account for this change?

Ostensible reasons

Evidence-based medicine is founded on an ideal - that decisions about the care of individual patients should involve the conscientious, explicit and judicious use of current best evidence. Much is claimed in favour of this approach, particularly in North America and Western Europe. The arguments in favour of it include 1) the more effective use of resources; 2) improvements in clinicians' knowledge; and 3) better communication with patients (Bastian, 1994). From an ethical point of view, the strongest argument in support of evidence-based medicine is that 4) it allows the best evaluated methods of health care to be identified and enables patients and doctors to make better informed decisions (Guyatt, Sackett, Cook and the Evidence Based Medicine Working Group, 1994; Hope, 1995). All these are good reasons but all were as relevant to medicine in the past as at the moment. So why the current emphasis?

The political background

The real driving force behind evidence-based medicine is unlikely to be a genuine concern for the quality of care. The movement appears to be largely driven by financial considerations and the hope of health care organizations to reduce escalating costs, by focusing on the most cost-effective options given a range of treatments. Governments and health funds find the notion of allocating health resources on the basis of evidence quite attractive. In North America, DK Eddy in an important JAMA editorial suggested that health care funds should be required to cover interventions *only* if there was sufficient evidence that they could be expected to produce their intended effects (Eddy, 1996). The Australian Health Minister, Dr Michael Wooldridge, adopted a very similar position stating '[we will] pay only for those operations, drugs and treatments that, according to available evidence, are proved to work' (Downey, 1997).

I believe that it is important to accumulate evidence in support of psychoanalytic interventions. I am sceptical, however, about the pressures brought on psychoanalytic clinicians as it seems unlikely that, even in the face of overwhelming evidence as to the benefits of this relatively expensive treatment, the resources would be available to provide psychoanalysis for many who require it. In this context it is important to review the philosophical basis of the search for evidence for psychoanalysis in order to gain a perspective on the entire enterprise of outcomes research.

Philosophical concerns

Evidence-based medicine represents a practical example of 'consequentionalism'. Consequentionalism refers to the proposition that the worth of an action may be assessed by the measurement of its consequences. There are at least three problems with the consequentionalist argument, all of which apply to psychoanalytic outcome research:

- the difficulty in measuring outcomes;
- the ownership of outcomes (whose interest should be considered?);
- and finally that consequentionalism may lead to unethical conclusions.

We shall take these in turn.

Philosophical questions concerning the measurement of outcome

The first concern is with the measurement of outcome. It is indisputable that many important outcomes of any medical treatment are unmeasurable.

Evidence-based medicine claims to provide a simple logical process for reasoning and decision making:

- systematic scrutiny of the available evidence;
- drawing conclusions leading to
- a clinical decision as to the appropriateness of a treatment.

Within this framework, for any decision to be balanced, all relevant consequences of a treatment must be considered. Unfortunately, in the current state of methods of psychological measurement, many important outcomes can only be very inadequately measured.

Psychoanalysis concerns complex internal states such as the degree of distress or pain experienced by an individual. Often these complex states are reduced to simpler, easily measurable ones such as depression (Beck, Ward, Mendelson, Mock and Erbaugh, 1961), anxiety (Spielberger, Gorsuch and Lushene, 1970) or total symptomatology (Derogatis, 1983). A valid objection to such measures (if used without sophistication) is that they are reified and researchers may conflate the measure with the phenomena it was aimed at quantifying. Thus, the BDI score is *not* depression and the total symptom distress score of the SCL-90 is not equivalent to mental pain. By having these measurements we have not at all done justice to the complex cognitive, affective and physiological processes that are implied by these terms.

Even if better measures were found for some domains of outcomes entailed in psychoanalytic treatment, other aspects of the process, such as an 'ethical life', a 'sense of purpose' or 'social justice', may be inherently unmeasurable. Even more troublesome are key domains that are not even well defined, let alone measurable. One such is the 'quality of life'. Attempts have been made to provide a metric for this, yet in the absence of a consensus as to what a reasonable quality of life might entail, it is hard to imagine how measurement is possible.

The philosopher Bernard Williams (1972), in an important book on morality, noted that values that can be quantified in economic terms may require comparison with values which are not quantifiable. His comments may be extrapolated easily to the current situation of psychoanalysis in some countries: 'Again and again defenders of such values are faced with the dilemma of either refusing to quantify the value in question, in which case it disappears from the sum altogether, or else of trying to attach some quantity to it, in which case they misrepresent what they are about and also usually lose the argument, since the quantified value is not enough to tip the scale' (p. 103). Some outcomes of psychoanalysis may indeed be costed, but these may be some of the least important. The cost saved may not 'tip the balance' in favour of psychoanalysis.

The ownership of outcome

The second common criticism concerns the ownership of outcome: 'Whose outcome is the outcome of psychoanalysis, anyway?' It may be *in principle* impossible to decide between the competing claims of different individuals. For example, a treatment that enhances the quality of life of one person may be deleterious to a spouse or an employer. This is particularly evident in the case of the psychoanalytic treatment of children where the treated child's desired outcome may be in conflict with that of the parent's, or indeed that of the sibling. Ideally, notwithstanding the insurmountable practical problems, all individuals significantly concerned with an analysand should be assessed as part of the outcome study. The research enterprise itself is clinician led. It is the clinician-researcher that decides whose outcome will form the basis of evidence-based practice. Thus all outcome investigations, perhaps particularly that of psychoanalysis, will be arbitrary, and limited by the selection of the individual(s) on whom outcome is measured.

An extension of the arbitrariness problem of outcome ownership concerns the status of client preference as an indication of outcome. It could be argued that the client is in a privileged position relative to the investigator in determining whether the treatment is helpful. Interestingly, when user groups are asked they tend to strongly favour approaches to most mental health problems which are psychologically rather than pharmacologically based, or at least they plead for a greater emphasis on psychological help (Seligman, 1995). When individuals perceive their difficulties arising out of psychosocial causes, they understandably seek redress in the same domain - the interpersonal. It is also worth noting that psychodynamic therapy often has greater prima facie acceptability than exposure-based cognitive behaviour therapy (for example, with patients with OCD, see Apter, Bernhout and Tyano, 1984). Yet the desire of the user, 'client satisfaction', is not generally acceptable as a criterion for outcome. By this criterion, many treatments known to be ineffective and even harmful (for example, recreational drugs such as nicotine to counteract anxiety) could be selected.

Psychotherapy researchers are particularly conscious of the danger of imposing ethnically rooted cultural biases on what is designated as 'needing treatment' and to be a 'good outcome' (Bernal, Bonilla and Bellido, 1995). For instance, the achievement of selfhood through the separation–individuation process is one of the cornerstones of psychotherapeutic interventions. Yet was Christopher Lasch (1978) correct that the emphasis on individual achievement in Western culture is excessive, and that submission to the goals of the family and community (Kagan, 1984) may be a far better indicator of healthy adaptation?

Ethical concerns

Finally, it is commonly asserted that a uniquely evidence-based treatment approach can lead to unethical activities. A good example of this is the success of aversive conditioning and other punishment-based techniques in the control of individuals with so-called 'challenging behaviour'. The fact that there is evidence supporting the efficiency of these techniques does not make them right.

More generally, ethical concerns arise out of the use of randomized control trials. While such trials can reduce worthless treatments, for example insulin coma therapy, they raise major ethical issues in the context of subject selection, consent, randomization and the continuing care of subjects once trials are complete. Randomized control trials require the clinician to act simultaneously as clinician and researcher. Patients are simultaneously invalids and research subjects. It is questionable if physicians' moral responsibilities towards patients can be consistent with the recommendation that their patients should participate in a randomized control trial, principally because of this conflict of interest (Hellman and Hellman, 1991).

It has been suggested that such trials may be recommended by clinicians if they are in a state of 'therapeutic equipoise', that is they are genuinely in doubt about the value of the interventions under scrutiny (Lilford and Jackson, 1995). Such equipoise may be achieved in the case of treatments with moderate effects, which might otherwise be obscured by bias and random effects. However, equipoise may not be achievable when interventions have great benefits or risks, and then alternative clinical procedures must be evaluated by other methods.

Is therapeutic equipoise applicable to the recommendation of psychoanalytic treatment? Interestingly, neither psychoanalysts nor the opponents of psychoanalytic treatment believe that this is the case. Psychoanalysts are so firmly convinced of the appropriateness of four or five times a week treatment that they tend to consider it unethical to recommend less intensive alternatives. Sceptics, on the other hand, feel that the sacrifice demanded of the patient and his/her family is such that randomization to psychoanalytic treatment is ethically unacceptable. In principle, the existence of these opposing views might somehow be combined to construct an attitude of therapeutic equipoise, but in reality it is tantamount to an insurmountable obstacle facing randomized controlled trials of psychoanalysis.

The need for persistence

Many other concerns could be raised about subjecting psychoanalysis to outcome evaluation. I raise some concerns here in part to demonstrate awareness of the issues, and in part to underscore that the clamour for evidence should be met with caution and sophistication. It needs to be recognized that objections to research will not win the day. It is unlikely that the prevailing view that places controlled studies at the top of the hierarchy of evidence will change, no matter what the strength of opposing arguments. The complexities of issues surrounding resource allocation, the drive to seek certainty and simplicity at the level of policy making, are such that alternative formulations will not be heard.

Psychoanalysis is not alone among medical treatments with a weak evidence base. Evidence, to the standards required, is available for relatively few medical interventions (Kerridge, Lowe and Henry, 1998). The drive for an evidence base for the selection of treatments will inevitably mean a biased allocation of resources in favour of those treatments for which rigorous evidence of effectiveness is relatively easily collected, or where funds are independently available to carry out more lengthy and complex effectiveness research. Brief therapy benefits from the former, pharmacotherapy from the latter. Psychoanalysis is further disadvantaged by opposition to many of its fundamental propositions from fellow mental health professionals and influential cultural figures. These considerations drive us to overcome our concerns with epistemological problems, and accept the imperfect solution of outcome research with the overriding objective of preserving the discipline.

The best strategy available to us is to collect all the data available rather than enter an epistemological debate amongst ourselves. The debate is inaudible to those outside the discipline. Further it would sap our energies when these are required for a collaborative effort to make the best case possible for psychoanalysis as a clinical method. Even those of us who are engaged in collecting evidence for the effectiveness of this discipline have major methodological as well as epistemological concerns. These should not be set aside, or forgotten about, but nor should they become an alternative focus.

The debate over the effectiveness of psychoanalysis is one of pragmatics not of principles. There is a clear danger that the therapy that is 'without substantial evidence' will be thought by all to be 'without substantial value' (Evidence Based Care Resource Group, 1994). Once this idea is allowed to flourish, a cultural change becomes inevitable - a change that at least temporarily has the power to stop the development of our discipline - through the rejection of psychoanalysis as a treatment of choice, through discouraging young people from entering the profession and through bringing psychoanalytic contributions to mental health disciplines and other subjects into disrepute.

References

Apter A, Bernhout E, Tyano S (1984) Severe obsessive compulsive disorder in adolescence: A report of eight cases. Journal of Adolescence 7: 349-58.

Bastian H (1994) The Power of Sharing Knowledge. Consumer participation in the Cochrane Collaboration. Oxford: UK Cochrane Centre.

Beck AT, Ward CH, Mendelson M, Mock J, Erbaugh J (1961) An inventory for measuring depression. Archives of General Psychiatry 4: 561-71.

Bernal G, Bonilla J, Bellido C (1995) Ecological validity and cultural sensitivity for outcome research: Issues for the cultural adaptation and development of psychosocial treatments with Hispanics. Journal of Abnormal Child Psychology 23: 67-82.

Derogatis LR (1983) SCL-90R: Administration, Scoring and Procedures - Manual II. Towson, MD: Clinical Psychometric Research Inc.

Downey M (10 May 1997) Trust me I'm a doctor. Sidney Morning Herald, p. 1.

Eddy DK (1996) Benefit language: Criteria that will improve quality while reducing costs. Journal of the American Medical Association 275: 650-57.

Evidence Based Care Resource Group (1994) Evidence-based care 1. Setting priorities: how important is this problem. Canadian Medical Association Journal 150: 1249-54.

Guyatt GH, Sackett DL, Cook DJ, the Evidence Based Medicine Working Group (1994) Users' guides to the medical literatures. Journal of the American Medical Association 271: 59-63.

Hellman S, Hellman DS (1991) Of mice but not men. Problems of the randomised clinical trial. New England Journal of Medicine 324: 1585-9.

Hope T (1995) Evidence-based medicine and ethics. Journal of Medical Ethics 21: 259-60.

Kagan J (1984) The Nature of the Child. New York: Basic Books.

Kerridge I, Lowe M, Henry D (1998) Ethics and evidence-based medicine. British Medical Journal 316: 1151-3.

Lasch C (1978) The Culture of Narcissism: American life in an age of diminishing expectations. New York: Norton.

Lilford R, Jackson J (1995) Equipoise and the ethics of randomizations. Journal of Research in Social Medicine 88: 552-9.

Sackett DL, Rosenberg WM, Gray JAM, Haynes RB, Richardson WS (1996) Evidence-based medicine: What it is and what it isn't. British Medical Journal 312: 71-2.

Seligman MEP (1995) The effectiveness of psychotherapy. American Psychologist 50: 965-74.

Spielberger CD, Gorsuch RL, Lushene RE (1970) The State-Trait Anxiety Inventory (Self-Evaluation Questionnaire). Palo Alto, CA: Consulting Psychologists Press.

Williams B (1972) Morality. Cambridge: Cambridge University Press.

PART 2

LONG-TERM PSYCHOANALYTIC THERAPIES: GERMAN STUDIES

CHAPTER 5
Introduction and overview

MARIANNE LEUZINGER-BOHLEBER

The worldwide *Zeitgeist* that we have described puts psychoanalysis once more under pressure to 'prove' its outcomes and its efficiency. This has met different political and psychoanalytic conditions in each of our countries: in the US, the UK, France, Germany and elsewhere. I will make a few remarks on the specific situation in Germany before introducing the chapters in Part 2, which represent some of the ongoing research activities there.

Bohleber (2001), summarizing the development of clinical psychoanalysis in Germany after 1945, discussed the specific historical situation of psychoanalysis in Germany after the Nazi persecution. This situation still influences discourse within psychoanalysis, an influence that often is not recognized and considered critically enough. It can also be observed within the epistemological debate on research in psychoanalysis in Germany. As Bohleber explains, German analysts like Wolfgang Loch, Helmut Thomä, Hermann Argelander and Alfred Lorenzer opened a new chapter within the clinical debate on psychoanalysis in the 1960s. Loch, Argelander, Lorenzer and others, developed a psychoanalytic hermeneutic approach in different papers, which were influenced by the general debate on hermeneutics in philosophy and the social sciences. This had been initiated by the publication of *Wahrheit und Methode* (*Truth and Method*) by Hans-Georg Gadamer in 1960 and *Erkenntnis und Interesse* (*Insight and Interest*) by Jürgen Habermas in 1968. In the concept of the 'szenisches Verstehen' (scenic understanding) by Argelander and Lorenzer, the position of the analyst as an 'objective observer' in the analytic situation was combined with a modern hermeneutic understanding of transference. In this view, transference is not seen as a static and already fixed psychic phenomenon, which means that the analysand reveals (static) past experiences in the presence of the transference relationship. Instead, transference, the 'scene', is a joint dynamic construction between analyst and patient, not a product of the past that simply has to be discovered in the present analytic relationship. The 'scenic understanding' by these authors is a modern constructivist understanding of the transference which was ahead of its time.

In my view, these concepts are not only clinically relevant but also touch the epistemological discussion on research, because of an analogous 'objective' position of researchers in relation to their research subjects. This argument was discussed extensively in the so-called debate on positivism (*Positivismusstreit*) starting in the 1950s, concerning research in social sciences, and in psychoanalysis. Lorenzer (1985) therefore defined psychoanalysis as a 'science between the sciences', between hermeneutics and science. For him, research in psychoanalysis is always partly a hermeneutic process because it is necessary to try to understand unconscious meanings connected with the idiosyncratic history of a specific individual. At the same time, psychoanalysis is also a science, offering generalized explanations for human behaviour. This dialectical position of psychoanalysis and the specificity of its scientific approach, hardly discussed internationally in the 1960s, was much later also postulated by American authors like Arnold Modell (1984), Arnold Cooper (1985), and the Israeli author Carlo Strenger (1991).

Strangely, this productive debate on research in psychoanalysis was hardly continued by the next generation of German psychoanalytic researchers, but remained in a kind of latency until a similar debate was 'imported' from psychoanalysis in the US. This was seen by many members of the younger generation of German analysts to be completely new, despite the extensive debate in Germany in the 1960s. During the late 1970s and 1980s, psychoanalytic research discussions in Germany showed a radical polarization between a purely hermeneutic, anti-empirical position (featuring an idealized reception of Kleinian psychoanalysis) on the one hand and, on the other, a fairly rigid positivistic position within a group of empirical researchers. These researchers identified exclusively with a particular tradition of empirical research in the US.

Bohleber (2001) discusses an interesting hypothesis with respect to a similar phenomenon in the reception of clinical psychoanalytic concepts. He suggests that the unconscious rejection of a productive psychoanalytic tradition in Germany by the younger generation of psychoanalysts is connected with a devaluation of their teachers after the discovery, in the 1980s, that not only some founders of the Deutsche Psychoanalytische Gesellschaft (DPG), but also a few of the German Psychoanalytical Association (DPV) had been involved with the Nazi regime. Idealization of Anglo-American psychoanalysis and a devaluation of German analysts and researchers were probably an unconscious consequence. Only searching reflection on these unconscious mechanisms could liberate the creativity of our generation of psychoanalysts in Germany, enabling us to use some of the productive continental traditions in psychoanalytic research, integrating them in a new way with the international psychoanalytic discussion.

The three-year period in the German Psychoanalytical Association (DPV) in which we planned and conceptualized the follow-up study presented in this part (Chapter 8 to Chapter 12) was an attempt at such critical self-reflection, integrating research traditions in our country with the research tradition of the IPA (for example, the discussion initiated by the Research Committee and the Research Advisory Board of the IPA). Only intensive discussion of the epistemological and methodological problems of empirical research in psychoanalysis finally convinced our DPV colleagues that a follow-up study - seen as an empirical approach to the complexity of psychoanalytic processes and its outcome - would be an interesting and relevant enterprise.

This discussion involved informing our colleagues about epistemological problems of research in psychoanalysis and the worldwide political situation of psychoanalysis. We also summarized some of the classical and current empirical studies in psychoanalysis (Leuzinger-Bohleber and Stuhr, 1997), demonstrating that despite the complex methodological problems involved, some of the most famous studies in the field of psychotherapy research were carried out by analysts. These include the Menninger Study, the Columbia Research Project, and the Boston Psychoanalytic Institute Prediction Study together with studies done at the New York Institute, at the Anna Freud Centre in London and in different places in the German-speaking community (see, for example, Wallerstein, Chapter 3 in this volume; Dahl, Kächele and Thomä, 1988; Krause et al., 1992). We also pointed out that several very sophisticated studies on psychoanalytical long-term therapies had been undertaken recently, or are currently under way. Many are presented in the present volume and are prospective studies that compare different psychotherapeutic treatments in an empirical design (some even randomizing the patients).

We discussed the fact that prospective studies have many advantages, particularly the measurement of the patient's state before, during and after treatment; but they also have some disadvantages, including the influence of the research setting on the psychoanalytic process, dropouts, the small affordable sample size, the long wait for the first results, with the risk that the instruments used may become out of date meanwhile. In contrast, follow-up studies have the advantage of not influencing the ongoing therapy; but the disadvantage is that the treatment is evaluated retrospectively by the patients themselves, their therapists and the independent observers. On the other hand the sample size can be large and results can be achieved quickly, and (especially important for many psychoanalysts) such studies are close to normal practice. This last was one of the major arguments convincing our colleagues to support an empirical follow-up study after intensive and controversial discussions. Following these discussions, we developed a design that integrated the different research traditions in German psychoanalysis, combining psychoanalytical with non-psychoanalytical, hermeneutic with nomothetic, qualitative and quantitative instruments (see below).

Much of this part of the book is dedicated to this naturalistic research project, the ***multi-perspective, representative follow-up study of psychoanalyses and long-term psychoanalytic therapies.*** We summarize some aspects of planning and implementing the study, developing a specific study design (Chapter 8 by Marianne Leuzinger-Bohleber), methodological considerations (Chapter 9 by Ulrich Stuhr), the statistical design and the control of representativeness (Chapter 10 by Bernhard Rüger), first results of the questionnaire sample (Chapter 11, Manfred Beutel and Markus Rasting) and the interview sample (Chapter 12 by Marianne Leuzinger-Bohleber).

Chapter 6, the case history 'Report on the analytical psychotherapy of a young girl' by Winfrid Trimborn, is also connected to the follow-up study: the epistemological debates focused on the critical discussion of this 'classical form' of communication within the psychoanalytic community, illuminating its advantages and disadvantages. Despite the well-known problems connected with this tradition (for example, selecting clinical information only to support and not to reject certain hypotheses) Trimborn's case history illustrates that some dimensions, complex clinical experiences and insights of our psychoanalytical practice can only be told and not measured, for example the transference–counter-transference dynamics, the many-sided relation between healing and the stabilization of this patient's late adolescent identity - a precondition for overcoming her symptoms and becoming a creative artist, and so forth. The case history also illustrates the subject of our book: long-term psychoanalytic therapies. Curative and developmental processes in certain patients need their own time in order to achieve stable and constant psychic changes! This clinically based thesis is tested empirically by the many studies of this book.

Chapter 7 is also close to clinical practice: Stavros Mentzos was professor of psychiatry and psychosomatics at the University of Frankfurt for many years and was a university colleague of Hermann Argelander and Alfred Lorenzer. He specialized in the psychoanalytic treatment of severely ill patients, such as psychotics and borderline personalities. He has developed concepts for psychoanalytic outpatient treatment of such patients. Most of the psychotic patients (6.2% of the interview sample of the DPV study) and some of the borderline patients (9.3% of the interview sample) were treated according to the concepts of Mentzos, often even supervised by him in a network of psychoanalysts working with such severely disturbed patients in Germany. In his chapter he offers a new diagnostic classification for borderline patients based on his rich clinical experience.

One aspect of treating these groups of severely disturbed patients is the current discussion on the cost effectiveness of long-term psychotherapies, a subject that is discussed in Chapter 13 by Markus Fäh, who has been active in health politics in Switzerland for years. This introduces some of the major topics in the ongoing controversies, also referring to some European and American theoreticians in this field. Wolfram Keller and his group summarize an empirical study on the mental health costs of Jungian long-term psychotherapies, replicating the classical study of Dührssen and Jorswieck (1965) showing that long-term psychotherapy proves to be cost effective for the health insurance companies.

In the last section of Part 2, two ongoing prospective studies are summarized: the research group of Gerd Rudolf and his co-workers reports a large prospective study comparing psychoanalyses (three and more sessions a week) with psychoanalytic long-term therapies (one to two session a week). They apply a large spectrum of different research methods, among them the operationalized psychoanalytic diagnostic, an elaborated psychoanalytic research instrument that has been developed by different research groups in Germany during recent years. Another prospective study is introduced by Dorothea Huber, Günther Klug and Michael von Rad in Chapter 16. This study focused on the treatment of depressed patients by psychoanalyses, psychoanalytic long-term therapies and behavioural therapies. The methods used, the design and first results of this ongoing study are summarized. The authors tried to fulfil the methodological requirements of the Society of Psychotherapy Research and thus to get into scientific exchange with the international community of psychotherapy researchers, which of course also includes non-psychoanalytic psychotherapy researchers.

References

Bohleber W (2001) 100 Jahre Psychoanalyse, 50 Jahre DPV - zur Situation der Psychoanalyse heute. In: Bohleber W, Drews S: 100 Jahre Psychoanalyse, 50 Jahre DPV - zur Situation der Psychoanalyse heute. Stuttgart: Klett Cotta, pp. 15-35.

Cooper A (1985) Historical Review of Psychoanalytic Paradigms. In: Rothstein A (ed.) Models of the Mind. Their relationship to clinical work. New York: International Universities Press, pp. 7-20.

Dahl H, Kächele H, Thomä H (1988) Psychoanalytic Process Research Strategies. New York: Springer.

Dührssen A, Jorswieck E (1965) Eine empirisch-statistische Untersuchung zur Leistungsfähigkeit psychoanalytischer Behandlung. Nervenarzt 39: 166-9.

Krause R, Steimer-Krause E, Ullrich B (1992) Use of affect research in dynamic psychotherapy. In: Leuzinger-Bohleber M, Schneider H, Pfeifer R (eds) 'Two Butterflies on My Head . . .' Psychoanalysis in the Interdisciplinary Scientific Dialogue. New York/Berlin/Tokyo: Springer, pp. 277-93.

Leuzinger-Bohleber M, Stuhr U (eds) (1997) Psychoanalysen im Rückblick. Methoden, Ergebnisse und Perspektiven der neueren Katamneseforschung. Gießen: Psychosozial-Verlag.

Lorenzer A (1985) Spuren und Spurensuche bei Freud. Fragmente 17(18): 160-97.

Modell AH (1984) Gibt es die Metapsychologie noch? Psyche 38: 214-35.

Strenger C (1991) Between Hermeneutics and Science. An essay on the epistemology of psychoanalysis. New York: International University Press.

CHAPTER 6

Report on the analytical psychotherapy of a young girl

WINFRID TRIMBORN

> Nobody is born just once. If you are fortunate,
> you will see the light in the arms of another:
> if you are unfortunate, you will awaken with the long
> tail of terror brushing against the inside of your skull.[1]
>
> (Anne Michaels, *Fluchtstücke*)

'There is no difference, day and night are the same', the young girl complained near the end of our first interview and added, 'I need somebody who understands more than my mother does'. Thirteen years later she sent me the first pictures she had painted and with which she can now express and show her inner experience. One picture is entitled *Grim on a Bright Day.*

Confusion and alienation – depersonalization and derealization

When Ann came to me, she had already made two attempts at therapy that had failed at the outset. She was a pale 17-year-old, who looked so forlorn and neglected that I found the term 'sloppy Miss' - as her mother teasingly called her - quite appropriate for her appearance. She produced her request in a soft, childish voice and in a very hazy way. Every now and again she hesitated and silently examined me. She said that a year ago she had taken LSD. Since then she had had the feeling that she didn't really exist. The world seemed to her to be strange, like in a dream. If she rode her bicycle, lost in thought, she would wake up suddenly and everything would seem to be strange, just as it appeared to her to be in this room. Before going to sleep it was particularly bad. If she was alone, she would panic and feel afraid of losing her mind. 'There is no difference, day and night are the same.'

Ann - as I shall call her here - also talked about feeling as if she were stumbling into a void, as if she were about to go crazy. Something was missing. There were no connections. She complained of feeling meaningless, empty, depressed, and she expressed thoughts of suicide. There was a feeling of futility. She would prefer not to wake up in the morning, but would rather continue dreaming. She did not know who she was.

One remark she made struck me, because it was a very significant and far-reaching statement. She said, 'I want to be alone with my mother. But I need someone, who understands more than my mother does.'

The biographical information she gave me was confusing and incomplete, and she was very vague about when things happened. She said she was born during the extended honeymoon of her parents in a foreign country. Her parents separated when she was two years old. Her mother then married an Englishman. She doesn't get on with her younger half-brother. Suddenly she asked me what I thought about that. After the birth of her brother her mother separated from her second husband. Subsequently seven-year-old Ann was put on a plane all by herself and sent to her grandparents. Later her mother also came back home to her parents. Ann continued to have close contact with her stepfather through her brother. Finally, Ann mentioned that her own father, whom she had met for the first time in the previous year, only lives a few hundred metres from her home at her grandparents' house.

One question occupied my mind throughout the first session: Ann had been registered under the name of Burger at the university clinic. However this name was crossed out on her clinic card and had been replaced by Smith. When I asked her what her name was, she explained in many vague words that her name was Smith, saying that this was what she was called at school. I was confused, because the name on her card was Burger. After I asked her again, she replied rather unclearly that her birth name was Burger. Smith seemed to be the name of her stepfather, her mother and her brother. I now asked myself what she would really like to be called. I had had the strong impression that she wanted to be called Smith as usual. However, I had the unpleasant feeling that I would be making a mistake, whatever name I used. I freed myself from this dilemma by confronting her at the end of the session with the question of what she wanted to be called. After hesitating a little she decided on Burger, her birth name. After all that she had told me I did not expect this reply. She also added that she had considered calling herself after her grandmother. When I talked about her father in this connection she said 'I don't really talk about him as "father". My mother refers to him merely as my procreator.' I felt convinced that Ann had dared to take a big step.

During the second session Ann told me that she had taken LSD three times with her stepfather and said that this was the reason for her symptoms. However, I myself had started thinking that her visit to her real father could have occurred at this time and might have confused her. She had taken this step without her mother knowing and in spite of the disapproval she feared her mother would show. After I cautiously suggested that there might be a connection, Anne said that the situation with her father had seemed strange to her. She was quarrelling increasingly with her mother, who drank. Only after nine months was she finally able to talk about the fact that her stepfather had slept with her in the previous year.

The unconscious conflict situation and diagnostic reflections[2]

In the application for medical aid I listed four factors as having triggered off the patient's breakdown:

- taking LSD with her stepfather;
- visiting her real father;
- finishing school and starting an apprenticeship;
- her relationship to her mother being endangered by these three events.

In her attempts to separate from her mother Ann had obviously tried to obtain help from her real father, taking the risk of thus reconnecting to her early childhood. This attempt had brought about an inwardly unresolvable situation in respect to her mother, to whom she remained even more closely tied by these conflicts.

In the first application for medical aid my diagnosis was: depressive syndrome; imminent psychotic breakdown. Structural: unresolved dependency/separation problems on the grounds of an unintegrated highly ambivalent relationship to her mother. Her defence is marked by a massive schizoid withdrawal intended to ward off the depressive fear of destroying her primary object with her ambivalence.

The results of this withdrawal were far-reaching inner emptiness and isolation, which turned therapy into a tricky, tiring and difficult procedure. Right at the beginning Ann had already emphasized that it was important for her to be able to take her own time and not to be pushed, so that she could do something herself.

The ensuing process and the pictures that Ann sent me long after her therapy was finished confirmed these thoughts in an impressive way. Her first therapy of 110 sessions - at one session a week - took almost three years. After four years the patient called me again. The second therapy took another three-and-a-half years at two sessions a week. The therapeutic process shows how much an early apparent success in therapy can be deceptive and the results shaky.

Establishing a therapeutic framework against the fear of being overcome

The patient was a juvenile so I decided on low-frequency therapy, at first half an hour, later one hour a week. At the back of my mind was Winnicott's remark that adolescence is not an illness but rather a crisis and a developmental process, both of which need sufficient time. In addition I was convinced that if therapy were too intensive, her unintegrated dependency wishes and fears would increase her fear of fusion and of being emotionally overcome,[3] and that this would endanger the therapeutic framework. If the therapy were too intensive, this would force her either to act or to flee. Therapy was meant to be a catalyst - the therapeutic relationship ought not to become the dominant relationship.

In retrospect I still adhere to these thoughts to a large extent. However I must also admit that Ann experienced an enormous amount of support in the apprenticeship she had started, where she worked quietly in her master's presence. Ann herself confirmed this 17 years later. Without this stable background the therapy would probably not have been intensive enough. In her second therapy a higher frequency proved to be necessary and helpful for working on conflicts within the therapeutic relationship.

Ann was a highly sensitive person who tested me out from the beginning and observed my surroundings meticulously. Due to her schizoid structure she used her hyperconsciousness to empathize with my role. Usually she did not speak about herself at the beginning of the sessions, instead she tried to understand me and the problems of my profession. She was solicitous and tried to spare me, for example if she saw somebody leave the therapy room before her session. Or she showed concern for her brother, her mother or her stepfather.

I thought it necessary to neither reject nor promote her attempts at identification, because I saw that she was trying to slip into my role while at the same time quietly withdrawing. At this stage it was important for me to share in her well-founded concern for the people around her, particularly since she recognized their difficulties and defences, especially her mother's, with acute sensitivity. On the other hand I turned down her requests for interviews with others, which she made out of concern for her brother, as well as her boyfriend's request for an interview. Repeatedly she told me about the lack of understanding and the distrust her mother as well as her boyfriend had about her therapy. It would not do to allow myself to be quietly taken in.

Ann tried to empathize with me and draw closer inconspicuously. Without saying anything about it, I listened with an amused smile, as she talked about a pop singer whom she liked to listen to and who spoke with a Frankfurt dialect. Apparently she had recognized the dialect I was prone to use. When she asked me why I did not use a more familiar tone in addressing her, although she came so often and talked about so many personal things, I pointed out the peculiarity of a psychotherapeutic situation, describing it as a form of doctor-patient relationship. Clever as she was, Ann said that one might become too dependent, making it difficult to leave later, which however she could not imagine doing at that point. In expressing this thought she was touching on her basic conflict. It was precisely this kind of experience - being dependent and interrelated with another person - which she was forced to ward off under all circumstances.

In this respect it was extremely important for me to be completely reliable in keeping our appointments. Ann came to the first session after my lunch break. She often sat in the waiting room unobtrusively for 20 to 30 minutes before her session, just keeping quiet. Despite her taking possession of my personal space, in a sensitive way, she did not seem to be clinging, because at the same time she was deeply afraid of becoming a burden. She made herself small and invisible. Even the smallest inattentiveness on my part caused her to withdraw immediately and made her try even harder to empathize with my therapeutic role so that she would be better able to spare me. Once when I accidentally began a session half-an-hour late, she told me about a dream in which I had died making her feel helpless. Punctuality, serenity and reliability were apparently essential conditions for her not to keep me permanently the object of her sensitive observation and control. Only in this way could Ann slowly be made to come to the fore. My approach was to be present as a person, but not to involve myself. When treating this kind of disturbance the primary task is not bringing the unconscious into consciousness or elaborating on oedipal conflicts and interpreting them. According to James (1964) this would merely promote intellectual defences, mythologizing and schizoid disruptions. After all, the danger that Ann might involve me in pseudo-oedipal rivalry, jealousy, and loyalty conflicts, was there at an early stage already. So I tried rather to open a space for her, that would allow her to gain access to herself and her life story.

From the beginning it was also important to keep within specific bounds and promote her responsibility for the therapy. In consideration of her limited resources we agreed on a fee of DM 15 (about £5), if she should miss a session. The first salient turning point came after she had had nine months of therapy, after the Easter holidays. Up until then Ann had come regularly and punctually. After the holiday of one week, however, she did not come for the following two sessions. In the sessions before the holidays she had expressed the fear of falling into a void. When I talked to her about her absenteeism in the first subsequent session she seemed to be completely surprised and helpless, saying that she had thought that there would be a break of two weeks. She was helpless in such a completely childlike, innocent way that I had to muster a great deal of inner strength to remind her of our agreement and insist on it. She brought me the money the following session, expressing some feelings of guilt. Then she told me about a lecture on psychotherapy she had heard on the radio. She had been relieved to realize that one has to participate. Until now she had thought I was doing something to her, guiding her. Then she asked me whether I also read books by Freud. She was apparently trying to reconnect to me through a common 'Father Freud'.

Another danger was that she might fall pregnant. On one occasion I took the initiative to point out the need for birth control, for which she was very grateful later on. At this point she also mentioned two abortions her mother had had. Only after the first therapy, however, did this topic come up in all its severity.

Missed meetings and incest

Ann's first therapy mainly revolved around her attempts at separating from her home and her mother. Inwardly she was unable to do so because, for her, separation was connected to unbearable feelings of insecurity and intangible fears, compelling her to control her mother in an insidious way. However, this made her feel controlled herself, and forced her to become even more invisible in her actions. As a result there were continuous, puzzling misunderstandings between her and her mother. They both avoided one other. They could not get together. If they agreed to meet, they would just miss one another. To Ann it seemed impossible to get a chance to talk to her mother, yes, even to be together with her, because she was always just going off or had just gone, when Ann came home. This she experienced as a form of rejection and injury. She complained about the futility of her effort to establish contact with her mother, finally accepting this as an unalterable fact.

Ann was afraid of the emptiness with which she was trying to defend herself against her feelings of ambivalence, but also of her symbiotic wishes of not being able to disassociate herself any longer. But in the end this habit of missing one another also served to keep up a minimum of individuation, independence and identity. That is why they could not talk to each other. However, Ann insisted that she needed her mother to obtain clarity. Unless her mother was there, she would not obtain any answers. When both of them were at home, it was apparently impossible for both Ann and her mother to be in the house and in the same room for any length of time. Her fear of fusion expressed itself in her continuously present fear of becoming a burden. She therefore had to avoid all closer relationships and at the same time control them. As though standing next to herself, she observed herself. Although she wished she could be more direct and spontaneous, she had a great fear of losing control.

She was very concerned about her brother. When he went to live with their stepfather in another town, because of the problems he was having with their mother, she herself fell into a deep, diffuse state of uncertainty, even panic. This in turn was connected to feelings of envy and guilt as well as hatred of her mother, who seemed to have no difficulty in giving away her son. Unconsciously, however, her brother's move suited her desire to have her mother all to herself. Especially because of this, Ann was overcome by a feeling of deep helplessness: she said she just felt rotten.

In therapy, however, she was now, at last, able to hint at an event that had endangered her integrity deeply and that she viewed with conflicting emotions. A year before therapy her stepfather had slept with her. Ann asked herself whether she had allowed this to happen to take revenge on her mother. Or had she wanted to comfort her stepfather, who seemed to be feeling rejected by his ex-wife, who was playing around with other men at the time? Were her actions an attempt at finding a new place for the unconscious guilt feelings she had, because she had gone to see her father? Ann had a positively coloured relationship to her stepfather, which was not endangered by any deep ambivalence. However she now felt deeply guilty towards her mother, and had simultaneously lost her stepfather as a form of support.

Every step she took towards becoming more independent entailed new confrontations with her home, of which she was afraid. For this reason she left all the initiative to her boyfriend Klaus, indeed she took refuge with him. She only took very cautious steps - with therapeutic help - in trying to come to terms with her mother. For the first time in her life she thus dared to talk to her mother about herself and their relationship, without at once taking flight to her boyfriend. Before this happened, she had dreamt that she had ridden her bicycle all by herself. In the same way she sought to talk to her stepfather, who was to help her bring some light into the darkness of her life history. Apparently he also felt that it was right for her to undergo therapy. He told her how she had cried, when her parents were divorced and her father had come to visit her. She felt and recognized her dependency on her home, but also on Klaus, and on therapy, experiencing herself as small and fettered.

After nine months Ann made the following statements about herself, having first looked around my room: 'I wonder if I missed something in my childhood? I remember reading that animals who have had no experience of mirroring, no mother, have no knowledge about themselves. I think the same applies to me. I have the feeling that I am only now getting to know myself. When I looked at myself in the mirror before the session, I had the feeling that I don't really exist . . . I got a fright just now, when I looked out of the window and saw the mountains and the sky in front of me. When Klaus said that was normal, I was relieved at first. Then I had the feeling that he doesn't really understand me. (I asked her to elaborate.) Yes, that he is entirely engrossed in me. Then I can't disassociate myself any longer . . . I am always frightened when I hear things about madness.'

Ann had made friends with Klaus when therapy started, and the relationship continued all the time the first therapy lasted. She made use of it to be able to leave home. Together the two of them went to live with a young married couple. Ann also made use of this relationship to protect herself from dependence within therapy. It was only later that it became clear to what extent she was living in his shadow and keeping herself hidden. Klaus supported her against her mother as well as against therapy. In this way she was able to avoid all personal initiative, which would have been associated with severe guilt feelings. Her inability to be alone became apparent. She said that this was so, because she did not have the necessary background.

When Klaus wanted to have a steady and binding relationship at the end of her apprenticeship, Ann provoked their separation by withdrawal and playing around with other young men. However she then felt abandoned in her empty room. She felt that Klaus had left her in the lurch. After all, she had left all initiative to him. The fact that I moved from the clinic to my own private practice at the time may also have been of great importance here. Her boyfriend had helped her to leave home, but he had projected all her problems on her mother and so he had lightened her burden, but had not helped her find access to her own innermost self or to find her inner mother.

The narcissistic restitution

Ann presented herself in the guise of the friendly child. Everyone tried to save her and thus she could achieve narcissistic restitution. However this proved to be deceptive - as became apparent later. Ann simply continued to withdraw and remained out of reach. In so doing she was refusing to be herself, because this would have meant losing or even destroying her mother. Due to her lack of individuation this would also have meant losing or destroying herself.[4]

It is appropriate to relate a significant episode towards the end of the first therapy in greater detail here. As a result of a change in my timetable Ann no longer had her sessions straight after lunch. I take the usual break of 10 minutes or more between sessions. Before long Ann began to come early to the sessions as before and sit quietly in the room in front of the consulting room. That is how she met the patient from the session before, Ms M, who was about the age of her mother and was pregnant.

When Ann rang the doorbell I had to press the buzzer to open the front door for her, causing a small interruption to the ongoing session. After I had talked to her about it she came to the next session during the break. However, she said she was afraid of having to be considerate and asked me, as she had done so often before, how I could work so much. I associated her question and her fear with the previous session and her meeting the other patient. Then I confronted Ann with the question of how she would feel if there were somebody else waiting outside during her session. She said that she would be fidgety and nervous and that she would withdraw. At the same time she said she was afraid of 'getting a proper dressing down from me'.

Ann came only a little earlier to her next sessions, but again it was before the end of the previous ones. In connection with her own previous session she suddenly said that for the first time she had not looked at her watch when leaving at the end. The end of the session had been like a lid on her head. She felt like sighing, but dared not come back in to say that this was the first time she had sighed and it had not mattered. Somehow personal things were not allowed.

In this episode Ann had succeeded in allowing direct emotional contact to occur. She had reacted with a 'sigh' to the end of the session - an expression of ambivalence between love and anger. She was surprised at herself but had to close up again quickly, because every time emotional contact occurs it is a highly dense moment, which - as became apparent at the end of the second therapy - for her meant an incestuous approach and destruction. By disregarding her time limit Ann was starting a limitless, soundless symbiosis with the other patient.

Ann thus once again came before her time and went to the toilet directly next to the surgery, loudly clattering with her wooden shoes, which she had never worn before. This was completely contrary to her usual behaviour. When I asked Ms M, who had never said anything about it, how she felt, she assured me that it did not worry her. On the contrary she made it clear that she felt a lot of sympathy for the girl. Ann on the other hand made some cautious, but at the same time apt, critical comments about Ms M. When I referred again to her early arrival Ann said in a firm but also saucy tone that, after all, she had needed to go to the toilet. In the rooms at the clinic she had not been able to endure it. Here she could make a noise, otherwise it was too sterile. It was possible, of course, that the woman might think that here was that girl coming again and making a disturbance. My comment was 'You don't seem to like the fact that you cannot come earlier and that there is somebody else with me then.' Ann: 'It was important, wasn't it, that you once said that this is my session.' My response: 'And now you don't like me to tell you that the time before your session is not yours, but instead of saying so, you create a disturbance.' Ann: 'Yes, when you say that you don't want me to come early, I have a sort of tingling sensation.' My answer: 'You are afraid that you could not endure it, if I should say that that is not allowed any longer. And you are afraid you would hurt me, if you then became angry with me.' Ann: 'Yes, that woman looks so sad.' My comment: 'You always want to know what is wrong with that woman, perhaps particularly when you are angry at her.' Ann: 'Yes that is possible.'

After the Easter holidays Ann had to cancel one session because of illness. After that she came 20 minutes early. Although both women seemed to have come to terms with the situation, the whole thing seemed uncanny to me and I felt increasingly uncomfortable because my interventions had not led to any changes. At the same time the boundaries of the experience were becoming diffuse. Was it perhaps my fear of hurting her, if I should insist that she refrain from coming before the end of the previous session? At the same time Ann told me that her boyfriend Klaus had moved out of their common room and that she felt as if she was all in a fog, especially since she was afraid that she would have to move out of the room she had with the young couple because they would need it for a child they were expecting. Nevertheless, I again confronted her with her coming too early. Ann was taken aback and almost began to cry: 'I was quiet, wasn't I? Would you rather I made a noise? I don't know what you want . . . you did say it was my time. Do you really want me to beat about the bush?' Then Ann vaguely referred to a dream: 'Tonight I saw my mother and what she is like, when the two of us are not together. Then my mother says what she wants.' Then I asked her, if she perhaps also experienced me as somebody who did not say what he wanted. She agreed, at the same time reproaching me for it. My comment: 'Maybe you are right and I must say what I want: I don't want you to come before the break between sessions in future.' Ann said she was happy to see that I was not so far above such petty things and compared the situation to the behaviour of her boyfriend's mother, who would say goodbye and then expect her to go. Then she suddenly asked: 'Was that your wish now, or that of the woman who comes before I do.' I said it was my responsibility to see that every patient could have an uninterrupted session. Ann reacted by saying that the woman had never felt interrupted - she had seen this in her eyes - and that this was such a contrast to Ann's usual experience of being a burden.

This session proved to be a significant turning point.[5] Before the following session, Ann sat waiting on the steps in front of my house. She said she had been angry and that I had betrayed her confidence because I had not said that she should not come early long ago, although I had known it all the time. It was just like at home, where her mother would also not say anything. Then Ann insisted on a comment from me. I affirmed her thoughts but added that I thought this course of action would not have been possible before. I associated her feeling hurt with the early separation of her parents, as well as with the pregnancy of the patient/mother, which had probably also surprised her and made her feel betrayed, especially because she may have felt something for a long time already. Ann: 'Yes, my mother is not open, it isn't possible to talk to her. With my father there is distance, a feeling of clarity.' My answer: 'Maybe you are not only angry because you experienced this as a breach of trust. Perhaps you are also angry because I have forbidden you to do something.' Ann: 'Yes, I see that.' My comment: 'You see it. And yet there is still anger.' Ann: 'Yes I experience that sort of thing as an attack, in spite of always trying to understand everything.'

She brought photographs from her childhood to the next session, describing and characterizing all the family members depicted there, but also taking a close look at herself as a child. By the look on her face on these photographs, she recognized her early withdrawal and quiet reproachfulness. She discovered similarities between herself and her father and said, 'Two years ago my dentist filed away a crooked tooth that my father also has. I wanted to hit him. Nobody understood that.' And: 'I used to have the feeling that my legs are too short. Now I can see that I have legs.' In the next session she talked about the final examination of her apprenticeship, in which she felt she had not done well. After the examination she had felt as if she was in a fog.

At the same time she quarrelled with Klaus, who had said that one also had to meet other people, and she said she was afraid that something could be taken away from her. The couple with whom she was living also thought that other relationships were important. She had dreamt that she had been together with someone else, another man, without uttering a word. There was only the feeling, nothing else. I gave the interpretation: 'I wonder if that is the same kind of feeling a mother has, when she is together with her baby.' Ann: 'That is just a dream. It will never come true for me.' I connected her wish to have somebody just for herself with her longing for the early mother of her childhood, but also with an attempt at comforting herself when she felt excluded because the young couple agreed with Klaus. This made her feel abandoned by everybody. Ann said that other things might come true, and then began to talk about her work. She was enjoying learning more than before. Where there had just been a fog, there were now holes. She now wanted to meet old friends. She hadn't had a relationship to other people before. Only now did she go to see her grandfather and grandmother. Earlier it had all been just like a dream.

Ann noticed that her dreams seemed to have changed since my statement about the mother and the baby. Her dreams had just been feelings before, nothing else. Now there were relationships. In one dream she had visited another boy. But there had not just been the feeling, but also a relationship. She connected the boy in her dream with a previous boyfriend, Micha, who had not matured however, but was still full of dreams. In this statement I think she was also referring to a split-off part of her personality.

After Klaus had moved out of their shared room she was able to live with her fear of emptiness. She did not have to pack it full right away, as she said, adding that she had had that feeling, that longing again. She had gone to see Micha to be able to make up her mind. Usually when that feeling had come over her, she had not been able to think or see anything. Everything had just reeled itself off like clockwork, it had flooded her. She would just hang on and wait for Horst, her young landlord, to say that she should stop it. Ann: 'Now I realize that all that had nothing to do with Micha, but that I am searching for something. I see the point in what you said about the mother and the baby, because I never had this feeling before.'

After Klaus had gone, she experienced her room as empty and said that she was not able to fill it, she was only pushing everything aside. Then she had the idea of running away and sighing. But then she put a table into the room and began to paint. Previously she had done nothing but make a perfect copy of a clown. But now she became afraid, when she saw that the eyes of the clown were diffuse and sad. She did not dare show this picture to anybody, especially not to her mother, who would invariably ask why she had painted it that way. She was afraid of losing herself in her pictures, but she did need somebody to whom she could show them. Ann had taken the risk of drawing herself and had discovered - as she said - her own cold and evil side in the picture, more so than even on the photos, because it did not have a setting. She had then rubbed it out. Previously Ann had discovered this side of herself in a photograph and had described it: a photograph that had been taken when she had not been feeling at all well. However, I was only to get to see her first pictures 10 years later.

Ann passed her apprenticeship examination and was awarded a state prize. She even succeeded in getting not only her mother and her brother but also her real father to attend the festivities. Thus she was able to bring her parents together, even if only for a moment. A short time later she ended the therapy.

Interruption, demolition and breakdown

More than three years later I received a letter from Ann from a foreign country. She cautiously asked if she could come back for more therapy. After having left the country with a new boyfriend, having had two self-administered abortions (like her mother) and a series of broken relationships, Ann was in a catastrophic condition. She felt completely lost. Probably, she said, she had been fooling herself in looking for the security that she wanted from her father in other relationships. She always wanted a degree of closeness and security to which no man could do justice and tended to give herself up entirely in a relationship. In this way she would become a burden and would be deserted, or she would force the man to desert her. Now, after the separation from her last boyfriend she had fallen into an inner void. Being afraid of becoming melancholic again, she had gone to her previous boyfriend and had done nothing but weep. She had longed to disintegrate. However she then had to get away quickly from his fatherly embrace, before she could be deserted. She was using sexuality to find security and create dependency. She was blocking herself and needed help.

With reference to the end of the first therapy Ann admitted that she had probably fled because of her fear of the therapeutic relationship. After the first therapy she had finally separated from B. and had gone overseas by herself to the place where she had been born to prove to herself that she was self-sufficient. After this her life was characterized by erratic behaviour, searching and running away, moving this way and that in her relationships. Much of this bore a frightening resemblance to her mother's behaviour.

Ann and I agreed to an analytic psychotherapy of two sessions a week. Without a doubt a higher frequency was indicated. But since Ann was unemployed and there was no other way she could pay for the sessions herself, a therapy of 240 to 300 hours in the course of three years, which her medical aid was prepared to pay for, was probably more appropriate. The progress of treatment showed that within this framework a decisive step could be taken: namely that of obtaining access to her depression. On the one hand the course of treatment shows that limitations can promote and accelerate the process. On the other hand it also proves that only long-term treatment can do justice to the inner process and also that even then the results within such limitations remain limited and fragile.

It became apparent that her renewed flight to Paris had led to inner deflation and destruction. Ann had tried to get away from her symbiosis with her mother and chaos at home (grandparents, mother, brother, cousin with child). She wanted to leave it all behind in one go and forget it. However, in doing so Ann had also robbed herself of all her inner resources. She acted out this destructive deflation in two abortions, which she brought about herself with the help of a method her mother had taught her. Only in these moments could she call her mother from outside the country.

Clarifying her relationships

Ann's destructive defence mechanisms became accessible to treatment in particular by interruptions to therapy caused by holidays or vacations. On the one hand she adjusted to circumstances without offering any resistance, because the merest hint of making demands or having negative feelings would trigger off her deep-seated fear of becoming a burden. On the other hand she anaesthetized herself by means of total emotional deflation, which brought her to a state of fogginess and withdrawal. It was on just such a weekend, when sessions had been cancelled, that she went to see her stepfather, who once again made sexual advances to her. In the last minute she was able to stop him. She had tried to deny the cancelled sessions and fill the resultant inner void by going to see her stepfather.

It became increasingly clear that Ann was adjusting to her surroundings in everyday situations in a quiet, almost 'invisible' way, nipping every wish of her own in the bud. She would not even allow herself to have her own mattress to sleep on or to have an egg for breakfast, because this would have meant having rights of her own, which she would then have had to acknowledge and express. By making no demands whatsoever, Ann tried to keep up a narcissistic, self-sufficient state, free of drives, which would enable her to live in the shadow of those people who were important to her, without having to come to terms or really get in touch with them. She avoided all distancing and individualization. As a result she experienced herself as worthless because every exchange of give and take was precluded. After I had confronted her repeatedly with her avoidance behaviour and she had increasingly gained insight into this mechanism, she began to do things for herself: she bought herself a ring and a mattress, she finally tried to talk to her boss. In the end she even dared to invite her aunt and her grandparents to her room for the first time - she had left home once again to be better able to distance herself - and later also her mother and her brother. This meant an increase of personal value, identity and individuality.

Because of her increased feeling of self-worth Ann was able to disassociate herself from her stepfather and confront him in a letter with his sexual infringements. She also refused to visit him on a special birthday and hinted to her brother what the real reason for this was.

After a year of withdrawal she resumed contact with her real father and talked critically to him about her childhood and the failure of his marriage to her mother. After this she felt that she had a dad - before that she had only referred to him as her father. Her first attempt at establishing contact with him almost 10 years earlier had led to her breakdown. At that time she had been afraid of losing her mind. Now she was also able to express her deep disappointment and anger at her ex-boyfriend Klaus because of the way he had deserted her then.

Apart from other relationships, which - because of her difficulties - had always been very problematic and susceptible to disturbance, it was now the relationship with her mother that increasingly came within the scope of her perception and reflection. Up until then this subject had been almost inaccessible. It now became clear that the patient was greatly involved in a pathological network of family relations. When Ann announced to her family that she wanted to move out - after her return from a foreign country she had again moved in with her grandparents and her mother - her mother responded with a mirroring reaction, completely surprising Ann with the news that she had met a man and was going to go to Greece with him two weeks later. Ann's mother always went to foreign countries with her male partners. On the one hand her mother's reaction relieved Ann's guilt feelings because not she but her mother was bringing about the separation; on the other hand she also felt bound to her grandparents, for whom she now felt responsible, but who also seemed to belong to her for this reason. Even when her mother came home again after three weeks, it turned out that she had not given up her plans entirely. A remark she made showed that in her eyes Ann was a non-individualized, manoeuvrable object, which she was trying to tie to herself: she said that if things did not work out with her boyfriend and the house in Greece, she could move there together with Ann. In spite of this Ann began to disassociate herself more clearly from her mother, surprising herself by being able to say that it was difficult having so many fathers, after her mother announced her intention of a third marriage.

It was new that Ann could now admit to her past and present identification with her mother, acknowledging the similarity between them, for example in the difficulties they had with men, in the way they dealt with sexuality and frigidity, in their problems with self-worth, in their fear of closeness together with the wish for absolute security and availability of a partner. In the same way she was able to see connections between herself, her mother and her controlling grandmother, for instance in the devaluation of all men, her fathers, and in the way her mother and grandmother ostracized her grandfather. By recognizing this identification Ann had taken a decisive step forward. Until now she had believed that, in being 'sloppy' and unassuming, she was completely different from her smart, superficial mother, who laid such store on clothing and external things.

It was another step forward when she set up her own workshop. In the end she even invited her mother to see it, despite the envy she feared. In retrospect she realized that her mother coming and talking to her there meant that their relationship had changed in a positive way. In the workshop she did not feel overwhelmed and so she did not have to avoid contact with her mother. Ann experienced the buying of material and machines as a process of taking on responsibility for herself - even as if she now had her own children. After a long battle she could now say that it was fun 'to be myself, that is: to live.'

Stagnation and boredom in therapy

The beginning of her vocational work was associated with an end to splitting-off processes in therapy. Until now she had treated me only as a neutral therapist and for a long time she kept her knowledge about my family a secret. However, as this splitting-off diminished, there was a strange standstill in therapy. Monotony and boredom spread. There was tangible tension, but it was impossible to get a grip on it. This oppressive but not resolvable atmosphere only improved when Ann began to occupy herself with me as a concrete person. She said that if she had seen the man in me before she would have thought that she had to be at my disposal sexually and would have to allow everything to be done to her, because that was what all men were like. That was the family ideology of her mother and grandmother. However, after she had dared see me as a man and at the same time become aware of my therapeutic abstinence, she could risk an approach. It was a remarkable phenomenon. On the one hand, in her naive innocence she was offering herself to me as a sexual object without actually saying so. If I was a man, then that was the way it was and the way it had to be. Then only was I truly a man. On the other hand she was relieved to find out that the admission of sexual wishes as well as the recognition of me as a person with my own sexuality did not automatically lead to sexual acts.

Two problematic areas had remained untouched so far. Ann had never even hinted to her mother that her stepfather had made sexual advances to her and seduced her. However she now felt that she would have to talk to her about it, in order to clarify their relationship. She had also not yet dared to tell her mother about her therapy. In both cases she was afraid of starting an avalanche, something she would not be able to control, especially because she did not know in how far she herself had contributed to the sexual events with her stepfather as a form of revenge against her mother. With the eyes of her mother she unconsciously also saw the therapeutic relationship more as a primal scene - a sexual encounter from which her mother was excluded, than a tripartite relationship - as a relationship with an uncontaminated third person, who could enable her to disassociate herself from her mother by helping her integrate her ambivalent feelings and the depressive fears that were associated with them. This was a decisive step that she still had to take. But again there was a tiring standstill and stagnation spread over a long time, which proved to be an expression of her comprehensive defence against contact, aggression and depression.

A 'poop in the universe' and the 'leaden cap' – clash and catastrophic change[6]

In all these years Ann had repeatedly thought about undergoing retraining, because she saw no future for herself in her present trade. However, she never actually did anything about it. Now she was also thinking about the imminent end of her medical aid and the possible end of therapy. In one session she told me that she had gone to the Labour Office, acting as if this had finally been a truly serious, if not decisive step. However, her action turned out to be just another sham manoeuvre. They had merely given her some brochures. I began to feel annoyed.

After pausing to reflect for a moment I became convinced that I needed to 'knuckle down' on this occasion. So I said, 'You can't expect me to believe that this action was a real decision, or a step towards the clarification of the retraining question!' In reality I was not concerned with the question of her retraining but was focusing on her behaviour towards me. Ann reacted in the typical way, cautiously giving in, yet also acting offended and defensive, by withdrawing into an attitude of naive childish innocence and bewilderment. But this time I harped on the matter, especially since her withdrawal further annoyed me. We 'squabbled', and the session ended without further clarification. My annoyance was obvious in my impetuous tone and could not be overlooked. Nevertheless my spontaneous reaction was still under control – it was not an impulsive outburst, although it was unplanned and unexpected, even by me.

At this point the question will surely be raised whether anything psychoanalytic happened during this session. After all, I did not take up any forms of transference or resistance but acted or reacted on a purely manifest level. My intervention seems to have been a purely pedagogic action, or a countertransference reaction in psychoanalytic terms. In addition this confrontation did some damage to the framework of my analytic neutrality and abstinence. Nevertheless the session did have its place in a specific setting and space within the long process of therapy. The discourse not only had an unconscious transference meaning, but it was also an event of personal experience and expression to substantiate this meaning within the psychoanalytic relationship itself – a formulation that I found in Foucault's introduction (1954: 28) to Binswanger's paper, 'Dream and existence' – which also means, however, that the meaning of the events of a certain session has to be found or even constructed within the psychoanalytic relationship and can never be objectively assessed.

Ann surprised me at the beginning of the following session with the direct question of whether I had been bad-tempered and annoyed the previous time. I was taken aback, because I had not known her to act in such a way before, and I was irritated, because I did not understand why she was asking such a question. So I first tried to save myself in the usual professional way by asking her to reflect on why she was interested in this and what came to her mind in that connection. Ann then said she thought that I was annoyed at the beginning of the session already but that she really could not tell the difference and she repeated her question once again without hesitation.

After thinking a little about whether there could be something to what she said and what good her question, put so directly, could do, I said, 'Yes, that is possible (I was probably a little bad-tempered at the beginning of the session). However, this does not make any difference to what I said.'

Ann was quiet for a little while and then said, 'You are probably right. What I did was probably no more than a poop in the universe.' I responded, 'Perhaps a poop, but it was not nothing. A poop in the universe can also be a storm.' There was a pause and then Ann said, 'There is a dream I did not want to talk about, because it gives away too much. We are in a therapy session and are talking. Suddenly you are very nice and friendly to me. You come over to me, probably wanting to embrace and kiss me. That clarified something for me: are you also one of those therapists that make passes at your patients.'

After another pause she associated this dream with her wish of finding acceptance and modified this statement by adding that, together with this wish, she would push everything else away. I replied, 'That means that there was also something like appreciation and closeness in my annoyance.' Ann: 'Yes, because you were not neutral any more, but also impatient.' Then she complained about my neutrality in the face of the end of therapy. On the other hand she also said that she was very sensitive and had been watching me closely to see whether I would act like an accomplice; in that case she would have taken off immediately. And she continued: 'After the last session I only thought about closing up. I asked myself why I should ever come back to a place where I had received such a talking-to. But there is something like responsibility at the end of therapy.' My response: 'In other words, there are not only passes, but also ties!' Ann: 'Yes, and that before the end, when everything is lost. I used to think that I was no more than a case for you, a file you can pack away when I go. Now I realize that there is also a relationship.'

The course of events clearly shows that the session before last was a turning point. Ann's remarks, her thoughts, and finally her dream show how complex and confusing the process was for her. Her remark, 'that was just a poop in the universe', shows how quickly she was ready to let everything disappear into endless space, an attitude that the English analyst Bion has described as characteristic of 'hallucinosis'. Bion, who occupied himself intensively with thought disturbances, has shown that such an experience will not be integrated, leading to 'hallucinosis', if the child does not find a counterpart it can use for its not yet integratable, immature and non-symbolized emotions. Obviously I had succeeded in becoming a 'container' for Ann's emotional reaction, when I attacked it with the interpretation, 'Perhaps a poop, but it was not nothing either. A poop in the universe can also be a storm.' It was necessary for both her and me to perceive her anger and at the same time to save it over a period of absence or separation. The anger was not allowed to be forgotten, discarded or denied during the interval between the sessions. Bion is of the opinion that the system of hallucinosis stems from the fact that the absence of the object - here the analyst - with the accompanying pain of frustration - here Ann's anger - cannot be borne (see Grinberg et al., 1973: 100ff. in this connection). Ann was angry and had been considering not coming back. This would have meant that the event would have been lost, and it would not have been possible to transform it into language. But then it would have continued doing mischief in endless space.

At first sight the session I have described seems to be simple and not at all exciting. Its explosiveness can only be understood in terms of transference and in the framework of the therapeutic process. Many things had become clear to Ann in the course of therapy, but she was still unable to establish a true relationship to her mother. However the further course of events confirmed the decisive experience contained in and the far-reaching significance of this session.

Ann was relieved - so she said - that she had insisted on asking me about my annoyance. She had told herself that she had nothing to lose. The previous day her mother had been drinking again. For the first time she had the clear feeling: 'I hate you!' and the clear thought: 'Why does she drink?'

In the following sessions, as well, Ann talked with satisfaction and pride about the change in her attitude and behaviour towards her mother. She had always felt that her mother let her down, which was an insoluble problem for her. Every attempt at contact failed, because - so Ann thought - her mother avoided her, immediately pushing things aside. Her mother never expressed anger. She was afraid of driving her mother into a corner whenever she saw her cynical mouth. Her mother always said that everything was OK, that she was not storing up grievances, that she would be able to get rid of it. Ann was not able to cope with that. Freud had talked about guilt feelings, she said, and she wanted to know if that applied to her as well. She always felt that she was a nuisance, for example if she forgot her key.

Now, when she came home late one night, having forgotten her key, she dared to wake up her mother for the first time by throwing pebbles against the window, even though her mother might have been upset or the window pane might have been broken. Until then she had seen the house as an impregnable fortress, against which she had not been able to do anything. But now she had taken the risk. She had felt paralysed with terror, when the door was opened and her mother appeared. Before then, she had always gone to stay with friends in such a situation. Now she could even quarrel with her mother, as well as recognizing and expressing her hatred, when her mother was drunk and took men into her bedroom.

Ann recognized her far-reaching and unconscious identification with her mother and how split off she was. She showed her mother a portrait of herself, in spite of her fear of being exposed after her friends had commented on how sad she was in the picture. She saw a connection between this sadness and her mother's denied depression. Ann was now also able to ask her mother why she had always felt so threatened: 'I was able to ask this question, because I had survived that horror here. It was like a leaden cap that was now gone.'

I will have to refrain from giving further material and commentary here. However I think the course of treatment does make it clear that the session I have described was a highly dense moment that can be interpreted on many different levels, but only - and that must be emphasized - in retrospect. Living contact had occurred making the primary object, that is the early mother, accessible (one goal of analysis according to Paula Heimann). The framework prevented incestuous fusion, making it possible for Ann to endure the absence of the object without having to deny the affect. Only during such an absence can the affect be connected to an object representation, while simultaneously creating distance. Both Ann and I had to endure and retain anger, and in the following session we had to talk about it. If the analyst does not give shape to anger and desperation, these will be lost like 'a poop in the universe'. They will disappear in a void and the subject will suffer from 'inner bleeding,' if no word, symbol or metaphor is found for the catastrophe.

After this phase another important stage followed, in which Ann felt overwhelmed by inner feelings and emotions. Her experience was connected to a compulsive feeling that she had to leave the room and vomit, which finally led to the memory of her breakdown.

After her medical aid was finished, Ann decided to extend therapy for another month at her own expense. I will now quote some of her comments on therapy that she made during these last sessions:

> Therapy was entirely different from what I thought it was going to be. In the beginning, and for a long time after that, I thought that you were going to take away my problems. I never imagined that I myself would be questioned and that I would have to query all my systems.
>
> I got a shock when I heard that in the USA half of the therapists sleep with their patients. Nothing can come of it then.
>
> There is a kind of intermediary world, from which I don't think I can escape without help: for example when I talk to Eva, who is pregnant, about death. Here for the first time I have found somebody to talk to about this world.
>
> I always used to surround myself with a cocoon.
>
> It's funny that one should have to give up on something to get something else. I used to feel threatened when talking about death.
>
> I never thought that I would have to deal with dependence to get where I am now. I have finally told my mother that I have gone back to therapy.

> I have succeeded in breaking through . . . but there is also the fear of going too far, of losing my mind; like an artist, that there are no limits any longer.
>
> It is difficult to be oneself. I used to make myself small; anything to prevent myself from having to be me. That made me a difficult patient, as I realize today.
>
> I have planted some flowers in Grandpa's garden.
>
> [Last session.] Something has happened at home again. I slapped my mother's boyfriend in the face - the one who had attacked her - and kicked him out. All the same, the police still had to be called.

Ann associated this event with memories of quarrels between her parents during her childhood.

> These were 10 important years. I want to give you something, not because I owe it to you, but because I am grateful. I have improved by vast steps this past half year: I want to live, even though not unconditionally as yet.
>
> Your concern for me, and that you expressed it, helped me take an important step forward and learn to trust. My gift is something tangible for you. Ten years, those were also 10 years of your life, after all.

She took her leave from me by giving me a present that she had made for me and my comfort in an almost professional way. It was entirely to my taste. She had added a card: 'Many thanks for your efforts. You have actually succeeded in bringing the little plant to life . . .' Ann had pasted a picture by Cezanne on it, showing a small house among trees over a suggested crack in the rocks with a fissure through the house from the top down to the bottom.

'Grim on a Bright Day' – pictures of emptiness and depression

Three years after the end of her therapy I received a letter from Ann with the photograph of one of her paintings that is reprinted here without further comment (see Figure 6.1). This was the very first picture I ever got from her. Ann had written 'It is one of my favourite pictures and I confidently leave its analysis to you.'

On thanking her I received another letter from her:

> your unexpected reply gave me a feeling of 'reality', a confirmation that the years I spent with you were not just a vague dream, but that I was dealing with somebody made of 'flesh and blood'! Clever as you are, you probably knew I needed such a signal?! In general I can now show people my pictures without fear. Only sometimes I am afraid of shocking them, if the pictures are rather 'gloomy' . . . You

Figure 6.1. Painting sent by Ann.

> ask me how I am getting on with my life. I only want to say that I am 'quite OK' and am still learning to live with myself. One day I hope to come to terms with the gnawing question deep inside me about the meaning of my existence (which I cannot make for myself), and perhaps I will one day understand where my deep indifference towards myself comes from. Maybe I will need your help again sometime for these questions, because they are very hard nuts to crack!

She sent me more pictures. One of them had the title *Grim on a Bright Day* (Figure 6.2). Ann wrote about it: 'It was created in Canada, during my first visit here. That was during the time after therapy. I am enclosing it as an expression of this period in my life . . .' At the same time she included an appreciative article out of a large foreign newspaper about the exhibition of her pictures by a renowned art association.

Seven years after the end of therapy – 17 years after our first contact – Ann spontaneously visited me in my consulting rooms. At her request we met outside the practice half a year later for a cup of coffee. In the course of our conversation we touched on the first session, during which I had brought up the question of her name. She could remember it all exactly. She had experienced the situation as confusing for herself as well as for me. For the first time, she had heard herself say that name. Without me this would not have been

Figure 6.2. *Grim on a Bright Day.*

possible. It was a step away from her mother and had frightened her very much.

At that time she had been standing at the edge of an abyss, on a ridge. She often thought about me and was very grateful.

She also mentioned that she had told her mother about her stepfather's behaviour. However, her mother had already known about it. She had read it in a letter that had been left lying around, unsealed. And Ann added: 'I can now also imagine having children of my own.'

Notes

1. Anne Michaels (1996) Fugitive Pieces. McClelland & Steward, Toronto.
2. This report is based on session records and applications for medical aid, which were written at the time. They have only been copy-edited.
3. In an important paper Martin James (1964) describes various fears that come up when juveniles are treated: the fear of incest, the fear of the dissolution of ego boundaries, the fear of being emotionally overcome and the fear of the phallic mother.
4. In another paper (Trimborn, 1995a) I have described excessive identifi-

cation as a defence mechanism against traumatic object losses. Every step towards autonomy is then experienced both as a loss of self and a destruction of the primary object.

5. A. Green (1978) has pointed out that patients with pronounced narcissistic disturbances will often only change in a noticeable way after having gone through a conflict about the framework of the treatment situation. He explicitly points out that the analyst can only bring about a transformation from the hopeless alternative between psychosis and death with the help of a non-ego, namely the spatially and temporally defined setting.
6. I have attempted a theoretical explanation of this section of therapy in my paper 'The framework and the psychoanalytic event' (Trimborn, 1995b).

References

Foucault M (1954) Einleitung zu L Biswanger (dt. Ausgabe ohne Jahresangabe) Traum und Existenz. Bern, Berlin: Gachnang und Springer.

Green A (1978) Potential space in psychoanalysis: The object in the setting. In: Grolnick SA, Barkin L (eds) Between Reality and Fantasy. Transitional objects and phenomena. New York, London: J Aronson.

Grinberg L, Sor D, Tabak DeBianchedi E (1973) WR Bion: Eine Einführung. Jahrb. d. Psychoanalyse (1993) Beiheft 17. Stuttgart: frommann-holzboog.

James M (1964) Interpretation and management in the treatment of preadolescents. Int. J. Psycho-Anal. 45: 499–511.

Trimborn W (1995a) Die Gefahr der Heilung. Pathologische Identifizierungs- und Mentalisierungsprozesse als Grenzen therapeutischer Möglichkeiten. In: Schneider G, Seidler GH (eds) Internalisierung und Strukturbildung. Opladen: Westdeutscher Verlag.

Trimborn W (1995b) Der Rahmen und das psychoanalytische Ereignis. In: Haas JP, Jappe G, Deutungs-Optionen. Tübingen: Edition Diskord.

Chapter 7

A clinically orientated psychodynamic classification of borderline states

Stavros Mentzos

This attempt at a psychodynamic classification of borderline states is not intended to stand in opposition to the descriptive classification: it is rather a complement to it. Although I will focus on psychodynamics, my assertions and considerations will always remain sensitive to the phenomenal level. Indeed this should go without saying: how else could one put forward psychodynamic hypotheses, if one did not designate the phenomena these hypotheses refer to? However, I should point out right at the beginning that the phenomena I have in mind are not only the behaviour and experience of the patient but also the recurring countertransference reactions as well as the relationship between the patient and the therapist.

In the big classificatory systems DSM-IV and ICD-10, borderline personality disorder stands out. One peculiarity of the borderline syndrome is that its definitions and operationalizations directly or indirectly reveal an otherwise unusual congeniality to psychodynamics. This obviously has to do with the fact that the concept of borderline was originally developed in psychoanalysis and that psychoanalysts, particularly Otto Kernberg, have attended it in its transfer to psychiatry (where it now really booms). Thus, in the course of the last 25 years, during the transfer of the concept to psychiatry, what was originally considered a psychodynamic personality structure has transformed into a descriptive syndrome. First, it was believed to be close to schizophrenic disorder and later close to the affective disorders. Finally, the view has developed that borderline syndrome is a specific personality disorder. In some places it is perhaps regarded as both the most important and most common personality disorder. The operationalization of the concept led to a considerable improvement in reliability, and stimulated a great number of research studies conducted by clinical psychiatrists, by behavioural and cognitive therapists and also by psychodynamically orientated therapists.

Critical voices did not fail to appear. The critique was not only directed against the concept of borderline personality disorder but also against the one-sided operationalization strategy in general. Parnas (1994), for instance, points out that, where classification is concerned, modern psychiatric research is dominated by an exaggerated quest for reliability at the price of validity. He asks for a renewed focus on clinical phenomenological observation. An even more important critique points to the fact that rather different clinical symptoms, which are often accompanied by different psychodynamics, are all classified as borderline as long as they exhibit the desired number of definitional characteristics. Through this, uncertainty and confusion in the diagnosis of this disorder is produced: the clinician is confronted by the fact that 'one borderline is not the same as another'.

Some diagnosticians and therapists accept only the core group of patients - with their characteristic enduring instability of self- and object assessment, their unpredictability, their groundless outbursts of rage, and their often seemingly acute suicidality and so forth - as the 'real borderliners'. Other clinicians, such as Akiskal (1992) for instance, associate borderline disorder primarily or exclusively with affective disorders - they are also committed to a narrow conception of borderline, but one close to the affective disorders. Many authors, clinics and institutions, however, lean towards a much wider concept of borderline, which embraces not only the two groups just described but also many schizoid or paranoid patients. Tyrer (1994), for instance, supports such a wide conception, asserting that overlaps between different disorders and so-called comorbidity cannot be denied. From this, he draws the conclusion that 'borderline state' is a diagnosis that can apply both to personality disorders and to other *syndromal* disorders. Hence, he argues, it would be wrong to use the concept exclusively for the designation of a personality disorder.

I do not want to go into further details of this debate. I want only to point out that, if we want to retain the wider conception of borderline, we must introduce a differentiation into subgroups. However, we must beware of resorting to new and even more disadvantageous formalisms. I believe that this aim can best be reached with a - somewhat new - 'psycho-dynamicization' of the borderline concept. In the following, I would like to make some suggestions on this, and offer a new model.

A division into three borderlines

In the last five years, through my activity as supervisor at different psychiatric and psychosomatic institutions, I have had the opportunity to gain a certain overview of the diagnostic customs currently in practice. I have worked in different clinics and have also had contact with psychiatrists, psychoanalysts, and psychotherapists in private practice who refer patients to these clinics. The patients that were diagnosed with borderline personality disorder can by no means be meaningfully lumped together under the same diagnostic category. The group is just too disparate. It includes patients better called schizoid as well as cycloid. Further, there are patients with slight paranoid features, as well as others whose experience and behaviour is markedly histrionic (hysterical). Amongst the patients diagnosed as borderline, there were some with dissociative disorders, and others who were clearly depressed. Finally, there was also a large group of currently emotionally unstable, strongly acting out, dramatizing, suicidal or pseudo-suicidal patients.

The model proposed several years ago by Otto Kernberg (1975) was received with enthusiasm within and in part also outside psychoanalysis, because it promised to remove these difficulties by providing a shared framework - at least on the psychodynamic level and dimension. According to Kernberg, the essence of the borderline syndrome is the missing integration of 'good' and 'bad' parts both in the self and in the object, while (in contrast to the psychoses) the differentiation of self and object is at least partially developed. I believe that for the most part this model is still valid today and can be of great benefit. Nevertheless, in my opinion, it is not sufficient to grasp adequately all the different forms of what is called 'borderline' today. A further psychodynamic differentiation within the global term 'borderline' is needed. Kernberg himself speaks of the 'group' of borderline states and personality structures. Thus, he obviously assumes that there is more than one of them.

I was confronted by a similar task, when I began to concern myself seriously with the psychodynamics and psychotherapy of psychoses about 15 or 20 years ago. In the meantime, a psychodynamic model in the field of psychoses has been contrived that obviously serves both theory and practice well. An extrapolation of this model to the group of borderline disorders was an obvious suggestion. This extrapolation - as I will explain in detail - corroborated the division into three of the borderline syndrome that had been assumed beforehand. Consider the fact that in the past borderline structures and states were believed to be close to schizophrenia whereas nowadays they are more commonly believed to be close to the affective psychoses. In actuality, there are good reasons for both accounts. Therefore, it seems reasonable to assume that borderline cases occur at all three respective borders to the psychoses (at the border to schizophrenia, the border to the affective psychoses, and also at the border to the schizo-affective psychoses). Indeed, there is every reason to believe that the main and core group borders on the schizo-affective psychoses. Thus, one could differentiate three groups of borderline patients: schizo-borderline, schizo-affective borderline, and thymo-borderline.

This division into subgroups is only partially based on descriptive characteristics and focuses mainly on the psychodynamics that stand behind them. In order to make this comprehensible it is necessary to outline the model of the psychoses just mentioned which will then be extrapolated to the borderline syndrome.

A psychodynamic classification of psychoses

If you ask a psychiatrist why a schizophrenic megalomania on the one hand and the ideas of grandeur in a mania on the other, belong to different nosological categories (schizophrenia and mania respectively), whereas such dissimilar clinical phenomena as autism and fusion or mania and melancholia belong to the same nosological category (schizophrenia and bipolar affective disorder respectively), they will most probably be embarrassed. They might try to give an answer in terms of statistical correlations and cluster analyses, or in terms of biological differences. However, I suspect, they would not really be satisfied with their answer themselves (and we would be even less so). But is a psychoanalyst or a psychodynamically orientated psychiatrist in a better position to give a convincing answer?

I maintain that the psychodynamic model of the psychoses to be outlined here makes it much easier to answer not only this but also many other important questions concerning the theory and therapy of the psychoses. The model is primarily based on observations and experiences, made over many years, of psychoanalytically orientated therapies of schizophrenic, affective and schizo-affective psychoses. Among other things, it struck us that the psychotic person is not primarily characterized by an ego-disorder and cognitive malfunctioning; rather the psychotic person is primarily entangled in a constellation of contradiction, of opposition, between fusion and autonomy. Furthermore we noticed that psychoses were brought about by external and internal constellations that were obviously potent for actualizing and intensifying the above mentioned intrapsychic oppositions. In most cases, it was either the opposition between striving for self-identity and autonomy versus striving for relatedness and unification with the object, or it was the opposition between an autonomous feeling of self-worth and a feeling of self-worth that was primarily dependent on the object (Mentzos, 1991, 1995, 1997, 1999).

I have designated these fundamental oppositions *basic dilemmas* in order to differentiate them from the conflicts that are usually found in neuroses. The pressure of such problematic constellations results in certain severe 'disorders of experience and behaviour'. However, for the most part these disorders are not functional losses but should rather be understood as active defence mechanisms and reactions, which aim at protection and restitution. On the descriptive level, they form the known psychotic symptoms.

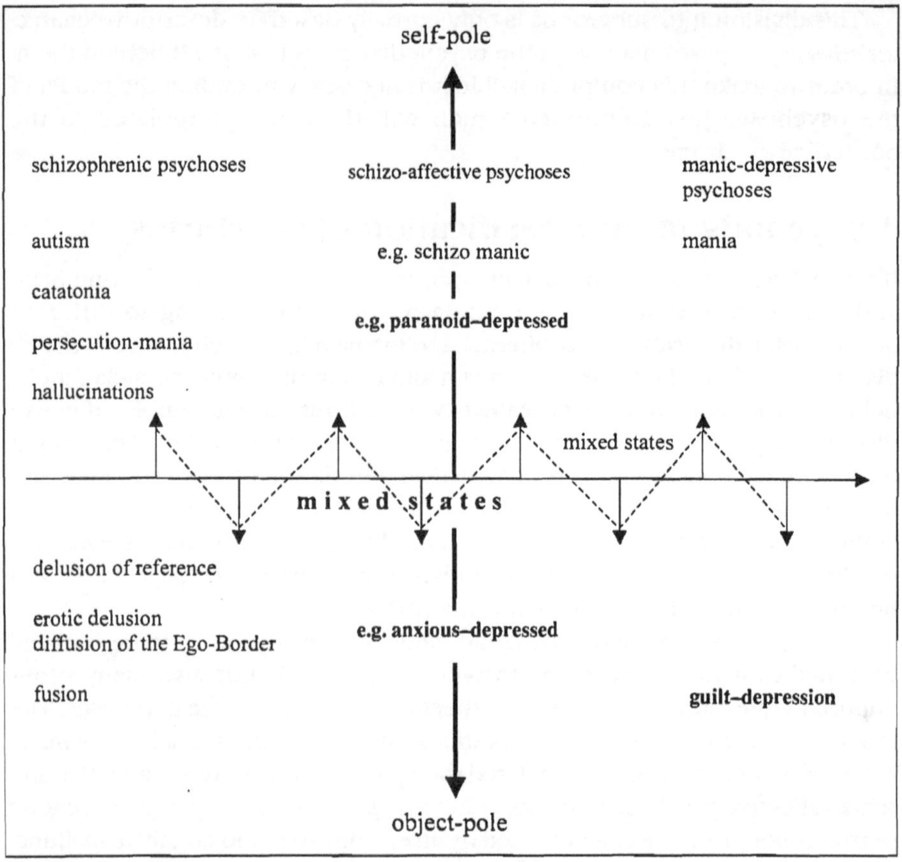

Figure 7.1. Classification of psychotic symptoms according to their 'closeness' to either the self-pole or the object-pole.

With the background of these observations and assumptions it is possible to systematize a wealth of psychotic cases meaningfully and convincingly along an axis, which is defined by a self-directed and an object-directed defensive orientation - this corresponds to a fundamental bipolarity that is also found in 'normal' persons. The 'self-pole' (at the top of Figure 7.1) represents the self-directed needs and strivings (for self-identity, autonomy, self-coherence, stability, and so forth) as they occur under normal conditions and, in the case of pathological processes, it also represents the mechanisms of defence, protection, restitution and compensation *directed at the self.* At the other end, the 'object-pole' (at the bottom of Figure 7.1) represents the object-directed needs and strivings (for example, for contact, closeness, relatedness, unification, and so forth) as they occur in general; and in pathological cases it also represents the mechanisms of defence, protection, and compensation *directed at the object.*

The clinical syndromes of autism or catatonia as opposed to the clinical syndrome of psychotic fusion - as for instance in an ecstatic psychosis - are examples of two extreme alternative pathological solutions of the dilemma of self-identity versus fusion. Much the same is true of the affective psychoses. Manic puffing up of the self and delusions of grandeur as opposed to the absolute submission to an archaic super-ego (internalized object), in melancholia, is a second example of two extreme alternative pathological pseudo-solutions of this dilemma - of the opposition between an autonomous feeling of self-worth and an object-dependent feeling of self-worth.

On the line between these extremes there are several pathological 'solutions', which are more like compromises. Delusion of persecution, for instance, constitutes a pathological compromise between autistic ignoring the object and submitting to and fusing with it. While the relationship between the pursuer and the victim is very intense, the dangerous closeness and the threat of fusion is avoided through hostile distancing. (By the way, this conceptualization of delusion of persecution is much closer to Freud's view than the more common exclusive emphasis on the projection of aggression. In the Schreber case, Freud (1911) talks about *Umkehr* and projection, not projection alone. According to Freud, Schreber's primary problem was not aggression but homosexuality. Nowadays we would say the problem is dependency on an object, which is both existentially important and dangerous - no matter whether it is homosexual or heterosexual.)

Now it is an obvious next step to supplement the vertical bipolar axis just described (self-directed versus object-directed) by a horizontal axis. The two endpoints of the horizontal axis might not be opposites in a strict sense of the term, but they nevertheless mark fairly divergent constellations, mentioned above. On the one hand (on the left side of Figure 7.1), we have the problem of self-identity versus fusion, on the other hand (on the right side of the figure), we have the problem of an autonomous feeling of self-worth versus an object-dependent feeling of self-worth. With this two-dimensional system, it is possible to classify psychotic patients in a way that is sensible from a psychodynamic point of view. Depending on the type of problem (self-identity versus fusion on the one side and autonomous versus object-dependent feeling of self-worth on the other), one assigns the patient either more to the left side or more to the right side. Depending on the mode of defence and compensation by which the patient 'answers' to this problem (self-directed versus object-directed), one assigns him either more to the upper or to the lower part of the diagram.

Apart from the arguments mentioned so far, the plausibility of this classificatory system is also confirmed by the following observation: the syndromes that psychiatrists have arduously worked out in the last 200 years can easily be located in this two-dimensional system. In other words: in general, the psychodynamic classification offered here corresponds well to the distinctions developed in descriptive psychiatry, with the advantage that the individual syndromes are no longer disjointed but can be conceptualized as alternative attempts at solving the two basic dilemmas referred to above.

Note that this dimensional (rather than categorical) classificatory system readily permits us to place the schizo-affective psychoses in the middle of the horizontal axis. Here we have a psychotic disorder of persons who have partially, but not completely, overcome the first dilemma. When the second dilemma is massively actualized, these persons 'drift' to the left side, so to speak, and thus develop symptoms typical for schizophrenics - they have to mobilize some of the psychotic defence and compensation mechanisms.

The question asked at the beginning - why such dissimilar syndromes as autism and ecstatic psychosis or expansive mania and guilt-depression belong together - can now very easily be answered. In both cases we have alternative solutions to the same problem. In the first case, we have the problem of self-identity versus fusion, and, in the second case, we have the problem of an autonomous versus object-dependent feeling of self-worth.

Extrapolation and application of the system to the borderline disorders

The decisive next step - namely the extrapolation of this conceptualization and psychodynamic classification of the psychoses to the borderline disorders - has unintentionally been facilitated by, among others, Otto Kernberg. Due to his work, it is not necessary to engage in a lengthy argument in order to elucidate the significance of a basic intra-psychic opposition for the borderline disorders. It suffices to refer to Kernberg's assertions on the insufficiency or lack of integration of the good and the bad in borderline cases.

One might well dispute certain, even important, aspects of Kernberg's model. One might, for instance, argue that anxiety, instead of aggression, is at the core of the borderline syndrome, as Dulz (1999) does. Or one might claim, as I do, that both the aggression Kernberg has in mind and the anxiety that Dulz sees are just reactions, violent or helpless attempts to cope with the enormous intra-psychic strain that develops on the basis of a conflictual constellation. Like Hoffmann (1998), one might hold that the existing technical terms are sufficient, and that there is no need for new concepts like splitting (which Kernberg conceives of as a central element of his model). One might also prefer alternative definitions of, and distinctions between, the good and the bad. Granting all this, the fact remains that Kernberg's central tenet - that the psychodynamics of the borderline syndrome consist essentially in an, at first insurmountable, fundamental opposition - has repeatedly been confirmed. This fact made it easier for me to carry out the extrapolation I will now describe.

Like Kernberg, I will assume that the level of personality organization is higher in borderline patients than in psychotic patients. This can be seen, for example, from the fact that the differentiation of self and object and the reality testing is considerably more developed in borderline patients than in psychotic patients. Still, the borderliners do not reach the level of neurotic or, more generally, so-called normal persons. Thus, if the personality structure - the mechanisms of defence, compensation and coping - matures from one level to the next, then the potentially conflictual bipolarities will always stay the same. However, they present themselves in different, more or less differentiated forms. The so-called healthy person, as well as the neurotic, and even more the borderliner, will all often become involved in the opposition between self-interest, self-identity and autonomy on the one hand and the wish for contact, relatedness and unification on the other. Likewise, everybody becomes involved in the opposition between an autonomous feeling of self-worth and the dependency on the opinions, the affection and the recognition of others. For this reason it seems justifiable to take the scheme for the psychoses and apply it also to the subsequent levels of personality organization.

In Figure 7.2 one can see the three possible conflictual constellations (self-identity versus fusion on the left, autonomous versus object-dependent self-worth on the right and a mixture of both in the middle). These three dilemmas can be answered by three different kinds of defence and

n = 20 (17 women, 3 men)

	Schizo-borderline	Schizo-affective borderline	Thymo-borderline
Self-directed defence and compensation	+ + + +		+
Mixture of and/or alternation between self- and object-directedness		+ + + + + + + + + +	+ + +
Object-directed defence and compensation	+		+

Figure 7.2. Psychodynamic classification of borderline cases.

compensation (self-directed at the top, object-directed at the bottom and, most frequently, a compromise between these in the middle). The 20 patients displayed in the figure are all the borderline cases I have treated during the last 10 years, either for a longer or a shorter time (the gender distribution of 17 women to three men corresponds with expectations). Of course, statistically significant results cannot be expected from such a small sample. Nevertheless, the apparent tendencies that I want to discuss in a moment are quite remarkable and correspond to the impressions of other clinical observers.

Before I come to this point, however, let me further explain Figure 7.2. The three dilemmas correspond to the three types of borderline patients I distinguished above: schizo-borderline, schizo-affective borderline and thymo-borderline. In addition, the figure depicts the mode of coping (self-directed, object-directed or more like a compromise, alternating, unstable). Thus, we get 3 × 3 = 9 fields. Noticeably, most cases accumulate very densely in the central field. Compare Figure 7.3, where I have classified 28 psychotic patients, whom I have diagnosed and treated. The distribution of those 28 patients over the nine fields is different. The patients are, again, not pre-selected. It is therefore reasonable to expect that, insofar as institutional, personal, economic and other factors have influenced the composition of this group, they will have been the same as in the borderline group.

As I said, in the case of the borderline patients we find an accumulation in the middle field. The group, which I have termed schizo-affective, with its permanent alternation between the self- and object-pole, and symptoms that call to mind both affective psychotic and schizophrenic psychotic patients, thus constitutes the majority of borderline cases. One might suspect that the most frequent 'border' of the borderliners is the 'border' to the schizo-

n = 28 (15 women, 13 men)

	Schizophrenia	Schizo-affective psychoses	Affective psychoses
Self-directed defence and compensation	+ + + + +	+	+ + + +
Mixture of and/or alternation between self- and object-directedness	+ + + + + +	+ + +	+ +
Object-directed defence and compensation	+ + +	+	+ + +

Figure 7.3. Psychodynamic classification of psychosis cases.

affective psychoses. Cautiously, I venture to generalize my results and claim that the majority of borderline patients we encounter, in clinics as well as in outpatient therapies, are to be found very close to the centre of the diagram. This is not only true concerning the horizontal axis - not only is the schizo-affective form of borderline the most frequent - but also with regard to the vertical axis. The inconstancy of borderline patients, their alternation between self-directedness and object-directedness, this permanent oscillating overestimation and underestimation of both the self and the object is known to be one of the greatest challenges for their therapists.

By the way, this instability and alternation is also characteristic of many schizo-affective psychoses. Under the heading 'psychoses with mixed symptoms' I have collected a very large group of such cases (over 300, see Mentzos, 1967) in the Hamburg university clinic, and analysed it statistically. The topic of this study was not, as one might be inclined to think, the mixture between schizo and thymo - the schizo-affective psychoses. Rather it concerned the mixture between the self-directed and object-directed mode of coping (however, at that time, I lacked the conceptual apparatus to differentiate clearly between these two modes). Of course, at that time, I could not define the group of patients I studied as precisely as I could today. Nevertheless, my clinical intuition told me that cases with mixed symptoms are of great importance for clinical research.

My experiences of the subsequent 34 years confirmed this impression. It is the mixed symptoms - both in the case of psychoses and, even more frequently, in the case of borderline - which are the reason for the very stressful experiences and counter-transference reactions therapists have to endure when they treat these permanently 'cycling' patients. What I am getting at is the great extent of psychic pressure on the therapists, the nurses, the spouse and the whole environment of such patients, which results from their permanently changing defences and their unpredictable alternations, particularly since they take the form of acting out in reality. Of course, the patient suffers even more from all this. Nevertheless, if one also tries to understand the positive, as it were 'functional', side of this kind of struggle for survival, one can easily see that it is precisely the flexibility and inconstancy characteristic of borderline patients that comes to their advantage. Compared to the highly secluded schizoid patients, for instance, or to the almost completely fused and dependent symbiosis patients, the borderliners are more lively, and they are capable of having contacts and relationships, although only for a short time. This is the reason why borderline patients, especially female borderline patients, have many, although unsteady, relationships, and why other people like, love and marry them, despite their disorder. What we regard as instability and inconstancy - and hence classify correspondingly according to ICD-10 and DSM-IV - often turns out to be also flexibility, and particularly an ability of the patients not to tie themselves down to something and not to let others tie them down. Some decades ago, the French psychiatrist Benoit (1960) made similar remarks about psychoses with mixed symptoms.

This conceptualization and elaboration of certain important aspects of the psychodynamics of borderline patients has not only theoretical consequences but also practical ones which are beyond the scope of the present contribution.

References

Akiskal HS (1992) Borderline. An adjective still in search of a noun. In: Silver D, Rosenbluth M (eds) Handbook of Borderline Disorders. Madison, WI: International University Press, pp. 155-76.

Benoit D (1960) L'état mixte de la psychose maniaque depressive. Ann Med Psychol 118: 637.

Dulz B (1999) Wut oder Angst - welcher Affekt ist bei Borderline-Störungen der zentrale? Persönlichkeitsstörungen, Theorie und Therapie 3 (PTT): 5-15.

Freud S (1911) Psychoanalytische Bemerkungen über einen autobiographisch beschriebenen Fall von Paranoia. GW 8: 240-316.

Hoffmann SO (1998) Die Angst des Borderline-Patienten und seine Beziehungen. Persönlichkeitsstörungen, Theorie und Therapie 1 (PTT): 4-9.

Kernberg O (1975) Borderline Conditions and Pathological Narcissism. New York: Aronson.

Mentzos S (1967) Mischzustände und mischbildhafte phasische Psychosen. Stuttgart: Enke.

Mentzos S (1991) Psychodynamische Modelle in der Psychiatrie. Göttingen: Vandenhoeck & Ruprecht.

Mentzos S (1995) Depression und Manie. Psychodynamik und Therapie affektiver Störungen. Göttingen: Vandenhoeck & Ruprecht.

Mentzos S (1997) Zur Psychodynamik der Psychosen. Zur psychodynamischen Differenzierung und Einordnung psychotischer Prozesse. Psychotherapeut 42: 343-9.

Mentzos S (1999) Operationalisierung versus 'Psychodynamisierung' in der Psychosendiagnostik. In: Mentzos S (ed.) Forum der psychoanalytischen Psychosentherapie. Band I. Göttingen: Vandenhoeck & Ruprecht.

Parnas J (1994) The concept of borderline conditions: A critical comment on validity issues. Acta Psychiatr Scandin 89 (Suppl. 379): 26-31.

Tyrer P (1994) What are the borders of borderline personality disorders? Acta Psychiatr Scandin 89 (Suppl. 379): 38-44.

THE PSYCHOANALYTIC FOLLOW-UP STUDY (DPV): A REPRESENTATIVE, MULTICENTRE STUDY OF LONG-TERM PSYCHOANALYTIC THERAPIES

CHAPTER 8
Short overview, aims and design of the follow-up study

MARIANNE LEUZINGER-BOHLEBER

Historical background and basic assessment

As already mentioned in Chapter 5, planning and carrying out the Psychoanalytic Follow-up Study was motivated by many different determinants: responding to the current *Zeitgeist*, our own research curiosity, and the wish to integrate different research traditions within German psychoanalysis and thus to bridge the gap between clinicians and researchers in our psychoanalytical society. Besides this, from a research perspective, we wanted to take up the claim of many contemporary psychotherapy researchers who, disappointed, had turned away from some methodologically sophisticated empirical and experimental studies because their results often seemed to be irrelevant for the 'real' treatments of 'real' patients. Some of them argued that only naturalistic studies could really offer true insights on the effects and important therapeutic variables of psychotherapies (these arguments are summarized in Leuzinger-Bohleber, Stuhr, Rüger and Beutel, 1999; Stuhr, Leuzinger-Bohleber, Rüger and Beutel, 2001; Leuzinger-Bohleber, Beutel, Stuhr and Rüger, 2000; Rudolf, 1996). Because only our psychoanalytical institutions enable us to do such naturalistic research (with 'real patients', qualified and experienced therapists, normal indications for certain treatments and so forth) the Research Committee of the German Psychoanalytical Association (DPV), after extensive discussions with our colleagues, decided to do a naturalistic follow-up study in 1997.

As a first step we had to ask the members of the DPV formally if they were willing to support such a study or not - and if not, what arguments they would put forward against such an empirical enterprise. Therefore we performed a *basic assessment* in the first months of 1997. We sent a questionnaire to all members of the DPV, first of all to test the feasibility of our study according to the level of co-operation of the members, and secondly to ascertain the total number of patients eligible for inclusion in the study: 91% of the members responded to the 'baseline-assessment' by questionnaire or by telephone. A great majority (89%) voted for the study. At the meeting of the German Psychoanalytical Association in Köln, in May 1997, the study was agreed officially and financially supported. We then contacted all former patients who had terminated their psychoanalytic long-term treatments between 1990 and 1993. We had not expected that over 300 of our colleagues and over 400 former patients would be willing and interested to participate actively in our study (see the following chapters).

As Bernhard Rüger discusses in Chapter 10, the data of this basic assessment helped us to monitor representativeness and to assemble a representative sample (n = 401) of all former patients in psychoanalysis and long-term psychoanalytic therapies who had terminated their treatments with DPV members between January 1990 and December 1993.

Aims and research questions

As Fonagy discussed in Chapter 4, one of the basic problems in psychotherapy research deals with the question: 'to whom do the results of a psychotherapy belong?' To the patient himself? His partner? His family? His firm? The mental health companies? And so on. We decided to focus mainly on the retrospective view of the patient himself in evaluating the outcome of his long-term therapy. As a second step we wanted to compare and contrast the patient's view with that of the treating analyst, psychoanalytic and non-psychoanalytic experts, questionnaires and tests from psychotherapy research and mental health data. In other words we decided on a *multi-perspective view* of the outcome of psychoanalyses and psychoanalytic long-term therapies (see Figure 8.1).

Thus, the *major aim of our project* is to study the patients' retrospective views of their experiences with psychoanalytic therapy and its effects at least four years after the end of their psychoanalyses or psychoanalytic long-term therapies. Do the subjective views of the former patients correspond to those of their former analysts, the independent psychoanalytical and non-psychoanalytical observers and the results of tests and questionnaires used in psychotherapy research? And do psychoanalytic long-term therapies reduce mental health costs in the long run?

Design overview

As already mentioned, our colleagues would not have been willing to support our study without the preceding extensive epistemological discussions and

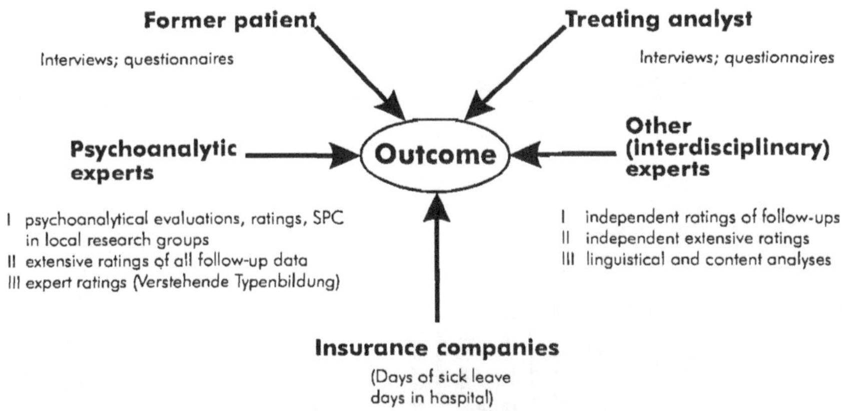

Figure 8.1. Multi-perspective approach to psychotherapy outcomes.

controversies. In the design of our study, described below, we have tried to combine psychoanalytical with non-psychoanalytical, hermeneutic with nomothetic, qualitative with quantitative approaches.

As you can see in Figure 8.2, our main method for gaining information on the outcome of psychotherapy consists of two psychoanalytic follow-up interviews which enable us *to perceive, and evaluate psychoanalytically, conscious and unconscious processes involved in evaluating therapy outcome, within the professional setting of interviews conducted by experienced psychoanalysts.* We also apply other psychoanalytic methods like supervision between the two interviews, assessing the psychodynamic hypotheses in the local psychoanalytic research groups and summarizing the findings of the follow-ups in 'psychoanalytically controlled' case studies (see Chapter 12).

The results gained by these *psychoanalytic* methods are compared and contrasted with those gained by *non-psychoanalytic* instruments: questionnaires (such as IRES, and the Sense of Coherence Scale), ratings by non-psychoanalytic experts and objective data on health costs.

Analysing our data we also compare psychoanalytic with non-psychoanalytic procedures such as content and linguistic analyses of the transcribed follow-up interviews.

In Chapter 9, Ulrich Stuhr summarizes one outcome of our controversial theoretical discussions but the reader will also find traces of our epistemological and methodological debates in the other reports of the results of our study (see Chapters 11 and 12).

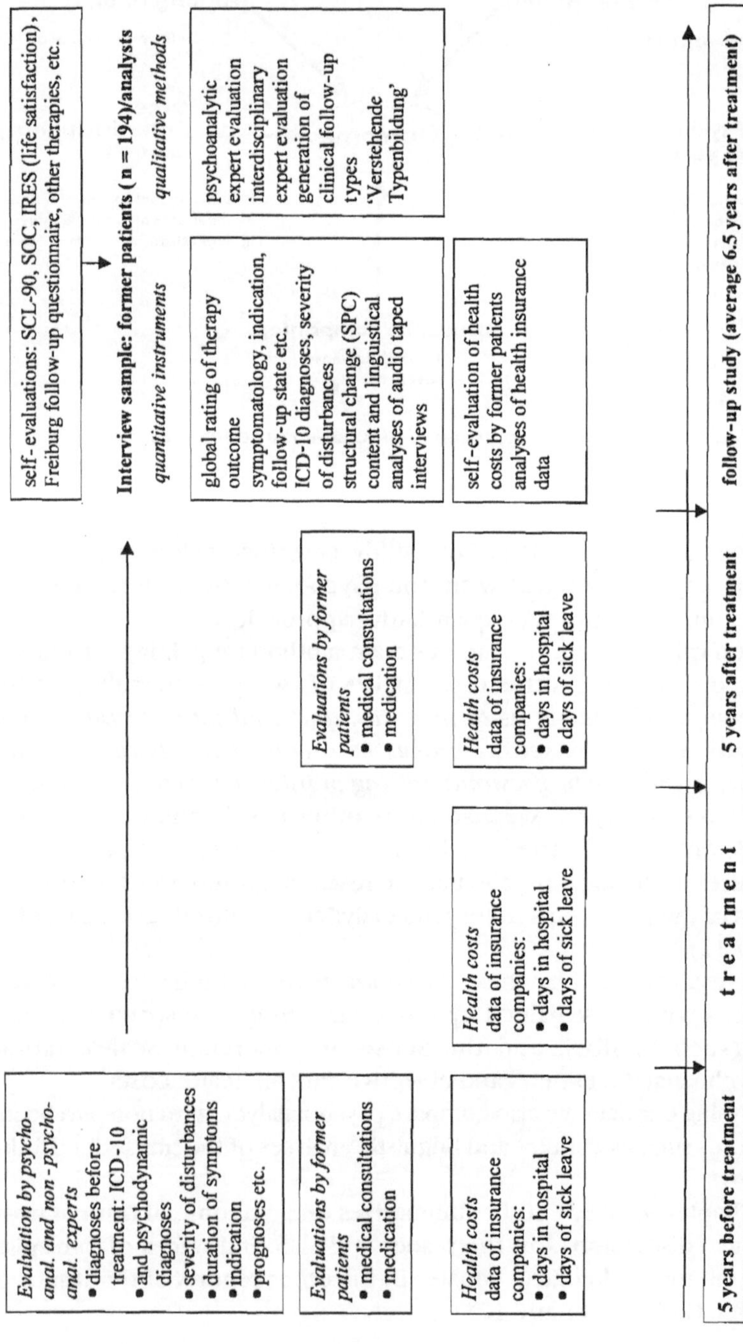

Figure 8.2. Long-term psychoanalytical treatments: a representative, multiperspective follow-up study (design and methods).

Questionnaire and interview sample

As I have said, many more colleagues and former patients were willing to participate in our study than we had originally dared to plan for. As a result we did not have the capacity to interview all of the 401 former patients, which would have meant performing 802 follow-up interviews. Therefore it was necessary to draw a representative subsample of those former patients, whom we could interview. Manfred Beutel and Markus Rasting report on the findings of the questionnaire sample in Chapter 11. I summarize some of our interview results in Chapter 12, where I focus particularly on the psychoanalytic outcome of our study.

We hope that the following chapters will give a vivid impression of our 'naturalistic' research enterprise, its opportunities and its problems, and that they will be of interest to our clinical colleagues and researchers in this complex field.

References

Leuzinger-Bohleber M, Stuhr U, Rüger B, Beutel M (1999) Long-term Effects of Psychoanalyses and Psychoanalytic Therapies: A representative follow-up study. Paper given at the Empirical Procongress of the IPA Congress in Santiago de Chile, 24 July 1999.

Leuzinger-Bohleber M, Beutel M, Stuhr U, Rüger B (2000) How to Study the Quality of Psychoanalytic Treatments: Combining qualitative and quantitative approaches in a representative follow-up study. Paper given at the Research Conference of the IPA in London, 4 March, 2000.

Rudolf G (1996) Psychotherapieforschung bezogen auf die psychotherapeutische Praxis. Psychotherapie Forum 4: 124–34.

Stuhr U, Leuzinger-Bohleber M, Beutel M (2001) (eds) Langzeit-Psychotherapie. Perspektiven für Therapeuten und Wissenschaftler. München: Kohlhammer Verlag.

CHAPTER 9

Combining qualitative and quantitative methods in psychoanalytic follow-up research

ULRICH STUHR

The well-trained medical doctor Sigmund Freud (1895a: 227) had a peculiar feeling about the observation that 'his case histories *read* like short stories'. Freud thought that this suggestion might be determined by the fact that he had not always been a psychotherapist but had begun professional life as a neuropathologist. So he tried to comfort himself by blaming the 'nature of the subject' for the novel-like character of his case reports.

This contradiction, which Freud himself felt, between the roles of a scientist and a narrative writer initiated a continuing dialogue. An example is the discussion, in 1996, between André Green and Robert Wallerstein (Green, 1996). Another example is the prominent review article by Bachrach and his collaborators (1991) about the effectiveness of psychoanalysis. On the one hand there is a demand for standardized, reliable and valid research methods within a formalized research strategy and, on the other, the perceived need for a specific psychoanalytic research methodology in which the idiosyncrasy of each single clinical case is emphasized. We can also find these contradictions in Fonagy's (1999) 'Open Door' review, in the so-called French versus Anglo-Saxon Position.

In our project, we tried to respect the warnings of Mertens (1995: 431) who says that in a follow-up project psychoanalytic colleagues do not expect useful information from an experimental design because they think their clinical work wouldn't be represented adequately by such a research methodology. He suggests replacing these methods by procedures that take more time and personal commitment. But such research strategies are dependent on the support of many researchers and colleagues. So in planning our research project, we had to consider whether our own scientific ideas would be acceptable in the community of our colleagues. Achieving such an acceptance took many discussions with our psychoanalytic colleagues. It was also the case that the analysts conducting the follow-up study wanted to make sure that they would not spend their time interviewing patients with senseless questions as part of an ineffective methodology. Within the German Psychoanalytical Association (DPV), we would not have been able to implement our research plans if we had chosen a purely quantitative and experimental design for our study. But thanks to these many, and often difficult, discussions, and to the decision to use a multi-perspective design close to psychoanalytic practice, it was finally possible to convince the DPV to support a research project that addressed its members' clinical work and the resulting outcomes.

During these discussions, and in the process of our study, it became clear that even among those of us responsible for conducting the follow-up study we had different scientific positions that we were reluctant to compromise. In consequence, a further result of the study is to examine which of these different positions and the derived research methods, including the statistical tests, has led to the most interesting results. This includes interpretation of the ICD System Codes as well as the sociodemographic factors, or the number of patients who, after termination of their therapy, met their therapists again or sought other therapies. Therefore the quality of interpretation, and the questions asked of certain results are most relevant.

Despite the fact that Freud often referred to physics as a scientific paradigm in his 'outline' (Freud, 1940: 127) and wanted to have the acceptance of the natural sciences, he often points to the psychological specificity of his research subject. Psychology, due to its complex issues, could not be studied only by 'a cool scientific interest'. Freud also writes that there is no way of recognizing, and describing a complicated set of simultaneous events instead of simplifying them.

Of course one could argue that at the start of the discovery of psychoanalysis there was justification for using case histories, 'novels', as a new way of communicating complex observations; but with the subsequent progress in psychoanalysis this form of communication would no longer be required. But have the basic characteristics of our discipline really changed since Freud's time? And do we really have a different situation from that of the first generation of analysts, trying to discover new, strange and uncommon events within their patients, and to understand them? Is the main function of case studies still to inspire communication between the author and readers, for example by using the author's counter-transference reactions evoked during the experience related in a case history (Overbeck, 1993; Kvale, 2001)?

Bude (1993b) shows how Freud keeps the reader in tension by the specific dramatic and other didactic strategies in his narratives: something surprising, strange or shocking constantly occurs. We proved the accuracy of this observation again and again in listening to the narrative summary of the follow-up interviews by our colleagues in our study (see Leuzinger-Bohleber in this volume).

Because a storyteller tells only what can be told, he points out that not everything can be explained, although it has a deep sense and meaning. The story, the narrative, as the case history of 'Dora' illustrates, manifests the relationship between the storyteller and his subject, the therapist and his patient. And the careful reader – according to Mahony (1989) – finds out that the main figure of the narrative is not 'Dora', but Freud himself, the author of the novel. Such understanding, which is the base and the aim of the psychoanalytic process, becomes relevant for the reader, and may become a contribution to the developing body of knowledge within the psychoanalytic community, for example in the analysis of the counter-transference reactions of the therapist which can be observed, and reflected on, by others. Since Paula Heimann's papers (1950, 1969) we know that we can use counter-transference reactions as research instruments, using our own unconscious sensibility to gain access to the unconscious of the patient, an access unattainable with any other method.

One basic argument for qualitative research, especially for a narrative approach (see, for instance, Bude, 1993a) is that the novel-like style adjusts precisely to characteristics of the subject. Gaining knowledge by narratives means 'telling only what can be told'. In contrast to this approach the methods predominantly used in psychotherapy research follow the specific logic of 'non-ambiguity': A is not not-A (negation). This means: statement A, for example an item in a questionnaire or in an observation, has to be defined without contradictions within itself. But we know from the field of rhetoric that there are language phenomena such as the paradox and the oxymoron, similar to that ambivalence, important in psychoanalysis, which cannot be described by formal logical systems such as algorithms. This means that it is not necessarily the complexity of the subject, but the logic of 'unmistakable, unequivocal statements' that limits traditional quantitative psychotherapy research. It was this that created the need for the scientist Freud to communicate his observations by novel-like case histories. I suppose he would have preferred, following the paradigm of physics, a precise and unequivocal description if this had made any sense. One of the best illustrations of this thesis is Freud's (1895b) paper, which he characterized as a 'psychology for neurologists'.

To illustrate this once again: if statement 'A' means 'I love you', then its negation means 'I don't love you'; and if A means 'I want to be alone' then its negation means 'I don't want to be alone'. But as we know, opposite phenomena and contradictions are often connected in psychology (the phenomenon of ambivalence). Love and hate, autonomy and wish for closeness; they cannot be separated from each other in a strict logical way, such as by the negation that statistical procedures afford. Therefore the operationalization of such psychological phenomena and their statistical testing creates insoluble problems. That's exactly the point: these phenomena can only be told and communicated by narratives. In this respect psychoanalysts are more closely related to philologists than to natural scientists. When the writer Thomas Mann speaks of the 'guiltless guilty' in order to illustrate the state of temporal contradictions, it becomes clear how difficult, or even impossible, it is to describe such phenomena with a mathematical formula. The contrasts in rhetoric, expressed in *paradoxes* and *antinomies,* create a limit to the capacities of logical and rational representations in our research subject, which is one that can only be represented adequately by what can be told, which means communicated by narratives.

The philosopher of science, Stephen Toulmin (1994) claims there is a denial of the humanistic acceptance of uncertainties and ambiguities in the logical strength and thematic precision of rationalism, as Wolfgang Mertens has also pointed out. When I was a young psychologist I went through an experience that can be a relevant and important example of this. In the 1970s, I was asked to develop a questionnaire on psychoanalytic sessions for colleagues in our department. The questionnaire returned by one of the analysts shocked me because he had consistently marked two numbers on the same bipolar scale. Indeed, I was unable to use this data in my statistical analyses. The analyst told me that first he had rated his conscious attitude in respect to the analytic session, then, in a second step, he had tried to evaluate his deeper, preconscious attitudes. The analyst had tried to express one of the dichotomies of psychoanalytic sessions, and as a result it was impossible for me to use my statistical instruments.

But of course, narratives and qualitative approaches do not only have advantages - they also have disadvantages.

The main methodological criticisms of qualitative research, for example to the inclusion of narratives, can be summarised in two points:

- Data analysis and interpretation is selective, which means that the authors consciously and unconsciously select only those facts that suit their preconceived ideas, so the results can neither be replicated nor falsified, and so are invalid.
- Results cannot be generalized. Qualitative results and generalizations are often based on single cases. Nevertheless, generalizations may well be derived from single cases in this approach, and therefore have no validity because the case may be atypical.

Ernst Federn, in a conversation with Tomas Plänkers, gives an informative example of this by reading the protocols of the Wednesday Society produced by his father (Plänkers and Federn, 1994: 34): 'it's amazing how rapidly the group leaves the single case and concentrates on the development of general theses in the sense of an average pathology.' To all such rushed conclusions and generalizations Freud always returned the answer: 'We do not understand enough, yet.'

This is exactly the site of the fracture where advocates of critical rationalism prefer quantitative scientific methods and set out their doubts about qualitative narrative methods. They see the particular danger of hollowing out the conception of truth. Albert and Stapf (1979: 108) explore the matter:

> the finding seems to be a collection of products from subjects that are able to enforce their preconceptions, irrespective of any truth that is independent from them. For they play their word-games according to rules where there is no necessity to regard the resistance of truth. The idealistic tendencies of such a science are obvious. The methodological effects, with respect to the development and gathering of knowledge, can only be opposed to scientific progress.

What does critical rationalism, which prefers the quantitative strategy, offer us for our specific research subject? The strategy of the critics opposed to the narrative approach is the emphasis on empirical methods that are supposed to deliver reliable, valid and objective data. But before we can conduct a measurement we have to decide on the scaling, operationalizations and so forth. This unfortunately leads us to a general question that is often neglected: how can we set out the relevant characteristics of mankind so that a measurement can be conducted at all?

In an operational definition, developed by the physicist Bridgman (1927), researchers have to define precisely how the terms used in research can be transformed to concrete operations of measurement for establishing facts – a precondition for any discussion about an 'objective' phenomenon. To define terms by operations of measurement is of course easy in physics. The length of an object can be defined by 'applying a scale of measurement'. But how can this strategy be transferred to psychology or further to psychoanalysis, when independent observation is supposed to be validated by precise and objective operations? One could, for example, define a tear as an indicator for a defended depressive reaction in a patient. The tear volume per patient, or the biochemical consistency of the tears, would be set by definition to quantify the reaction. It would be an interesting examination, but there is one crucial point: tears have a very individual meaning within the psychological experience of the person who cries. How can we know, from the measurements described above, if the patient's tears are tears of joy, tears of rage or just tears of melancholy? And how about patients who never cry or those who cry very easily? Of course, one could argue that tears are generally not useful indicators for certain emotions. But the example is useful to illustrate the problems of the approach of operational definitions in psychology. We leave the psychological base to gain more objectivity. The wish for exactness and objectivity threatens the detectable psychological content of a statement.

We are observing here a tension which Freud anticipated, and which Theodor Adorno experienced in a very concrete way after his emigration to the US. He was disqualified as a 'social commentator' because he, as a social scientist of the critical theory (so-called 'Kritische Theorie') of the Frankfurt School, felt close to the interpretative method. Applying this method he was disqualified as a 'social scientist' because interpretation is always determined by this tension between the concrete and the general; aiming at generalizations from the concrete single case, in contrast to the basic principle of 'science as measurement' (see Adorno et al., 1950).

This is where the problems really start, for we have to produce not only objective data, the so-called scaling within the operational definition, but also the subsequent measurement itself, which, in psychology, is difficult.

Measurement is defined as an operation in which there are events or persons on one side and on the other side numbers or groups, classes or clusters, which are related to each other. The relevant question for those of us using this exact, but at the same time lapidary arithmetical definition mathematically is the relation between the inner and outer world of our patients and the relation of those phenomena to numbers and statistical operations. For this relationship, an exact representation would be an unalterable precondition for the conduct of measurements that make sense. The numbers representing attributes and/or relations must exist equally in the real objects or within our patients, and the statistics must exactly represent the real dynamic in the objects. The measured values in the attributes of our patients should only be averaged, if - to give an easy example for a mathematical operation - we can assume for the measured attributes that they can change in units, and the interval between two successive single units is always the same. Only in this way can we be sure that the mean really represents the average attribute exactly. Even the advocates of empirical psychology know that this precondition for measuring (so called interval scaling) is not to be accomplished for the measurement of relevant psychological phenomena: 'Most of the time we are able to give only ranking scaled information' (Hofstätter and Wendt, 1966: 233). It is not surprising that even Mittenecker (1971: 6), who propagated the introduction of measurement methods in psychology, named the restrictive conditions himself: 'Only if a situation is very complex and is continuously changing for the observed time, will it not be possible to produce sensible quantitative statements.'

Our research subject is indeed very complex, and for the unconscious dynamic, continuously changing. So empirical psychology using quantifying measurement operations does not do justice to psychoanalytic research issues.

If 'hard science' could convince us, and could put an end to the chronic discussion between 'correlators' and 'interpreters', we would not protest. But, so far, our specific research subject has never been adequately investigated by quantitative methods – if indeed it ever will be.

Besides the problem of developing an approach suitable for the investigation of our specific discipline, we have another problem in psychotherapy research. This is the specificity problem. In a direct comparison of different therapy methods, we obtain similar results although the procedures differ fundamentally, and are expected to lead to specific results. In order to avoid this problem, differential psychology research since Kiesler (1969) has in fact created a research strategy, the so-called grid model, which is very differentiated. But the problem here is that the pattern is too elaborate to allow later comparison of the patterns of different patients with each other in a meaningful and statistically plausible way. It was for this reason that Westmeyer (1979) and Eysenck (1991) asked if the perfect resolution of our research problems is utopia. The idea is great, but while on the way to realizing it we get results that are already outdated in psychotherapeutic practice (see Eckert, 1993).

It is a crucial fact that, *a priori*, there is no fundamental system of therapeutic techniques or definitions of patients' symptoms and their interaction. The drug metaphor tells us that it is not single variables in therapies that are similar; rather that the dose of a therapeutic technique is decisive for the success or failure of the intervention; hence the claims of some researchers for therapy manuals. There is a risk in this that research goes far beyond clinical practice and will therefore never lead to any clinically relevant results.

Russell (1995) and other well-known psychotherapy researchers, for example Stiles, Greenberg or David Shapiro in the book *Reassessing Psychotherapy Research*, reject the scientific operational definition paradigm and the drug-metaphor paradigm for psychotherapy research. For the fourth phase of psychotherapy research, Orlinsky and Russell (1995) demand an innovation – a reform of the qualitative approach that is not orientated to the operational definition paradigm of the natural sciences. Not either/or, but, as Faller (1994: 56) stresses, a gradual differentiation between quantitative and qualitative methods could be one solution, because the difference between the two approaches is not absolute; it is only a matter of the point at which interpretation is applied.

We should be sceptical of myths of uniformity as well as of the specificity thesis in psychotherapy research. We should use empirical research to attain more differentiated knowledge, applying qualitative and quantitative procedures. My suggestion is a balanced empirical position that can be defined as a taxonomic strategy within psychotherapy research. Far from the utopian grid model, we are looking for a differentiated solution in our follow-up study. We do not expect to find all cases reflected in one result such as N = 1 nor, taking the extreme other possibility, to postulate that every case can stand for itself. Such extreme heterogeneity would be clinically interesting, but is scientifically dissatisfying because we would have as many solutions as we have patients. The taxonomy approach I favour is theoretically based on the hypothesis that there are reasonable solutions possible between N = 1 and N = n with various meaningful subgroups.

To answer the question of how to combine qualitative and quantitative methods, we did not have to start from scratch, for we could learn from the classic studies in social research, such as from Adorno and his co-workers (1950) about authoritarian personalities. This study integrates quantitative and qualitative methods, by taking samples derived from certain data from a large heterogeneous sample of more than 2000 subjects sorted by quantitative methods, and by carrying out clinical examinations with qualitative methods. The study used standardized psychometric instruments such as the ethnocentric scale, the f-scale and the scale for registering political and economic ideology. The high scorers and the low scorers were further explored with qualitative methods in intensive interviews.

The simplest model for combining quantitative and qualitative procedures is to select the high and low scorers of the relevant psychometric scales, as was done in Adorno's study using, for example, the depression scale from the SCL-90, or other clinical ratings, and then, in a second step, to examine the selected subjects as above intensively, looking at data from the interviews and describing them in a clinical, psychodynamic way. The result is a broad quantitative description that is illustrated with small novel-like case histories, giving detailed information about the outcome of the therapy (see Stuhr, Oppermann and Höppner-Deymann, 2002). By this procedure we can localize one specific single case in a sample, which we can then describe by applying quantitative methods. This procedure therefore gives a picture of the subject where the qualitative information is integrated in the quantitative description of the sample. The fascination in such a combined strategy is the mutual illumination of quantitative and qualitative descriptions that complement each other.

There is also the option of putting more weight on the qualitative approach, and differentiating subgroups with an empirical qualitative approach, as I did with Ms Wachholz in the *Journal of Psychotherapy Research* for follow-up studies of short-term psychotherapies (Wachholz and Stuhr, 1999).

In this case we used the taxonomic approach, but differentiated subgroups not with a quantitative method but a qualitative one. In our department in Hamburg, we have worked for several years on the task of using Max Weber's concept of the creation of ideal types on clinical narrative material. We combine this concept with Uta Gerhardt's (1986) thoughts about how to approach the issue of ideal types, and aim for a 'qualitative cluster-analysis'. The poignant clinical cases among the samples are identified and described as prototypes that are used to sort the samples and build a structure for subgroups of successful therapies (Wachholz and Stuhr, 1999). We then use quantitative variables for the qualitatively described and extracted subgroups of so called ideal types. In illustration, such ideal-type subgroups could be formed of former patients who have a perceived inner picture of a certain kind of their therapists in the follow-up interview. For example the former therapist may be described as a 'severe and demanding father' or as 'a symbiotic motherly object'. In this example, the qualitative methods play a major role in the whole research project.

The transcription of the follow-up interviews, and their analysis by this method, takes a lot of time, and is not yet complete. For that reason, I cannot present results from that qualitative study in this chapter (see Stuhr et al., 2002).

The reader might have noticed that I, personally, sympathize with the qualitative approach within the possible combinations of quantitative and qualitative instruments. This is because what seemed to be a 'preliminary emergency solution' for the neurologist Freud a hundred years ago has proved to be an excellent research strategy in itself: case histories, narratives, are a means of telling only what can be told, and preventing the over-simplification of our psychoanalytic knowledge. This is one of the reasons why we are using narrative methods in our follow-up study, illustrating all kinds of quantitative findings (see Leuzinger-Bohleber and Beutel/Rasting in this volume). By this procedure we try to bring to life the 'objectivity' of numbers, opening them up to a broader understanding by telling and illustrating.

References

Adorno T, Frenkel-Brunswik E, Levinson DJ, Sanford RN (1950) The authoritarian personality. In: Tiedemann R (ed.) Theodor W Adorno: GS, Soziologische Schriften II (9.1). Frankfurt/Maine: Suhrkamp, pp. 143–509.

Albert H, Stapf KH (eds) (1979) Theorie und Erfahrung. Beiträge zur Grundlagenproblematik der Sozialwissenschaften. Stuttgart: Klett-Cotta.

Bachrach HM, Galatzer-Levy R, Skolnikoff A, Waldron S (1991) On the efficacy of psychoanalysis. J Am Psychanal Assoc 39: 871–916.

Bridgman PW (1927) The Logic of Modern Physics. New York: Macmillan.

Bude H (1993a), Freud als Novellist. In: Stuhr U, Deneke F-W (eds) Die Fallgeschichte. Beiträge zu ihrer Bedeutung als Forschungsinstrument. Heidelberg: Asanger, pp. 3-16.

Bude H (1993b) Die soziologische Erzählung. In: Jung T, Müller-Dohm S (eds) Wirklichkeit im Deutungsprozeß. Frankfurt/M.: Suhrkamp: 409-29.

Eckert J (1993) Zur Begutachtung der psychotherapeutischen Verfahren im 'Forschungsgutachten' zum Psychotherapeutengesetz. Viele sind gar nicht erst angetreten, drei haben gewonnen und zwei bekommen den Preis. Psychother. Forum 1: 87-91.

Eysenck H-J (1991) Meyer's taxonomy of research into psychotherapy. Z Klin Psychol 20: 265-7.

Faller H (1994) Das Forschungsprogramm 'Qualitative Psychotherapieforschung'. Versuch einer Standortbestimmung. In: Faller H, Frommer J (eds) Qualitative Psychotherapieforschung. Heidelberg: Asanger, pp. 15-37.

Fonagy P (1999) (ed) An Open Door Review of Outcome Studies in Psychoanalysis. IPA. London: University College.

Freud S (1895a) W Bd. 1. London: Imago, pp. 75-312.

Freud S (1895b) Entwurf einer Psychologie. GW Ergänzungsband. London: Imago, pp. 375-486.

Freud S (1940) Some Elementary Lessons. G.W. Bd. 17. London: Imago, pp. 139-47.

Gerhardt U (1986) Patientenkarrieren. Frankfurt/M.: Suhrkamp.

Green A (1996) Welche Forschung für die Psychoanalyse? Int. Psychoanalyse. The Newsletter of the LPV 5, 1: 10-14.

Heimann P (1950) On counter-transference. Int J Psychoanal 31: 81-4.

Heimann P (1969) Gedanken zum Erkenntnisprozeß des Psychoanalytikers. Psyche 23: 2-24.

Hofstätter PR, Wendt D (1966) Quantitative Methoden der Psychologie. München: J.A. Barth.

Kiesler DJ (1969) A grid model for theory and research in psychotherapies. In: Eron LA, Callahan R (eds) The Relation of Theory to Practice in Psychotherapy. Chicago: Aldine Publ. Comp.

Kvale S (2001) The psychoanalytic interview as qualitative research. In: Frommer J, Rennie DL (eds) Qualitative Psychotherapy Research: Methods and methodology. Lengerich: Pabst; 9-31.

Mahony PJ (1989) Der Schriftsteller Sigmund Freud. Frankfurt/M.: Suhrkamp.

Mertens H (1995) Warum Psychoanalysen lange dauern. Psyche 5: 405-33.

Mittenecker E (1971) Planung und statistische Auswertung von Experimenten. Wien: F. Deuticke.

Orlinsky DE, Russell RL (1995) Tradition and change in psychotherapy research: Notes on the fourth generation. In: Russell RL (ed.) Reassessing Psychotherapy Research. New York, London: Guilford Press: 185-214.

Overbeck G (1993) Die Fallnovelle als literarische Verständigungs- und Untersuchungsmethode - Ein Beitrag zur Subjektivierung. In: Stuhr U, Deneke F-W (eds) Die Fallgeschichte. Beiträge zu ihrer Bedeutung als Forschungsinstrument. Heidelberg: Asanger: 43-60.

Plänkers T, Federn E (1994) Vertreibung und Rückkehr. Interviews zur Geschichte Ernst Federns und der Psychoanalyse. Tübingen: Edition Diskord.

Russell RL (1995) (ed.) Reassessing Psychotherapy Research. New York, London: Guilford Press.

Stuhr U, Oppermann M, Höppner-Deymann S (2002) Zur Kombination qualitativer und quantitativer Daten. Was nur erzähltwerden kann. In: Leuzinger-Bohleber M, Stur U, Beutel M (eds) Wieforschen und heilen Psychoanalytiker? Bericht und Ergebnisse aus einer repräsentativen Katamnesestudie. Stuttgart: Kohlhammer (in press).

Toulmin S (1994) Kosmopolis. Frankfurt/Maine: Suhrkamp.

Wachholz B, Stuhr U (1999) The concept of ideal types in psychoanalytic follow-up research. Psychotherapy Research 9(3): 324-41.

Westmeyer H (1979) Die rationale Rekonstruktion einiger Aspekte psychologischer Praxis. In: Albert H, Stapf K (eds) Motiv und Erfahrung. Beiträge zur Grundlagenproblematik der Sozialwissenschaften. Stuttgart: Klett-Cotta: 139-61.

Chapter 10
Statistical design and representativeness of the DPV follow-up study

Bernhard Rüger

Introduction

The aim of the statistical design of studies of this type is the creation of one or more representative samples within the available resources. Essentially there are two procedures to accomplish this: drawing *random samples,* which are representative by nature, and selecting *representative controls* from non-random samples. The latter procedure is often a painstaking exercise but it can hardly ever be avoided because of dropouts and missing values. In the statistical design of the DPV follow-up study, both procedures have been employed. Random samples, if possible, or controls that are representative with regard to evaluations of therapy outcomes. The checks for representativeness are carried out by comparing the samples of co-operating analysts and patients with the total population of analysts and patients, whose structure (including evaluations) had been previously established by a basic assessment. Similar verification of representativeness is used to exclude biases due to dropouts. The applied random samples are stratified samples with respect to evaluations of therapy outcomes by the analysts and the patients. The results of these two procedures in the statistical design are representative patient samples for follow-up interviews and questionnaires. Our procedure is described in detail below.

The basic population

The basic population of the follow-up study consists of all long-term *psychoanalyses* (three, four, or more than four sessions per week) and long-term psychoanalytic *psychotherapies* (one or two sessions per week), conducted by members of the DPV, and terminated between January 1990 and December 1993. (Training analyses and supervised cases during training have been excluded.) The size of the basic population is approximately 6400 cases. The follow-up study began in 1998 and is still in progress. Between five and nine years have passed since treatment terminations. This amount of elapsed time is generally recommended for the investigation of the long-term effects of psychotherapies.

The basic assessment (January–April 1997)

In the first phase of the study, questionnaires were sent to all 751 psychoanalysts of the DPV (774 minus 23 who were unobtainable). The questionnaires consisted of questions concerning the analysts' identities (questions numbers 1-3), their attitude towards the study (question number 6), their willingness to take part in the study (question number 7), the total number of cases they had treated (question number 5), the number of patients they had currently in treatment (question number 4), the number of patients they had had, who terminated therapy between 1990 and 1993 (question number 8), their global evaluation of the severity of the mental disorders of these patients, and their global evaluation of the outcome of these patients' therapies (question number 9).

Although many of the findings of the basic assessment are interesting in their own right, in what follows only the issue of how the questionnaire data were used for planning the sample and controlling its representativeness will be discussed. A high return rate of the basic assessment was crucial for the feasibility of obtaining representativeness: 521 analysts (return rate: 69.4%) returned the questionnaire (however some did not answer it completely). In a subsequent round, a further 161 analysts (additional return rate: 21.4%) returned at least an abbreviated questionnaire with question 9 missing. Thus, a total return rate was yielded of almost 91%.

The basis of the test of representativeness is especially question 7, where the analysts could state reasons for not participating in the study, and question 9, where the analysts had to evaluate therapy outcome. The high return rate is correlated with question 7, which was answered by 92% of all the analysts who returned the questionnaire. A total of 303 analysts agreed to take part in the study (244 of these belong to those 521 analysts who returned the complete questionnaire; the remaining 59 belong to those 161 analysts who returned only the abbreviated questionnaire without question 9). Regarding the answers of the non co-operating analysts to the questions about the reasons why they didn't want to participate in the study, at worst in 5% of all cases a bias concerning the therapy outcome can be suspected.

This result alone justifies the conclusion that the participating analysts are a balanced sample with respect to success of therapies. This conclusion can be substantiated when question 7 is considered *together with* question 9 (though for this, only the answers of those 521 analysts who responded to the complete version of the questionnaire, including question 9, can be taken into account and not the 161 analysts who answered the abbreviated questionnaire). The corresponding table is shown in Table 10.1.

Table 10.1. Crosstabulation of question 7 and question 9 (absolute frequencies)

Question 7: co-operating	Responded to question 9 yes	no	Sum
Yes	207	37	244
No	114	163	277
Sum	321	200	521

Table 10.2 shows a comparison of the 207 co-operating analysts and the 114 non co-operating analysts regarding their answers to question 9 (evaluation of therapy outcome).

Table 10.2. Spontaneous global evaluation of therapy outcome by the analysts (question 9) separated into number of cases (absolute and in %) and according to co-operation

Evaluation	All 321 analysts responding to question 9		Among them 207 co-operating		Among them 114 not co-operating	
Bad	184	8.4 %	127	9.2 %	57	7.2 %
Middle	705	32.4 %	446	32.2 %	259	32.6 %
Good	981	45.0 %	620	44.8 %	361	45.4 %
Very good	309	14.2 %	191	13.8 %	118	14.8 %
Sum	2179		1384		795	

The fact that the two frequency distributions are almost identical corroborates the representativeness of the treatment cases of the 207 participating analysts: their (subjective global) evaluation of therapy success does not lean towards 'more successful' cases. In fact there is even a slight (statistically not significant) tendency towards 'less successful' cases in the participating group.

On the basis of these highly satisfactory results the project group decided to limit the basis for the patient sample to those 207 participating analysts who had returned the complete questionnaire and answered question 9 (and to exclude the other co-operating analysts who did not answer it). Through this (regrettable) limitation it is even possible to control the representativeness of the later assembled patient samples (despite their relatively high dropout rates), because this control is based on the answers to question 9, as will be shown below.

The patient survey (May 1997–January 1998)

The 207 co-operating analysts had indicated a total of 1399 patients in the basic assessment (Table 10.2 shows only 1384 because in 15 cases the evaluation of therapy outcome was missing). Unfortunately, only 154 out of the 207 participating analysts were able (or willing) to include their own patients in the study. In order to exclude trainee analysts, we had contacted only analysts who had finished their training before 1990. Nevertheless there were quite a lot of analysts in the sample who had not conducted any independent therapies that terminated between 1990 and 1993. This is one major reason for the 53 dropouts. The corresponding cases are shown in Table 10.4 under the category 'dropouts due to therapist'. The remaining dropouts were due to the patients, who were either 'unobtainable', 'began a new therapy' or submitted 'no response'. However, this dropout rate did not lead to a bias in favour of 'more successful' cases, as Table 10.3 shows. Actually there are more cases with a negative outcome evaluation in the sample of the remaining 154 analysts than in the original sample.

Table 10.3. Spontaneous global evaluation of therapy outcome by the 207 co-operating analysts separated into number of cases and into analysts with/without patients for the study

Evaluation	207 co-operating analysts		Among them 154 with patients for the study		Among them 53 without patients for the study	
Bad	127	9.2 %	113	10.9 %	14	4.0 %
Middle	446	32.2 %	315	30.3 %	131	37.9 %
Good	620	44.8 %	479	46.1 %	141	40.8 %
Very good	191	13.8 %	131	12.6 %	60	17.3 %
Sum	1384		1038		346	

Table 10.4. Dropouts separated into different cases and valid cases among the 1399 treatment cases of the 207 co-operating analysts

	Number of cases	
	Absolute	Percentage
Dropouts due to therapist	358	25.6
Dropouts due to being unobtainable	278	19.9
Dropouts due to no response but being obtainable	248	17.7
Dropouts due to starting a new therapy	62	4.4
Valid cases	453	32.4
Sum	1399	

Only the 453 remaining 'valid cases' in Table 10.4 could be included by the project group. The first contact with these patients was established via their analysts, who sent them a letter and a short questionnaire. (Of course, the confidentiality of the patients was preserved throughout the study. They were assigned a code number, which only their analyst could decipher. Later contacts were established via the head of the statistical team, who was handed out the code-keys on permission of the patients.) An astonishingly high proportion of the 453 patients contacted, 401, agreed to take part in the study. But before the actual follow-up phase (comprising interviews and questionnaire surveys) could begin, it was necessary to examine whether the sample of 453 patients and the subsample of 401 participating patients could be seen as representative, despite the high dropout rate of almost 68%. This especially important test of representativeness was performed by two methods.

First the analysts' evaluations of therapy outcome (question 9 of the basic assessment) for the 453 and 401 cases respectively were compared to the outcome evaluations for all 2179 cases, for which the answer to question 9 was available. This comparison is shown in Table 10.5 (only the relative frequencies are indicated).

The frequency distributions of the analysts' evaluations of therapy outcome for the first three patient samples are, as already indicated, very similar. These samples were essentially determined by the analysts. By contrast, samples (4) and (5) were primarily determined by the patients. The frequency distributions of these two samples are again very similar but there is a considerable shift towards 'more successful' cases from the first three samples to sample (4) and (5). In view of the high dropout rate from sample (3) to sample (4), such a shift was to be anticipated. However, this shift is moderate enough to be controllable, and it is by no means big enough to indicate a bias toward the 'good' or 'very good' cases. On the basis of the

Table 10.5. Spontaneous global evaluation of therapy outcome by analysts (question 9) separated into different patient samples. (The first three patient samples can already be found in tables 2 and 3.)

Patient samples	Global evaluation of therapy outcome by analysts (question 9 of basic assessment)			
	Bad (%)	Middle (%)	Good (%)	Very good (%)
(1) All patients with statements to question 9 (n = 2179)	8.4	32.4	45.0	14.2
(2) Among them patients of the co-operating analysts (n = 1384)	9.2	32.2	44.8	13.8
(3) Among them patients who potentially can be included (n = 1038)	10.9	30.3	46.1	12.6
(4) Among them the actually contacted patients (n = 453)	7.5	28.0	49.4	15.1
(5) Among them the participating patients (in the study) (n = 401)	6.6	26.8	50.6	16.0

known differences between the frequency distributions of sample (3) and sample (4) it is furthermore possible to perform an, admittedly imprecise, statistical bias correction. Therefore, all in all, patient samples (4) and (5) can still be regarded as representative.

The second check on representativeness is based on an evaluation of therapy outcome by the patients themselves, which was part of the short questionnaire they received from their analysts. Table 10.6 shows the result of this survey for the whole sample of 453 identified patients (sample 4 in Table 10.5) and for the subsample of 401 patients who agreed to participate in the study (sample 5 in Table 10.5). The high level of similarity in the corresponding frequency distributions again corroborates the representativeness of the samples of participating patients.

Table 10.6. Self-evaluation (spontaneous global evaluation) of therapy outcome by former patients (in percentages of all cases)

	Evaluation				
	Bad (%)	Middle (%)	Good (%)	Very good (%)	Without statements (%)
All patients contacted (n = 453)	4.2	27.2	44.2	22.3	2.2
Participating patients (n = 401)	4.0	25.4	45.1	23.9	1.5

The patient sample (follow-up survey between April 1998 and October 1999)

All 401 (former) patients who agreed to participate were included in the follow-up study. However, within the limits of the available financial and personal resources it would have been impossible to include them in the full research procedure, which includes two follow-up interviews (one 90 minutes, one about 60 minutes), an interview with the analyst mostly by telephone, and a supervision and an evaluation session for the local research team for each case. Thus, it was necessary to draw a subsample of patients (sample size 194), who could be administered the complete research procedure (***interview sample***). The remaining patients (sample size 207) were asked to fill out several questionnaires, one of which contained open questions (***questionnaire sample***). The two subsamples were put together according to the ***random principle:*** the interview sample consists of two stratified random samples, one of which includes only psychoanalyses, and the other only psychotherapies. The two variables that were used for stratification are 'analyst's evaluation of therapy outcome' and 'patient's evaluation of therapy outcome'. For the psychoanalyses this procedure is set out in Tables 10.7 and 10.8. For the psychotherapies it is set out in Tables 10.9 and 10.10.

Table 10.7. Former patients in psychoanalysis (three, four or more hours of treatment) willing to participate in the study (n = 207)

	Spontaneous global evaluation of therapy outcome by the patients					
By the analyst	-	Bad	Middle	Good	Very good	Sum
-	0	0	3	4	1	8
Bad	0	2	5	4	2	13
Middle	1	3	20	31	7	62
Good	1	1	17	53	27	99
Very good	1	1	0	7	16	25
Sum	3	7	45	99	53	207

Table 10.8. Random sample (plus three consciously chosen extreme cases*) from Table 10.7 (n = 123)

	Spontaneous global evaluation of therapy outcome by the patients					
By the analyst	-	Bad	Middle	Good	Very good	Sum
-	0	0	1	2	1	4
Bad	0	1	3	3	2*	9
Middle	0	2	12	19	4	37
Good	0	1	12	34	10	57
Very good	1	1*	0	5	9	16
Sum	1	5	28	63	26	123

Table 10.9. Former patients in psychotherapy (1-2 hours per week) willing to participate in the study. (n = 194)

	Spontaneous global evaluation of therapy outcome by the patients					
By the analyst	-	Bad	Middle	Good	Very good	Sum
-	0	1	6	4	1	12
Bad	0	2	5	5	0	12
Middle	2	4	14	15	5	40
Good	1	1	23	44	25	94
Very good	0	1	9	14	12	36
Sum	3	9	57	82	43	194

Table 10.10. Random sample (plus four consciously chosen extreme cases •) from Table 10.9 (n = 71)

	Spontaneous global evaluation of therapy outcome by the patients					
By the analyst	-	Bad	Middle	Good	Very good	Sum
-	0	0	3	2	0	5
Bad	0	0	3	2	0	5
Middle	2	2	5	5	2•	16
Good	0	1•	9	19	9	38
Very good	0	1•	2	3	1	7
Sum	2	4	22	31	12	71

Certainly the information in the contingency tables, in which the analysts' evaluation of therapy outcome is contrasted with the evaluation by the patients themselves, is also significant in its own right. In order not to dismiss the infrequent but nonetheless interesting extreme cases, where the evaluations of the analyst and the patient are extremely divergent, some of these cases were subsequently added to the two samples. The complement of the interview sample is the questionnaire sample.

As a result of the procedures described there are now four random subsamples of the 401 patients who agreed to take part in the study (the size of each subsample is shown in Table 10.11).

Table 10.11. The four random subsamples of the 401 patients participating in the study

	Psychoanalysis patients	Psychotherapy patients	Sum
Interview sample	123	71	194
Questionnaire sample	84	123	207
Sum	207	194	401

It is these four subsamples that are currently being surveyed, investigated and analysed (the survey of the questionnaire sample has already been completed, and most of the interviews of the interview sample have been conducted). If there are further dropouts, these will be analysed in the way described above so that it can be determined whether the finally remaining valid cases can still be viewed as an unbiased representative sample, or whether it will be necessary to perform a bias correction.

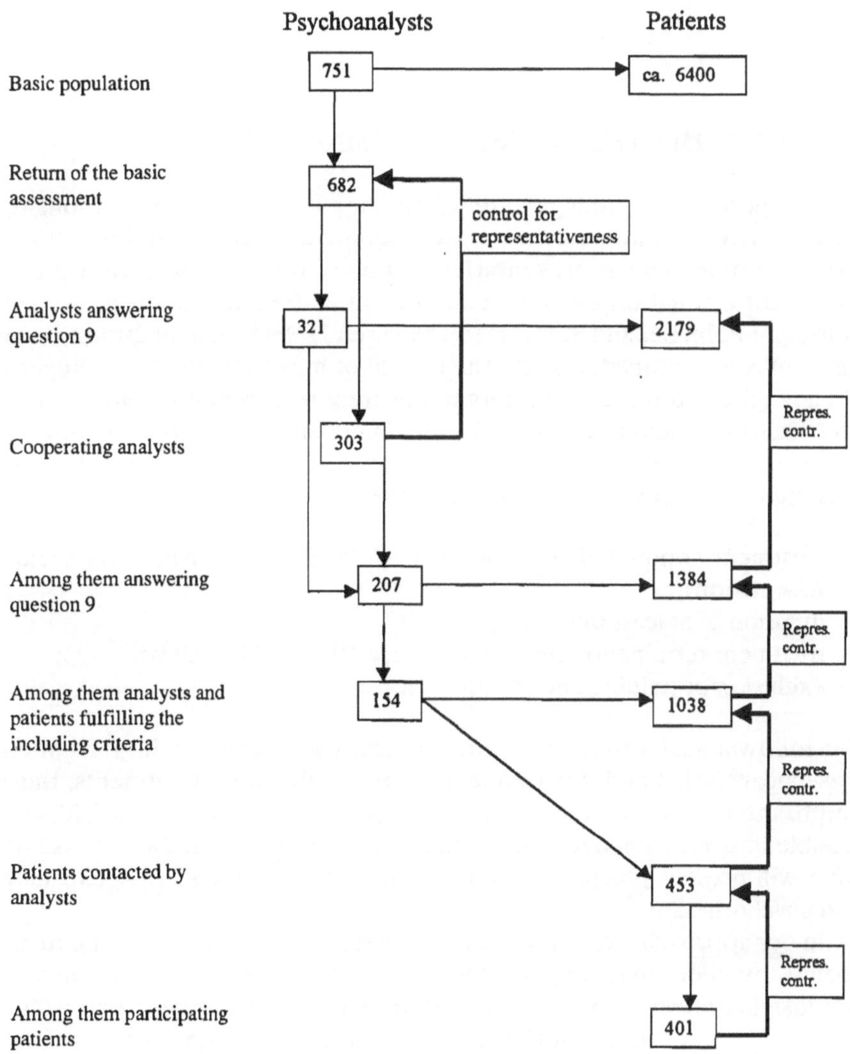

Figure 10.1. Sample design and control for representativeness.

CHAPTER 11
Long-term treatments from the perspectives of the former patients

MANFRED BEUTEL, MARCUS RASTING

The purpose of our study is to determine the long-term results of long-term psychoanalytic treatments. We have attempted to avoid the limitations of former studies (no representative samples, reliance on training cases, treatment evaluation by the treating analyst) (see Bachrach et al., 1991; Leuzinger-Bohleber and Stuhr, 1997) by careful selection of inclusion criteria, data collection procedures and the choice of measures. Professor Rüger has already reported on our attempts to ensure a representative sample. Ulrich Stuhr has presented procedures for relating quantitative and qualitative data. Our *inclusion criteria* were defined with the purpose of including long-term treatments by experienced psychoanalysts:

- treatment conducted by a member of the DPV (German Psychoanalytic Association);
- duration of at least one year;
- treatment termination between January 1990 and December 1993;
- exclusion of training and teaching cases.

We follow usual procedures and differentiate between high-frequency ('psychoanalysis') and low-frequency ('psychotherapy') treatments, but we emphasize that we do not intend to compare their effectiveness. This is not feasible in a retrospective design. Rolf Sandell, Dorothea Huber and Günther Klug will present prospective studies on different effects of psychoanalysis and psychotherapy.

In our approach we include several *perspectives:* the patients, the treating analyst, psychoanalytic experts and independent observers. Thus we follow the insights of recent psychotherapy research, that different perspectives reflect different aspects of the treatment process. A major criterion for the evaluation of psychotherapeutic treatment is the patients' satisfaction. Based on the patient questionnaire we want to pursue the following issues:

- How do former patients evaluate their psychoanalysis or long-term psychotherapy at least five years after termination?
- Do the patients' views differ from the analysts'?
- Is there a reduction of direct or indirect health costs?

Study design and measures

Study participants

As Professor Rüger has shown, we had a total sample of 401 former patients willing to participate in our study (Figure 11.1). We drew a stratified random sample for intensive interviewing (see Marianne Leuzinger-Bohleber). Another project, which we can only mention briefly, refers to the health data that we collect with the patients' consent at from their insurance companies. This allows us to assess direct health costs such as hospital days and work disability days before, during and after treatment.

We contacted the patients whom we could not interview for reasons of limited resources and asked them to fill out questionnaires. We offered all of these patients a personal interview, which few accepted. In this presentation we will restrict ourselves to this questionnaire sample. Forty-four patients did not respond; nine patients had to be excluded later because their treatments did not fulfil the inclusion criteria. We achieved a return rate of 154 patients (75%). From these patients we received 141 questionnaires from the treating analysts (92%).

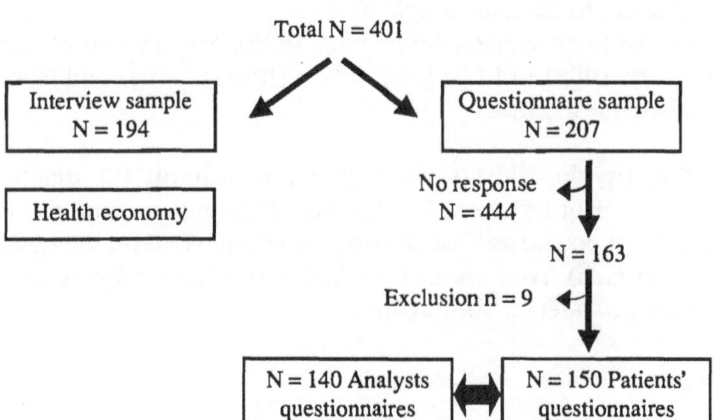

Figure 11.1. Overview of subsamples.

Measures

Table 11.1 gives us an overview of the questionnaire measures.

Table 11.1. Instruments of the questionnaire subsample

• **Former patients**	
- Open-ended questions *(based on interview)*	Goals, course of treatment, relationship with analyst etc.
- Treatment satisfaction	Well-being before/after treatment, treatment satisfaction, post-treatment course, work disability, utilization of medical services
- Questionaires	SCL-90R, SOC, life satisfaction (IRES)
• **Analysts**	
- Diagnosis, severity of disorder	
- Treatment setting (frequency, duration etc.)	
- Treatment course and satisfaction	

All former patients who had agreed to participate received the following questionnaires:

- *Open-ended questions* regarding goals, course of treatment and relationship with analyst (questions were based on the interview questions);
- *Well-being, utilization of medical services* before, during and after treatment and *treatment satisfaction;*
- *SCL-90R* (German version by Franke, 1995), *SOC* (Sense of Coherence; Antonovsky, 1988) and *Life Satisfaction* (IRES) (Gerdes and Jäckel, 1995) as standard questionnaires.

The treating psychoanalysts were questioned about the diagnosis, the severity of the disorders, treatment setting (frequency, duration, modifications), treatment course and satisfaction (wording based on the questions for the former patients). They were also asked to send us the forms submitted to the insurance providers before treatment.

Results

Treatments

Treatments with one, two and three or more sessions per week were about equally represented. The mean duration of treatment was comparable (about four years average). The total number of treatment sessions therefore increased with the weekly frequency. Treatments had been terminated an average of 6.5 years before follow-up, irrespective of treatment setting. It is interesting to note that 20% of the treatments were modified in their course. These were mostly (40%) beginning or termination of treatment in a setting with low frequency, reduction of frequency in order to increase the length of treatment or a change of frequency as a response to a therapeutic crisis. Patients who had a modification of their setting were assessed as more severely disturbed by their analysts at the beginning of treatment (regarding their symptoms and relationships), and they had less favourable treatment results than the other patients according to patients and analysts. The termination of treatment was usually based on mutual agreement according to the patients' views and prepared from a longer perspective.

As the treatment for three and more sessions took place in the recumbent position these were termed 'psychoanalysis group' (N = 74); about the same number of former patients with one and two sessions per week (N = 80) formed the 'psychotherapy group'.

According to our inclusion criteria the treating analysts were clinically experienced. They had an average experience of 13 years and they had completed 47 treatments (without training or supervision cases) since graduation. At the follow-up assessment the average age was 54 years (between 44 and 77 years) with equal numbers of men (N = 35) and women (N = 33).

Study participants

Table 11.2 gives an overview of the study participants. These had an average age of 45 years at the follow-up assessment (34.2 years at the beginning of treatment). As in other psychotherapy studies, about two-thirds were women. Slightly more than half were married at follow-up, one in three was unmarried and one in six was divorced. The majority (approximately 82%) had a college education, while approximately 19% had completed high school or junior high school. The majority of patients were working at least part-time. Psychoanalysis and psychotherapy patients did not differ in terms of their sociodemographic characteristics. Preliminary ratings of diagnosis according to ICD-9 or ICD–10 (based on analysts' reports) showed the necessity of further differentiation (for example, severity of the disorder with the BSS (Beeinträchtigungs-Schwere-Score).

Well-being before and after therapy from the patients' viewpoint

As Figure 11.2 shows, the majority of the patients (75%) reported retrospectively that their general well-being had been severely compromised before treatment; at follow-up, however, the majority (65%) reported good well-being. About two-thirds reported that their well-being had remained stable from termination to follow-up. We found comparable improvements of physical and psychological complaints, relationships, work, and so forth

Table 11.2. Sociodemographic characteristics

	Psychoanalysis (n = 74)	Psychotherapy (n = 80)	Total (n = 154)
age	44.9 (30-69)	44.3 (29-64)	44.6 (29-69)
male	32%	26%	29%
female	68%	74%	71%
married	60%	48%	52%
single	28%	36%	33%
divorced	12%	16%	15%
full-time job	56%	55%	56%
part-time job	30%	30%	30%
home maker	8%	8%	8%
others	6%	7%	6%

based on the views of the former patients and their psychoanalysts. We could not find consistent differences between psychoanalysis and psychotherapy patients regarding the retrospective assessment of their impairment before treatment.

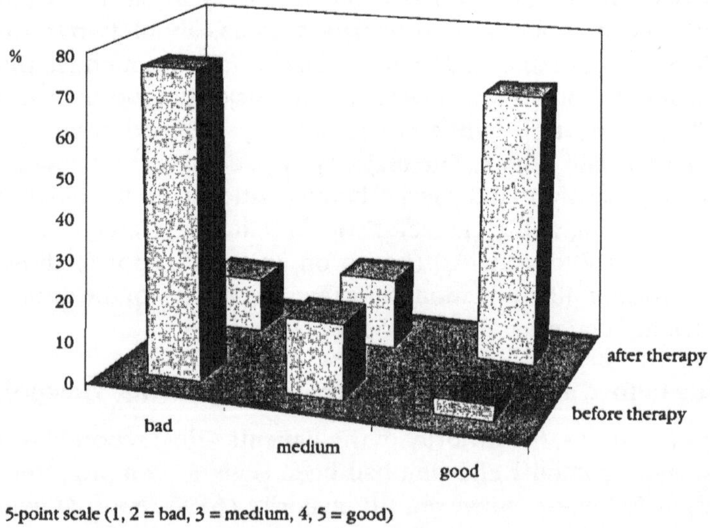

Figure 11.2. Well-being before and after treatment: participants of the follow-up study (N = 154).

Which changes could be achieved in different life areas from the patients' perspectives?

About 80% of the former patients reported positive changes (Figure 11.3) regarding well-being, personal development and relationships with others, 70% to 80% regarding coping with life events, self-esteem, mood, life satisfaction and work ability. The proportion of patients with a stable partnership increased from beginning of treatment to follow-up from 67% to 76% (chi-square $p<0.05$).

Patients added idiosyncratic accounts to their ratings of areas of symptomatic improvement which we wish to illustrate with two examples:

- A former patient had been on sick leave for several months before the beginning of treatment because of chronic back pain. She wrote: 'Through my psychoanalysis I have developed a feeling for me, for my needs and particularly for the limits of my capability for the first time in my life. The word "no" acquired a special meaning in my life, even when it took a long time from thinking "no" to saying "no" . . . My daily life has changed completely. Today there is a shift from tension to relaxation which I did not know before. This process of becoming myself was supplemented by that of becoming a woman. I gained a positive access to my own gender.'

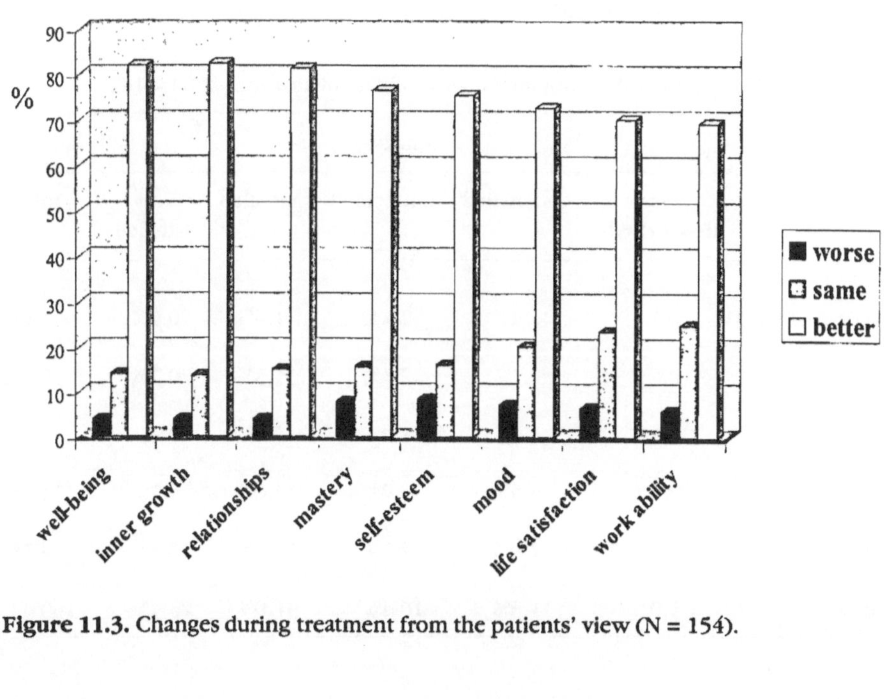

Figure 11.3. Changes during treatment from the patients' view (N = 154).

- Former patients did not only take the presence or absence of symptoms and complaints into account but also their means of coping with symptoms. Thus a former patient who had been able to overcome 'constant obsessive thoughts' and complete her final thesis and studies, wrote 'I still have problems with self-esteem and unreasonable fears. But I do not hate myself for them any longer, and they have not led to such a deep depression again.'

Table 11.3 compares treatment satisfaction of patients and analysts regarding treatment results: 76% of the patients were satisfied with the treatment (only 15% unsatisfied); with a 64% satisfaction rate the analysts were clearly more critical. The overall agreement was good; evaluation differed more than one scale point only in 26% of patients and analysts (on a five-point scale from 'very dissatisfied' to 'very satisfied').

As former psychoanalysis and psychotherapy patients were equally satisfied with their respective treatment, these two groups are not differentiated in the figures. Yet from the former patients' perspectives the treatment setting played a major role in the process and in their satisfaction with the therapy. This is testified by a number of statements such as: 'I definitely needed the long time and the intensity of the frequent sessions in order to be able to touch on my "inner life" and to understand it better'. The high weekly frequency of sessions was experienced as a basis for trust 'which did not allow for avoidance and gave support'. A number of former patients also emphasized the long time they needed in order to build a trustful relationship with the analyst.

Table 11.3. Treatment satisfaction in the view of patient and analyst (N = 141)

Patient	Analyst					
	very dissatisfied	dissatisfied	undecided	satisfied	very satisfied	total
very dissatisfied	0%	1.4%	2.1%	1.4%	0.7%	5.6%
dissatisfied	0%	2.1%	2.1%	4.3%	0.7%	9.2%
undecided	1.5%	1.4%	1.4%	5.0%	0%	9.3%
satisfied	0.7%	3.5%	5.7%	15.6%	5.7%	31.2%
very satisfied	2.8%	2.9%	7.1%	15.6%	16.3%	44.7%
total	5.0%	11.3%	18.4%	41.9%	23.4%	100%

Contact between patients and analysts after termination of treatment

According to professional consensus 'successful' patients are not seen again by their analysts after termination of treatment. Due to the structural change achieved they are supposed to be able to cope with stresses and life events themselves.

As Figure 11.4 shows, 37% turned to their analyst again after termination of treatment; 8% had a telephone consultation, 19% one or two sessions and another 10% went back into psychotherapeutic treatment. These contacts frequently followed serious life events (such as a breast cancer operation, death or serious accident of a close person, separation crisis). The contacts were judged as beneficial by the analysts (with just one exception) in order to deal with the acute conflict, resolve lasting transferences and encourage further development.

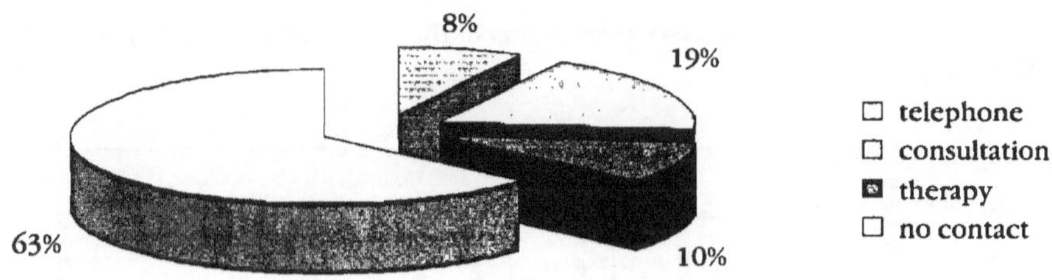

Figure 11.4. Contact with the analyst after termination of treatment (N = 154).

Current distress and life satisfaction of the study participants

Current distress was based on the total score of the SCL-90R (GSI). As Figure 11.5 shows, study participants were slightly above the norm (German community sample of Franke, 1995); however on average they were below the clinical range (90th percentile of the community sample). They were far below unselected psychosomatic ambulatory patients, patients of psychoanalytic practices, psychosomatic outpatients and inpatients taken from the Department of Psychosomatic Medicine of the University of Gießen in 1998.

As Figure 11.6 shows, *life satisfaction* was high at follow-up; 70% to 80% were satisfied with various life areas. Patients were in the range of a sample matched from the community sample of the German general population (N = 1800) according to age, sex and education.

Utilization of health care and absence from work

In the last part of our presentation we wished to turn to another set of outcome criteria. As Figure 11.7 shows, the number of outpatient physician

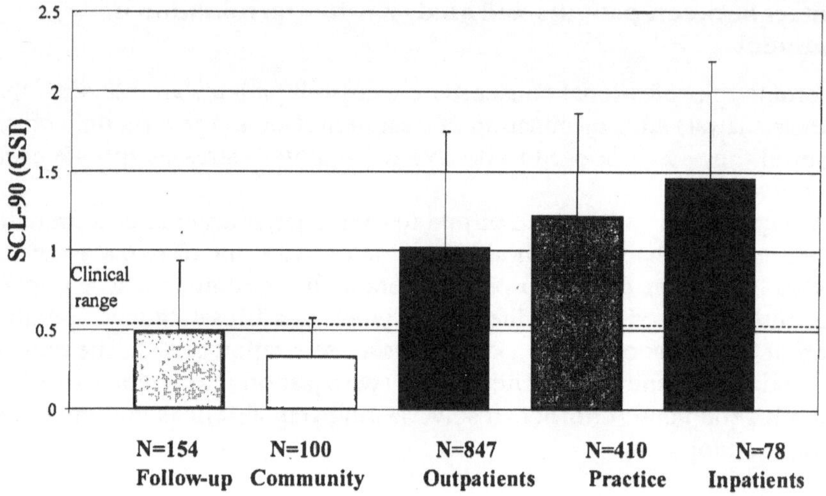

Figure 11.5. Current distress (GSI): participants of the follow-up study (DPV) compared to other samples.

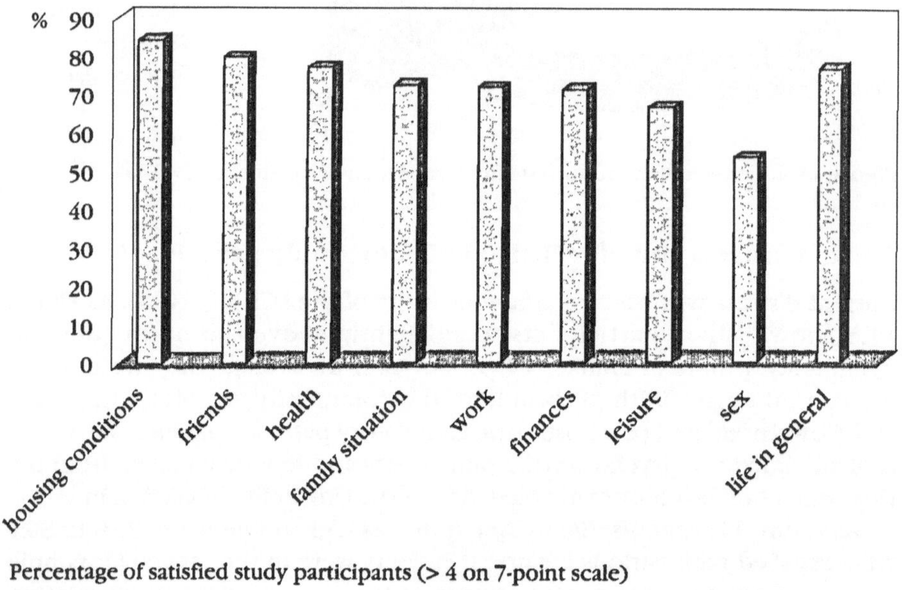

Percentage of satisfied study participants (> 4 on 7-point scale)

Figure 11.6. Life satisfaction (IRES) at follow-up (N = 154).

consultations was already significantly reduced in the first year of treatment compared to the year before treatment. This reduction was maintained to the follow-up.

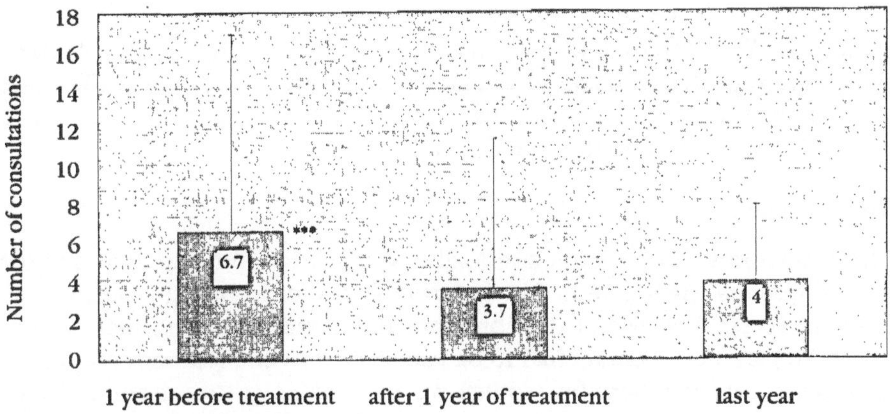

*based on patient data; *** p <0.001

Figure 11.7. Number of outpatient medical consultations per year (N = 111)*.

We found comparable reports concerning the days of sick leave. These were reduced accordingly (Figure 11.8).

At this point the reader might object that patients' reports are of a subjective nature and have been assessed retrospectively over a long time period. With the consent of the patients we therefore contacted the insurance companies and asked them for the data on hospital days and days

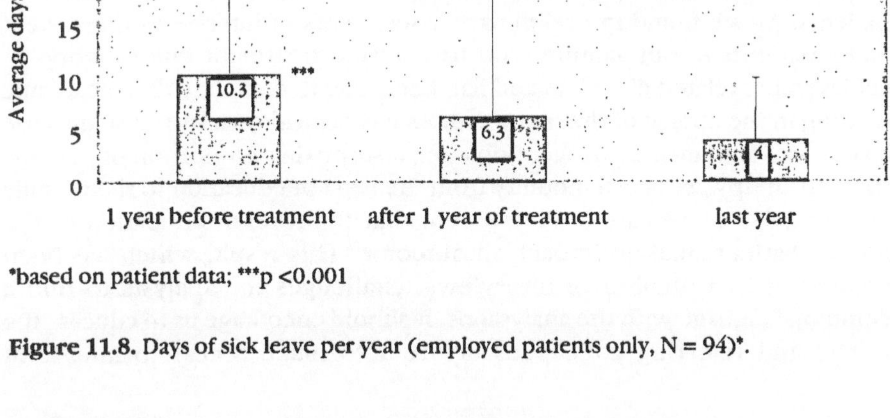

*based on patient data; ***p <0.001

Figure 11.8. Days of sick leave per year (employed patients only, N = 94)*.

of sick leave for the time periods before, during and after termination of treatment. We thereby followed the procedures of Keller and colleagues, which are reported in detail in Chapter 14. In order not to cover the same ground, we want only to remark that our pilot assessments of insurance data showed similar trends to those in the patients' reports.

To summarize

The return rates of patients and analysts exceeded our expectations for several reasons. Treatment had been terminated a long time ago (mean more than six years). Because of the confidentiality issue we did not have direct access to patients - contact had to be established by the treating analysts. In contrast to other follow-up studies we did not have the opportunity to remind patients to fill out the questionnaires. The success of the data collection was only possible because of the unflagging support of the treating analysts, whom we wish to thank on this occasion.

A total of three quarters of the patients were satisfied with their psychoanalysis or long-term psychotherapy. Seventy to eighty per cent reported positive and lasting changes regarding well-being, personal development and relationships with others, coping with life events, self-esteem, mood, life satisfaction and work ability. There was good agreement with the treating analysts, even when the latter tended to evaluate results more critically (self critical). The validity of the positive evaluations of the former patients is underscored by the fact that the total distress at follow up was in the normal range and therefore differed significantly from various samples of psychotherapy and psychoanalysis patients treated in various outpatient and inpatient settings.

In our sample there was a predominance of patients with a higher education. This result is in accordance with the general result that outpatient psychotherapy is more frequently used by patients with higher education (for example, Rudolf et al., 1994; von Rad et al., 1998). The selection of long-term treatments may have further increased the proportion of well-educated patients. As we found in preliminary assessments of interviews there were many patients in our sample who had started treatment due to work- or achievement-related disorders and had been able to complete their academic training in the course of the treatment. As has been shown by the single case analyses of Marianne Leuzinger-Bohleber, a surprising proportion of patients showed an upward social mobility from the level of education to their family of origin (37 of 43 cases). Please note that the level of education of the former patients had no impact on outcome. This result, which has been confirmed in a number of interviews, challenges the analysts to find a common language with the analysands. It should encourage us to educate the public and referring colleagues in order to make access to long-term psychotherapy easier for patients without higher education. The interpretation of this factor also has to take into account that treatment usually started in the 1980s, at a time when the utilization of psychotherapy may have been even more limited by education than it is today. As we know from the basic assessment, the participating analysts do most of their work with lower frequency or duration, so that our results do not reflect the overall range of their psychotherapeutic treatments. In order to assess this we are surveying co-operating analysts according to the education of their current patients.

Interpretations of the retrospective written assessments have to reflect a number of methodological restrictions. We had to limit ourselves to global outcome evaluations and, for example, could not include individual therapy goals. Despite the multitude of data, our interpretation has to contend with ambiguities (for example, diagnosis, severity of disease) that cannot be resolved without detailed analysis of the individual cases. That we could not find differences in satisfaction with treatment between analysis and psychotherapy may mislead parts of the audience into the assumption that more intensive analytic treatment might not be necessary. This conclusion cannot be supported by our data. As the type and duration of treatment are based on the agreement of analysts and patients, the patients' high satisfaction only testified that, apparently in both groups, the choice was 'correct'. Patients gave detailed accounts of the personal meaning of treatment setting, frequency and duration for their treatment outcome. This is underscored by the high agreement with the analysts about the kind and timing of termination. Marianne Leuzinger-Bohleber will show on the basis of interview data that from the views of the external evaluators there are indeed significant differences between psychotherapeutic and analytic treatments, referring to the psychic representations of treatment and related mental processes and so forth. These differentiated processes, of course, cannot be represented with simple ratings of treatment success or current symptoms on scales. The detailed responses of patients to the open-ended questions (on treatment course and results) provide an access to their inner world that goes beyond the rating scales presented and will be analysed by systematic and qualitative procedures in detail. Let us conclude with a former patient's statement.

> I encountered an overwhelming feeling of concern and empathy which did not restrict me in any way or force me into a defensive stance, which at the same time was distant and would not become dominated by me. There was the liberating possibility of reflecting, of probing arguments that were received with concentration, and occasionally questioned in a surprising way. I have very much learned to change perspectives and not to be frozen in the first impression. I would not say that this behaviour is always available to me, however I often succeed in changing my position and thereby gain insight and new options for action.

References

Antonovsky A (1988) Unraveling the Mystery of Health. How people manage stress and stay well. San Francisco: Jossey-Bass.

Bachrach HM, Galatzer-Levy R, Skolnikoff A, Waldron S (1991) On the efficacy of psychoanalysis. Journal of the American Psychoanalytic Association 39: 871–916.

Franke G (1995) SCL-90-R: Die Symptom-Checkliste von Derogatis - Deutsche Version - Manual. Beltz Test, Göttingen.

Gerdes N, Jäckel WH (1995) Der IRES-Fragebogen für Klinik und Forschung. Rehabilitation 34: 13-24.

Leuzinger-Bohleber M (1997) Psychoanalytische Katamneseforschung und die 'Wissenschaft zwischen den Wissenschaften'. In: Leuzinger-Bohleber M, Stuhr U (eds) Psychoanalysen im Rückblick. Gießen: Psychosozial Verlag, pp. 125-63.

Rad M von, Senf W, Bräutigam W (1998) Psychotherapie und Psychoanalyse in der Krankenversorgung: Ergebnisse des Heidelberger Katamnese-Projektes. Psychotherapie Psychosomatik Medinische Psychologie 48: 88–100.

Rudolf G, Manz R, Öri C (1994) Ergebnisse psychoanalytischer Therapien. Zeitschrift für Psychosomatische Medizin 40: 25–40.

Chapter 12

A follow-up study – critical inspiration for our clinical practice?

Marianne Leuzinger-Bohleber

Introduction

The focus of this chapter is on the relevance of the findings from the follow-up study for clinical practice. I want to concentrate on summarizing how we collected and analysed data from two psychoanalytical follow-up interviews. I shall illustrate our procedure by one shortened example of such a follow-up. Afterwards I shall summarize how we tried to analyse these psychoanalytic, qualitative data, comparing them with results collected by our quantitative instruments, and I shall present some selected results.

I hope to convey a first impression of our attempt to deal with the fundamental tension between empirical researchers in psychoanalysis mentioned in our introduction above. This tension derives from, on the one hand, demonstrating convincingly and with confidence, that psychoanalysis, as a unique form of knowledge, has developed its own idiosyncratic clinical research strategies, a characteristic combination of therapy and research within the psychoanalytic situation (the so called *Junktim-Forschung*), and, on the other hand, from trying to open up clinical findings to empirical and interdisciplinary research. As described above, we have combined *psychoanalytic* and *non-psychoanalytic* research methods as well as *qualitative* and *quantitative* instruments addressing this issue in our project.

It was our intention to conduct a *psychoanalytic* and 'naturalistic' research project ('real patients', qualified, trained and experienced therapists, realistic indications for certain treatments, and so forth) and a critical reflection on the research problems that convinced our psychoanalytical colleagues within the German Psychoanalytical Association (DPV) to support our project (see Chapter 10). We would never have dared to expect that over 300[1] of our DPV colleagues would be willing to have their former patients in psychoanalyses and psychoanalytic long-term therapies participating in our study. Even more surprising for us was that so many of our colleagues were willing to engage intensively in our project as follow-up interviewers or as members of the local research groups all over Germany - two in Frankfurt, Hamburg, Gießen, Tübingen, Freiburg, Munich, Cologne and Kassel. In order to guarantee confidentiality interviewers of one city (let us say Frankfurt) travelled to different cities (for example, to Hamburg) thus ensuring the anonymity of the therapist. This was extremely time consuming.

For our colleagues the main reason for devoting so much time to these interviews was probably that the follow-up interviews proved to be very interesting and clinically relevant. Most of our colleagues told us how much they had felt inspired by listening to the former patients in the follow-up interviews. Therefore we think that the close relationship between research and clinical practice is the key factor of our study, as Figure 12.1 tries to illustrate.

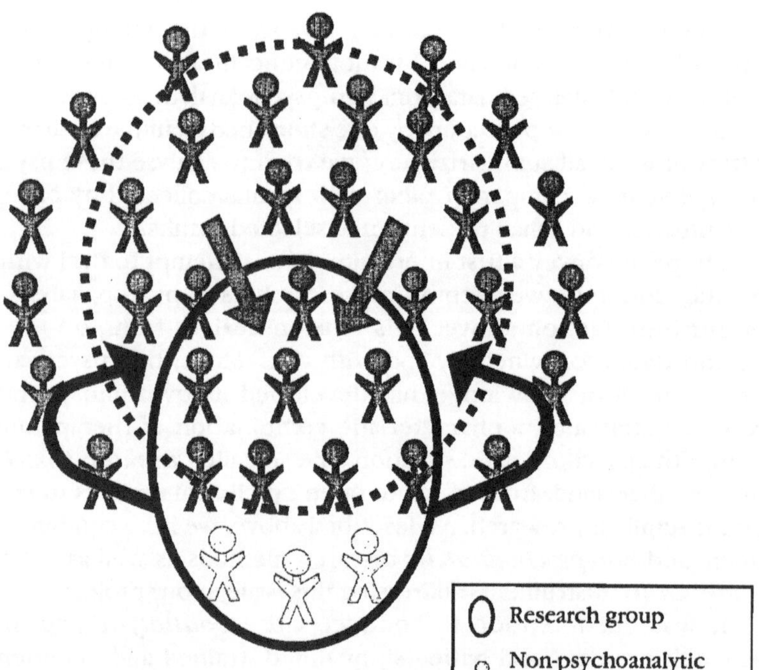

Figure 12.1. Close relationship between research and clinical practice in our follow-up study.

Our project was designed democratically, after long, intensive and often very controversial discussions within our project group and among the members of our psychoanalytical society (DPV). We reported on the progress of the study at every congress of the DPV. Gradually, other forms of transmitting the findings of our study to clinicians have developed spontaneously. In Frankfurt, Tübingen, Gießen and Cologne for example, members of the local research groups have offered to present the follow-up study in detail at their institutes and to discuss several follow-ups intensively with the candidates during a regular training course. We think, therefore, that an intensive transfer from our study back to clinical practice and to psychoanalytical training has taken place. Of course we - nevertheless - did not limit ourselves to discussing the results of the study within the psychoanalytical community. Our presentations at different congresses of psychotherapy researchers (for example, of the Society of Psychotherapy Research in Braha, Portugal, 1999 and Chicago, 2000) aimed at discussing the results of our study within the broader scientific and public community.

Psychoanalytic follow-up interviews: procedure and clinical illustration

As already mentioned data were collected mainly through the use of *two psychoanalytical follow-up interviews*.[2]

Our observations confirm the common findings of preliminary studies (for instance, by Pfeffer, 1959, 1961, 1963; Schlessinger and Robbins, 1983; Norman et al., 1976; Oremland et al., 1975), according to which the major transference constellations of the psychoanalytic treatment replicated themselves very quickly in the follow-up interviews and allowed us - as a sort of 'mini-analysis' - to look at some of the major (conscious and unconscious) outcomes of the former psychoanalytic treatments. As the interviewers and the researchers (who evaluate the data) in our study are experienced psychoanalysts, we wanted to use follow-up interviews as our major methodological approach, a decision which has proved to be wise. Incidentally, we can also show theoretically that using interviews is an excellent method for studying complex psychic and psychosocial phenomena, taking into account the current discussion on the narrative revolution in psychoanalysis, the social sciences and the neurosciences (see, for example, Koukkou, Leuzinger-Bohleber and Mertens, 1998).

We have gained rich and interesting information and insights concerning relevant aspects of psychoanalytic treatment. The 129 'single case studies' offer a good opportunity to recognize the highly individual and idiosyncratic experiences of a therapeutic process and its outcome, and therefore to offer insights into clinically relevant issues. Within the framework of this chapter we can only offer a illustration of our procedure, using an abridged clinical example.

In the first follow-up interview (about 90 minutes) we encourage the former patients by a more or less unstructured interview to tell us (consciously and unconsciously) their views of their experiences in their psychoanalytic treatment (about 60 minutes). We try to obtain manifest as well as latent (unconscious) information about the interaction between the former patient and the follow-up interviewer. In the last part of the interview (about 30 minutes) some follow-up topics are addressed (for example, asking for the reasons and motives for treatment, the patient's subjective evaluation of the therapy, motivation for participating in our study and so forth). The interviews are tape-recorded.

> Mrs X, a social worker, mother of two grown up daughters, married to an unemployed banker, is content with her psychoanalysis (four sessions a week, 720 sessions altogether). In a personal, clear language, filled with very individual metaphors, she summarizes her psychoanalytical experiences, her self-finding, and self-healing processes as well as her life history, a biography dominated by suffering. 'I changed a lot during psychoanalysis. Therapy has given a totally new direction to my life. I didn't really feel alive before treatment but perceived everything as though I was looking through a windowpane . . . During analysis I discovered my feelings and now I feel in the midst of life and enjoy every day even during these weeks of my husband's unemployment which have been quite a heavy strain for us.' She had suffered from severe depressions with a serious suicidal impulse to crash her car against a tree for some years and – in her words – 'compulsive masturbation'. One crucial event prompting her decision to look for therapeutic help was this: her nine-year-old daughter came in a fury to her bedroom where she lay in bed – depressed – as was usual at that time. She showed her a report in the local newspaper about a mother who had killed herself jumping from a high bridge. She said: 'If you ever do something similar, then I will beat your dead body as much as I can and will hate you forever.' Mrs X, shocked by her daughter's fantasy, decided to look for help in a psychiatric clinic. Nevertheless she refused the advice of the doctors to be hospitalized and treated with drugs. Without any help from experts she then looked for an outpatient psychotherapeutic treatment and tried out several different therapies. She reports how she watched a TV report on different psychotherapies, concluding that psychoanalysis would be the best form of treatment for her. She then looked for an analyst and started her psychoanalysis.
>
> She reports in detail on different sequences of her psychoanalysis that helped her to discover her feelings and her creativity and to understand the 'language of my unconscious'. She started to write a 'dream-book' and poems – one way for her and her analyst to approach her severe infantile traumas. She now understands that the years of severe depression had been unconsciously determined partially by archaic identification with her depressed mother who was overstrained by

giving birth to three children within three years. Her mother also had a very burdened biography being one of the twelve children of a poor working class family. Being chronically depressed, her mother was not able to care 'well enough' for her youngest daughter. Another severe trauma was sexual abuse by a colleague of her father's whom he knew from his SS group during World War II. After she had understood in psychoanalysis how, for example, her symptom of compulsive masturbation was unconsciously connected with these infantile traumas, 'the symptom just disappeared'.

With tears in her eyes she then speaks extensively about the death of her beloved father a few months ago. He, a warm-hearted man, had always been her confidant within the family. Once in his life he also had suffered from severe depression. This was shortly after the end of World War II. He, a deserter from the SS, could not endure psychically that he had been involved in killing civilians before his desertion. During the last weeks before his death he once more told his daughter some details of these horrifying experiences.

It was one of the insights gained in psychoanalysis that her good relationship with her father is one reason for her good marital relationship with her husband 'in spite of all the ups and downs we have already gone through'. Her husband had first rejected her plan for psychoanalysis, but after he had seen how fruitful therapeutic work turned out to be for Mrs X, overcoming her depression and finding a new and more cheerful relationship with her daughters and with him, he actively supported her psychoanalysis. He even drove her to her sessions when, during periods of heavy resistance, she did not want to go.

Due to psychoanalysis she ventured to qualify further professionally (she had been a medical secretary) and became a social worker for elderly people, an achievement that fills her with pride. She also likes her job in an old people's home very much. She seems proud and happy that she is now able to support her family financially although, nevertheless, her husband's unemployment has been a great burden for the whole family. 'During the 33 years of depression before treatment I would have never been able to cope with all this. I am very grateful for my inner stability now.'

'But I have to add that in spite of all these positive outcomes of psychoanalysis the treatment was sometimes very hard for me.' After a short pause in the interview Mrs X says: 'on some occasions my analyst also hurt me, although, looking back at the whole psychoanalysis - she generally did a good job.' It is important for Mrs X to communicate an experience to us, making it more public: she feels that analysts should offer their patients an opportunity for crisis interventions during long-lasting holidays. For her, the first summer holidays during psychoanalysis had been a catastrophe. In this context she mentions that she still has one 'remaining symptom': she panics when she has to go to the dark basement, a symptom that arose during the period when her father was diagnosed with cancer.

After the first interview the follow-up analyst tape-records his impressions and information gained from the interview (identifying important subjects, psychodynamics, and also hypotheses concerning his own countertransference reactions and so forth). He also rates some questions concerning his first overall evaluation of the possible outcome of the treatment and the Scales of Psychological Capacities (Wallerstein et al., 1996) in order to find out which important subjects remain to be addressed in the second interview.

> As already mentioned above, the transference is mostly very intensive during the follow up interviews.[3] I cannot go into detail here, but only want to mention that the possibility of 'abuse' had already been present during our telephone calls before the follow-up interviews. I had the fantasy of 'abusing' the patient by asking her to meet in a town where I could have used a room in the psychoanalytical practice of a colleague for the interviews. Mrs X rejected this proposal very definitely. Therefore I had to organize a room for the interview in a psychiatric clinic next to the place where Mrs X lives ('abusing' the slight acquaintance of a psychoanalytical colleague who knew one of the psychiatrists in this clinic . . .). The first direct contact with Mrs X was also striking: she dominated the interaction from the beginning, took my small case and carried it upstairs, asked the nurse for our interview room, installed the tape recorder, and so forth. After these initial interactions she was able to get involved in a dense and close dialogue, showing intensive emotions (crying, smiling, joking). Due to my counter-transference feelings, sometimes the inner borders between us seemed to blur a bit; at times it seemed to me that Mrs X could read my thoughts, for example when I was asking myself during a certain sequence of the interview whether Mrs X had experienced some kind of sexual abuse, Mrs X started to talk about this subject in the very next moment. These observations were quite irritating. I was glad to have the opportunity of supervision with one of my colleagues in the local research group.

The interviewer then meets one member of the *research group* for *supervision* and summarizes the interview in narrative form. In the subsequent dialogue the two exchange their impressions, evaluations, psychodynamic hypotheses, open questions, and so forth, in order to help the interviewer to test some of these hypotheses clinically in the second interview and obtain more information to deepen or correct the preliminary hypotheses.

> We talked - among other things - about the striking vitality and capacity for self-reflection of Mrs X in spite of her severe experiences of childhood trauma. After she had taken the initiative in the interaction with the interviewer, and was probably able to 'prove to herself' unconsciously that she didn't have to fear another traumatic experience (and was able to dominate in spite of being dominated internally by a depressed, helpless object), she was able to enter an intensive dialogue with the interviewer. She could even talk about her sexual abuse or having lost her father recently, communicating her feelings and thoughts in an effective and open way. Did she have some experiences with 'good-enough' objects in her early childhood (perhaps with a grandmother?) in spite of all the traumatizing events. What does the phobia concerning the 'dark basement' unconsciously mean? What kind of relationship did she have with her siblings?

The *second interview* is again unstructured in the beginning so that the possible effect of the first interview on the former patient can be observed and considered. The interviewer then poses a set of questions regarding the patient's view of the former therapy, the therapist-patient relationship, the symptoms, the personal significance of the treatment for the patient, the life events before, during and after therapy, and the overall evaluation (part of the semi-structured interview).

Summarizing the second interview with Mrs X: I had to cancel the date for the second interview on her answering machine. When I finally succeeded in talking to her personally on the phone, Mrs X expressed her anger very directly; she had given up a weekend with her husband because of the interview - and then it was cancelled by me! Nevertheless she is willing to see me for a second interview. (For me it is remarkable that Mrs X, a formerly depressed woman, is able to communicate her anger to me so directly and effectively!)

During the interview she tells me how much our first interview had been in her mind afterwards, for example, my question as to whether she still sometimes feels she is having 'an inner dialogue with her analyst'. She thought this to be true; in certain conflictual situations she suddenly remembers analogous sequences from her psychoanalysis. These memories then often prove to be helpful to her.

Later in the interview I ask her about her relationship with her grandparents. She indeed had quite a good relationship with her grandmother (the mother of her father), but what seems more important to her concerning her vitality and 'her capacity to fight for her basic needs' is the fact that she always felt herself to be her father's favourite daughter. He was very proud of her and helped her, as when his 'SS-friend' tried to abuse her again when she was 14 years old. 'Unfortunately he was working when that happened the first time - and I didn't dare to talk to anyone about these experiences because I felt very ashamed . . . but the second time I was screaming - and my father came immediately and stopped him. This man was finally caught and put into jail soon afterwards because he had abused other girls, too.' I ask whether her feeling 'as though she lived behind a window-pane' was one psychic reaction to her being sexually abused. After a short pause she denies this; the basic feeling must have been there before. She then talks about other traumatic experiences, for example a very painful and frightening rheumatic illness when she was five years old. The doctors first thought that she might have polio because she was unable to walk. But then her tonsils were removed and after one week she was able to walk again.

In reply to my question concerning her relationship with her siblings she tells me that her brother (14 months older than her) was very jealous. He had almost killed her when she was a baby, hitting her with a burning hot bar while her mother was in the basement. Nowadays she has a fairly good relationship with both her brothers but - compared to their lives and problems - she feels that she was very privileged to be able to undergo psychoanalysis. In this context she mentions her phobia of 'the dark basement' again. She thinks that her phobia might have to do with unconscious memories of her being sexually abused in a dark basement. 'And my irrational resentment that my beloved father was not able to protect me at that time. This resentment must have become alive within me once more - troubling me - because my father had become so ill at that time.' She says that she is still looking for other unconscious motives within herself, 'but perhaps you are not able to understand everything in your soul . . . and I can ask my husband to accompany me when I have to go to the basement - that is not such a big thing, after all . . .'

During a long sequence of the interview Mrs X deals with the question of guilt feelings towards her daughters because she had neglected them so much during the years of her depression. Both children have vivid memories of the period of analysis, and of the positive effect the treatment had on the atmosphere at home. 'They both understand a lot about psychoanalysis but have chosen quite different professions; one is an artist and the other one will be an engineer.' Obviously Mrs X is very proud of her daughters. 'Psychoanalysis also helped me to deal with my guilt feeling and to see also the positive aspects of giving us all a second chance.'

At the end of the interview Mrs X shows a great interest in our follow-up study. She thanks me for having the chance 'to look back to psychoanalysis once more with you in such great detail' and gives me two poems she wrote about her changes during psychoanalysis.

Another member of the research group interviews the former analyst of the patient (semi-structured interview), without knowing anything about the patient.

Afterwards the *local research group meets.*

The interviewer reports his experiences in narrative form, with observations and hypotheses gained in the two interviews. Then the group listens to *five minutes of the tape-recorded interview.* After that, the (six to eight) *members of the research group rate some questions concerning the overall evaluation of treatment outcome* before starting discussion. Finally they *exchange their ideas* concerning, for example, diagnosis, indication, and results of the treatments. The interviewers of the former patient and her analyst are silent - only the other group members associate and discuss (30 minutes).

The *group member who interviewed the analyst summarizes his findings*:

The report of Mrs X's analyst was in accord with most of the details and most of the important events related by this patient in her interviews (for example, the traumatic first summer holidays, feeling hurt during a sequence of negative transference, the relevance of writing poems etc.). In addition, the analyst mentioned the patient's fantasies of being beaten and having very terrifying sensations 'as if electricity was flowing through her whole body'. The analyst summarized her impression of the biography of the patient: 'She must have been a forgotten, lonely and neglected child. On her initial entry to her school her teachers discovered that her parents had forgotten to register her birth officially. Therefore officially Mrs X did not exist at all until then.' The mother of the patient must have been severely traumatized herself because she had had to look after her terribly handicapped

> sister for years. She had two abortions 'lying on the table in the kitchen'. Some of Mrs X's dreams suggested that she had observed these abortions when she was a little girl. The analyst, too, is quite satisfied with the outcome of the analysis but seems to be absorbed by the question of whether Mrs X will ever be able to manage certain life events connected to a loss of an object without coming back to her for a few sessions. She had come to see her again when she got the news that her father would die soon.

By this procedure we try to use a kind of a '*natural, narrative control*', because we have two completely independent 'stories' of the same therapy; one told by the patient and one told by the analyst. One of the striking clinical observations is that in successful treatments (as the one just mentioned) both partners, patient and analyst, seem to remember and tell 'the same story' (they report independently the same key events of the treatment and share their view of the overall results of the treatment). When the treatment was not so successful (especially with severely disturbed patients), we found many more divergences between the narrative of the patient and that of the analyst.

All the group members discuss the case again and finally try to find a common clinical view of the follow-up (about 15 minutes):

> Because of confidentiality I cannot cover the discussion of the local research group in this paper. The group dealt with the above-mentioned question of the analyst concerning the definitive separation of severely traumatized patients from their analysts. Briefly, according to the members of the group, the outcome of this psychoanalytic work with this not very highly educated and severely traumatized patient was 'good'. The group members shared the impression, that patient and analyst had been a 'well matched psychoanalytic couple'.

Finally *the group members independently rate their 'global evaluations' again and the Scales of Psychological Capacities*. Afterwards the group tries to find a 'consensus' concerning the Scales (according to the method developed by Leuzinger-Bohleber, 1989).

After the session *one member of the group summarizes the discussion* and hands his summary back to the members of the group to be corrected.

The sessions of the research group were tape-recorded. Thus the process of clinical judgement can also be analysed by different methods. Of course, the follow-up interviews have also been tape-recorded. This allows us on the one hand to monitor our clinical summaries of the follow-ups (see above) and important aspects of applying psychoanalytical methods in an empirical study; on the other hand, it enables us to analyse the transcripts of the interviews by different non-psychoanalytical research methods, such as content and linguistic analyses.

Analysing the follow-up interviews: combining psychoanalytical and non-psychoanalytical, qualitative and quantitative methods

We see this representative sample of all patients who terminated their treatment between 1990 and 1993 as a chance to combine psychoanalytical with non-psychoanalytical, clinical with extra-clinical and qualitative with quantitative approaches. We are applying a variety of such combinations.

Narrative psychoanalytic single case studies, each related to the representative sample

Many qualitative psychotherapy researchers and psychoanalysts point out that some complex clinical findings, especially the discovery of unconscious psychodynamics and phantasies, can best be communicated by narratives - one reason why psychoanalysis has developed the tradition of communicating by case studies (see, for example, Leuzinger-Bohleber, 1995). Using the case study approach is a very ambitious and difficult task (hardly anyone is as gifted a writer as Freud). In regard to the scientific quality referred to above, it is important that these case presentations can be related to the whole sample and that the selection and condensing of the information in the narratives can be monitored by listening to the tape-recorded interviews and is discussed carefully in the local research groups. In the Frankfurt research groups we have been working for several months on writing and discussing such preliminary versions of narratives. We have also been looking for a solution to the difficult problem of dealing with the confidentiality of our data. Unfortunately, we cannot present an example of such a case narrative within the frame of this chapter - they are often impressive, idiosyncratic stories of life and therapy offering, at the same time, a highly focused insight into the opportunities and dangers of psychoanalytic treatment, even communicating - as usually only art and literature do - unconscious observations of the follow-up interviewer, the author of the narrative.

Narrative case presentation as illustration for findings in the questionnaires

This combination of qualitative and quantitative data is common practice in psychotherapy research. Usually statistical analyses of the quantitative data are taken as the first step, adding some case presentations in a second step as illustrations of statistical findings (such as the illustration of prototypes found in a cluster analysis) (see Chapter 11).

Systematic evaluation of qualitative findings by the 'bottom-up procedure of clinical clustering' (*Klinische Typenbildung*)

Applying this method, we tried to take into account the basic 'philosophy of our study' in relating our psychoanalytic (qualitative) findings to the non-psychoanalytic (quantitative) ones. We favoured a strategy opposite to the one just mentioned, where qualitative single case studies 'only' serve as illustrations of the quantitative data. We tried to turn the whole perspective the other way around, defining our psychoanalytical, qualitative findings as our basis, the 'bottom', then trying to evaluate systematically this psychoanalytical discovery step by step, from 'bottom' to the 'top' of the quantitative data of our representative sample. We have described this procedure elsewhere (Leuzinger-Bohleber, Beutel, Stuhr and Rüger, 2000). Selected results based on it are presented below.

Applying the qualitative assessment of *Verstehende Typenbildung* (Stuhr) studying the image of the analyst using a representative subsample of transcribed follow-up interviews

Ulrich Stuhr has developed this specific, elaborated qualitative method in recent years (see, for example, Stuhr, 1995 and Chapter 9 of this volume). He has also applied this method to verbatim protocols of follow-up interviews in our study and compared its findings with those gained by a quantitative cluster analysis.

Narrative case presentation combined with 'objective data' (costs for the insurance companies) and quantitative data from the questionnaires

Inability to work and hospitalization data, collected from the health insurance companies, become more meaningful when combined with single case reports (see Chapter 11).

Comparing psychoanalytic qualitative hypotheses to structural change in narrative psychoanalytic single case studies with quantitative findings gained by the Scales of Psychological Capacities (Wallerstein et al., 1996)

In our presentation at meetings before the opening of the IPA congress in Santiago de Chile (July,1999) on research and at the Congress of the Society of Psychotherapy Research in Chicago (June 2000) we set out how we try to combine our clinical psychoanalytical findings on the structural change of the former patients with the ratings on structural change measured by the Scales of Psychological Capacities (Wallerstein et al., 1996)

Combining narrative single case studies with quantitative, theory guided computerized content analyses (Leuzinger-Bohleber, 1989) using a representative subsample of transcribed follow-up interviews

We also use the same transcribed subsample of the follow-up interviews for systematic analysis by a modified form of a theory-guided, computerized content analysis developed some years ago (Leuzinger-Bohleber, 1989). This analysis aims at comparing the extra-clinical, non-psychoanalytical analysis of the follow-ups with our psychoanalytic expert evaluation.

Selected results

A variety of possible outcomes of psychoanalyses and psychoanalytic long-term therapies: prototypes of follow-ups

Applying the above mentioned bottom-up procedure, systematically evaluating the follow-up interviews, we discovered the following three dimensions* that describe central aspects of the patient's change during psychoanalytic long-term psychotherapy:

- self-reflection: limited or high self-reflection
- object-relations: limited or high capacity to live in satisfying relationships
- creativity and working ability: limited or high creativity and work ability

We found all the eight prototypes that can be defined logically by combining these three dimensions systematically in our follow-ups. We can only summarize these different prototypes, briefly illustrating that - by this step of generalization - our understanding of different follow-ups and different kinds of therapeutic outcome has been enlarged. In the following graphs (Figures 12.1–12.9) these prototypes are shown, as well as their 'therapeutic development' ('starting' and 'end-point' of therapy) (based on ratings).

Type I: 'sound and positive' - the successful follow-up

Description: creativity and the ability to work are no longer disturbed by symptoms and conflicts: good self-reflection and capacity to experience satisfying object-relations.

*Note: We cannot describe the procedure used to discover these three dimensions in detail here. It is a similar procedure to the one used in 'normal' clinical psychoanalytical research, comparing similar single cases and discovering their similarities and differences ('aggregated single cases', see Leuzinger-Bohleber, 1995).

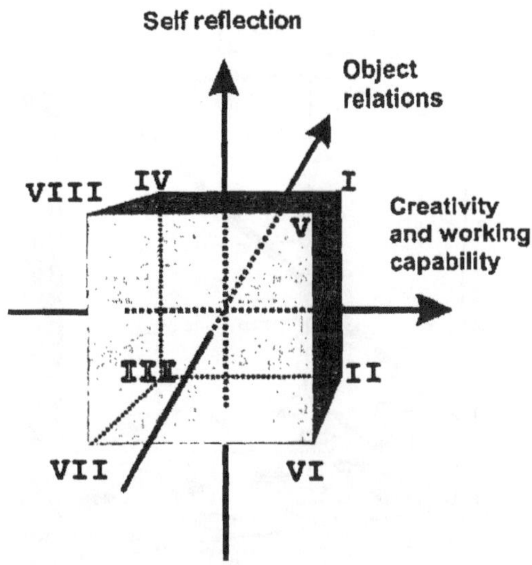

Figure 12.2. First generalization: eight prototypes of follow-ups.

Clinical prototype I: 'the artist'

> Mrs A had gone through severe early traumatic experiences, being a replacement child for a girl with the same name. She was given away shortly after birth for the whole first year of life. The symptoms and problems that prompted her to seek treatment (total breakdown after a reactivation of the early traumas, symptoms of depersonalization, promiscuity, severe depressions, inability to work and so on) have disappeared; one reason why she now is able to live 'in a deep, satisfying and stable relation with a man' (Mrs A). Important to her was that she had found a creative way to deal with her separation anxieties, which also liberated her professional creativity as an actress.

Using these ratings we can take into account an important issue in follow-ups: not all the patients with good outcomes start at the same point when they begin their treatment.[4]

Type II: 'successful, but why?' - the unreflective success

Description: creative and able to work, no longer bothered by symptoms, living in satisfying relationships, very content with treatment outcome but cannot tell what the helpful insights in psychotherapy had been.

Clinical prototype II: 'Dr X has saved my life . . . I have had no symptoms for ten years'

> Mrs B, daughter of a poor farmer, had a total psychotic breakdown during late adolescence with several psychiatric hospitalizations (presenting with hallucinations,

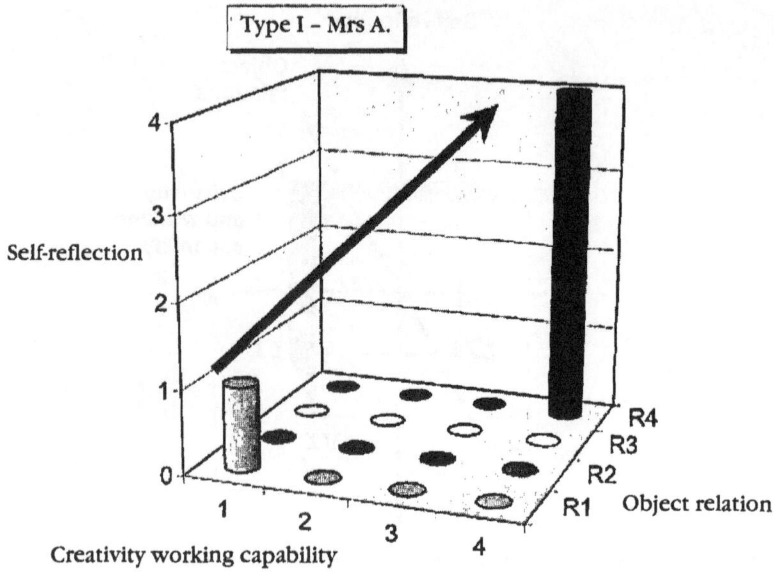

Figure 12.3. Type I - Mrs A.

de-personalizations, severe obsessional symptoms, suicidal impulses, and so forth). She is grateful that psychoanalytic treatment has helped her to overcome this crisis and 'saved her life'. She is proud that she is able to live without any medication, lovingly supporting her husband and working at home as a seamstress. The most important achievement for her is that she is a good mother for her two children, in contrast to her own mother, an alcoholic, who had left her and her five siblings suddenly when Mrs B was four years old (since when she has never seen her). She is very grateful to her analyst but she cannot tell 'what exactly Dr X has done with me . . . it was just good and whenever I have some kind of crisis and feel a bit uncertain I am still talking with Dr X without anybody knowing this - it's just inside me . . .' The expert group discussed this follow-up intensively, and the question of why Mrs B had gained such an amazing stability without being separated in her inner world from the analyst.

Type III: 'successful with respect to creativity and working ability but within clear limits', 'successful without much in the way of self-reflection or satisfying object relations'

Description: hardly any symptoms or complaints that would impair creativity and achievements, but little self-reflection and unable to live in satisfying human relations.

Clinical prototype III: 'the manager'

Mr C had started therapy during a severe crisis in his job (massive conflicts with the head of his department, unable to work any more, suicidal and so forth). All

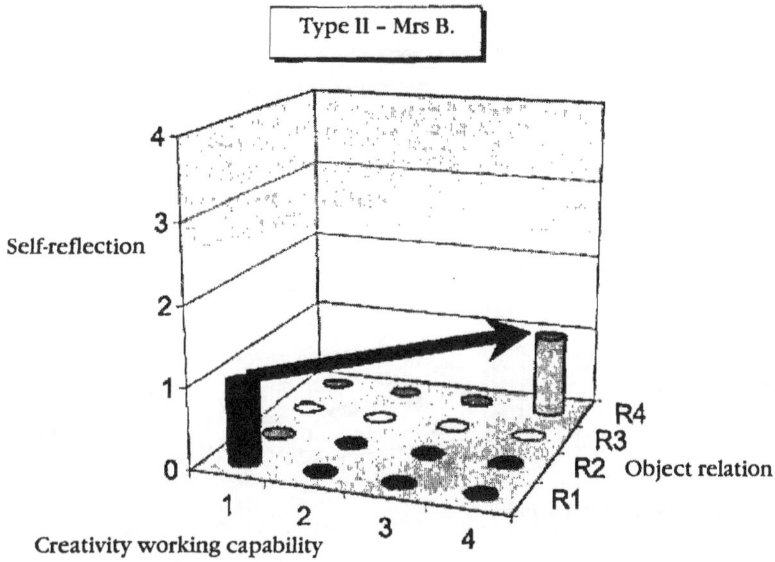

Figure 12.4. Type II - Mrs B.

these symptoms have disappeared. Mr C is able to work creatively in his job again. On the other hand the interviewer notices that Mr C cannot tell why and how these changes took place during therapy. He hardly seems to have any critical self-reflection. For example he irritates the interviewer by telling her that he was happy when his father committed suicide during his adolescence. Another important observation was that Mr C was not able to develop any kind of emotional relationship with the interviewer. His external relationships also seem to be quite unusual for he is married but has a lot of promiscuous love relations.

Type IV: 'creative and able to work, but still alone. Reflective and successful without satisfying love relations'

Description: this type of patient is creative and able to work but still suffers from being alone in his private life. He reflects on why close object relations are too difficult for him (for example, because of extreme infantile traumas).

Clinical prototype IV: 'but nobody tells you that you have to marry'

Mr D, a writer, reports in the interview that his psychoanalysis helped him to overcome his serious working inhibitions and that he is now a successful writer. He is very proud and satisfied with his professional situation. He describes in detail the analytic process and his insights - also concerning some of his serious traumatic experiences (chronically absent mother). He still suffers from his 'Lolita

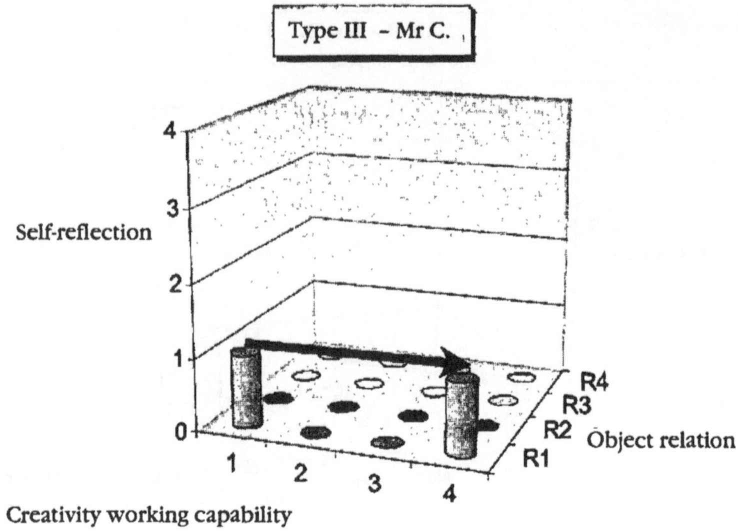

Figure 12.5. Type III - Mr C.

> Syndrome' (as he calls it), as it has not been modified, although he understands some of the unconscious determinants of the specific sexual attraction that very young girls have for him. This problem does not allow him to live in love relationships over a longer period of time - a source of personal suffering on the one side; a source of his creativity on the other (from his point of view).

Type V: 'the tragic ones - accepting their fates'

Description: creativity and ability to work are still very limited because of severe symptoms and complaints or renewed tragic life events. Nevertheless the self-reflection gained helped these former patients to accept their fate and to live within satisfying relationships.

Clinical prototype V: 'I am still suffering from the same symptoms which brought me into therapy - but nevertheless it helped me to live my life . . .'

> Mrs E suffers from an organically deformed arm and hand, and had the illusory hope of losing these symptoms as well as her severe nightmares and sleeping disturbances. Only the sleep disturbances disappeared during therapy. Nevertheless, as Mrs E told the interviewer, her whole life had changed. She had learnt to live with her symptoms and to accept that 'they are my personal marks of the war and of what I had gone through as a little child'. (She had been severely traumatized by bombings, flight, getting lost, and so on) . . . 'This makes such a big difference - I have found my inner peace and so has my family.'

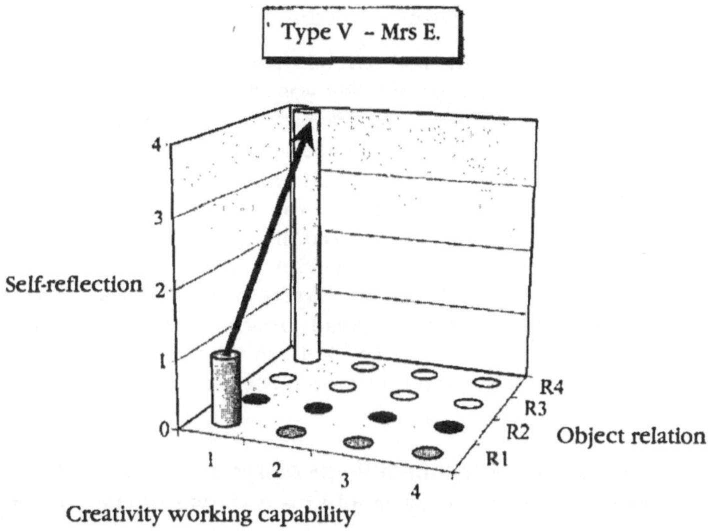

Figure 12.6. Type V - Mrs E.

Type VI: 'without success, but socially well integrated. Unreflective people with the capacity to establish relationships, but with limited creativity and ability to work.'

Description: Continuing symptoms and complaints that impair creativity and working ability, not much self-reflection but relatively good human relationships.

Clinical prototype VI: 'the singer from the East'

> Mrs F is a refugee from a socialist country - an opera singer. She is grateful that therapy helped her to overcome the separation from her husband (who had left her for a younger actress). She now lives again in a love relationship, which seems to be more satisfying to her. During the follow-up interviews she is barely able to reflect upon the reasons why therapy was helpful to her (she explains her life events magically, using horoscopes etc.). She also seems limited in respect to her creativity (as a singer) and seems to be able to work only if she is told what to do in detail by an authoritarian personality. Her Oedipal conflicts were regarded by the expert group as unresolved.

Type VII: 'the therapy did not have any positive effect . . . the unsuccessful ones'

Description: still has severe symptoms and complaints that impair creativity and working ability. Unable to have satisfying relationships, hardly any self-reflection.

Clinical prototype VII: 'the woman in catastrophes'

> Mrs G is in a terrible psychic and psychosocial situation - unemployed, and separated from a very cruel partner. She was able to finish her studies during treatment but was never able to 'make something positive out of it'. She is full of hatred towards her analyst who 'did not help me'. The expert group is very touched by this follow-up because analyst and patient are in agreement that Mrs G had been in a better inner and psychosocial state right after termination. Was the negative transference not worked through well enough? Was there a reason why the positive outcomes of therapy had to be devalued afterwards? Was the analyst's understanding of the several severe traumas suffered by the patient 'good enough'? (She was sexually abused and emotionally severely neglected.) Or had Mrs G become psychotic in the meantime? (She is openly paranoid during the follow-up interview.) Our study cannot answer these questions.

Fortunately, we only have few follow-ups of Type VII (about 4%) - but these few cases are nevertheless very troubling because of their tragic therapy experiences.

Type VIII: 'the extremely traumatized'

Description: Severe symptoms or complaints, not able to live in satisfying relationships, some capability of self-reflection.

Clinical prototype VIII: 'I am still suffering from depressions'

> Mrs H suffers from severe depression. She has been unemployed for about a year. She was seriously suicidal when she started analysis. Her brother committed suicide and both parents and her sister were suffering from depression. In the follow-ups we find out that she had overcome her depression during analysis and had 'four good years' afterwards. She is surprised to discover that the loss of her unborn child (in the sixth month of pregnancy, she is 45 years old) could have triggered her decision to give up her job and evoked her renewed depression. This insight motivates her to look for therapeutic help again.

Frequencies of the different follow-ups in the interview sample

An expert and a 'naive' rater (a social scientist without psychoanalytic training) evaluated all the 129 follow-ups according to these three dimensions and a variety of different questions. From these ratings we are able to gain an overview of the therapeutic outcome of all the 129 patients of the interview sample:

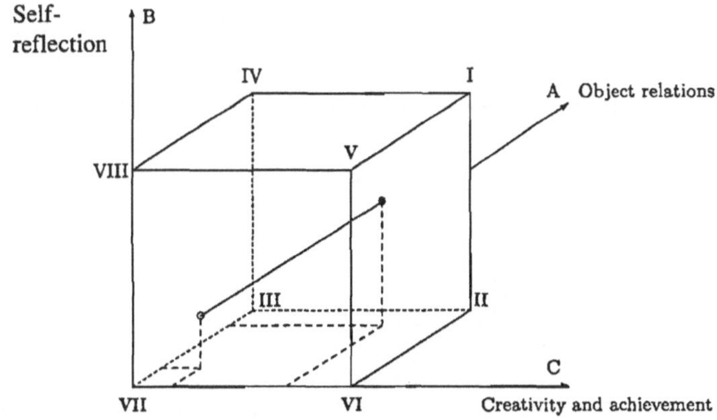

Figure 12.7. The three dimensions with the eight prototypes. One case of a therapy: 0 means rated score before treatment, black 0 means rated score after treatment.

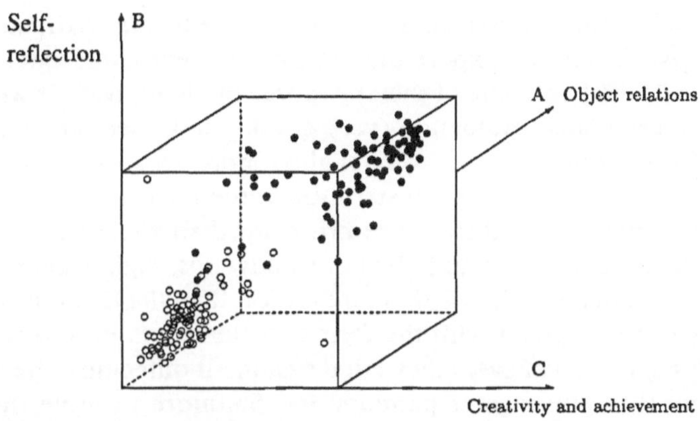

Figure 12.8. Former psychoanalyses, n = 91, scale 0-50, 0 means rated score before treatment, black 0 means rated score after treatment.

Selected clinically relevant results

Outcome - a multi-perspective approach

In our retrospective study we focused mainly on the views of the former patients themselves because we are convinced that patients are best qualified to evaluate the long-term effects of their treatments. Nevertheless, we tried to combine the patients' perspectives with others - that of the treating analyst, that of the psychoanalytical and non-psychoanalytical experts, and

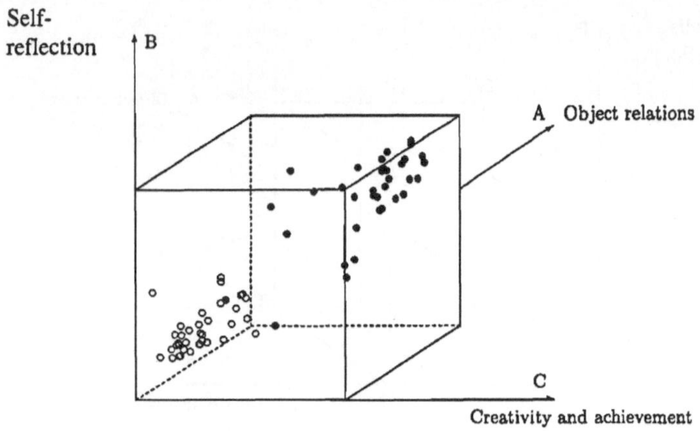

Figure 12.9. Former patients from psychoanalytic long-term therapies, n = 37, 0 means rated score before treatment, black 0 means rated score after treatment.

from other 'objective' criteria. In 89% of cases the former patients, their analysts, the psychoanalytic expert and the independent raters agreed with respect to the general outcome of therapy (good, medium, bad). If we asked for a more differentiated evaluation (very good, good, medium, bad, very bad), 46% of the former patients were slightly more satisfied with therapy outcome than their treating analysts; 44% agreed with them and 10% evaluated the outcome slightly more critically than their analysts. The psychoanalytical experts were, in 50% of the follow-ups, slightly more critical than the former patients and, in 25%, more critical than the treating analysts. In 40% of cases they agreed with the former patients and in 60% with the treating analysts. In 10% of cases they rated treatment outcome to be slightly more positive than the former patients, in 15% more positive than the treating analysts. Although we have not tested this result statistically yet, according to our preliminary observations the psychoanalytical experts evaluate therapy outcome most strictly, and the former patients most mildly of all our different groups of raters.

Degree of disturbances

According to an extensive rating of the pre-treatment state and patients' self-evaluations, the patients of our sample had been severely disturbed before treatment (GAF: average score before treatment: 52; after treatment: 78). The severity of the disturbances can also be observed looking at the ICD-10 diagnoses of the patients before treatment.[5] In our first results we found the following primary diagnoses in our sample: 51.2% personality disorders (of which: 28.7% were narcissistic personality disorders, 9.3% were borderline personalities and 12.0% other severe personality disorders); 27.9% were severely depressed; 8.5% had psychosomatic disturbances; 6.2% psychoses; 5.4% phobia and anxiety disorders and 1.6% obsessional disorders. Considering also the 'minor diagnoses' we see that we have severely disturbed patients - mostly with multiple disorders - in our sample. We found the whole range of psychopathology: very often several psychosomatic symptoms, but also bulimia, obsessional symptoms, drug abuse, sexual disorders and post-traumatic stress disorders. We have therefore developed the thesis that our data support a *patient-centred rather than a symptom-centred* indication for psychotherapy (see Leuzinger-Bohleber, Stuhr, Rüger and Beutel in press). Our study has shown that about 80% of these disturbed patients with multiple symptoms and personality disorders, treated by psychoanalyses and psychoanalytic long-term treatments, had good and stable outcomes. But still relevant is the question of contraindications, a question on which we continue to work.

Matching between patient and analyst

In keeping with Kantrowitz's (1997) overview of her different follow-up studies, our raters found that successful analyses seem to depend on a good 'matching process' between analyst and analysand. The idiosyncrasy of the different psychoanalytic processes and outcomes is amazing. We have the impression that these processes can lead to a satisfactory outcome if the analyst is capable of a skilful adaptation of his psychoanalytic technique to the individual characteristics, needs and conflicts of his specific patient, and can avoid following in a rigid and narrow way his own 'stereotyped' technique or his ideological view of how psychoanalysis should be. In particular, the treatment of severely disturbed patients seems to require much personal flexibility, creativity and sensitivity on the part of the analyst. Even with less disturbed patients, the summary of Mrs M seemed to hit the mark. 'It was the combination of warmth and emotionality on the one hand and absolute professionalism on the other hand.'

Differences between psychoanalyses and psychoanalytic therapies

Importance of the post-analytic phase

As already mentioned we did not find a statistically significant difference in the outcomes of psychoanalyses and psychoanalytic therapies in our questionnaire sample. This finding cannot be interpreted as a 'proof' that such a difference does not exist. In our retrospective study we can only say that about 80% of the former psychoanalyses and psychotherapy patients had a stable positive outcome at an average 6.5 years after the end of treatment. In other words, if the indication for either psychoanalysis or psychoanalytic therapy was correct, both therapeutic treatments were highly successful.

Analysing 43 follow-ups of the interview sample in detail, we did observe clear differences between former psychoanalysis and former psychotherapy patients. With two exceptions, the former psychoanalytic patients had internalized the analytic function in a more extensive and intensive way. Therefore their self-reflective functions were rated as 'deeper', 'more elaborated' and 'more differentiated' than those of the therapy patients. We suggest that this observation can contribute to the interpretation of the findings of the Stockholm study on why former psychoanalytic patients increasingly improve more than the therapy patients in proportion to the length of the follow-up period (see Sandell, Chapter 19 in this volume). As in the Stockholm study, we also found how important the post-analytic phase and the internalization of the analytic function of treatment were for a stable therapeutic outcome.

Length of treatments

Most of the treatments had been terminated by the agreement of patient and analysts: 43 of the 118 former patients, whose data we have analysed in this respect said that treatment had been too short for them; 11 said that treatment had been too long. Some psychoanalyses with medium or bad results were terminated after the insurance companies stopped paying (after 240 or 300 sessions). We also had some bad results from very long treatments (over 10 years).

Negative treatment outcome

Of the former patients in the interview sample, 11% were not satisfied with therapy outcome. In some cases obviously tragic life events (such as loss of a partner, unemployment and so forth) had influenced this negative view of therapy outcome. But others led us to reflect on the indication for psychoanalytic long-term psychotherapies and psychoanalyses, or for different techniques of treatment, and other questions that we discuss in more detail in later publications (see Leuzinger-Bohleber, Stuhr, Rüger and Beutel, 2002).

In 4% of the follow-ups either the former patient or his analyst were 'very unsatisfied' with therapy outcome. The five patients (out of the 129 interviewed) are especially on our minds in analysing our data further because it seems inadequate to harmonize these findings by arguing that 4% is an extremely small number compared with other risks in medical treatment - especially considering the long follow-up period of an average 6.5 years. Interviewing these five former patients we received a vivid impression of the tragic and desperate situation of these persons, their disappointments and resentments caused by the negative therapy outcome. Of course, wounds opened by long-term therapies or psychoanalyses are much deeper than those perhaps evoked by short-term psychotherapies. Often the long-term psychotherapy was seen as a 'last chance' for these patients, a chance that unfortunately did not turn out to be really a chance for them but was, rather, a disappointment again.

One more brief observation: in the group of the 11% unsatisfied patients we found persons with all kinds of diagnoses. It surprised us, however, that all the five patients with the extremely negative therapy outcome had been borderline patients. Even if seven borderline patients in our interview sample had good and stable therapy outcomes (even 6.5 years after the end of treatment), borderline patients seem to cause extreme difficulties in psychotherapies. First, single case analyses show that those analysts treating borderline patients with satisfying therapy outcomes had good institutional supports (for example, co-operation from psychiatric clinics, and regular supervision with experts in this field, which helped them cope with the extremely aggressive behaviour of these patients), and used a special technique for treating these patients (developed by Mentzos, see Chapter 7). Within the limits of this chapter we cannot contrast the therapeutic outcomes with these borderline patients with those of the unexpectedly large group of psychotic patients (6.2%) in our sample. Our results seem to support the experience of Mentzos over many years, that psychoanalytic therapies with psychotic patients often prove to be less difficult than those with borderline personalities (see his chapter). We have some very impressive and stable outcomes from psychoanalytic long-term psychotherapies with psychotic patients in our study (see Leuzinger-Bohleber, Stuhr, Rüger and Beutel, 2002), although these treatments were based on substantial institutional support (see above) and, of course, a modified psychoanalytical technique (e.g. using medication at the beginning of the treatment).

Severely traumatized patients

Another unexpected finding is the number of severely traumatized patients (externally traumatic events in the context of World War II, long separations from primary objects, psychiatric illnesses of caregivers, sexual abuse, illness during childhood and so forth): 81 of the 129 former patients belonged to this subgroup. Many of the analysts seem to have treated these patients with a modified psychoanalytic technique. It was interesting that there seemed to be two groups of severely traumatized patients with good therapeutic outcome. In the first group (76 patients), the trauma was reactivated and worked through in psychoanalysis itself. Another small group of patients (five patients) seems to have protected the analytic relationship from the enactment of the severest traumas and, instead, used the analytic relationship as a 'holding function', reflecting with the analyst on the reactivation of the trauma in an external relationship. All these analysts told us that they regretted that, although analysis had proved to be quite successful, negative transference was not worked through thoroughly.

Another feature was that the inner dialogue that these patients maintained with the analyst sounded, unlike dialogues described by other patients, quite concrete to the experts. It seemed somehow protected and isolated from inner destructive impulses, and was therefore not *fully* integrated psychically. We will have to analyse these findings further.

Finally, we would like to mention a positive finding that corresponds well with the one reported by Peter Fonagy and his co-workers from studies using the Adult Attachment Interview (Fonagy, 1998). Even in psychoanalyses with only medium results in the eyes of the patient and the analyst, it was nevertheless possible at least partially to understand severely traumatic experiences. The analytic process offered the patient the opportunity to interrupt the unconscious transgenerational transmission of the traumas. To quote just one of these patients:

> In my psychoanalysis I gained the insight that it is not possible to really restore some of my deepest psychic wounds. My mother became psychotic after the loss of my father in Russia (during the Second World War) and she abused me psychologically, for example by threatening to commit suicide over a period of many years. My brain is not able to eliminate these experiences. I probably will have problems really trusting my beloved partner deeply, and in feeling some closeness with him, for the rest of my life. But I am so happy that I can at least deal with these problems much better in relation to my two children. I can let them grow up and find their own ways of life - not having to abuse them unconsciously as my mother did with me. I am so grateful that psychoanalysis enabled me to cut the terrible and tragic umbilical cord with my family.

Concluding remarks

Can a follow-up study inspire psychoanalytic practice? Are findings of a naturalistic empirical psychoanalytical study of any relevance for it? These are the questions that I have tried to pursue in this chapter, covering some of the facets of our naturalistic follow-up study. I hope that I have been able to give an impression, if only fragmentary, of the complexity of our study and its clinically relevant findings. These seem, in my view, to belong to its very specific 'quality' although it leads us into a much darker and more challenging research labyrinth than studies applying exclusively quantitative instruments. I have tried to show our attempt at the pro-active argument that *psychoanalytic issues* (like studying the outcome of psychoanalytical treatments) have to be studied by *psychoanalytical* instruments, because only an application of the unique research methods of psychoanalysis will allow us to perceive, and to investigate systematically, manifestations of the unconscious. This was the reason why we chose to use two psychoanalytic follow-up interviews as the major method of collecting data in our study, interviews done by experienced analysts who were able to work with their professional tools (such as the systematic observation and interpretation of transference and counter-transference reactions). We also applied other 'classical' psychoanalytic methods in our study: supervisions between the two follow-up interviews, psychoanalytical expert evaluations in the local research groups, and the communication of the complex psychoanalytical findings in (systematically controlled) narrative case studies. We also illustrated how we try to combine and contrast these psychoanalytic qualitative approaches with non-psychoanalytic quantitative ones. We think that the results gained by these procedures are of direct clinical interest. They are 'naturalistic', provided by real former patients and experienced analysts in a clinical psychoanalytic situation - the follow-up interviews. Many of our colleagues share our perspective. They have confirmed how valuable it has been for them to listen to former patients and what they have to tell us, consciously and unconsciously, about their positive and negative experiences in their psychoanalytic treatments. Listening to former patients helps us to appreciate the brighter aspects of our clinical work and the potencies of our psychoanalytic treatment approach; but it also confronts us with many neglected, taboo and difficult aspects of our profession.

The richness and clinical relevance of our results are major advantages of our study. One of the disadvantages is the difficulty in summarizing and communicating its complexity adequately, without losing a feeling for the idiosyncrasies of the findings on the one hand, and the representative position of the single case studies in the larger group on the other hand. We also have illustrated that a naturalistic, retrospective study (with only one point of measurement) may evoke more questions than it is possible to answer definitively. Another critical point is that we have focused on the *retrospective* view of former patients. Because of ethical considerations we did not want to disturb the intimacy of current treatment situations by our study, and therefore planned a retrospective study. We also are convinced that the former patient himself is the best expert in judging whether and how therapy has helped him, even 6.5 years after the end of treatment. We know that from a methodological point of view, retrospective evaluations might not be considered to be 'objective', which leads us right into the middle of a current debate in psychoanalysis and the neurosciences on 'narrative versus historical truth' (see, for instance, Leuzinger-Bohleber and Pfeifer, 1998 and in preparation). Even if the patient has 'reworked' the 'historical truth' of his treatment experiences, the direction this 'reworking' has taken, and whether it still helps him to solve his former problems in current conflict situations in a more productive way than before treatment, is extremely relevant. And who should judge this better than himself? Nevertheless, it seemed valuable to compare the view of the patient with that of his former analyst, independent psychoanalytic and non-psychoanalytic experts, together with a number of objective data (like health costs, but also content and linguistic analyses of the interview transcripts and so forth). We see this multi-perspective procedure as an attempt to approach the complexity of therapy outcome, which is for us a 'naturalistic task' with many different facets and aspects, including conscious and unconscious dimensions. Studying unconscious conflicts and fantasies in the evaluation of therapy outcomes seldom leads, of course, to definitive answers, but often rather to new questions and the need to observe and study specific phenomena in greater detail. Is this peculiar to naturalistic, *psychoanalytic* research? Or does innovative research always raise more questions than it definitively answers? In any case we are eager to discuss our findings intensively and rigorously with our psychoanalytic colleagues as well as with non-psychoanalytical psychotherapy researchers. It would, for example, be interesting to compare our results with those collected in a 'naturalistic control group', such as former patients from behaviour therapies, at an average of 6.5 years after the end of therapy, applying the same research methods as in our study.

We hope, therefore, to have transmitted our impression that naturalistic studies - despite the methodological and practical problems - are a fruitful and exciting enterprise. They often create unusual and inspiring communications between researchers and clinicians and may also open some new perspective on our everyday clinical practice. Therefore, clinical and scientific work can, according to Ulrich Moser (1992), be described using the same metaphor: as psychoanalysts and psychoanalytic researchers, we can only work in a creative and fruitful way if two butterflies are sitting on our heads at the same time - art and science!

Notes

1. Unfortunately we had the resources to include only 201 of them in our study (see Rüger, Chapter 10 in this volume).
2. In order to give a first impression of the follow-ups I have tried to summarize the interviews descriptively without interpreting the material psychoanalytically to any degree. I have also tried to protect the confidentiality of the former patients and their analysts by leaving out or actively changing certain details in the information.

3. One preliminary hypothesis is that, at the beginning of the first follow-up interview, some of the 'original' pathology of the former patient becomes visible because it is enacted in some way or another in the developing transference. Afterwards - especially with former patients with 'good enough outcome' of psychoanalysis - some of the most important transference constellations of the treatment seem to be reactivated and are therefore observable in the follow-up interviews. In the local research groups we often discussed the observation that, in the two follow-ups, the psychoanalytical process redeveloped unconsciously in a very condensed and, of course, fragmentary form.
4. We thank Bernd Böttger, Frankfurt, for drawing the charts.
5. We found a very detailed and precise description of the original symptoms and complaints in the follow-up interviews with the former patient (and independently with his analyst) so it was possible to rate reliably the ICD-10 diagnoses before treatment (a possibility that we had not expected when planning our study). Using conservative and relatively strict criteria, we considered only those symptoms that were mentioned by the patient as well as by the analyst in the rating. The above mentioned first analyses of these ratings only contain the dominant diagnoses. In many cases we rated several minor diagnoses, especially the so called z-diagnoses containing traumatic 'real' events in the patient's childhood, see Leuzinger-Bohleber, Stuhr, Rüger and Beutel, 2002).

Bibliography

Argelander H (1970) Das Erstinterview in der Psychotherapie. Darmstadt: Wissenschaftliche Buchgesellschaft.

Bachrach HM et al. (1991) On the efficacy of psychoanalysis. J Am Psychoanal Assn 39: 871-916.

Beenen F (1997) Die Amsterdamer PEP Studie. In: Leuzinger-Bohleber M, Stuhr U (eds) Psychoanalysen im Rückblick. Gießen: Psychosozial-Verlag, pp. 336-47.

Beutel M (1989) Was schützt Gesundheit? Zum Forschungsstand und der Bedeutung von personalen Ressourcen in der Bewältigung von Alltagsbelastungen und Lebensereignissen. Psychother Psychosom med Psychol 39: 452-62.

Bohleber W (1997) Zur Bedeutung der neueren Säuglingsforschung für die psychoanalytische Theorie der Identität. In: Keupp H, Höfer R (eds) Identitätsarbeit Heute. Frankfurt a.M.: Suhrkamp, pp. 93-120.

Bohleber W (1999) Trauma und Trauer. Unpublished paper.

Breyer F, Heinzel R, Klein T (1997) Kosten und Nutzen ambulanter Psychoanalysen in Deutschland. Gesundh. ökonom. Qual Manag. 2: 59-73.

Dreher AU, Sandler J (1997) Zum Problem des Behandlungsziels von Psychoanalysen. In: Leuzinger-Bohleber M, Stuhr U (eds) Psychoanalysen im Rückblick. Gießen: Psychosozial-Verlag, pp. 73-89.

DeWitt K (1997) Interrater Reliability of the Scales of Psychological Capacities. Support for a measure of structural change. Unpublished paper given at the IPA Research Conference, UCL, March 1997.

Fonagy P (1998) Die Bedeutung der Entwicklung metakognitiver Kontrolle der mentalen Repräsentanzen für die Betreuung und das Wachstum des Kindes. Psyche 52, 4: 349-69.

Fonagy P, Target M (1997) Voraussagen über die Ergebnisse von Kinderanalysen: Eine retrospektive Studie von 763 Behandlungen am Anna Freud Center. In: Leuzinger-Bohleber M, Stuhr U (eds) Psychoanalysen im Rückblick. Gießen: Psychosozial-Verlag, pp. 366-407.

Gerhardt U (1996) Patientenkarrieren. Frankfurt a.M.: Suhrkamp.

Heinzel R, Breyer F, Klein T (1996) Ambulante Psychoanalyse in Deutschland. Eine katamnestische Evaluationsstudie. Fakultät für Wirtschaftswissenschaften.

Huber D, Klug G, von Rad M (1997) Münchener Psychotherapie-Studie (MPS). In: Leuzinger-Bohleber M, Stuhr U (eds) Psychoanalysen im Rückblick. Gießen: Psychosozial-Verlag, pp. 454-69.

Kaarento K, Aalberg V, Hannula J, Kaipainen M, Lindfors O, Järvikovski A, Pylkkänen K (1995) The Helsinki Psychotherapy Study. Unpublished manuscript.

Kächele H (1995) Klaus Grawes Konfession und die psychoanalytische Profession. Psyche 49: 481-92.

Kantrowitz J (1995) The beneficial aspects of the patient-analyst match. International Journal of Psycho-Analysis 76: 299-313.

Kantrowitz JL (1997) The Symmetrical Aspect of the Therapeutic Relationship: It takes two to have a therapeutic alliance. Paper given at the 7th IPA Research Conference, London, 7 March 1997.

Kantrowitz JL, Katz AL, Paolitto F (1990a) Follow-up of psychoanalysis five to ten years after termination: I: Stability of change. Journal of the American Psychoanalytic Association 38 (2): 471-96.

Kantrowitz JL, Katz AL, Paolitto F (1990b) Follow-up of psychoanalysis five to ten years after termination. II: development of the self-analytic function. Journal of the American Psychoanalytic Association 38(3): 637-50.

Kantrowitz JL, Katz AL, Paolitto F (1990c) Follow-up of psychoanalysis five to ten years after termination. III: the relation between the resolution of the transference and the patient-analyst match. Journal of the American Psychoanalytic Association 38(3): 655-78.

Keller W, Dilg R, Westhoff G, Robner R, Studt HH (1997) Wirksamkeit und Kosten-Nutzen-Aspekte ambulanter (jungianischer) Psychoanalysen und Psychotherapie. eine katamnestische Studie. In: Leuzinger-Bohleber M, Stuhr U (eds) Psychoanalysen im Rückblick. Gießen: Psychosozial-Verlag: 432-53.

Keupp H, Höfer R (eds) (1999) Identitätsarbeit heute. Frankfurt a.M.: Suhrkamp.

Koukkou M, Leuzinger-Bohleber M, Mertens W (eds) (1998) Erinnerung von Wirklichkeiten. Psychoanalyse und Neurowissenschaften im Dialog. Bd. 1: Bestandsaufnahme.

Leuzinger-Bohleber M (1989) Veränderung kognitiver Prozesse in Psychoanalysen. Band 2: Fünf aggregierte Einzelfallstudien. Ulm: PSZ Verlag.

Leuzinger-Bohleber M (1995) Die Einzelfallstudie als psychoanalytisches Forschungsinstrument. Psyche 49(5): 434-81.

Leuzinger-Bohleber M, Beutel M, Stuhr U, Rüger B (2000) How to Study the Quality of Psychoanalytic Treatments: Combining qualitative and quantitative approaches in a representative follow-up study. Paper given at the Research Conference of the IPA in London, 4 March, 2000.

Leuzinger-Bohleber M, Pfeifer R (1998) Erinnern in der Übertragung – Vergangenheit in der Gegenwart? Psychoanalyse und Embodied Cognitive Science im Dialog. Psyche 52(9/10): 884–919.

Leuzinger-Bohleber M, Pfeifer R (in press) Remembering a depressive primary object? Psychoanalysis and Embodied Cognitive Science. A dialogue on memory. Int Journal of Psychoanalysis.

Leuzinger-Bohleber M, Stuhr U (eds) (1997) Psychoanalysen im Rückblick. Methoden, Ergebnisse und Perspektiven der neueren Katamneseforschung. Gießen: Psychosozial-Verlag.

Leuzinger-Bohleber M, Stuhr U, Rüger B, Beutel M (1999) Long-term Effects of Psychoanalyses and Psychoanalytic Therapies: A representative follow-up study. Paper given at the Empirical Precongress of the IPA Congress in Santiago de Chile, 24 July 1999.

Leuzinger-Bohleber M, Stuhr U, Rüger B, Beutel M (2002) Wie forschen und heilen Psychoanalytiker? Berichte und Ergebnisse einer repräsentativen Katamnesestudie. Stuttgart: Kohlhammer, in press.

Meyer AE (1981) The Hamburg Short Psychotherapy Comparison Experiment. Psychother Psychosom 35(2–3): 81–207.

Meyer AE, Stuhr U, Wirth U, Rüster P (1988) 12-year follow-up study of the Hamburg Short Psychotherapy Experiment: An overview. Psychother Psychosom 50: 192–200.

Moser U (1992) Two butterflies on my head, or, why have a theory in psychoanalysis? In: Leuzinger-Bohleber M, Schneider H, Pfeifer R (eds) 'Two Butterflies on My Head ...' Psychoanalysis in the Interdisciplinary Dialogue. New York: Springer, pp. 29–47.

Norman H, Blacker K, Oremland J, Barrett W (1976) The fate of the transference neurosis after termination of a satisfactory analysis. J Amer Psychoanal Assn 24: 471–98.

Oremland J, Blacker K, Haskell F (1975) In completeness in 'successful' psychoanalyses: A follow-up study. J Amer Psychoanal Assn 23: 819–44.

Pfeffer AZ (1959) A procedure for evaluating the results of psychoanalysis: A preliminary report. J Am Psychoanal Assn 7: 418–44.

Pfeffer AZ (1961) Follow-up-study of a satisfactory analysis. J Am Psychoanal Assn 9: 689–718.

Pfeffer AZ (1963) The meaning of the analyst after analysis. J Am Psychoanal Assn 9: 229–44.

Rudolf G (1996) Psychotherapieforschung bezogen auf die psychotherapeutische Praxis. Psychotherapie Forum 4: 124–34.

Rüger B (1994) Kritische Anmerkungen zu den statistischen Methoden in Grawe, Donati und Bernauer. 'Psychotherapie im Wandel. Von der Konfession zur Profession'. Zeitschrift für Psychosomatische Medizin und Psychoanalyse 40: 368–83.

Rüger B (1996a) Eine Erwiderung auf Grawes Artikel 'Psychotherapie und Statistik im Spannungsfeld zwischen Wissenschaft und Konfession'. Zeitschrift für Klinische Psychologie 25: 61–5.

Rüger B (1996b) Fragen und Anmerkungen zu einigen statistischen Methoden in der Psychotherapieforschung. Psychotherapie Forum 4(3): 135–43.

Sandell R (1994) A follow-up evaluation of psychoanalysis and psychoanalytic psychotherapy. Unpublished paper given at the Workshop Process and Effect Research in Psychoanalysis, Stockholm, 27/28 May 1994.

Sandell R (1997) Langzeitwirkung von Psychotherapie und Psychoanalyse. In: Leuzinger-Bohleber M, Stuhr U (eds) Psychoanalysen im Rückblick. Gießen: Psychosozial-Verlag, pp. 348–65.

Sandler J, Dreher AU (1996) What Do Psychoanalysts Want? The problem of aims in psychoanalytic therapy. London: Routledge.

Schlessinger N, Robbins FP (1983) A Developmental View of the Psychoanalytic Process: Follow-up studies and their consequences. Madison, CT: International Universities Press.

Stern D (1997) The Motherhood Constellation. New York: Basic Books

Stuhr U (1995) Die Fallgeschichte als Forschungsmittel im psychoanalytischen Diskurs. Ein Beitrag zum Verstehen als Methode. In: Kaiser E (ed.) Psychoanalytisches Wissen. Opladen: Westdeutscher Verlag, pp. 188–204.

Stuhr U (1997) Psychoanalyse und qualitative Psychotherapieforschung. In: Leuzinger-Bohleber M, Stuhr U (eds) Psychoanalysen im Rückblick. Gießen: Psychosozial-Verlag, pp. 164–81.

Stuhr U, Deneke FW (1993) Die Fallgeschichte. Beiträge zu ihrer Bedeutung als Forschungsinstrument. Heidelberg: Asanger.

Stuhr U, Leuzinger-Bohleber M, Beutel M (2001) (eds) Langzeit-Psychotherapie. Perspektiven für Therapeuten und Wissenschaftler. München: Kohlhammer Verlag.

Stuhr U, Meyer AR (1991) University of Hamburg. Hamburg short-term psychotherapy comparison. In: Beutler LE, Crago M (eds) Psychotherapy Research. An international review of programmatic studies. Washington, DC: Annual Psychol Ass: 212–25.

Thomä H, Kächele H (1996) Lehrbuch der psychoanalytischen Therapie. Separatum aus Kapitel 9. Berlin: Springer, pp. 470–597.

Tschuschke V, Heckrath C, Tress W (1997) 'Zwischen Konfusion und Makulatur': Zum Wert der Berner Psychotherapie-Studie von Grawe, Donati und Bernauer. Göttingen: Vandenhoeck & Ruprecht.

Varvin S (1977) Die Oslo-Psychotherapiestudie. In: Leuzinger-Bohleber M, Stuhr U (eds) Psychoanalysen im Rückblick. Gießen: Psychosozial-Verlag, pp. 407–14.

Wachholz S, Stuhr U (1996) The concept of ideal types in psychoanalytic follow-up research. Paper at the First International Congress of Qualitative Psychotherapy Research. In: Frommer J (ed.) (1998) Qualitative Research In Psychotherapy. London: Sage.

Waldvogel B (1997) Längere Psychotherapien werden als nützlicher erlebt. Zu den Ergebnissen und der Diskussion einer unabhängigen Umfrage in den USA. Forum der Psychoanalyse 13: 172–82.

Wallerstein RS (1986) Forty-two Lives in Treatment: A study of psychoanalysis and psychotherapy. New York: Guilford Press.

Wallerstein RS (1989) Follow-up in psychoanalysis: Clinical and research values. J Am Psychoanal Assn 37(4): 921–43.

Wallerstein RS (1999) The Generations of Psychotherapy Research: An overview. Unpublished manuscript.

Wallerstein RS, DeWitt K, Hartley D, Rosenberg SE, Zilberg NJ (1996) The Scales of Psychological Capacities. Version 1. Unpublished manuscript.

Weber M (1904) Die 'Objektivität' sozialwissenschaftlicher und sozialpolitischer Erkenntnisse. In: Gesammelte Aufsätze zur Wissenschaftslehre. Tübingen: Mohr, pp. 124–214.

Weber J, Bachrach H, Solomon (1985) Factors associated with the outcome of psychoanalysis: Report of the Columbia Psychoanalytic Center Research Project. I and II. International Review of Psychoanalysis 12: 127–41 and 251-62.

Zielke M, Kopf-Mehnert C (1978) Veränderungsfragebogen des Erlebens und Verhaltens. Heidelberg: Springer.

STUDYING THE MENTAL HEALTH COSTS OF LONG-TERM PSYCHOTHERAPIES

CHAPTER 13

Mental health – its significance for society and conditions for its development

MARKUS FÄH

As Chapter 2 explained, an intensive debate is currently taking place within psychoanalysis as to the aims of psychoanalytic treatment. This debate also touches upon society, in an endeavour to gain greater insight into so-called 'postmodernity'. Hence, leading sociologists are also looking into the changes that are coming about in the relationship between the individual and society and, more particularly, between the demands imposed by society and the individual's psychological make-up. Thus, Sennett (1998: 31) writes:

> How is it possible to strive for long-term goals in a society that is orientated towards brevity? How can lasting social relationships be maintained? How can a person in a society that is made up of episodes and fragments integrate his identity and biography into a story? The conditions prevailing in the new economic order promote an experience which drifts from place to place and from job to job over time. Hence capitalism, with its short-term actions, threatens particularly those personality traits that bond people to each other and give an individual stable self-esteem.

According to Sennett, current social conditions represent a serious danger to the mental health of a large number of individuals. In addition to this, stable personality traits seem to have become dysfunctional for social survival: superficial loyalty and weak bonds make it easier for people to switch flexibly and with mobility from one place of employment to another, and to swap relationships. In his *Postmodernity and Its Discontents,* the Polish sociologist and postmodernity theorist, Zygmunt Bauman (1999: 18), writes: 'acquired competencies to act represent a considerable asset in a stable and predictable world; but would be veritably suicidal if events were suddenly to break out of their causal relationships, elude any type of prediction and hit us unexpectedly'. I cannot go into further detail about this discussion within the scope of this chapter, but will simply point out that this gives rise to aspects of relevance for the topic under consideration in this book, namely, an analysis of the concept of health, and the economic reflections on the care of the sick that stem from this.

In this connection, mention must also be made of a number of empirical findings showing that long-term psychoanalytic treatment promotes mental health on a lasting basis. We have the account of the impressive results of the study conducted by Rolf Sandell and his co-workers in Stockholm. We also have the findings of the Konstanz Study, carried out by Heinzel, Breyer and Klein, and the Berlin Study conducted by Keller and co-workers, all showing how positive changes result in different areas of mental behaviour after long-term psychoanalytic treatment. The results of the DPV study also show which lasting and long-term, positive mental changes and health changes come about with long-term psychoanalytic treatment.

By way of an introduction to the issue of the health-economic aspects of long-term psychoanalytic treatment, I would like to draw your attention to a number of more general considerations, such as the question 'can the benefit of long-term psychoanalytic treatment be viewed in a meaningful manner from a health-economic and health-sociological angle too?'

Certain conflicts will always be inherent in the interdisciplinary discussion between psychoanalysis and other fields of knowledge, bringing problems of translation and understanding with them, so I shall restrict myself, within the limited scope available, to two aspects that seem particularly important to me, namely the positive concept of health and the interface between health-economic and psychoanalytic concepts. I will not go into a detailed analysis of the concept of health and its social significance, nor will I give a theoretical and empirical analysis of the development of creative and resilient mental resources in the framework of long-term psychoanalytic treatment (for example, Bollas, 1992).

First of all, I would like to give a brief introduction to the 'salutogenetic' understanding of health that, in my opinion, has a kind of bridging or hinging function between the psychoanalytical health discussion and the health economics discussion.

The concept of 'salutogenesis' is set against the concept of 'pathogenesis', a frequently used term in medicine. It leads on to the question: how does health develop or how is health maintained? Which are the factors that promote health? Viktor von Weizsäcker wrote back in 1930 (cited in Sack and Lamprecht, 1998: 325): 'The health of a person is not simply capital that can be spent, but will only be present at all if it is generated at each moment of life. If it is not generated, then the person is already ill.'

Working on the basis of system-theory and action-theory model assumptions, Rimann and Udris (1998: 352) conceive of health as: 'a transactionally-caused dynamic equilibrium between the physical and mental protection and defence mechanisms of the organism, on the one hand, and the potentially pathogenic influences of the physical, biological and social environment, on the other hand'.

Viewed in this way, health is an uninterrupted constructive process of self-organization and self-steering. It has to be produced by the organism on a permanent basis in the form of defence in the immunological sense and as adaptation or purposive change of the environment by the individual. This equilibrium is a function of the availability and use of health-protecting or health-restoring factors within the individual and the environment, in other words of internal (personal) and external (situational) resources.

According to the salutogenetic understanding of health, mental health is a personal resource. It takes in the cognitive and emotional capacities of individuals to master the stresses of life and repeatedly generate and maintain their health through their own particular life orientation and lifestyle. Research within the framework of the salutogenetic paradigm is aimed at determining the factors that generate health on a long-term basis.

The Israeli sociologist, Aaron Antonovsky (1987; Antonovsky et al., 1971), is regarded as the founder of the salutogenetic paradigm. In the framework of a sociological-sociopsychiatric study, he established that women who had survived the Holocaust and were traumatized adjusted less well to the menopause than non-traumatized study participants. Within the traumatized group, there were nonetheless 29% of women who coped well with the changes brought about by the menopause. On the basis of these research results, Antonovsky increasingly focused his interest on the question of what enables people to remain healthy despite being subject to very serious stress.

First of all, he attempted to describe resources that are deployed to offset pathogenic influences or to resist illness. When he realized that these resources were individually different ways of coping with potentially pathogenic influences, he began to develop a global concept, which he termed 'sense of coherence'. This concept is generally translated into German as *Kohärenzsinn* (Becker, 1982; Hurrelmann, 1998) or *Kohärenzgefühl* (Antonovsky, 1993; Faltermeier, 1993). In line with Rimann and Udris (1998), I prefer the translation 'Kohärenzerleben' because I feel that this term best reflects the integration of the cognitive and emotional aspects of a salutogenic way of living or a salutogenic life orientation. This 'sense of coherence' is defined as:

> A basic orientation which expresses the extent of the comprehensive, lasting and simultaneously dynamic feeling of confidence in such a way that
>
> 1. life events are structured, foreseeable and explainable

2. resources are available to cope with the demands stemming from these events
3. these demands are challenges which are worth intervention and commitment.

(Antonovsky, 1987)

The sense of coherence is made up of three components, which Antonovsky designates 'comprehensibility', 'manageability' and 'meaningfulness'. 'Comprehensibility' relates to the cognitive component. The individual experiences the information from their internal and external world in a sufficiently structured manner and in an inherently logical way, so that it can be placed in a context; in other words, it is neither chaotic nor random, neither arbitrary nor inexplicable. Antonovsky coined the image 'that we are all in the dangerous river of life and never stand safely on the bank'. Anyone who experiences the river of life and hence 'the world in which they live' as comprehensible, has fulfilled a key prerequisite for keeping his or her head above water, for avoiding the rapids and for remaining healthy over the long term. 'Manageability' describes the feelings experienced by the actor in the 'river of life'. Can I 'handle' the world in which I live? Have I inner or external resources? To keep to the same image: how well can I dive and swim, have I got life belts, dinghies, fellow swimmers who can help me keep my head above water in the flow? 'Meaningfulness' relates to the emotional component. Is it worthwhile committing myself? Do I experience swimming in my river of life as a meaningful challenge, or do I consider it to be a meaningless torment, a dull struggle?

In order to subject his concept to an empirical test, Antonovsky developed a questionnaire of 29 items which was first published in 1983 and the structure of which was described in detail in 1987. In the meantime, more than 100 studies with the SOC have been published worldwide and the standard test quality criteria, such as test/retest reliability and internal consistency, are good. The correlation between sense of coherence and health indicators is high. Results of new studies also show that the sense of coherence is not just – as Antonovsky originally postulated – an experience constant based on habit, acquired during the first ten years of life, but can undergo a positive change in the course of psychotherapy (Sack and Lamprecht, 1994, 1998; Sandell, 1997; Fäh, 2000).

Lack of space prevents me from going into detail here on the correlation between the sense of coherence and psychoanalytical health concepts, and I would like to restrict myself to showing that a number of aspects of psychoanalytic maturity goals can be associated with the 'sense of coherence' concept.

Experiencing the world and one's own position within it in a coherent manner marks the outcome of a complex cognitive and emotional capacity to assess one's perception of oneself and one's transaction with one's surroundings in both affective and cognitive terms. Serving as a moderating emotional and cognitive resource, the sense of coherence has an influence on the individual's appraisal of life's stresses (see Bohleber, 1992, inter alia). This appraisal, in turn, influences the individual's inner stress state, which impedes or supports the assessment and implementation of coping strategies. The effective development and deployment of personal and situational resources, in turn, serves to promote a sense of coherence. Figure 13.1 shows the correlation between the sense of coherence and the ability to cope with life.

Finally, I would like to turn my attention to a number of health-economic aspects of long-term psychoanalytic treatment.

The health-economic discussion is focused on the following questions, inter alia. Does quality of life and health correspond to economic values? Expressed in more specific terms: which types of treatment on offer make which contribution to improving health, and at what cost? Health economics provides decision makers in the health system with data that are used to take health policy decisions regarding the allocation of resources to particular types of treatment. If it is seen, for instance, that two treatment methods, which are equally effective, differ solely in respect of their cost, then the more expensive method can be struck off the list of publicly financed treatments. If treatments differ in respect of their effect and their cost, which is evidently the case for psychotherapy, then the cost carriers are interested

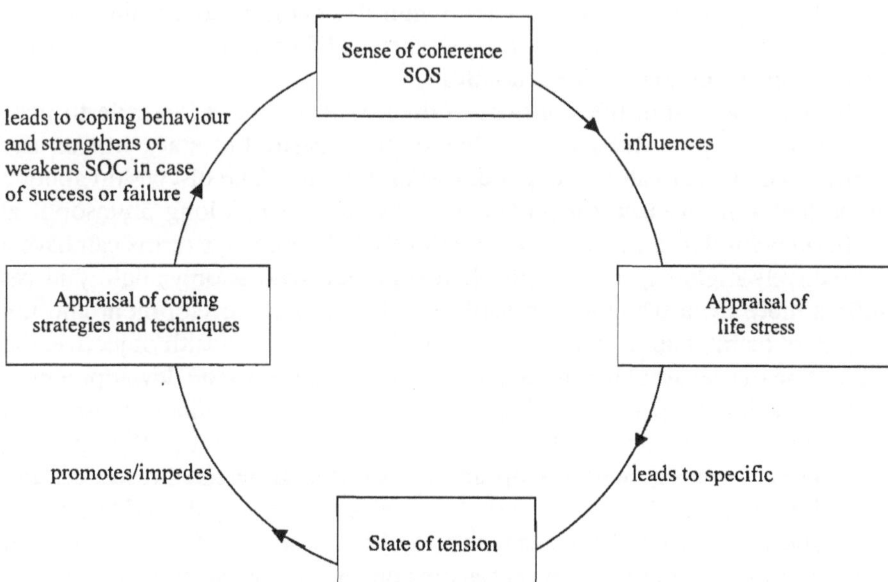

Figure 13.1. Function of sense of coherence in the salutogenetic process.

in more differentiated considerations in order to establish the treatment method that works out cheapest for them.

At the level of research instruments, a distinction must be made between different types of study (Hargreaves et al., 1998): 'cost-benefit studies' in the strict sense of the term can only be conducted if the costs of treatment and the benefit derived from treatment can be compared with each other on the basis of economic measurements. In the case of mental health, this is only possible to a limited extent. Only part of the 'mental health benefit' can be measured, at best indirectly, in cost-benefit studies through the savings made on other costs (for example, doctors' fees, cost of drugs, hospital costs, lost working hours). Cost-benefit studies in the field of psychotherapy systematically underestimate the value of psychotherapy, because a large portion of the quality of life - for example satisfaction with relationships - has no economic equivalent (see below).

Most studies in the health field are thus 'cost effectiveness' studies in which the costs are compared with 'natural' outcome measurements (scales of perceived state of health, symptom lists). The problem with these studies lies in the translation of their results into criteria that are of relevance for the decision makers in the health system, such as cost savings. In the case of pure cost effectiveness studies, this translation has to be performed by the decision makers themselves and is thus often at the mercy of political and economic interpretations.

A third type of study attempts to counter this danger: 'cost-utility' studies are designed in such a way that they integrate different outcome variables in units of relevance to health economics.

In this discussion, the concept of quality of life has a key role to play. Health is not perceived as an objectively measurable state but as the experience of the quality, the 'goodness' of one's life. The discussion about a 'good life' - or *eudaimonia* in Greek - has, of course, a long philosophical tradition behind it. A person who is seriously ill in objective terms can have a subjectively higher quality of life than someone who is only slightly ill yet suffers more from his illness in subjective terms. The development and the long-term maintenance of a feeling of 'quality of life' as a health objective, the realization of the 'art of living' (Schmid, 1998), is linked to the development of highly individual capacities to shape one's life. These capacities are associated with personal ideas and wishes, with the realistic appraisal of the opportunities open to oneself, with the optimum activation of personal resources and with the selection of action aimed at satisfying wishes capable of fulfilment. The concept of quality of life can take on a different specific form as a function of the individual - in the same way as the concept of a sense of coherence.

One attempt at achieving 'comparability of the quality of life on the basis of measurements' - an attempt that, in my opinion, is fraught with problems

- is the operationalization of the gain in quality of life expressed in the measuring unit of 'quality-adjusted life years' (QALYs) (Walker and Rosser, 1993). The basic idea behind QALYs is to view the 'good' life gained through a treatment measure - the health that is generated - as the mathematical product of qualitative aspects of life (subjective well-being) and quantitative aspects (duration of life). Cost-utility studies using the instrument of QALYs have developed into a special branch of research in the context of health economics. Whether this concept can really be of use for studying the cost and benefit of long-term psychoanalytical treatment by comparison with other treatment methods is something I regard as highly doubtful, but it is something that needs to be discussed in a public and proactive manner. If we think of the individual statements made by a large number of former patients from the DPV study mentioned, these would seem to provide far more information than attempts to measure qualitative phenomena, such as the quality of life, in quantitative terms.

Several questions arise in connection with studies in this book.

Can long-term psychoanalytical treatment be justified as a method that promotes and develops health on a lasting basis? Is it in a position to generate a fundamental salutogenic life orientation that individuals have not been able to create for themselves on account of their life history, and how does it do this? Can it make any sense to correlate this salutogenic effect of psychoanalytic treatment with economic parameters?

Let me conclude with two statements made by patients in follow-up interviews. One patient reported amongst other things that, upon completion of her psychoanalysis, she was able to recognize the correlations between physical symptoms and what was going on in her mind, with the successful outcome that the symptom then disappeared: 'I frequently suffer constipation as well at the weekend. So I see there are still latent associations there, but not so strongly pronounced as before. I know about it now, and the moment it becomes clear to me, I can go to the toilet again. Sometimes it's quite phenomenal.' The patient then mentions that her mother frequently stuffed her full of tablets. She was never able to accept that her daughter was able to look after herself when she was ill. The patient had evidently been able to recognize and correct her pathological identification with her mother's attitude as a result of the analytic treatment she received. She states that she can now look 'after herself' and 'inside herself' and understand her state of health, instead of silencing her physical symptoms by taking medication.

Another patient reports: 'All in all, I have become more stable in terms of my health. I also look after myself better. I keep an eye on myself more. I eat only healthy food - something on which I place great value. Before, I used not to look after myself and now it is very important to me that I should feel well.' The interviewer notes at this point that her health has now obviously become her own concern, distancing her from the attitude of her mother, who regarded the patient's body as her particular concern and worried her with the fear that she could become anorexic.

Both these examples show how the patients' attitude to themselves and to their own physical state of health has changed by virtue of their psychoanalytic treatment. The way they feel is not something morbid, which needs to be warded off, but a matter for concern about themselves, for self-perception and for self-analytic reflection. These examples suggest the value of considering the question of whether and how long-term psychoanalytical treatment can intensify salutogenic factors and thus prove relevant for health economics too.

References

Antonovsky A (1987) Unraveling the Mystery of Health. How people manage stress and stay well. San Francisco: Jossey-Bass.

Antonovsky A (1993) The structure and properties of the sense of coherence scale. Social Sciences and Medicine 36: 725-33.

Antonovsky A, Maoz B, Dowty N, Wijsenbeek H (1971) Twenty-five years later. A limited study of the sequelae of the concentration camp experience. Social Psychiatry 6: 186-93.

Baumann Z (1999) Das Unbehagen in der Postmoderne. Hamburg: Hamburger Edition HIS.

Becker P (1982) Modelle der seelischen Gesundheit. Band 1: Theorien, Modelle, Diagnostik. Göttingen: Hogrefe.

Bohleber W (1992) Identität und Selbst. Die Bedeutung der neueren Entwicklungsforschung für die psychoanalytische Theorie des Selbst. Psyche 46: 58-84.

Bollas C (1992) Being a Character. Psychoanalysis and self experience. London: Routledge.

Fäh M (2000) Verbessert Psychotherapie die Moral? Inwiefern können grundlegende gesundheitsrelevante Lebensbewältigungseinstellungen durch psychologische Interventionen erworben bzw. verbessert werden? In: Wydler H, Kolip P, Abel T (eds) Kohärenzgefühl und Salutogenese - Grundlagen, Empirie und Praxis eines gesundheitswissenschaftlichen Konzeptes. München: Juventa, pp. 149-60.

Faltermeier T (1993) Gesundheitsbewusstsein und Gesundheitshandeln. Über den Umgang mit Gesundheit im Alltag. Weinheim: Psychologie Verlags Union.

Hargreaves WA, Shumway M, Hu T, Cuffel B (1998) Cost-Outcome Methods for Mental Health. San Diego: Academic Press.

Hurrelmann K (1988) Sozialisation und Gesundheit. Somatische, psychische und soziale Risikofaktoren im Lebenslauf. München: Juventa.

Rimann M, Udris I (1998) Kohärenzerleben (Sense of Coherence): Zentraler Bestandteil von Gesundheit oder Gesundheitsressource? In: Schüffel W, Brucks U, Johnen R, Köllner V, Lamprecht F, Schnyder U (eds) Handbuch der Salutogenese. Konzept und Praxis. Wiesbaden: Ullstein, pp. 351-64.

Sack M, Lamprecht W (1994) Lässt sich der 'sense of coherence' durch Psychotherapie beeinflussen? In: Lamprecht F, Johnen R (eds) Salutogenese - ein neue Konzept für die Psychosomatik. Frankfurt: VAS, pp. 186-93.

Sack M, Lamprecht W (1998) Forschungsaspekte zum 'Sense of Coherence'. In: Schüffel W, Brucks U, Johnen R, Köllner V, Lamprecht F, Schnyder U (eds) Handbuch der Salutogenese. Konzept und Praxis. Wiesbaden: Ullstein, pp. 326-40.

Sandell R (1997) Langzeitwirkung von Psychotherapie und Psychoanalyse. In: Leuzinger-Bohleber M, Stuhr U (eds) Psychoanalysen im Rückblick: Methoden, Ergebnisse und Perspektiven der neueren Katamneseforschung. Gießen: Psychosozial, pp. 348-65.

Schmid W (1998) Philosophie der Lebenskunst. Eine Grundlegung. Frankfurt: Fischer.

Sennett R (1998) Der Flexible Mensch. Die Kultur des neuer Kapitalismus. Berlin: Verlag.

Walker SR, Rosser RM (1993) Quality of Life Assessment: Key issues in the 1990s. Dordrecht: Kluwer.

CHAPTER 14

Efficacy and cost effectiveness aspects of outpatient (Jungian) psychoanalysis and psychotherapy – a catamnestic study

WOLFRAM KELLER, GISELA WESTHOFF, REINER DILG, ROBERT ROHNER, HANS HENNING STUDT AND THE STUDY GROUP ON EMPIRICAL PSYCHOTHERAPY RESEARCH IN ANALYTICAL PSYCHOLOGY[1]

Despite a large number of studies on the effectiveness of psychodynamic psychotherapy, when we began our work there were no studies on the efficacy and effectiveness of long-term psychoanalysis in a naturalistic setting, including Jungian psychoanalysts and psychotherapists in private practice. The reasons for this paucity of research include the long duration of prospective case studies and the high costs involved, as well as methodological difficulties involved in research in the field of private treatment practice. Psychoanalysis and psychoanalytic psychotherapy are increasingly under pressure to offer convincing evidence of their effectiveness. The study presented here is an effort to close this gap for Jungian therapy. The study was financed by independent funding (Bosch Family Foundation).[2]

Objectives

There were three objectives for this study:

- To prove the effectiveness of long-term analyses (more than 100 sessions) in routine treatment practice and to examine the stability of treatment results by a follow-up study six years after the end of therapy.
- To evaluate some aspects of cost effectiveness.
- To implement research strategies in the area of outpatient psychotherapeutic care for quality assurance purposes.

Methods and design

Central components of the study were, on the one hand, the follow-up of former patients via a questionnaire six years after the end of psychotherapy or psychoanalysis and, on the other hand, the recording of objective administrative data from health insurance claims (number of days off work or in hospital) five years before and after therapy. All members of the German Society for Analytical Psychology, the umbrella organization of Jungian psychoanalysts (DGAP), were asked to participate in the study: 78% answered our request, 24.6% participated.

Measures and sample

On the basis of their clinical notes, participating therapists in private practice documented all their cases (including dropouts) which terminated in 1987 and 1988. They completed a basic questionnaire regarding clinical and sociodemographic data, and setting characteristics, at the onset of therapy and gave a retrospective global assessment of their patients' state at the end of therapy.

Based on the diagnosis given in the funding claims of the former therapists, two independent raters reached a consensus concerning a retrospective ICD-10 classification. The severity of disease before treatment was also assessed using the Schepank impairment severity index (BSS) (1987, 1994)).

In 1994, 111 former patients who had finished either psychoanalysis or long-term psychotherapy in 1987 or 1988, and who agreed to take part in the study, were sent a follow-up questionnaire that included measures of life satisfaction, well-being, social functioning, personality traits, interpersonal problems, self-rated health care utilization and some psychometric tests (SCL-90R, VEV, Gießen-Test). In 33 cases (in the Berlin region), a follow-up interview was carried out and actual health status was rated by two independent psychologists trained in Jungian psychoanalysis.

Objective data on the utilization of health care services were also recorded from health insurance companies (number of days off work through sickness and inpatient hospital days) five years before and after therapy. Data were unavailable for a significant proportion of patients. In this comparison only those cases with complete data pre- and post-therapy were included. Thus, for this calculation, the sample was reduced to 47 (for analysis of sick days) and 58 (for analysis of hospital days). Neither subgroup differed from the complete sample in terms of sociodemographic data, pre-treatment characteristics or other criteria of treatment success.

The selection of the follow-up sample was controlled by comparing the study patients with the total of 351 therapist-documented therapies that finished in 1987 and 1988 with respect to sociodemographic and clinical characteristics. The selection of therapists participating in the study was controlled by an independent survey of all DGAP members with respect to characteristics of the therapists and settings. There was no difference between the groups, supporting the assumption that the study sample was representative of the clinical population.

Results

Status before treatment

A third (34%) of the patients had had symptoms for more than 10 years; 17% had a personality disorder and 46% were classified as affective disorders according to ICD-10.

In 96% of the patients psychotherapy was necessary because disturbance of emotional, psychosocial and physical functioning was above the clinical cut-off point. The mean impairment-severity score (BSS) for the total sample was 6.8. The clinical cut-off point for this measure is 5.0 or above (Schepank, 1987, 1994). Figure 14.1 shows the distribution of the BSS impairment-severity score prior to therapy and indicates that a substantial proportion of the sample were very severely handicapped, normally warranting hospitalization or partial hospitalization (score of nine or above).

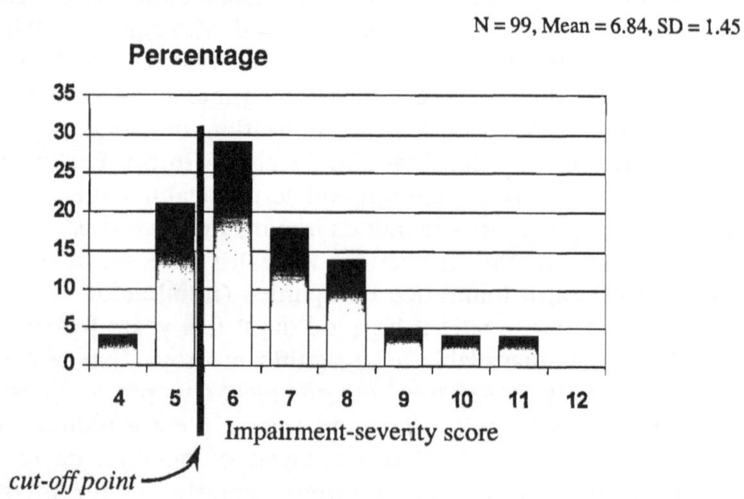

Figure 14.1. Total mean of impacts on emotional, psychosocial and physical functioning prior to psychotherapy.

Self-assessment of the patients at follow-up

Compared with their state before therapy, six years after the termination of treatment 70–94% of the former patients reported good to very good improvements with respect to physical or psychological distress, general well-being, life satisfaction, job performance and partner and family relations as well as social functioning.

Global state of health

The self-reported global state of health of the patients at follow-up was compared with a representative randomly assigned calibration sample drawn from a 'normal' population (Gerdes and Jäckel, 1992) adapted to the study with regard to sex and age. Overall, 88% of the follow-up sample's ratings fell within the 75th percentile of the reference sample, indicating that the global state of health of 88% of our sample could be seen as normal as rated by 75% of the calibration sample.

Clinical significance of global well-being

Global well-being was assessed using a six-point Likert scale (from very poor to very good). Of 60.4% ($n = 67$) of patients reporting their well-being as very poor prior to therapy, 86.6% ($n = 56$) rated their global well-being at follow-up (six years after termination of psychotherapy) as very good, good or moderate. This indicates improvement in global well-being long after the termination of treatment. These results have been confirmed by the Consumer's Report Study by Seligman (1995).

Relation between global success and treatment length

The addition of three total scores (ranging from 0 to 100) of different self-reported global ratings (degree of improvement of the complaints leading to need for psychotherapy, how much psychotherapy helped the patient, satisfaction with actual psychological and emotional state) created a global variable of therapy success. The relationship of therapy success to treatment length indicates the longer the treatment, the better the treatment success six years after termination of psychotherapy ($p < 0.05$) (Figure 14.2).

With regard to this criterion, long-term psychotherapy was more successful than short-term psychotherapy. Similar results were found by Seligman (1995) and Sandell (this volume).

The global assessment by former therapists

The global assessment by former therapists of the patients' state at the end of therapy shows a comparatively good agreement in terms of distribution with

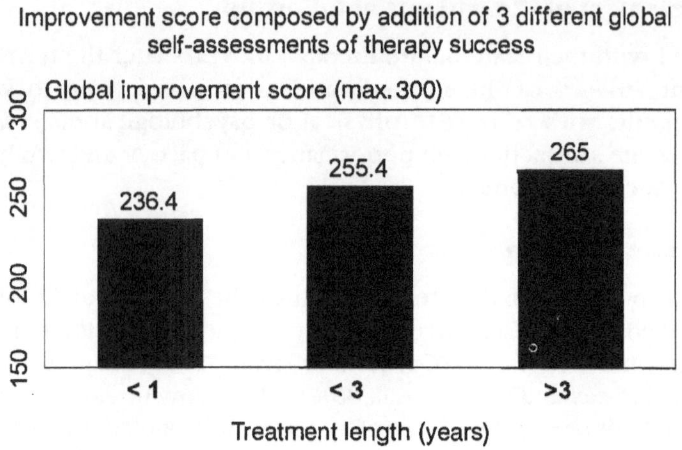

Figure 14.2. Treatment length and global therapy success.

the patients' own assessment at the time of follow-up six years after the end of therapy (*therapists:* 64.9% good, 29.7% moderate, 5.4% unchanged or deteriorated overall state; *patients:* 70.3% good, 22.5% moderate, 7.2% unchanged or deteriorated).

Results of psychometric test examinations at follow-up

SCL-90R

On standardized psychometric tests of state of health at follow-up, the sample tested lies within the range of healthy standard random samples and compares favourably with other clinical groups with respect to the relevant alteration qualities of symptoms. Figures 14.3 and 14.4 show the means of the nine subscales and global severity scores on the SCL-90R for the study sample compared with relevant standardization samples.

The global severity scores and the subscale scores of the Jung study sample indicate that, six years after treatment, this group with a relatively severe set of diagnoses pre-therapy was quite well-adjusted on all scales of psychopathology, and more like the normal comparison group than any of the clinical groups with which it shared diagnoses prior to therapy.

Gießen personality test (GT)

Standardized for sex and age, the Gießen test scales (T-values) range within the calibration values of two SDs from 50 for normal sample. Clinically significant disturbance is indicated by deviations greater than two SDs from

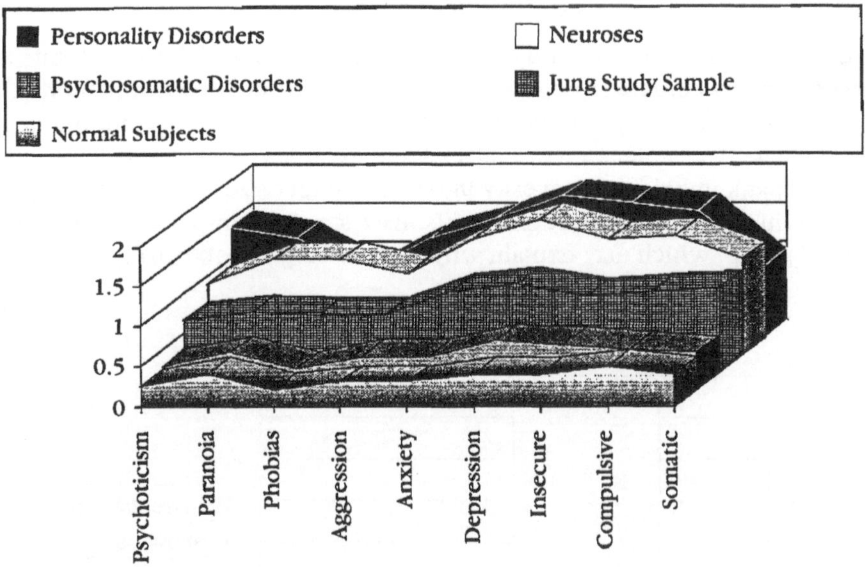

Figure 14.3. Mean SCL-90-R Scales on follow-up compared with standardization samples.

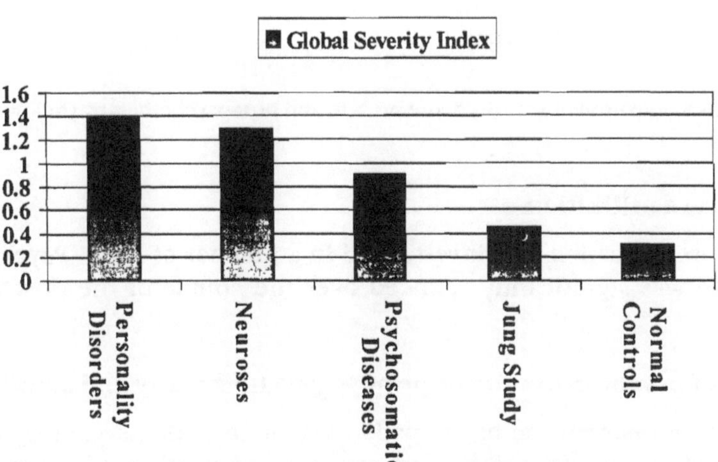

Figure 14.4. Mean SCL-90-R Global Severity Index on follow-up compared with standardization samples.

the mid-point of 50. The results obtained from the Jung study follow-up indicate that the means of these subjects fell within the normal range on all scales.

Change of the impairment severity score

In the comparative pre- and post-treatment expert rating of the actual state of disturbance by clinical interviews during the follow up, an examination of a subsample of n = 33 patients (regional sample of Berlin) by independent raters showed a significant ($p < 0.01$) decrease in severity of disturbance on the Schepank impairment severity index. The effect size was 2.1 (see Figure 14.5), which is large, although in this instance the comparison was not a control group, which may explain why the ES is larger than usual.

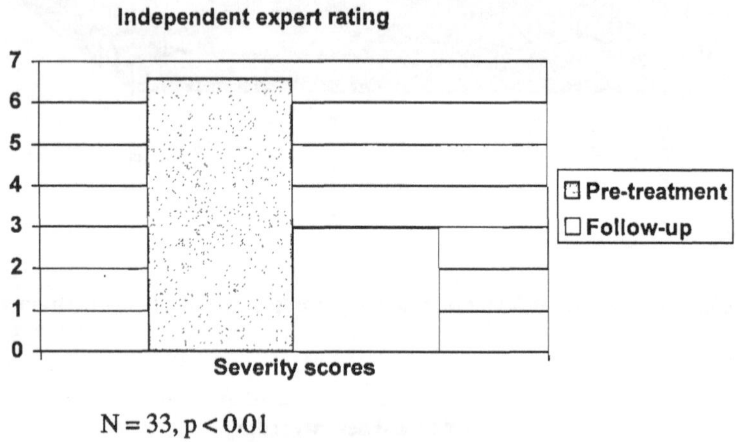

Figure 14.5. Impairment severity score prior to and post-psychotherapy (follow-up).

Healthcare utilization

Healthcare utilization was investigated in a number of ways. Psychotropic drug use was significantly reduced over the course of the post-therapy period.

Intake of psychotropic drugs prior to psychotherapy and at follow-up

An increased percentage of the patients no longer use psychotropic drugs compared to pre-psychotherapy and the proportion of those taking medication regularly reduced most substantially (Figure 14.6).

Frequency of medical visits (comparison of the year prior to psychotherapy and the year prior to follow-up)

Neurotic and personality-disordered patients often use resources by presenting at primary care physicians for physical symptoms or support.

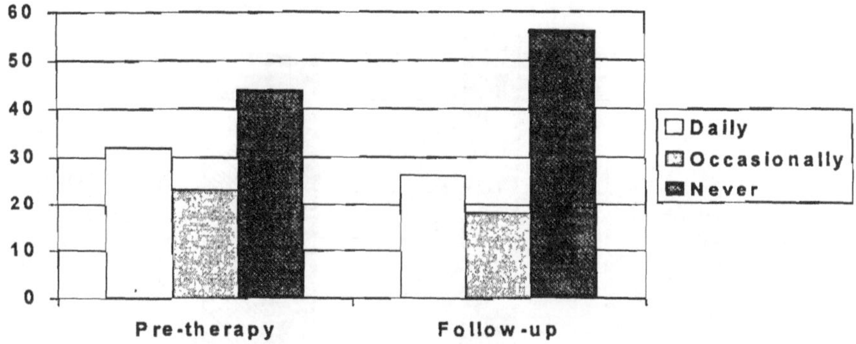

N=111

Figure 14.6. Intake of psychotropic drugs prior to psychotherapy and at follow-up.

More than half of the patients reported a substantial reduction in the frequency of doctor visits compared with the frequency of visits prior to psychotherapy. Only 8.1% had a higher frequency and nearly 40% reported an unchanged frequency in the year before the follow-up (Figure 14.7).

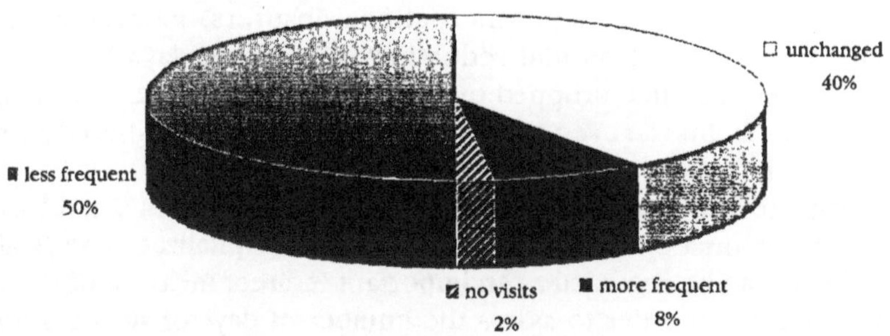

Figure 14.7. Frequency of medical visits (comparison of the year prior to psychotherapy and the year prior to follow-up).

Frequency of medical visits in the past year compared with two German studies of general practice attendance (DHP and EVas-Study)

The frequencies of medical visits in the year before follow up were substantially below the frequencies that would be expected on the basis of two representative studies of private practice patients (Hoffmeister et al., 1988; Schacht et al., 1989) (Figure 14.8).

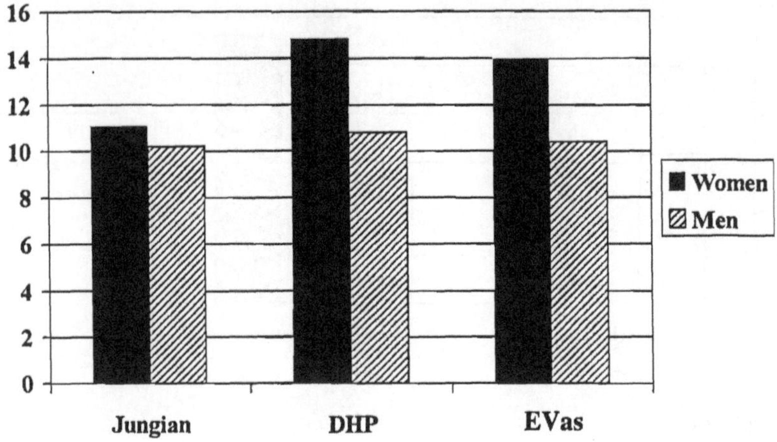

Figure 14.8. Frequency of medical visits in the past year compared with two German studies.

Mean number of work days lost per annum due to sickness and mean number of days of hospitalization

Perhaps the most meaningful index of resource use is days lost from work due to illness (sickness absence) and cost of hospitalization. An examination of the data recorded by third-party payers (national insurers) before and after treatment revealed a substantial reduction of working days lost due to sickness. Sickness absence dropped by 50% (from an average of 16 to eight days). At the same time an even greater reduction in hospitalization days was observed. The reduction was 87.5%, from an average of eight days per year before therapy to an average of one day per year after (Figures 14.9 and 14.10).

Generally, a reduction of sickness absence and hospitalization days after psychotherapy can be regarded as an important indirect measure of therapy success. However, in order to assess the number of days of sickness using insurance records, the study participants had to be continuously employed. Part of the sample therefore could not be included in this analysis. Thus the sample was reduced from 111 to 47 patients for analysis of sickness absence and to 58 patients for days of hospitalization.

Comparison with the mean values of the average population from a large health insurance company (Barmer Ersatzkasse)

An additional comparison with the mean values of the average population from a large health insurance company (Barmer Ersatzkasse) showed a reduction in objective work disability and hospitalization days for the Jung study sample against the mean population average (Figure 14.11).

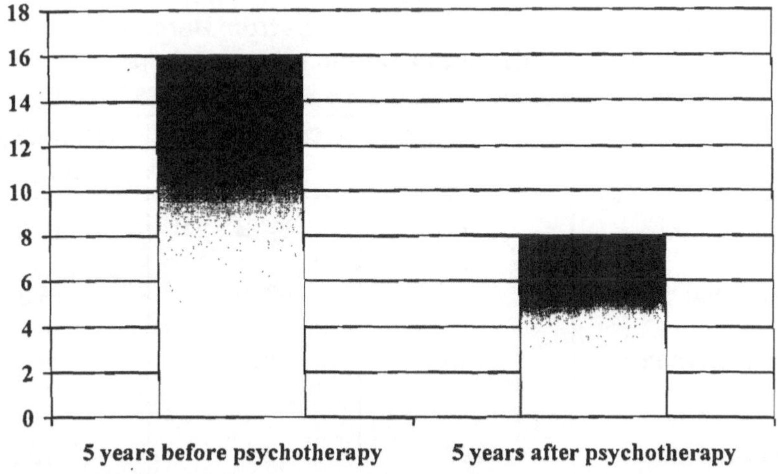

Figure 14.9. Mean number of work days lost per annum due to sickness five years before and five years after psychotherapy.

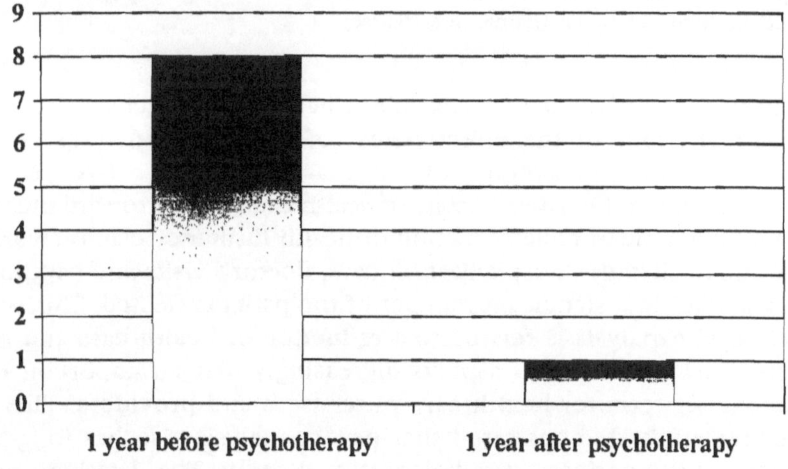

Figure 14.10. Mean number of days of hospitalization (one year before and after psychotherapy).

Conclusion

The effectiveness of Jungian psychoanalysis and psychotherapy was determined on the basis of a number of different perspectives and success criteria in a selected and not necessarily representative sample. Three

Comparison of the mean of work disability (WD) days 1 year before and after psychotherapy with the mean values from Barmer Ersatzkasse (BEK) Objective data from the care takers

	sum of WD (sum/100)	WD cases/100	WD duration (days)
1 year before	1456.1	61.4	41.6
1 year after therapy	819.6	59.6	13.5
1985 BEK mean ('pre')	1083	68	16
1989 BEK mean ('post')	1229	83	15

Sample N = 47 rounded to 100 patients

Figure 14.11. Comparison with the mean values of the average population from a large health insurance company (Barmer Ersatzkasse).

quarters (76%) of the patients examined had Jungian psychoanalysis so that empirical proof of the effectiveness of long-term analyses could be examined after an average of six years. Even after five years, the improvement in the patients' state of health and attitude toward the disease resulted in a measurable reduction of health insurance claims (work days lost due to sickness, hospitalization days, doctor's visits and psychotropic drug intake) in a significant number of the patients treated. This suggests that psychoanalysis is related to a reduction of health care and related costs. Cost effectiveness aspects increasingly play an important role as outcome criteria for health care purchasers and providers. This retrospective study demonstrated that psychoanalysis also has long-lasting effects on the patients' psychological wellbeing. The data here provide some convincing arguments for the effectiveness of psychoanalysis.

Notes

1. D. Baldus, R. Väth-Szusdziara, C. Weitze, R. Huntzinger, G. Betzner, H. Krause, P. Affeld-Niemeyer, A. Göttke, S. Loesche.
2. Foundation for Research on Education and the Handicapped: Robert Bosch; German Society for Analytical Psychology (DGAP).

References

Gerdes N, Jäckel WH (1992) 'Indikatoren des Reha-Status (Ires)' - Ein Patientenfragebogen zur Beurteilung von Rehabilitationsbedürftigkeit und -erfolg. Rehabilitation 31: 73-9.

Hoffmeister J, Hoeltz J, Schön D, Schröder E, Güther B (1988) Nationaler Untersuchungs-Survey und regionale Untersuchungs-Surveys der DHP (Deutsche Herz-Kreislauf-Praeventionsstudie). DHP Forum 3. Heft 1.

Schacht E, Schwartz FW, Kerek-Bodden HE (1989) Die EVaS-Studie. Eine Erhebung über die ambulante medizinische Versorgung in der BRD. Zentralinstitut für die kassenärztliche Versorgung: Köln.

Schepank H (1987) Psychogene Erkrankungen der Stadtbevölkerung - eine epidemiologische Studie in Mannheim. Heidelberg, New York, London, Paris, Tokyo: Springer.

Schepank H (1994) Der Beeinträchtigungsschwere-score (BSS) für psychogene Erkrankungen. Weinheim: Beltz.

Seligman MEP (1995) The effectiveness of psychotherapy - The Consumers Reports Study. American Psychologist 50: 965-74.

Prospective studies in psychoanalysis and long-term psychoanalytic treatments

CHAPTER 15

Structural changes in psychoanalytic therapies – the Heidelberg-Berlin Study on long-term psychoanalytic therapies (PAL)

GERD RUDOLF, TILMAN GRANDE, REINER DILG, THORSTEN JAKOBSEN, WOLFRAM KELLER, CLAUDIA OBERBRACHT, CLAUDIA PAULI-MAGNUS, SABINE STEHLE, STEFANIE WILKE

Introduction

The Heidelberg-Berlin study investigates the course taken and the results produced by high-frequency psychoanalytic psychotherapies in comparison with psychodynamic psychotherapies. The study is prospective and naturalistic in its design. The initial impulse for embarking on such a study was provided by the DGPT (Deutsche Gesellschaft für Psychoanalyse, Psychosomatik und Tiefenpsychologie - German Society for Psychoanalysis, Psychosomatic Medicine and Psychodynamic Psychology). In 1994 the society recognized the need for a study on the efficacy and efficiency of high-frequency long-term analytic therapies and invited proposals for such a study. This undertaking was a response to the increasingly heated political debate about the costs and benefits of the various forms of psychotherapy. That same year (1994) the Heidelberg research group put forward its proposal. Conditional upon the fulfilment of certain requirements (notably the conduct of a pilot study testing potential study instruments for their suitability), the project was granted financial support as of 1997. (Since then, further funding for the main project and related part projects was approved by the Robert Bosch Foundation, the German Research Council (DFG), the International Psychoanalytic Association (IPA) and the International Society for Analytic Psychology (ISAP).)

The study is being conducted in Heidelberg and in Berlin. The participants are experienced in psychotherapy research. The Berlin group has recently concluded an efficacy study on Jungian analyses concentrating *inter alia* on the cost-benefit aspect against the background of objective data on utilization of medical services (see Chapter 14). The experience gathered by the Heidelberg group dates back initially to the Berlin Psychotherapy Study investigating the course and outcomes of outpatient psychoanalyses and inpatient psychotherapies (Rudolf, 1991a). Since then, a number of studies of decisive importance for the preparatory stage of the present project have been carried out, all relating to inpatient psychotherapy (Grande, Oberbracht and Rudolf, 1998; Grande et al., 2001; Rudolf et al., 1996). Of equal significance was the group's involvement in the development of the Operationalized Psychodynamic Diagnostics instrument (OPD) (OPD Task Force, 2000; Grande and Jakobsen, 1998; Grande and Oberbracht, 2000; Rudolf, Oberbracht and Grande, 1998; Rudolf, Grande and Oberbracht, 2000), one of the central research tools of the present study. The OPD is one of the first investigative procedures to allow the systematic conduct of psychoanalytic diagnostics in a standardized form.

A crucial consideration at the planning stage of the project was the fact that so-called dose-effect models as proposed by Howard et al. (1986) are patently inadequate to the task of delineating the specific effects of psychoanalytic therapies. The reason for this is that while the customary measuring instruments used in psychotherapy research (for example, to test for symptom changes) are able to capture pronounced changes in the initial phase of therapy, they obviously fail to reflect, to any significant degree, effects achieved in the further course of therapy. The premature conclusion frequently drawn from such studies is that short-term therapies are sufficient because the essential effects are achieved in a short space of time. It is thus a central concern of the present study to capture more fundamental changes at the personality-structure level over and above more obviously perceptible symptom and behaviour changes. In the so-called Heidelberg Structural Change Scale (Grande, Rudolf and Oberbracht, 1997; Rudolf, Grande and Oberbracht, 2000), described in more detail below, we have at our disposal an instrument enabling us to capture the therapeutic changes in a way that is valid with regard to the intentions and aims of psychoanalytic treatment.

The main issues around which the study revolves are the specific effects of long-term analytic psychotherapies in general and the question of structural changes in particular. This further prompts inquiry into the way in which symptomatic and structural changes interrelate and structural (as opposed to 'merely symptomatic') changes have a bearing on the lives of the patients.

Such an inquiry of course necessarily implies a comparison between the effects of high-frequency and low-frequency analytic therapies. Recent studies (Sandell, Blomberg and Lazar, 1999) strongly suggest that frequency and setting differences make themselves most clearly felt in the years following the termination of therapy. Accordingly, a further central line of inquiry examines the changes taking place in that period; hence the research design also extends to follow-up studies. Another major issue addressed by the study is the cost–benefit ratio of high-frequency long-term analytic therapies.

Study design

Figure 15.1 shows the study design. It involves 30 patients receiving psychoanalysis at least three hours a week and 30 psychotherapy patients in a one-hour sedentary setting. At the outset of therapy the patients are examined diagnostically and a detailed clinical picture elaborated in each case. In the further course assessments are made at three- or six-monthly intervals all the way up to termination. Follow-up studies are to take place one and three years after the termination of therapy. The data collected during and at the end of therapy stem from four different vantage points: patient self-assessment, analyst assessment, objective data supplied by the health insurance institutions on the use made of medical services, and assessment by independent raters. The last-named information source is certainly unusual in connection with psychoanalytic therapies and represents an important contribution to the present study. An external rater interviews the patients, initially at three-month intervals, later at six-month intervals. These interviews are recorded on video for later assessment.

The patients admitted to the study display severe neurotic, psychosomatic and personality disorders. They are assessed for these before admission on the basis of pre-established criteria. Experienced psychoanalysts from the two regions (Heidelberg and Berlin) treat the patients. Every analyst is requested to contribute both a psychotherapy case and an analytic case, thus ensuring comparability on the therapist side. Both groups are matched for sex, age, education and severity of disorder so that patient comparability is also assured. The alternative - randomized group allocation - is hardly feasible under normal outpatient conditions and also carries substantial scientific risks (distortion of the object of study). Hence the decision in favour of a naturalistic design plus subsequent group matching. In many other details of the study care is also taken to ensure protection of the therapeutic situation and as little interference from our research as possible. Where a degree of impact is unavoidable this is documented both by the external raters and the analysts and included in the evaluation.

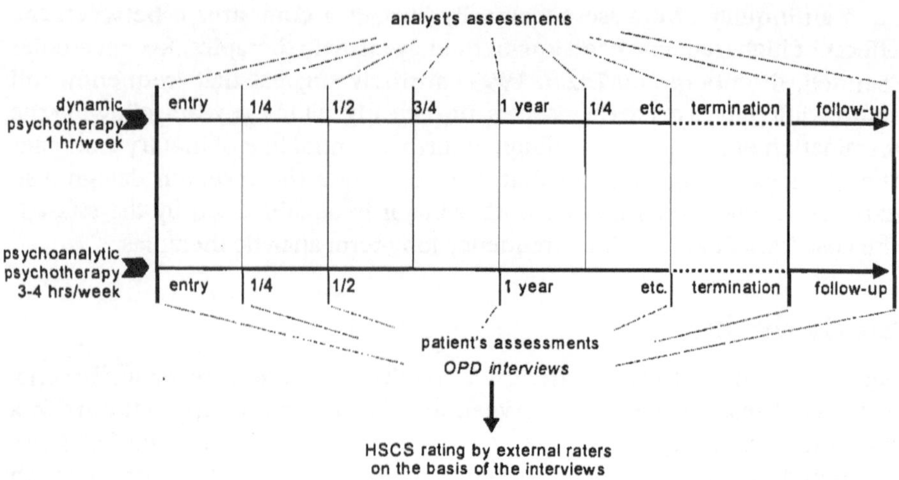

Figure 15.1. Study design.

Table 15.1 lists the instruments drawn on in the study. As noted earlier, psychoanalysis-specific instruments and assessment procedures were developed especially for the project, thus ensuring *congruence* between the description of the treatment object (psychoanalytic definition of disorder), the therapy intention (structural change), and the outcome (PTO-congruence, cf. Strupp, Schacht and Henry, 1988). The central areas covered by these instruments at the various levels of observation are:

- *Patient self-assessment* at the beginning and in the course of therapy: symptoms/personality traits/social status/socio demographic data/quality of life/SCL90-R, PSKB-Se (Psychic and Social-Communicative Questionnaire), IIP (Inventory of Interpersonal Problems).
- *Analyst assessment* at the outset: symptoms, diagnoses, conflicts, structural level, severity of impairment, initial working relationship, initial counter-transference.
- *Analyst assessment* in the course of therapy: session protocols, working alliance, counter-transference, therapeutic change.
- *Assessment by external raters* at the outset: OPD rating, diagnosis of personality disorders, focus selection.
- *Assessment by external raters* in the course of therapy: OPD rating, assessment of therapeutic change on the Heidelberg Structural Change Scale (HSCS).

Table 15.1. Measurement timetable and instruments

Time points	Patient self-assessments	Analysts' assessments	External raters	
Prior to therapy	Pat-1: social data, illness behaviour, SCL-90R, SG scale			
Therapy onset	Pat-2: PSKB-Se, IIP, SASB-Introject, ZSU	Analyst-1: initial diagnosis, TAB, SGRT	Ex-1: Significant life events	Ex-2: OPD, Focus selection, HSCS
3 months	Pat-3: illness behaviour, PSKB-Se, IIP, SASB-Introject, ZSU	Analyst-2: session protocols Analyst-3: notes on setting, symptomatology, process/themes, techniques/targets, therapeutic changes, TAB, SGRT	Ex-1: Significant life events	Ex-2: OPD, Focus selection, HSCS
6 months	Pat-3: illness behaviour, PSKB-Se, IIP, SASB-Introject, ZSU	Analyst-2: session protocols Analyst-3: notes on setting, symptomatology, process/themes, techniques/targets, therapeutic changes, TAB, SGRT	Ex-1: Significant life events	Ex-2: OPD, Focus selection, HSCS
9 months		Analyst-2: session protocols Analyst-3: notes on setting, symptomatology, process/themes, techniques/targets, therapeutic changes, TAB, SGRT		
1 year	Pat-3: illness behaviour, PSKB-Se, IIP, SASB-Introject, ZSU Pat-3x: SCL-90, SG scale	Analyst-2: session protocols Analyst-3: notes on setting, symptomatology, process/themes, techniques/targets, therapeutic changes, TAB, SGRT	Ex-1: Significant life events	Ex-2: OPD, Focus selection, HSCS
3 months		Analyst-2: session protocols Analyst-3: notes on setting, symptomatology, process/themes, techniques/targets, therapeutic changes, TAB, SGRT		

(contd.)

Table 15.1. (contd.)

Time-points	Patient self-assessments	Analysts' assessments	External raters	
6 months	Pat-3: illness behaviour, PSKB-Se, IIP, SASB-Introject, ZSU	Analyst-2: session protocols Analyst-3: notes on setting, symptomatology, process/themes, techniques/targets, therapeutic changes, TAB, SGRT	Ex-1: Significant life events	Ex-2: OPD, Focus selection, HSCS
9 months		Analyst-2: session protocols Analyst-3: notes on setting, symptomatology, process/themes, techniques/targets, therapeutic changes, TAB, SGRT		
2 years	Pat-3: illness behaviour, PSKB-Se, IIP, SASB-Introject, ZSU Pat-3x: SCL-90R, SG scale	Analyst-2: session protocols Analyst-3: notes on setting, symptomatology, process/themes, techniques/targets, therapeutic changes, TAB, SGRT	Ex-1: Significant life events	Ex-2: OPD, Focus selection, HSCS
Further ratings every 3 months (Analyst-2, Analyst-3) or every 6 months (Pat-3, Ex-1,Ex-2), every 12 months Pat-3x additionally				

Notes:

- *Contents of sheet Pat-1:* information on personal details, job, health insurance, social situation, health and health behaviour (items from the Berlin Jung study and the Berlin psychotherapy study, cf. Keller et al., 1997; Rudolf, 1991a); symptom checklist SCL-90R (Derogatis, Lipman and Covi, 1975); SG scale (from the TPF, Becker, 1989)
- *Contents of sheet Pat-2:* Psychic and Social-Communicative Questionnaire PSKB-Se (Rudolf, 1991b); Inventory of Interpersonal Problems IIP (Horowitz, Strauß and Kordy, 1993); INTREX-Introject questionnaire (Benjamin, 1974; Tress, 1993); Questionnaire on satisfaction in social environment (ZSU, newly developed for the project)
- *Contents of sheet Pat-3:* information on health and health behaviour (items from the Berlin Jung study and the Berlin psychotherapy study, cf. Keller et al., 1997; Rudolf, 1991a); Psychic and Social-Communicative Questionnaire PSKB-Se (Rudolf, 1991b); Inventory of Interpersonal Problems IIP (Horowitz, Strauß and Kordy, 1993); INTREX-Introject questionnaire (Benjamin, 1974; Tress, 1993)
- *Contents of sheet Pat-3x:* symptom checklist SCL-90R (Derogatis, Lipman and Covi, 1975); SG scale (from the TPF, Becker, 1989)

- *Contents of sheet Analyst-1:* ICD-10 (Dilling, Mombour and Schmidt, 1991); physical symptoms and psychic/social symptoms (lists from the Berlin psychotherapy study, Rudolf, 1991a); structural level (short version of OPD structural axis); mode of coping with conflict (Rudolf, Laszig and Henningsen, 1997); impairment/severity score BSS (Schepank, 1995); major social strains/entrapments and physical limitations; prognostically positive features (Rudolf, Laszig and Henningsen, 1997); psychodynamics and psychodynamic diagnosis; Initial Therapeutic Alliance iTAB (Grande, Porsch and Rudolf, 1988; Rudolf, Grande and Porsch, 1988; Rudolf, 1991a); Questionnaire on Therapist's Spontaneous Emotional Reactions SGRT (Grande, 1992).
- *Contents of sheet Analyst-2:* session protocols
- *Contents of sheet Analyst-3* (free descriptions and item lists): information on setting and interruptions in the last 3 months; significance of, and changes in, symptomatology over last 3 months; analytic process and co-operation; themes in therapeutic work; patient's approach to important themes; Therapeutic Alliance TAB (Grande, Porsch and Rudolf, 1988; Rudolf, 1991a); Questionnaire on Therapist's Spontaneous Emotional Reactions SGRT (Grande, 1992)
- *Contents of sheet Ex-1:* events and changes in various life spheres (item list)
- *Contents of sheet Ex-2:* assessment of the OPD axes 'relationships', 'conflict' and 'structure' (OPD Task Force 2000); focus selection; Heidelberg Structural Change Scale HSCS (Rudolf, Grande and Oberbracht, 2000)

- *Health insurance data:* number of days in hospital, sick leave, use of medical services three years prior to therapy and three years after termination of therapy.

With regard to statistical power, the number of patients (N = 30 for each group) is small in terms of experience with instruments customarily used to measure differential change. But the drawbacks of a small number of patients can be offset by the fine tuning of the differential hypotheses made possible in this project by the use of study instruments specifically designed for the psychoanalytic approach, notably the Structural Change Scale (HSCS, see below). Restricting the study to a relatively small number of cases also means that the use of time-consuming study procedures becomes a viable proposition. For example, the rating of one single videotaped interview (and the number of interviews per analysis can be anything from six to 12 and more, depending on length) takes 16.5 hours on average. No less time consuming are the qualitative text evaluation procedures used to study the written reports of the analysts on the course of therapy. The material thus gathered is so extensive and detailed as to make individual case studies feasible over and above group statistics.

A case study

As the data-collection phase of the study is not complete we cannot as yet present any final results. By drawing on an individual case study we can illustrate how the course taken by psychoanalysis shows up against the background of the various observation levels and data sources. The case in question is a course of therapy now entering its third year and not yet terminated. It is the analysis of a young man with pronounced somatic complaints, anxieties and an identity and self-esteem problem. For reasons of confidentiality we shall not disclose any further details at this point. In the following we describe the patient's self-assessment, the analyst's description of the course taken by therapy and the assessments by the external raters.

First observation level: patient's self-assessment

Figure 15.2 shows the progress of the symptomatology over the first two years of psychoanalysis, measured on the scales 'somatic anxiety symptoms', 'depression' and 'somatization' taken from the Psychic and Social Communicative Questionnaire (PSKB; Rudolf, 1991b). The ratings are expressed as T-values; scores below 60 can be regarded as clinically normal. The figure shows a drop in the initially very high physical complaint scores to a normal range after a period between six months and one year; thereafter

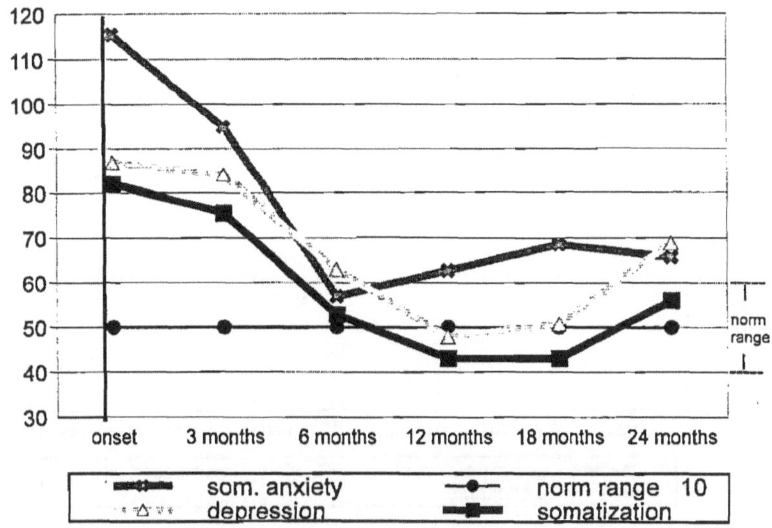

Figure 15.2. Somatic anxiety symptoms, depression and somatization in the course of therapy.

we have a reactivation of the symptomatology to a clinically abnormal score with respect to 'depression' and 'somatic anxiety symptoms'.

We find a very similar curve for the scales 'over-introverted', 'over-exploitable' and 'over-submissive' in the Inventory of Interpersonal Problems (IIP-D) (Horowitz, Strauss and Kordy, 1993), where the patient again had quite a high score at the outset (Figure 15.3). Here the reactivation trend in the second year of treatment was even more marked.

Second observation level: psychoanalyst's descriptions of the process

The analysts describe and assess the course of therapy with the aid of standardized questions and questionnaires; their main tool is, however, freely formulated written reports whose structure is only loosely predetermined. These texts have to be processed and condensed with the help of qualitative procedures to delineate the significant lines of the analytic process. The procedure is geared to content-analysis methods, thus generating content categories from the analysts' texts (Wilke, 1992; Strauss and Corbin, 1996).

Table 15.2 summarizes process notes made by the analyst on the course of treatment. These notes are allocated to two categories that resulted from the qualitative analysis: 'experience of relationships' and 'therapeutic

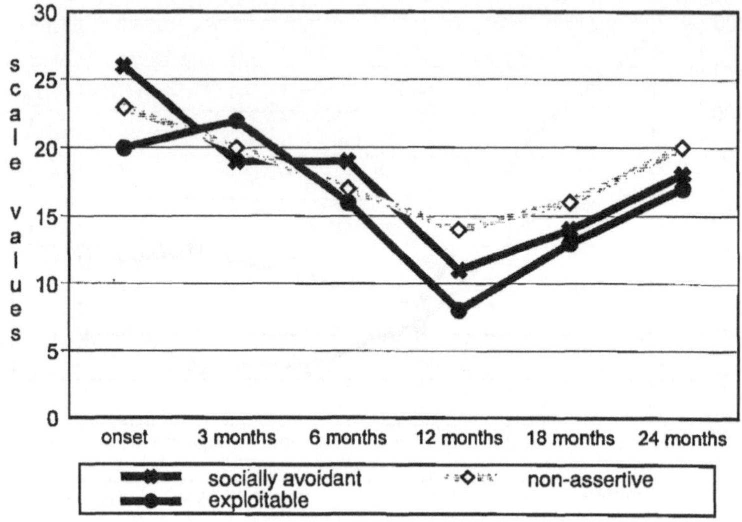

Figure 15.3. IIP scales 'socially avoidant', 'exploitable' and 'non-assertive' in the course of therapy.

Table 15.2. Qualitative evaluation of analyst's commentaries (brief summary)

	Experience in relationships	Therapeutic relationship
Onset	Marked guilt feelings in attempts at self-differentation from mother, accompanied by suicidal crisis	
3 months	Attempts at self-differentation from mother fail repeatedly, incipient anger at mother	Sudden onset of rage and self-distancing impulses versus guilt and shame feelings; fear of being overwhelmed; longing for a good father figure
6 months	Incestuous fantasies vis-à-vis mother more conscious; Pat moves out into an apartment of his own	Fear of engulfing less marked
1 year	Greater ability to sustain distance and independence without breaking off contact with mother	Thoughts of separation in the face of anxiety about severe internal aggression; at the same time increasing acknowledgment of therapist
1.5 years	Increasingly able to keep mother at a distance without breaking with her altogether; new: mourning over the difficult relationship with mother	Pat. moving between progression and regression; able to speak more openly about feelings; less anxiety about confiding in others, but fear of regressing too far
2 years	Pat. has applied for a scholarship so as to be more financially independent of mother	Torn between need for distance and longing for love; hardly any anxieties in the therapeutic relationship

relationship'. Naturally, numerous other content categories are of significance for the case in question. The two categories set out here have been selected for the purposes of the present description and the process notes much condensed. Both categories show a development in which the patient initially sets himself apart defensively and then achieves a greater ability to enter more deeply into the relationships. The latter process is bound up with the onset of feelings of depression.

Third observation level: assessments by external raters

A further stage in the study complements the viewpoints of patient and psychoanalyst with observations by external raters. In the following a degree of familiarity with the methodology used is required, so we shall now explain this in a brief excursus. The method can be represented as a sequence of four stages (for details see Grande, Rudolf and Oberbracht, 1997; Grande, Rudolf and Oberbracht, 2000; Rudolf, Grande and Oberbracht, 2000).

First stage: interview

The basis for the external rating is an interview linking aspects of the relationship episode interview according to Luborsky (see Dahlbender et al., 1993) with aspects of the Operationalized Psychodynamic Diagnostics (OPD) interview (Janssen et al., 1996). The patient is invited to report on episodes connected with encounters and interpersonal experiences. These episodes form the point of departure for a frank exchange about the patient's experience of self and objects; the interviewer also addresses various life spheres of significance for an assessment in accordance with OPD.

Second stage: OPD rating

On the basis of this (videotaped) interview, two raters assess independently of one another the findings of the OPD in relation to dysfunctional relationship patterns, life-determining conflicts and structural capacities/vulnerabilities (OPD axes II to IV). Table 15.3 shows these three diagnostic categories and their contents.

Third stage: focus selection

Table 15.3 lists a total of 30 individual features allocated to the three OPD axes 'relationship', 'conflict' and 'structure'. We call this the 'focus list' because it is used to select for each patient individual focal problems of central significance for the definition of his or her personality structure. Once the OPD rating has been established, the raters select five focal problems per patient from this list. The selection takes the form of an individualized psychodynamic hypothesis. The assumption is that the problems defined as

Table 15.3. OPD axes and focus list

Relationship Individualized formulation of a core dysfunctional relationship pattern	
Life-determining conflicts	
1. dependence/autonomy conflict	5. guilt conflicts
2. submission/control conflict	6. oedipal-sexual conflicts
3. care/autarchy conflict	7. identity conflicts
4. self-value conflicts	8. deficient awareness of feelings and conflicts
Structural capacities/vulnerabilities	
1. capacity for experience of self	4. capacity for object experience
self-reflection	*self-object differentiation*
image of self	*empathy*
identity	*awareness of total objects*
differentiation of affects	*object-related affects*
2. capacity for self-regulation	5. capacity for communication
affect tolerance	*contact*
regulation of self-esteem	*decoding other's affects*
regulation of impulses	*encoding own affects*
anticipation	*reciprocity*
3. capacity for defence	6. capacity for attachment
intrapsychic defences	*internalizations*
flexibility	*detaching*
	variability of relationships

focal are centrally instrumental in causing/sustaining the patient's present disorder and that they *must* be changed if any substantial improvement is to be brought about. In trials of this method the choice of five focus problems has proved to be satisfactory clinically and lends itself well to the requirements of research practice.

Fourth stage: assessment of structural change in the focal areas

To delineate the changes in the focal areas we use a scale that presents at the same time a general (not school-specific) model of therapeutic structural change in psychoanalytic psychotherapies. The scale (Figure 15.4) is an adaptation of a similar instrument by Stiles et al. (1992), the (significant) modification providing a much closer orientation to psychoanalytic theory. This Heidelberg Structural Change Scale (HSCS) enables us to assess the level of working-over and working-through attained by the patient at any given point in his/her engagement with the five focal areas. The procedures underlying focus selection and restructuring assessment have been tested in large-scale preliminary studies and have proven both practicable and reliable

Stages		Excerpt from the manual
1. *Focus problem warded off*	exact 1 match 1+ tendency↓	The problem is completely unconscious; experiences connected with it are evaded; problematic behaviour is ego-syntonic; the patient has 'no problems' with the critical area
2. *Unwanted preoccupation with the focus*	tendency↑ 2- exact 2 match 2+ tendency↓	Unpleasant feelings and thoughts in connection with the problem area can no longer be immediately rejected; but preoccupation with the problem is reluctant; external confrontations with the problem take place but are rejected as disturbances; no realisation that the problems might be associated with pat.'s own person
3. *Vague awareness of the focus*	tendency↑ 3- exact 3 match 3+ tendency↓	Patient notices/suspects the existence of a problem that is part of him/herself and cannot simply be rejected; in the course of repetition the problem takes on a continuing existence; negative affects originate from the tension between the insistent nature of the problem and the pat.'s defensive/aversive attitude
4. *Acceptance and exploration of the focus*	tendency↑ 4- exact 4 match 4+ tendency↓	The problem starts to take on a new shape in the pat.'s consciousness; incipient indications of an active, 'head-on' preoccupation with it; the problem can now be formulated as an 'assignment' and hence be made the subject of therapeutic work; destructive, rejecting responses may interfere with this attitude but can no longer undermine it altogether
5. *Deconstruction in the focus area*	tendency↑ 5- exact 5 match 5+ tendency↓	Querying and disintegration of accustomed coping modes; uncertainty about evaluations of own person and others; perception of own limitations and deficiencies; resignation and moods of despair alternate with urges toward reparation; old modes are lost and cut off, new ones not yet accessible
6. *Reorganisation in the focus area*	tendency↑ 6- exact 6 match 6+ tendency↓	Abandonment and final relinquishing of accustomed coping modes; in his/her own experience pat. is increasingly self-reliant and able to take in hand and assume responsibility for his/her own life in the problem area; increasingly conciliatory approach to problem area; problem solutions spontaneous and unexpected; re-integration
7. *Integration of the focus problem*	tendency↑ 7- exact 7 match	Dealing with the problem has become something natural; the area has lost its special significance in the eyes of the patient; the problem is something belonging to the past, as a memory

Figure 15.4. The Heidelberg Structural Change Scale (HSCS).

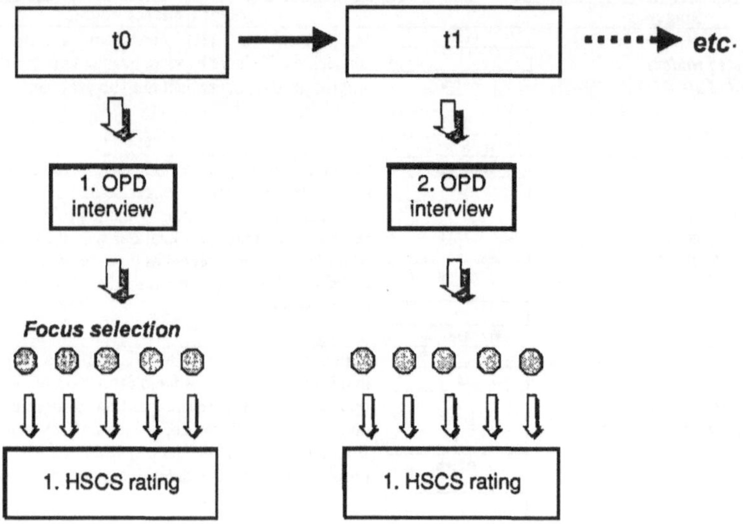

Figure 15.5. Overview of stages in measurement of structural change.

(Rudolf, Grande and Oberbracht 2000); validity evidence has also been adduced (Grande et al., 2001).

Figure 15.5 shows the procedure in overview. At the outset of therapy an interview is used to assess the OPD rating, the focal problems and the level of engagement on the Heidelberg Structural Change Scale (HSCS). At each new rating time-point the five focuses are reassessed on the basis of new interviews, thus pointing up the changes in the patient as shifts within the focal areas on the Structural Change Scale. The two raters are asked to arrive at a consensus on the basis of their independent judgements and to record this in a written commentary, thus producing a brief description of the level of engagement achieved for each of the focal areas.

Table 15.4 shows a condensed version of these commentaries for one of the focal problems of the young patient presented here for illustration purposes. The focus in question is 'detaching', figuring in the focus list (Table 15.3) as a structural capacity/vulnerability allocated to the OPD structure axis. As in the analyst's process description, we see here a development in which, over the period of two years, the patient moves through a defensive/anxious, and, at the same time, aggressive distancing from the object, to a more intensive involvement accompanied by ambivalence and feelings of depression.

The text information recorded in Table 15.4 is quantified through the data provided by the Heidelberg Structural Change Scale (HSCS). Figure 15.6

Table 15.4. External raters' commentaries on development with respect to the focus 'detaching' (condensed version)

	CT score[1]	Patient's management of focus problem
Onset	2+/A	Despair, depression and thoughts of suicide following separation from girlfriend; inability to live a life of his own; responsibility for this attributed to mother
3 months	4-/C	First rift in the union with the mother through realization that she will die some time; acknowledgement of having a part in this dependence; purchase of own washing machine; twin-like relationship with a friend
6 months	3-/B	Engagement with the focal problem has become vaguer again, much acting out in this connection; first meeting with father; welcomes analytic break because of fear of dependence on analyst
1 year	4-/D	Reflection on his 'fateful union' with the mother; hate and conciliatory reports on the mother, more differentiated, three-dimensional description of mother; interest in sexuality and own attractiveness; loosening of bonds with friend, more clearly delimited relationship; first emphasis of autonomy vis-à-vis interviewer
1.5 years	5-/D	Mourning over contradictory relationship with mother and guilt feelings; disappointed at relationship with father; feels wrongly treated in the analysis; makes indirect accusations in interview (dryness of mouth!); expresses longing for a girlfriend
2 years	6-/D	Describes being in love with new, object-related quality; mourning over lack of primary trust; systematic boundary-setting, aggression vis-à-vis mother followed by pangs of conscience

[1] cf. Figures 15.6 and 15.7

shows the shifts within the five focal topics over an observation period of 24 months. According to the raters' assessments there was successful progress in that period of psychoanalysis from a status of low awareness and absence of responsibility in connection with the focal problems to a conscious and responsible approach to them (Stage 4 of the Scale). In three focal areas the development has progressed to the stage where, according to our hypothesis, genuine structural change in the framework of a psychoanalytic process actually begins: at Stage 5 of the Scale processes are set in train in which the accustomed coping modes practised hitherto disintegrate, thus creating the preconditions necessary for the kind of re-integration resulting from genuine structural change. The Manual (see abridged version in Figure 15.4) speaks in this connection of uncertainty, resignation and despair, perception and ultimate acknowledgement of the patient's own limitations and impairments and depressive affects bound up with this.

Figure 15.6 gives a graphic representation of the degree of structural change achieved, and Figure 15.7 also shows the changes initiated by the patient in his outside life. This representation reflects growing awareness of the fact that what has been achieved in the analytic space must be implementation of the outside world in order to take on practical form in reality. We thus speak of the Structural Change Implementation Matrix. Figure 15.7 shows this matrix for the two focal areas where the patient displays a particularly high degree of development up to Stage 5 in the Structural Change Scale (detaching and Oedipal-sexual conflicts). We see the correlation between external changes and therapy progress: the patient is making concrete attempts to implement what he has achieved; in some significant instances he has already effected changes in the outside world.

Fourth observation level: health insurance data

This level reflects social and health policy implications; the use made of the health system and the cost-benefit aspect are of central significance here. The demands made by the patient on the healthcare system and the costs accruing from this behaviour prior to therapy are compared with the corresponding data after termination of therapy. This level has as yet no relevance

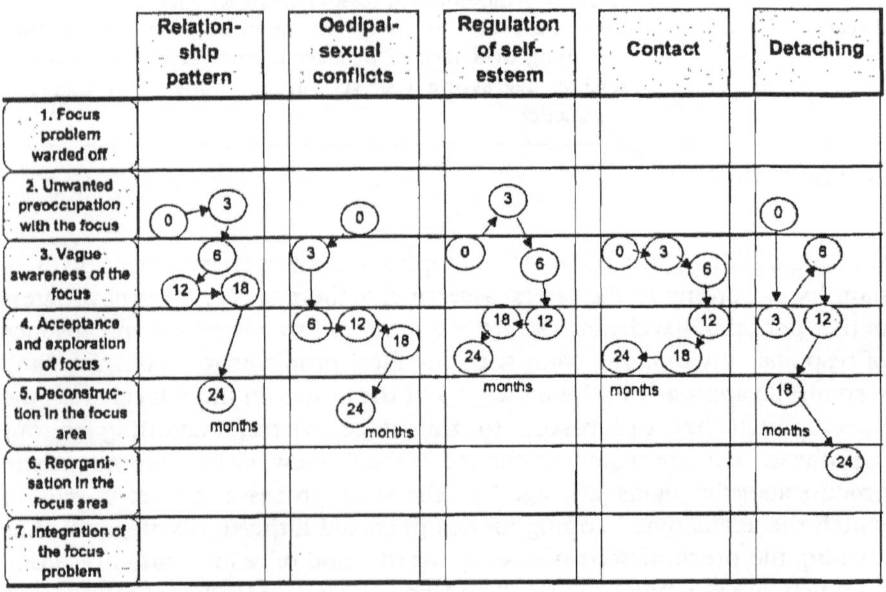

Figure 15.6. Structural change in the five focal areas.

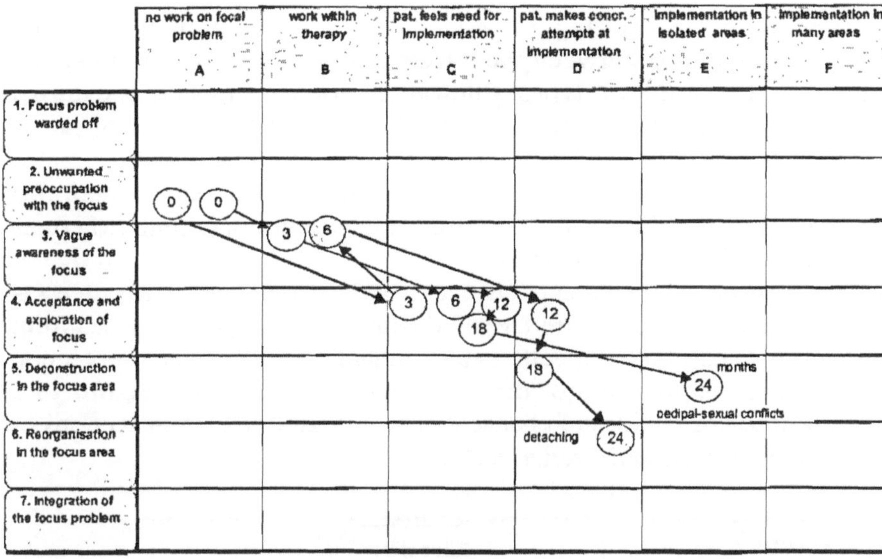

Figure 15.7. Development in two focal areas on the Structural Change Implementation Matrix.

for the ongoing therapy case discussed here and can only be reported on in the aftermath of the follow-up studies.

Synopsis of the case

We can summarize the course taken by our example case on the various observation levels as follows. In the first year the patient develops from a more 'unwanted preoccupation' with his problem areas (Stage 2 of the Structural Change Scale, Figure 15.4) to acceptance and exploration of his problems (Stage 4). During this period the somatic, psychic and interpersonal complaints disappear almost totally. At the beginning of the second year of therapy we see a qualitative difference. The patient experiences his problems more intensively. On the basis of the more firmly established therapeutic relationship he now ventures to, as it were, 'expose' himself to them. At the symptom level this goes hand in hand with a moderate reactivation of symptomatology and a clear increase in the interpersonal difficulties experienced by the patient. A phase of more intensive analytic working through has begun, which we allocate to Stage 5 ('deconstruction in the focus area') on the Structural Change Scale.

Structural and psychotherapeutic changes

In our discussion of a sample case, Stage 5 of the Structural Change Scale, and the temporarily destabilizing processes bound up with it, mark a caesura allowing a distinction between the effects of psychotherapies and psychoanalyses in terms of ideal types. Clinical experience shows that external changes may take a long time to materialize in psychoanalyses, appearing spontaneously at a later date when a solution has had sufficient time to mature inwardly. In terms of the process model we have developed, this occurs at Stages 6 and 7 when old, consolidated defence or coping structures have been deconstructed (Stage 5).

The spontaneous character of changes deriving from an analytic process is quite conceivably one feature clearly distinguishing psychoanalyses from other forms of psychotherapeutic treatment aiming at a specific therapeutic change either via focusing or direct educative intervention. Figure 15.8 shows how various modes of change can be allocated to certain sections of the Heidelberg Structural Change Scale.

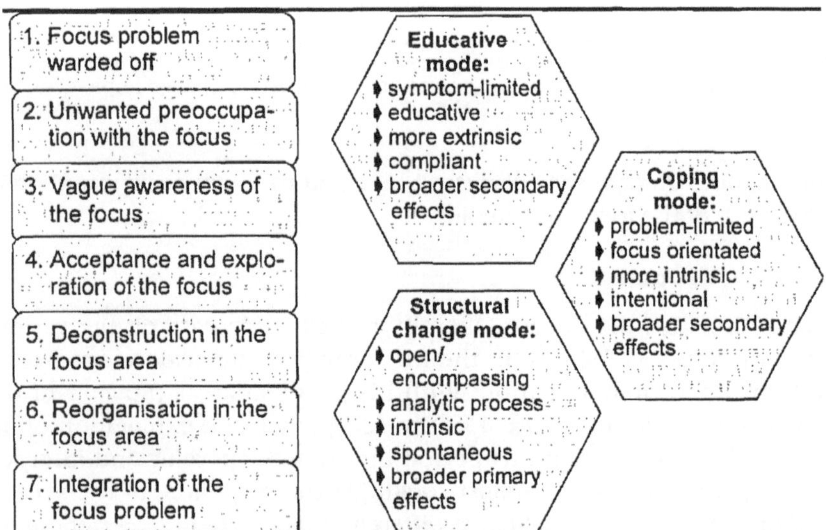

Figure 15.8. Modes of therapeutic change.

- At Stages 1 and 2 of the Scale, positive changes are most likely to be achieved if the therapeutic approach is symptom-related and educative. Here the patient is more extrinsically motivated in his attempts to bring about change and (in productive instances) behaves in a 'compliant', co-operative way. The changes themselves are correspondingly symptom-related. At a secondary level, however, coping with symptomatic impairments can definitely trigger notable other effects, for example via a gain in the subjective awareness of personal competence and an improvement in self-esteem, which in its turn may then generate further favourable effects of a nature not necessarily specific to the intentions of the therapy (educative mode).

- Distinct from this is a coping mode where the therapeutic approach is geared to the inner psychic problems connected with the symptomatology and sets out to uncover this focally. Patients' insights into their own problems gained via focal insights enable them to attain greater ability to manage these problems in the form of conscious regulation and to bring about change deliberately. Here the motivation is more intrinsic. From this mode broader positive effects may derive, as described above (coping mode).
- The third mode is the mode of structural change proper. Here the therapeutic approach is basically open and characterized by the willingness of the therapist to take comprehensive account of the personality of the patient in its conscious/unconscious forms of expression and to allow for an analytic process. Here again, the patient's changes are more intrinsically motivated but essentially they are not consciously desired but transpire spontaneously, sometimes surprising the patients themselves. The effects triggered by this mode are primarily broad in scope and at the same time specific to the equally broad therapeutic intention (structural change mode).

In principle, however, our working hypothesis for the study as a whole is that *in psychoanalysis there is a higher incidence of developments corresponding to the third change mode (structural change) and described by Stages 5 to 7 on the HSCS.* Vice versa, for psychotherapies we expect a higher frequency of changes taking place at Stages 3 and 4 and corresponding to the *coping mode.* This specific hypothesis is the central distinctive assumption of the study and will be subjected to verification via comparison between the groups.

Conclusions

In a recent paper, Wallerstein (1999) has listed a series of criteria psychoanalytic studies should satisfy in order to qualify as being up to date (he calls them 'third-generation' studies). A comparison between this list and the features of the study under discussion here shows that the Heidelberg-Berlin Long-term Analytic Therapy study largely matches the criteria and can hence be said to satisfy the requirements of modern psychoanalytic research. In line with Wallerstein's categories, the PAL Study:

- is a prospective, systematic study of psychoanalytic therapy;
- looks at clinically indicated therapies;
- has a significant number of cases;
- contains a comparison of psychoanalyses and psychotherapies;
- covers outcome and process equally;
- allows for individual longitudinal studies of each individual case;
- combines group-statistical techniques and presentations of individual cases;
- is grounded on well-defined psychoanalytic concepts and operationalizes them in rating scales;
- includes a thorough diagnostic description of the patients at the outset of therapy;
- distinguishes between outcomes achieved at the termination of therapy and developments in the post-analytic phase (follow-up);
- permits identification of process and outcome predictors.

We anticipate that this approach will do more than merely furnish global evidence for the superiority of one form of therapy over another. We expect it to supply a better understanding of the way in which various different processes achieve their effects, of the processes they set in train, and of the likelihood, not only of a good sustainable therapy outcome but also of the risks of standstill and failure. The structural change model developed by the authors and condensed in the Heidelberg Scale represents a viable method of imaging change processes beyond the symptom development level and hence of capturing the specific outcomes traceable to psychoanalysis in the therapeutic change process.

References

Becker P (1989) Der Trierer Persönlichkeitsfragebogen TPF. Göttingen: Hogrefe.

Benjamin LS (1974) Structural analysis of social behavior. Psychological Review 81: 395–425.

Dahlbender RW, Torres L, Reichert S, Stübner S, Frevert G, Kächele H (1993) Die Praxis des Beziehungsepisoden-Interviews. Zeitschrift für Psychosomatische Medizin und Psychoanalyse 39: 51–62.

Derogatis LR, Lipman RS, Covi L (1975) SCL 90. An outpatient psychiatric rating scale. Psychopharmacology Bulletin 9: 13–28. (The revised version, SCL 90-R, by LR Derogatis appeared in 1983 as an academic print.)

Deutsche Gesellschaft für Psychoanalyse, Psychotherapie, Psychosomatik und Tiefenpsychologie DGPT (1994) Ausschreibung eines Forschungsprojektes zur Effektivität und Effizienz höherfrequenter analytischer Langzeitpsychotherapie. Öffentliche Ausschreibung.

Dilling H, Mombour W, Schmidt MH (1991) Internationale Klassifikation psychischer Störungen. Bern etc.: Huber.

Grande T (1992) Fragebogen zu den spontanen gefühlshaften Reaktionen des Therapeuten auf den Patienten SGRT. Not published.

Grande T, Jakobsen Th (1998) Zur Notwendigkeit einer psychodynamischen Diagnostik und Veränderungsmessung in quantitativen Studien zur analytischen Psychotherapie und Psychoanalyse. In: Fäh M, Fischer G (eds) Sinn und Unsinn in der Psychotherapieforschung - Eine kritische Auseinandersetzung mit Aussagen und Forschungsmethoden. Gießen: Psychosozial-Verlag, pp. 125-37.

Grande T, Oberbracht C (2000) Die Konflikt-Checkliste. Ein anwenderfreundliches Hilfsmittel für die Konfliktdiagnostik nach OPD. In: Schneider W, Freyberger HJ (eds) Was leistet die OPD. Bern etc: Huber, pp. 74-102.

Grande T, Oberbracht C, Rudolf G (1998) Einige empirische Zusammenhänge zwischen den Achsen 'Beziehung', 'Konflikt' und 'Struktur'. In: Schauenburg H, Freyberger HJ, Cierpka M, Buchheim P (eds) OPD in der Praxis. Konzepte, Anwendungen, Ergebnisse der Operationalisierten Psychodynamischen Diagnostik. Bern: Huber, pp. 121-38.

Grande T, Porsch U, Rudolf G (1988) Muster therapeutischer Zusammenarbeit und ihre Beziehung zum Therapieergebnis. Zeitschrift für Psychosomatische Medizin und Psychoanalyse 34: 76-100.

Grande T, Rudolf G, Oberbracht C (1997) Die Praxisstudie Analytische Langzeittherapie. Ein Projekt zur prospektiven Untersuchung struktureller Veränderungen in Psychoanalysen. In: Leuzinger-Bohleber M, Stuhr U (eds) Psychoanalysen im Rückblick: Methoden, Ergebnisse und Perspektiven der neueren Katamneseforschung. Gießen: Psychosozial Verlag, pp. 415-31.

Grande T, Rudolf G, Oberbracht C (2000) Veränderungsmessung auf OPD-Basis - Schwierigkeiten und ein neues Konzept. In: Schneider W, Freyberger HJ (eds) Was leistet die OPD. Bern etc.: Huber, pp. 148-61.

Grande T, Rudolf G, Oberbracht C, Jakobsen T (2001) Therapeutische Veränderungen jenseits der Symptomatik - Wirkungen stationärer Psychotherapie im Licht der Heidelberger Umstrukturierungsskala. Zeitschrift für Psychosomatische Medizin und Psychotherapie 47: 213-33.

Horowitz LM, Strauß B, Kordy H (1993) Inventar zur Erfassung interpersoneller Probleme. Manual of the German Version.

Howard KI, Kopta SM, Krause MS, Orlinsky DE (1986) The dose-effect relationship in psychotherapy. American Psychologist 41: 159-64.

Janssen PL, Dahlbender RW, Freyberger HJ, Heuft G, Mans EJ, Rudolf G, Schneider W, Seidler GH (1996) Leitfaden zur psychodynamisch-diagnostischen Untersuchung. Psychotherapeut 41: 297-304.

OPD Task Force (ed) (2000) OPD - Operationalized Psychodynamic Diagnostics. Foundations and Manual. Seattle, Toronto, Bern, Göttingen: Hogrefe & Huber.

Rudolf G (1991a) Die therapeutische Arbeitsbeziehung. Untersuchungen zum Zustandekommen, Verlauf und Ergebnis analytischer Psychotherapien. Unter Mitarbeit von T. Grande und U. Porsch. Berlin: Springer.

Rudolf G (1991b) PSKB-Se - ein psychoanalytisch fundiertes Instrument zur Patienten-Selbsteinschätzung. Zeitschrift für Psychosomatische Medizin und Psychoanalyse 37: 350-60.

Rudolf G, Grande T, Oberbracht C (2000) Die Heidelberger Umstrukturierungsskala. Ein Modell der Veränderung in psychoanalytischen Therapien und seine Operationalisierung in einer Schätzskala. Psychotherapeut 45: 237-46.

Rudolf G, Grande T, Porsch U (1988) Die initiale Patient-Therapeut-Beziehung als Prädiktor des Behandlungsverlaufs. Zeitschrift für Psychosomatische Medizin und Psychoanalyse 34: 32-49.

Rudolf G, Laszig P, Henningsen P (1997) Dokumentation im Dienste von klinischer Forschung und Qualitätssicherung. Psychotherapeut 42: 145-55.

Rudolf G, Oberbracht C, Grande T (1998) Die Struktur-Checkliste. Ein anwenderfreundliches Hilfsmittel für die Strukturdiagnostik nach OPD. In: Schauenburg H, Freyberger HJ, Cierpka M, Buchheim P (eds) OPD in der Praxis. Konzepte, Anwendungen, Ergebnisse der Operationalisierten Psychodynamischen Diagnostik. Bern: Huber: 167-81.

Rudolf G, Grande T, Oberbracht C, Jakobsen T (1996) Erste empirische Untersuchungen zu einem neuen diagnostischen System: Die Operationalisierte Psychodynamische Diagnostik (OPD). Zeitschrift für Psychosomatische Medizin und Psychoanalyse 42: 343-57.

Sandell R, Blomberg J, Lazar A (1999) Wiederholte Langzeitkatamnesen von Langzeitpsychotherapien und Psychoanalysen. Zeitschrift für Psychosomatische Medizin und Psychotherapie 45: 43-56.

Schepank H (1995) BSS - Der Beeinträchtigungs-Schwere-Score. Göttingen: Beltz-Test.

Stiles WB, Meshot CM, Anderson TM, Sloan WW (1992) Assimilation of problematic experiences: The case of John Jones. Psychotherapy Research 2: 81-101.

Strauss A, Corbin J (1996) Grounded Theory: Grundlagen Qualitativer Sozialforschung. Weinheim.

Strupp HH, Schacht TE, Henry WP (1988) Problem-treatment-outcome congruence: A principle whose time has come. In: Dahl H, Kächele H, Thomä H (eds) Psychoanalytic Process Research Strategies. Berlin: Springer-Verlag, pp. 1-14.

Tress W (ed.) (1993) SASB - Die Strukturale Analyse Sozialen Verhaltens. Heidelberg: Asanger.

Wallerstein RS (1999) The Generations of Psychotherapy Research: An overview. Unpublished lecture to the Rapaport-Klein Study Group in Stockbridge, MA.

Wilke S (1992) Die erste Begegnung. Eine konversations- und inhaltsanalytische Untersuchung der Interaktion im psychoanalytischen Erstgespräch. Heidelberg: Asanger.

Chapter 16

The Munich Psychotherapy Study: a process–outcome comparison between psychoanalyses and psychodynamic psychotherapies

Dorothea Huber, Günther Klug, Michael von Rad

Introduction

The Munich Psychotherapy Study (MPS) has an unusual history because its beginning was a rare instance of therapists approaching researchers to evaluate empirically what they were doing in their everyday practice. They were, of course, especially interested in the effectiveness of their psychoanalyses and whether they achieved the outstanding results they were supposed to achieve. To answer this question a therapy comparison study was designed. The main research questions were:

- Are there any differences in effectiveness between psychoanalysis and psychodynamic psychotherapy? And if so, are those changes psychoanalysis brings about based on 'structural changes' and, because of this, are they more profound and more stable than those that psychodynamic psychotherapy brings about?
- Are there any links between therapeutic process and outcome? If so, what are they?

Study design

In order to answer the first research question a randomized control design was chosen to compare the two experimental groups.

One group of patients was treated with psychoanalysis (PA). Frequency was at least three times a week and in a recumbent position, with an average duration of 240 hours.

Another group of patients was treated with psychodynamic psychotherapy (PT). Frequency was once a week, and in an upright position, with an average duration of 80–120 hours.

As already stated, the effectiveness of the two treatments can only be evaluated correctly if the patients are assigned at random to the two experimental groups. Because of the relatively small number of patients in each group a strict allotment at random would lead to an uneven distribution of important patient variables, which was one of the main issues in the NIMH depression study (Elkin et al., 1989). Therefore we decided to stratify the patients with regard to severity of symptoms and age.

Please note that it is the therapies, and not the therapists, which are assigned at random so as not to interfere with the important, individual patient–therapist match.

Each patient of the outpatient department of the Institute for Psychosomatic Medicine, Psychotherapy and Medical Psychology of the Technical University of Munich who meets the inclusion criteria receives an extensive clinical intake interview that is recorded. Based on this recorded interview a board of three experienced psychoanalysts (the so-called 'indication board') decides if the patient can be randomly assigned to the two experimental groups. This decision process is documented as precisely as possible.

Each experimental group will comprise 30 patients in order to ensure a sufficient statistical power for the design.

The inclusion criteria are as follows:

- between 25 and 45 years of age;
- ICD-10 diagnosis: depressive episode or recurrent depressive disorder/ DSM-IV diagnosis: major depressive disorder (MDD);
- Beck Depression Inventory > 16;
- previous psychotherapy to be finished at least two years before entering the study;
- without anti-depressive medication;
- location in Munich or nearby;
- adequate German language skills.

The 12 therapists who are participating in the study are experienced psychoanalysts and psychotherapists in private practice and have been working with patients for at least five years. They were trained at an approved institution and graduated there. They apply only those therapies they are used to, and nobody is forced to apply a therapeutic modality he does not consider as suitable for a specific patient who has been referred to him.

Study measures

The data come from three different sources of observation: the patient, the therapist and the researcher ('external investigator'). The test battery of outcome measures is adapted to the core battery suggested by the Society of Psychotherapy Research (SPR) to be comparable with other ongoing studies. A main goal of the study is to measure not only symptoms and behaviour but especially mode-specific effects; therefore special instruments to measure structural change and individual therapeutic goals were administered. Structural change was measured with the Scales of Psychological Capacities (SPC), developed by Wallerstein and the PRP II group because there is some evidence from the reliability-studies of the PRP II group and other validity studies (Huber and Klug, 1997) that it is reliable and valid, and, on the whole, a very promising instrument. Individual goals are assessed by means of the Goal Attainment Scaling, developed by Kiresuk and Sherman in 1968, which in the Heidelberg Study of von Rad et al. (1998) showed an interesting discrimination between PA and PT.

Assessing structural change with the Scales of Psychological Capacities (SPC)

The Scales of Psychological Capacities (SPC; Wallerstein, 1988, 1991; Zilberg et al., 1991; DeWitt et al., 1991) are expert-rated measures that are theoretically informed but not theory specific, and evaluate the level of psychic structure. They have been developed from the research methodology of the Psychotherapy Research Project (PRP) of the Menninger Foundation (Wallerstein, 1986), and aim to operationalize the concepts of 'psychic structure' and 'structural change' as independently as possible of the differing theoretical perspectives in psychoanalysis, to be able to assess reliably the specific changes after psychoanalyses and psychodynamic psychotherapies - and after other psychotherapies, like behaviour therapy as well (Wallerstein, personal communication, 1999). Bound to an empirical research strategy these Psychological Capacities are designed to be as low-level (experience-near) constructs as possible, and readily inferable from observable behaviours and conscious states of mind so that underlying 'hidden' intrapsychic structures and their changes after treatment and after follow-up periods can be reliably captured.

The Psychological Capacities consist of 17 dimensions, 13 of which are divided into two subdimensions and three of which are divided into three subdimensions. One dimension is not divided; in all 36 subdimensions are assessed.

The assessment of all subdimensions is based on a tape-recorded, one-hour clinical intake interview, together with a special semi-structured SPC interview with probe questions, of one to two hours, developed by the test author and his group, and translated into German by the second author (of this article).

The material gained in this way will be scored for each subdimension on a seven-point scale from '0' for 'normal' or fully adaptive functioning to '3' for functioning that is seriously and obviously disturbed. The dimensions are constructed so that one subdimension is designated for different degrees of inhibited functioning and another for different degrees of exaggerated functioning. Both directions have to be assessed and both subdimensions can be scored simultaneously (corresponding to the concept of splitting). The rating procedure requires an extensive manual with a detailed description of each subdimension together with one or more clinical vignettes to anchor each scale point.

The first authors (DH and GK) have attended a rater training according to the formal method (Mercer and Loesch, 1979) with the PRP-II group at the California Pacific Medical Center in San Francisco, and are training new German raters. An inter-rater reliability study with these three raters is in progress. At the moment the manual is used in the English original version; a German translation is planned, together with a back-translation into English controlled by the test author to comply with generally accepted research standards.

A construct validity study of the SPC was performed by Huber and Klug in 1997. They demonstrated with a sample of 41 depressed patients that there are no significant correlations between the SPC and symptoms measured by the Symptom Check List (SCL-90; Derogatis, Lipman and Covi, 1975) and the Symptom Severity Score (BSS; Schepank, 1995) respectively. There was no significant correlation between the SPC and the Global Assessment of Functioning (GAF; American Psychiatric Association, 1994). There were 10 significant medium-range correlations (rr: 49–64) between the SPC and the Inventory of Interpersonal Problems (IIP; German version, Horowitz, Strauß and Kordy, 1994). This evidence of the discriminant and convergent construct validity confirms the theory, and there is therefore substantial evidence that the SPC measures neither symptoms nor their influence on the personality, and measures something similar but not identical to interpersonal functioning.

Convergent construct validity was examined in a further study by prospectively (that means before the respective subdimensions were scored based on empirical material) constructing hypothetically expectable 'prototypic' profiles of neurotic depressive patients. 'Prototypic profiles' predicted - with one exception - the empirically found, calculated mean profiles of depressive patients very well, demonstrating a high consensus between clinical judgement and SPC ratings (Klug, Huber and von Rad, 1997).

The procedural plan (schedule) of the study is shown in Table 16.1.

Table 16.1. Procedural plan of the study, MPS (see text for abbreviations of the instruments)

Pre-treatment measurement	External investigator 1 and patient: intake interview, ICD-10 and DSM-IV diagnosis, GAF, BADO, BDI (>16), BSS, HAMD Board of three experienced analysts: decision on patient's inclusion in the study and on randomized allocation External investigator 1 and patient: SPC interview; informed consent Patient: self-report questionnaires: BDI, SCL-90-R, IIP, FKBS, INTREX, SOZU, BADO, FLZ, FPI-R External investigator 1 and patient: assessment of individual goals (goal attainment scaling GAS) Referral to therapist Therapist: documentation of diagnosis, psychodynamic hypothesis, level of personality organization, treatment goals, prognosis, HAQ-T
Process measurement	Audio-recording of every session Patient: self-report questionnaires: BDI, SCL-90-R, IIP, GAS and HAQ-P every 6 months Therapist: therapy card to be filled out after every session; periodical process rating scale with HAQ-T every 6 months
Post-treatment measurement	External investigator 2 ('blind' to applied therapy) and patient: post-treatment interview, SPC interview, life events checklist, ICD-10 and DSM-IV diagnosis, GAF, BSS, HAMD, BADO Patient: self-report questionnaires: BDI, SCL-90-R, IIP, FKBS, INTREX, SOZU, BADO, FLZ, FPI-R, GAS, HAQ-P, VEV Therapist: periodical process rating scale and HAQ-T, assessment of termination of treatment
Follow-up measurement (every year)	External investigator 2 and patient: follow-up interview, SPC interview, life events checklist, ICD-10 and DSM-IV diagnosis, GAF, BSS, HAMD, BADO Patient: self-report questionnaires: BDI, SCL-90-R, IIP, FKBS, INTREX, SOZU, BADO, FLZ, FPI-R, GAS, VEV

After the intake interview with ICD-10 and DSM-IV diagnosis and a positive decision by the 'indication board', the external investigator interviews the patient with a semi-structured SPC interview to get the necessary information to score the SPC scales. The self-report questionnaires are handed out to the patient and they sign the informed consent. In a last pre-treatment session, the external investigator and the patient assess together the individual goals the patient wants to achieve during the therapy.

Afterwards the patient will be assigned to one of the experimental groups so that the external investigator is 'blind' for therapeutic modality during the pre-treatment measurement.

Before the treatment starts the patient fills out the following self-report questionnaires:

- Symptom Check List (SCL-90-R, Derogatis; Lipman, Covi and 1975; German version Franke, 1995).
- Beck Depression Inventory (BDI; Beck, Ward, Mendelson, Mock and Erbaugh, 1961; German version Hautzinger, Bailer, Worall and Keller, 1995).
- Inventory of Interpersonal Problems, short version (IIP-C; Horowitz, Rosenberg, Bauer, Ureno and Villasenor, 1988; German version Horowitz, Strauß and Kordy, 1994).
- Introject questionnaire (INTREX and Benjamin, 1974; German version Tress, 1993).
- Questionnaire for Coping Strategies (FKBS; Hentschel, 1998).
- Freiburg Personality Inventory, revised version (FPI-R; Fahrenberg, Selg and Haempel, 1986).
- Questionnaire of Life Satisfaction (FLZ; Huber, Henrich and Herschbach, 1988).
- Basic documentation of the German College of Psychosomatic Medicine (BADO; Broda et al., 1993).
- Questionnaire of Social Support, short version (F-SOZU-K-22; Sommer and Fydrich, 1991).

The therapist fills out the Helping Alliance Questionnaire (HAQ-T) (Alexander and Luborsky, 1986; German version: Bassler, Potratz and Krauthauser, 1995) and a documentation form with psychodynamic diagnoses, main defences, level of personality organization, motivation, main psychodynamic hypotheses, treatment goals and prognosis.

During the ongoing therapeutic process neither the patient nor the therapist will be contacted personally, so as to minimize interference with the process; of course, research itself as an observation inevitably influences the process. The process measures will be sent to patient and psychotherapist by mail.

The therapist records each session on an audio-recorder and fills out a therapy card immediately after each session comprising the patient's code, therapist's code, date, number of session, main session theme, special events, intensity of work with transference and assessment of session's quality.

Every six months the therapist will receive the Periodical Process Rating Scales with questions about transference, resistance, analytic work, technique, setting, sessions relevant for patient change, counter-transference, dealing with current life events and with treatment parameters and main unconscious themes.

Every six months the patient will receive the following five measures already mentioned:

- Symptom Check List (SCL-90-R; Derogatis, Lipman and Covi, 1995; German version Franke, 1995).
- Beck Depression Inventory (BDI; Beck, Ward, Mendelson, Mock and Erbaugh, 1961; German version Hautzinger, Bailer, Worall and Keller, 1995).
- Inventory of Interpersonal Problems, short version (IIP-C; Horowitz, Rosenberg, Bauer, Ureno and Villasenor, 1988; German version Horowitz, Strauß and Kordy, 1994).
- Goal Attainment Scaling (GAS; Kiresuk and Sherman 1968; Kiresuk, Smith and Cardillo, 1994).
- Helping Alliance Questionnaire (HAQ-P; Alexander and Luborsky, 1986; German version Bassler, Potratz and Krauthauser, 1995).

Measurement points for the outcome measures are at pre-treatment, at post-treatment and at follow-up each year after the end of treatment. The external investigator 2 at post-treatment and follow-up will not be the same as at pre-treatment, and will be 'blind' to the therapeutic modality that has been applied.

At post-treatment and follow-up the patient and external investigator 2 meet, and the pre-treatment instruments will be used again. In addition, a retrospective life event checklist and a self-report questionnaire of Change in Experiencing and Behaviour (VEV) (Zielke and Kopf-Mehnert, 1978) are added.

The therapist evaluates the transference–counter-transference situation at the end of treatment.

Results

Preliminary results from the first process measurement, half a year after beginning of treatment will be set out - with all the necessary qualifications regarding an ongoing study with incomplete recruitment of patients.

The research question to be answered is the following: are there any differences between psychoanalysis and psychodynamic psychotherapy during the first half-year of treatment regarding: the attainment of the individual patients' goals; the therapists' assessment of the therapeutic process; and the patients' assessment of the therapeutic alliance?

The first hypothesis is that patients' attainments of their individual therapeutic goals do not differ between the two experimental groups, because in the opening phase of psychoanalysis its typical curative factors have not yet developed. The second hypothesis is that there are differences in the therapeutic process between the two experimental groups as regards

- therapists' assessment, even when the typical features of the psychoanalytic process could not yet develop; and
- the patients' experience of the therapeutic alliance

because the more problem-centred and goal-directed technique of psychodynamic psychotherapy, with fewer possibilities for regression, produces fewer unpleasant affects and in this way leads to a higher level of satisfaction with the therapeutic alliance.

Data from the first process measurement, performed half a year after the beginning of treatment have been selected to investigate this question: 42 patients passed the first six-month measurement, 21 of them in the psychoanalysis group, and 21 of them in the psychotherapy group. According to the inclusion criteria they have an ICD-10 diagnosis of depressive episode or recurrent depressive disorder; mean age is 34 years, mean BDI is 24; there are 13 men and 29 women in the sample. There is no significant difference in age, BDI-score or sex distribution between the groups.

Patient and external investigator together defined individual therapy goals in three different domains, and formulated five steps to reach this goal (any deterioration, no change, first step towards reaching the goal, reaching realistic goal, and one step further than expected in reaching the realistic goal). The external investigator's task was to operationalize the goals together with the patient and to formulate a series of equidistant steps to reach the goals; it was the patient's task to define the goals as precisely as possible.

As expected (first hypothesis), there was no significant difference between the two experimental groups at that measurement point in any of the three domains (first domain: $\chi^2 = 2.65$, df = 3, n.s.; second domain: $\chi^2 = 2.97$, df = 4, n.s.; third domain: $\chi^2 = 3.41$, df = 2, n.s.). Out of 42 patients, 29 have reached the first step, 10 patients have reached the realistic therapy goal and three patients are beyond the realistic therapy goal as conceived of at beginning of treatment.

The Periodical Process Rating Scales, filled out by the therapists every half year, were selected to evaluate the therapeutic process from the therapists' points of view. Eighteen out of 218 variables in the Periodical Process Rating Scales, which could be expected to give an idea of the therapist's technique, and of the intensity of the patient's reactions to it, were chosen and compared for the two experimental groups. Luborsky's Helping Alliance Questionnaire (HAQ-P, German version) with its two factors - satisfaction with relationship, and satisfaction with success of treatment - published by

Bassler, Potratz and Krauthauser (1995) was chosen to give another window on to the continuing therapeutic process.

The variables of the two experimental groups were compared on an ordinal scale level by a non-parametric test, the Wilcoxon test. There were no significant differences between the 18 variables of the Periodical Process Rating Scale for a two-way test and a 5% significance level, except for the variable 'affective tone of transference' ($W = 291.5$, $Z = -2.03$, $p = 0.042$). It is clearly more negative in the psychoanalysis group, showing more variance (mean = 3.0; SD = 1.48) than in the psychotherapy group (mean = 2.11; SD = 0.83). No significant differences could be found in the two factors of the HAQ-P between the two experimental groups.

The first part of the second hypothesis can be regarded as partly confirmed. The more negative tone of transference in the psychoanalysis group can be interpreted as an indication of the growing tension in the therapeutic dyad. It has to be attributed to the analytic attitude of the therapist, because the data do not point to a generally increased disposition towards negative transference on the patients' side in the psychoanalysis group. Interestingly enough the patients themselves do not seem to recognize the tension; they do not score a more negative experience in the helping alliance measured with the HAQ-P.

Obviously, the second part of the second hypothesis was refuted. There seems to be some evidence that in the opening phase of a psychoanalysis the positive affects of the therapeutic 'honeymoon' prevail in the patient's consciousness whereas the negative affects in this group are still unconscious and only recognized by the therapist.

Finally, the validity of the later findings is qualified because:

- although the therapists consider the Periodical Process Rating Scales a useful and feasible instrument, and although the essentials of psychoanalytic theory were used in constructing our instrument, an examination of their psychometric properties certainly needs to be done; and
- a lot of process variables could not be controlled and many alternative explanations for the findings are therefore possible.

On the whole, these findings are to be regarded as a trend, and not as a definite result, because not all patients of the two experimental groups could be analysed statistically to this point. Therefore, more sophisticated research questions will be investigated only when data from all patients are available.

Acknowledgement

The rater training of the first two authors (DH and GK) with the PRP-II group in San Francisco at the California Pacific Medical Center was supported by the German Research Foundation DFG (444 USA 111/3/98). The inter-rater-reliability study with the SPC is funded by a grant of the IPA.

References

Alexander LB, Luborsky L (1986) The Penn Helping Alliance Scales. In: Greenberg LS, Pinsof W (eds). The Psychotherapeutic Process: A research handbook. New York: Guilford Press, pp. 325-66.

American Psychiatric Association (1994) Diagnostic and Statistical Manual of Mental Disorders, 4th edn, Washington, DC: APA.

Bassler M, Potratz B, Krauthauser H (1995) Der 'Helping Alliance Questionnaire' (HAQ) von Luborsky. Psychotherapeutics 40: 23-32.

Beck AT, Ward CH, Mendelsohn M, Mock J, Erbaugh J (1961) An inventory for measuring depression. Arch Gen Psychiat 4: 561-71.

Benjamin LS (1974) Structural analysis of social behaviour. Psychological Review 81: 392-425.

Broda M, Dahlbender RW, Schmidt J, Rad M von, Schors R (1993) DKPM-Basisdokumentation. Eine einheitliche Basisdokumentation für die stationäre Psychosomatik und Psychotherapie. Psychother Psychosom Med Psychol 43: 214-23.

Derogatis LR, Lipman RS, Covi L (1975) SCL-90. An outpatient psychiatric rating scale. Psychopharmacology Bulletin 9: 13-28.

DeWitt KN, Hartley D, Rosenberg SE, Zilberg NJ, Wallerstein RS (1991) Scales of psychological capacities: Development of an assessment approach. Psychoanalysis and Contemporary Thought 14: 334-43.

Elkin I, Shea MT, Watkins JT, Imber SD, Sotsky SM, Collins JF, Glass DR, Pilkonis PA, Leber WR, Docherty JP, Fiester SJ, Parloff MB (1989) National Institute of Mental Health Treatment of Depression Collaborative Research Program: General effectiveness of treatments. Arch Gen Psychiat 46: 971-82.

Fahrenberg J, Selg H, Hampel P (1986) Das Freiburger Persoenlichkeitsinventar (FPI-R). Göttingen: Hogrefe.

Franke G (1995) Die Symptom-Checkliste von Derogatis. Deutsche Version. Manual. Göttingen: Beltz.

Hautzinger M, Bailer M, Worall H, Keller F (1995) Das Beck-Depressions-Inventar (BDI). Göttingen: Hogrefe.

Hentschel U (1998) Fragebogen zu Konfliktbewältigungsstrategien. Göttingen: Hogrefe.

Horowitz LM, Rosenberg SE, Bauer BA, Ureno G, Villasenor VS (1988) Inventory of Interpersonal Problems: Psychometric properties and clinical applications. J Clin Consul Psychol 56: 885-92.

Horowitz LM, Strauß B, Kordy H (1994) Inventar zur Erfassung interpersonaler Probleme (IIP-D). Göttingen: Hofgrefe.

Huber D, Henrich G, Herschbach P (1988) Measuring the quality of life: A comparison between physically and mentally chronically ill patients and healthy persons. Pharmacopsychiatry 21: 453-5.

Huber D, Klug G (1997) How to measure structural change. Vortrag, gehalten auf dem 28. Jahrestreffen der Society for Psychotherapy Research, Geilo, 25-29 June 1997.

Huber D, Klug G, von Rad M (1997) Münchner Psychotherapie-Studie (MPS). In: Leuzinger-Bohleber M, Stuhr U (eds) Psychoanalysen im Rückblick. Gießen: Psychosozial.

Kiresuk TJ, Sherman RE (1968) GAS: A general method for evaluating comprehensive community mental health programs. Community Mental Health Journal 4: 443-53.

Kiresuk TJ, Smith A, Cardillo JE (1994) Goal Attainment Scaling: Applications, theory, and measurement. Hillsdale, NJ: Lawrence Erlbaum.

Leuzinger-Bohleber M, Stuhr U (eds) (1997) Psychoanalysen im Rückblick. Gießen: Psychosozial.

Mercer RC, Loesch LC (1979) Audiotape ratings: Comments and guidelines. Psychotherapy: Theory, Research and Practice 16: 79-85.

Rad M von, Senf W, Bräutigam W (1998) Psychotherapie und Psychoanalyse in der Krankenversorgung. Ergebnisse des Heidelberger Katamnese-Projektes. Psychotherapie Psychosomatik Medizinische Psychologie 48: 88-100.

Schepank H (1995) Der Beeinträchtigungs-Schwere-Score (BSS). Göttingen: Beltz

Sommer G, Fydrich T (1991) Entwicklung und Überprüfung eines Fragebogens zur Sozialen Unterstützung (F-SOZU). Diagnostica 37: 160-78.

Tress W (1993) Die strukturale Analyse sozialen Verhaltens: SASB. Ein Arbeitsbuch für Forschung, Praxis und Weiterbildung in der Psychotherapie. Heidelberg: Asanger.

Wallerstein RS (1986) Forty-two Lives in Treatment. New York: Guilford Press.

Wallerstein RS The Scales of Psychological Capacities. Version 1. Unpublished manuscript.

Wallerstein RS (1991) Assessment of structural change in psychoanalytic therapy and research. In: Shapiro T (ed.) The Concept of Structure in Psychoanalysis. Madison: International Universities Press, pp. 241-61.

Zielke M, Kopf-Mehnert C (1978) Veränderungsfragebogen des Erlebens und Verhaltens, VEV. Weinheim: Beltz.

Zilberg NJ, Wallerstein RS, DeWitt KN, Hartley D, Rosenberg SE (1991) A conceptual analysis and strategy for assessing structural change. Psychoanalysis and Contemporary Thought 14: 317-42.

PART 3

FOLLOW-UP AND PROSPECTIVE STUDIES AND THEIR FINDINGS IN OTHER INTERNATIONAL RESEARCH CENTRES

CHAPTER 17
Introduction and overview

MARY TARGET

This section of the volume includes five studies from four countries: the UK, Sweden, Germany and the US. Chapters 18, 19 and 20 concern either prospective or follow-up studies of psychoanalytic outcome. Chapters 21 and 22 are studies of the process of analytic work - that is, how the treatment material evolves during long-term therapy.

Chapter 18, by Mary Target from the Anna Freud Centre in London, concerns a very under-researched area, the outcome of child psychoanalysis. The chapter describes a programme of research carried out at the Anna Freud Centre over several years, begun by Dr George Moran and Dr Peter Fonagy with a series of highly innovative studies of treatment of brittle diabetes in young people. Subsequently, Peter Fonagy and Mary Target carried out a retrospective study of the outcomes of all treated cases over 40 years, then a follow-up of some of these treated cases and the groundwork for a prospective study of child analysis.

Rolf Sandell reports data from the Karolinska Institute in Stockholm, where he and his colleagues have carried out research that is vitally important to the future of psychoanalysis. This very large and careful study demonstrated the greater effect of psychoanalysis in comparison with less intensive psychoanalytic psychotherapy, using perhaps the most widely used measure of change in adult mental health research (the SCL-90), and investigated the impact of therapist and other factors on the degree of changes observed. The chapter included here focuses on highly important issues of the effects of frequency of session, length of treatment, and means of payment, in relation to treatment outcome. Among the very interesting results are that, to over-simplify, shorter non-intensive therapies work, and longer, intensive analysis works, but short analyses or long once-weekly therapies are associated generally with worse outcomes. Also that the outcome of treatment, and the relationship between factors associated with outcome, change substantially depending on when the follow-up assessments are carried out. As Sandell tells us, outcome is a process, not a stable state, and that process is different depending on how much treatment has been delivered over what period of time. These are fascinating matters for clinicians and researchers alike.

Norbert Freedman's chapter, which follows, draws on the research programme of the Institute for Psychoanalytic Training and Research (IPTAR), in New York. Their clinic offers low-cost psychoanalytic psychotherapy for up to three years. The present report offers some findings from a recently completed study relating three aspects of change (improvement in presenting problems, satisfaction with therapist, and more general improvement) to quantitative aspects of the treatment provided. The findings were based on replies from 99 out of 241 patients who had attended the clinic, or were currently in therapy, and who agreed to complete a questionnaire. The chapter raises pertinent criticisms of this questionnaire study, especially the vexed question of cognitive dissonance (while investing so much time, money and hope in therapy, patients are likely to slant their evaluations in a positive direction to justify their behaviour). Freedman then presents some early material from the Recall Project, a one-year follow-up - still in progress - of patients who had terminated treatment at the clinic, in which the former patients were interviewed by a clinical researcher about aspects of the experience of treatment. In the second part of the chapter, Freedman raises deep and central questions, such as the nature of internalization of the therapeutic process, the nature of clinical facts, and forms of evidence in psychoanalytic work.

The following two chapters use the Psychotherapy Process Q-Sort method, developed by Enrico Jones at the University of California, Berkeley. Chapter 21 is centred on the idea of an interaction structure, which bridges the intrapsychic and the interpersonal domains within the therapy relationship. In most patient–analyst dyads, one dominant interaction structure emerges over time. This chapter elegantly explains how the method he has created allows the tracking of interaction patterns over time, within and across cases. The method allows rigorous measurement and powerful analysis, while staying very close to the clinical material so that the interaction patterns, the items on which they are based, and the descriptions of change, are all immediately comprehensible to a clinical therapist. This is a very remarkable achievement in the field of psychotherapy research, which fulfils one of the major aims of this book: to demonstrate that research and clinical practice do not have to be poles apart, with languages and tools that cannot be understood across the boundary. Jones makes a convincing argument for the usefulness of the concept of the interaction structure in clinical work, supervision, and in collaborative reflection between patient and therapist, within the session.

Chapter 22, by Cornelia Albani and colleagues from Ulm in Germany, describes the application of Jones' Q-Sort method to a 'specimen case' of psychoanalysis, known as Amalia X, a case which has already been investigated by a number of other psychotherapy research methods. This case study both offers a more detailed example of the application of the Psychotherapy Process Q-Sort, and allows its results to be compared with other studies of this same audio-recorded case.

Taken together, the research reports in Part 3 impressively illustrate the creativity and productivity of research on the psychoanalytic situation, using follow-up and prospective methodologies, and process studies. The outcome studies offer us compelling grounds for seeing long-term, intensive treatment as an effective intervention for many patients, and the studies using one approach to describing psychoanalysis material offer one fascinating window on how this process may be achieving its effects.

Chapter 18

The problem of outcome in child psychoanalysis: contributions from the Anna Freud Centre

Mary Target

In past decades there have been impressive systematic studies of the outcome of psychoanalysis across groups of patients and analysts (for example, Wallerstein, 1989; Sashin et al., 1975; Weber et al., 1985a, b; Kantrowitz et al., 1987a, b, 1990a, b, c), in addition to those included in the present volume. However, the studies carried out to date have almost all been with adult patients. There is very little information even on the short-term outcome of psychoanalytic treatment for children (Target and Fonagy, 1996). The information that does exist has largely emerged from the research tradition of the Anna Freud Centre (formerly the Hampstead Clinic) in London. The early studies will first be mentioned, then our current programme of research.

Heinicke and Ramsey-Klee (1986) evaluated psychoanalytic treatment for latency children referred for reading retardation associated with emotional disturbances. In separate groups the frequency of treatment sessions was set at either once a week for two years, four times per week for two years, or once a week in the first year followed by four times a week in the second. All patterns of treatment led to gains in self-esteem, adaptation and the capacity for relationships but the gains were significantly greater, and better sustained, for the groups treated four times per week for one or both years. This study paved the way for later work on child psychoanalytic outcome, but has been regarded in the literature as flawed by the lack of definition of disorders and treatment procedures, and the use of outcome assessments that had not been validated.

Moran and Fonagy conducted a series of studies of psychoanalytic treatment with children suffering from so-called brittle diabetes (for a detailed account, see Fonagy and Moran, 1991a, 1994). These young patients cannot maintain their blood sugar levels close to normal, and therefore their lives are constantly disrupted by life-threatening episodes of hypoglycaemia and ketoacidosis. The children in the study were referred for psychoanalysis after many other physical and psychological treatments had been shown not to be ineffective. The problem of measuring the outcome of psychoanalysis was circumvented by using physical measures: a simple biochemical index of average blood glucose levels, and accurate indicators of growth.

The first study explored the relationship between metabolic control and the process of psychoanalysis in a single case study of a diabetic adolescent girl. Process reports were rated for the presence of dynamic themes. The association of these themes with independently obtained measures of diabetic control was examined using time-series analysis. The study revealed a close statistical relationship between week-to-week fluctuations of metabolic control and the presence of key themes in the patient's analytic material. Most significantly, the analytic narrative predicted the child's subsequent diabetic control: the presence of conflict in the analytic material was reliably followed by an improvement in diabetic control one to three weeks later.

The second study by these authors compared two equivalent groups of 11 diabetic children with grossly abnormal blood glucose profiles, requiring repeated admissions to hospital. Patients in the treatment group were offered an intensive inpatient treatment programme that included three to four times weekly psychoanalytic psychotherapy. Treatment was brief, lasting on average 15 weeks. Patients in the comparison group were offered only inpatient medical treatment. The children in the treatment group showed considerable improvements in diabetic control, maintained at one-year follow up. The comparison group children, in contrast, returned to pre-treatment levels of metabolic control within three months of discharge from hospital.

The third of these studies was an independent series of experimental single case studies. This assessed the impact of treatment on growth rate (measured by changes in height and bone age) in three children whose height had fallen below the fifth percentile for age. Medical intervention had been of little value, as was shown by charts of the children's heights over two to three years prior to their treatment. In order to illustrate the causal relationship between the psychoanalytic therapy and their growth measures, changes in three indicators were recorded for six-month periods before, during and after treatment. For all three children, treatment was associated with an acceleration of growth and a substantial increase in predicted adult height (in the case of one boy, an increase of over 10 centimetres).

Taken together, these studies of diabetic children illustrated one important method of assessing the effectiveness of psychoanalysis. The crucial components of this approach were:

- a patient group who responded poorly to alternative treatments;

- an outcome variable independent of the treatment process;
- process studies that offered pointers to the effective component of the treatment.

These studies illustrate that as well as producing evidence of efficacy that was 'hard' enough to convince the sceptical medical carers of these patients, and to be published in major psychiatric journals, an empirical study was able to yield data of clinical psychoanalytic interest, probably extending to other patients engaging in self-harming behaviour and perhaps well beyond.

The ongoing work on outcome at the Anna Freud Centre

Identifying predictors of therapeutic outcome

The first of our studies to be described used retrospective chart review methodology; 763 cases already treated at the Anna Freud Centre in either four-to-five times per week psychoanalysis or one-to-three times per week psychodynamic therapy were systematically reviewed. The procedures and results of this study have been more fully described elsewhere (Fonagy and Target, 1994, 1996; Target and Fonagy, 1994a, b). In approaching this vast collection of clinical material (many case records covering hundreds of pages), we decided to use standardized psychological and psychiatric, as well as psychoanalytic, descriptions of the children treated. This allowed much easier comparison between these children and those offered other forms of psychiatric treatment, and therefore readier acceptance of the findings in the wider psychiatric community. The sacrifice initially was in acceptance within the psychoanalytic world, but this we hope is being rectified by our further studies, to be mentioned later.

Three main studies of the closed case records were reported.

Emotional disorders (Target and Fonagy, 1994a)

This study examined the effectiveness of psychoanalysis for children and adolescents with DSM-III-R diagnoses of anxiety or depressive disorders: 352 charts were reviewed and independently rated for a wide range of demographic, clinical, process and outcome measures. The study showed that:

- 72% of those treated for at least six months showed reliable, clinically significant improvement in adaptation, and only 24% had a diagnosable disorder at termination;
- phobic disorders were most likely to remit, and depressed children least likely;

- children under 11 years were significantly more likely to be well at the end of treatment;
- while longer treatment was predictably associated with good outcome (not only extra treatment, but also spontaneous improvement, might have produced this), more frequent sessions also led to greater improvements independently of the child's age and length of treatment;
- intensive treatment was significantly more helpful for children who presented with more severe disturbance, in terms of a psychoanalytic diagnosis of atypical personality development, multiple psychiatric diagnoses or pervasive impairment, usually affecting social, emotional and cognitive functioning.

A number of demographic and clinical variables helped to identify children most likely to improve. These included higher IQ, younger age, longer treatment, good peer relations, poor overall adjustment of the mother, the presence of anxiety symptoms in the mother, concurrent treatment of the mother, and absence of a history of maternal antisocial behaviour. Groups of children with depressive, overanxious and specific anxiety disorders had different predictors of favourable outcome, underscoring the heterogeneity of this group, and the different processes at work in their psychotherapeutic treatment.

Disruptive disorders (Fonagy and Target, 1994)

Here 135 children with disruptive disorders were matched on demographic, clinical and treatment variables with children presenting with emotional disorders. Overall improvement rates were lower for disruptive disorders, and nearly one-third of the children treated terminated within one year of starting treatment. Premature termination was associated with older age, non-intensive treatment, a less well-functioning mother, fewer learning difficulties at school and lack of concurrent parental guidance. Of those disruptive children who remained in treatment, 69% were no longer diagnosable on termination. Predictors of improvement included the presence of an anxiety disorder, absence of other disorders, younger age, intensive treatment, longer treatment, maternal anxiety disorder, child having been in foster care, and psychotherapeutic treatment of mother.

Developmental considerations (Target and Fonagy, 1994b)

This third report examined the way in which the age of a child or adolescent when treated in psychoanalytic psychotherapy related to the outcome of that treatment: 127 children were selected from each of three age bands (under six, six to 12, and adolescents); they were matched on broad diagnostic grouping, gender, socio-economic status, global adaptation and frequency of sessions. Outcome was indicated by diagnostic change and clinically significant change in adaptation. Younger children generally improved to a greater extent. Children under 12 benefited from intensive treatment more than from non-intensive treatment, but this was not true of adolescents. Division into age groups improved the accuracy of prediction of improvement. Within the limitations of a retrospective design, this study suggested that, in psychodynamic treatment, younger age is an advantage and that developmental factors considerably affect the outcome of this form of therapy.

A number of themes ran through the various analyses of this data. Younger children appeared to improve more during psychodynamic treatment. Anxiety disorders, particularly specific rather than pervasive symptoms, were associated with a good prognosis, even if the primary diagnosis was of a different type, for example disruptive. Children with pervasive developmental disorders (such as autism) did not do well, even with prolonged, intensive treatment. However, among children with emotional disorders there was evidence that severe or pervasive symptomatology did respond well to intensive treatment, but did not show satisfactory rates of improvement in non-intensive psychotherapy.

Outcome studies should always be carried out within a theoretical context. Anna Freud's work formed the backbone of our research, and of our understanding of the findings. The Anna Freud Centre's mission has always been to provide psychoanalysis for children with a view to restoring them as far as possible to the path of normal development (Freud, 1965; Kennedy and Moran, 1991). While recognizing the place of less intensive therapy, which was indeed confirmed and clarified by some of our chart review findings, clinical experience supported by other results of the above study suggests that intensive treatment may sometimes be essential if we are to influence pathological developmental processes.

Anna Freud's model assumed that emotional disorders of childhood arose in association with the arrest or distortion of lines of normal development for which the child may find maladaptive solutions. Anna Freud therefore conceived developmental anomalies as risk factors for neurotic disorders. Our work with case records in conjunction with other research has led a group working at the Anna Freud Centre to extend psychoanalytic assumptions about psychic change in child analysis (Fonagy and Moran, 1991b; Fonagy et al., 1993). We delineated two models of the psychoanalytic treatment of emotional disturbance in children. The first (the classical model) involves the patient recovering threatening ideas and feelings, which have been repressed or distorted as a result of conflict and defence. Non-intensive and intensive treatments seem to be equally effective for this group, although for younger children intensive treatment may have an added advantage. The second model (the mental process model) draws attention to inhibited, underlying mental processes. The gradual engagement of these in treatment occurs primarily through patient and analyst focusing on the thoughts and feelings of each person, and how the child understands these. Patients with disorders that involve the inhibition or decoupling of essential mental processes, such as reflective capacities, or aspects of awareness of the mental states of others, show more pervasive (though not necessarily more severe) psychopathology, and require intensive psychoanalytic intervention. The distinction roughly corresponds to the traditional psychoanalytic distinction of neurotic versus developmental disorder. On the basis of the retrospective study, we have reached a clearer definition of such disorders in diagnostic terms and we have been able to confirm the theoretical expectation that these patients really do need long-term and intensive intervention.

This retrospective study is now being followed by a group of further research initiatives, which aim to extend the findings considerably. The main ongoing studies are outlined below.

The establishment of a prospective study of treatment effectiveness in child psychoanalysis

The only method of evaluation of therapeutic outcome that meets strict scientific requirements in the wider mental health community is the randomized controlled trial (RCT). There are great practical and ethical difficulties in using RCTs to evaluate intensive, long-term therapies (see Fonagy, Chapter 4 in this volume). These include the identification of outcome measures appropriate to psychoanalytic treatment, the need for very long-term follow-up to demonstrate subtle changes in personality functioning, difficulties in describing complex treatment procedures sufficiently clearly for others to be able in principle to replicate the study, and the very great expense of mounting an investigation with sufficient statistical power to produce conclusive results. Peter Fonagy and myself have been working for some years to overcome these problems.

- *Measurement of outcome.* Measures applied in the evaluation of other therapies, such as change in symptoms, must be included when assessing the outcome of psychoanalytic treatment. However, if one is to test our belief that analysis does much more than reduce observable symptoms, then an attempt must be made to measure parameters identified by analysts as relevant (particularly intrapsychic functioning). Some such measures are: the quality of object relationships, adaptiveness of defences, the range and regulation of the child's emotional responses, the development of morality, and social understanding. This poses a formidable challenge, in that normative data are not yet available on many measures. The approach we have taken is to make more extensive use of recent progress in developmental psychology, to adapt measures that were devised to chart the cognitive and social capacities of children, and to collect normative data on these measures.

- *The specification of treatment technique*, or manualization. Although there is a vast literature on technique in adult and child psychoanalytic treatment, this is not written in the explicit 'operational' terms that are required to define a treatment approach in studies of efficacy. Paulina Kernberg and her colleagues have prepared an excellent manual on supportive-expressive psychotherapy for children with moderate to severe conduct disorders (Kernberg and Chazan, 1991). In some respects this manual is appropriate for other childhood disorders and retains the distinction between insight-oriented treatment and developmental help proposed in this chapter. We have, however, prepared a manual of the approach adopted at this Centre, for the full range of developmental and neurotic disorder in latency children (Fonagy et al., unpublished). It consists of 17 chapters, five providing historical and theoretical background, 12 taking an important aspect of technique, offering a definition, the aims the analyst would have in mind in using that form of intervention, the ways in which it is implemented, and finally situations in which it is not likely to be helpful. The manual made extensive use of the many years of work at the Centre spent in systematizing child psychoanalytic treatment, for instance the Hampstead Index Project (Sandler, Kennedy and Tyson, 1980). Work on validating the manual was carried out by subjecting individual chapters of the manual to formal assessments of comprehensibility, accuracy and comprehensiveness with current senior and junior clinicians at the Centre (Miller, 1993).
- *Monitoring of treatment integrity.* As well as specifying the technique involved in this treatment, it was necessary to devise measures of the content and technique of analytic sessions in order to learn to what extent the technique described in our manual is in fact being used. This involves developing scales for recording the process of treatment. We have developed a measure named the Session Rating Scale (Fonagy, Phipps-Buchan and Target, unpublished), which represents an attempt to quantify the psychoanalytic experience of children treated at the Centre. The scale provides a measure of the content and quality of the work with each patient, which may help to identify what type of treatment was most successful in which sort of case. It also offers a way of excluding cases where the therapeutic work, for whatever reason, was not within the range of accepted psychoanalytic technique.

The very long-term outcome of child psychoanalysis

A further research study we have undertaken is to follow up as many people as possible who were treated at the Anna Freud Centre as children, their siblings, and a further group of untreated, referred children with apparently similar psychopathology in childhood. Our theoretical stance leads us to predict that there will have been clear differences in technique, levels of change, and rates of change depending on the depth of personality disturbance in a child. In the context of the follow-up study, we have predicted that those children who appeared to be suffering from pervasive and deep-seated psychopathology would show substantial impairment of emotional and social adjustment as adults, unless they had received long-term and intensive psychoanalytic intervention, whereas differences between intensive and non-intensive long-term treatment outcome would be much narrower in the treated children with less severe pathology. We are therefore expecting considerable differences in outcome between the groups in the sample, to the extent that different types of pathology in childhood can be assessed, and we have looked to test the hypothesis that the differences in immediate outcome observed in our chart review study would persist into adult adjustment and functioning. This has been assessed by extensive interviews (with established reliability and validity) to cover a wide range of child and adult personality and social functioning.

This ongoing follow-up study aims to evaluate two contrasting expectations about the long-term outcome of child psychoanalysis. It was Anna Freud's view that analytic help could provide a vital bridge back to a normal developmental path, removing both developmental and neurotic obstacles. However, she did not believe that the child was then any less vulnerable than other normal children to the later vicissitudes of life events, relationships, and so forth, which might cause a breakdown in adolescence or adulthood. In contrast to this view, we have suggested that psychoanalytic therapy might enhance resilience in the face of later events, enabling the child to understand, predict and plan for his own and others' responses, particularly within relationships, through for instance facilitating the capacity for mentalization, or reflection on mental states, and through enhancing the security and autonomy of internal working models of attachment relationships.

We are using three types of measures. First, and perhaps most central, in-depth interview-based objective measures of life events, transitions and plans, current personality functioning, psychiatric and personality disorder diagnosis. Second, self-report measures of symptomatology (SCL-90), physical health (SF-36), IQ, personality (SCID-II) etc. And third, psychodynamic measures of attachment and internal representations of object relationships that provide relatively reliable data on the quality of object relationships, the coherence of object representations, expectations of others' behaviour, morality, perspective taking, hostility and mentalizing capacity.

Preliminary results

We are still collecting data, and any results are very preliminary. In particular, the difficulties in recruiting referred but untreated subjects makes comparisons invalid for this group. We feel more confident of the comparisons between treated and untreated siblings and between treated subjects who were rated in our earlier study as having achieved a clinically significant change in their child therapy, and those whose outcome was at the time considered poor.

We found evidence that, although in childhood the vast majority of treated subjects suffered more adversity than their siblings, in adulthood the siblings were more likely to experience negative life events than the treated subjects. In terms of personality functioning, in the work domain all of our sample with the exception of those whose childhood outcome was poor are doing well. In the love relationship domain, individuals with successfully treated psychiatric disorders in childhood appeared to be doing somewhat better than both their siblings and the untreated controls. None of those unsuccessfully treated in childhood appears to have an adequate love relationship. In terms of friendships, even those successfully treated appear to be somewhat disadvantaged relative to their siblings.

In terms of attachment security, those children whose immediate outcome was relatively good appear to do as well as their siblings in terms of the likelihood of secure attachment in adulthood. Those unsuccessfully treated appear to be predominantly preoccupied and entangled, whereas those untreated appear to be predominantly dismissing. In terms of the capacity to mentalize, to understand events in psychological terms, as predicted, the successfully treated group does somewhat better than all the others, whereas those whose outcome was poor in childhood remain unable to conceive of thoughts, feelings or intentions accurately. In brief, childhood treatment which was independently rated in the retrospective study as successful does appear to be protective. However, it is possible that unsuccessfully treated individuals are even worse off than those whose disorders were untreated. We should bear clearly in mind that the samples are small and further interviews may yield different conclusions.

We have made a number of other preliminary observations. For example, we were able to compare the information about childhood gained from these retrospective interviews with the original observations carefully recorded by clinicians on the basis of parent and teacher interviews and family work. It seems that the agreement in recall between case files and adult recollection was relatively high, particularly for physical abuse and parental discord. Ratings also matched case files in terms of the extent to which childhood experiences were regarded as loving, rejecting, pressuring or involving. Thus we may conclude, with respect to the current controversy concerning the accuracy of childhood memories, that these are broadly reliable. Is there evidence that the forgetting (repression) of adverse experience is associated with psychopathology or poor personality functioning? The answer seems to be no. It seems that individuals who are better functioning remember somewhat *less* well: their recollections are very coherent but tinged with idealization. They appear to smooth over or forget adverse experiences noted at the time of their assessment - even quite objective events, for example the prolonged psychiatric hospital admission of the mother when the subject was 12 years old, or divorce in adolescence. These idealizing subjects were much less likely to come from the treated group, even from those with successful outcome. The good-outcome treated cases, as adults, seemed to have retained an accurate and balanced, although still inevitably more painful memory than their siblings.

Conclusion

Despite the 90 years that have passed since the publication of Freud's case study of Little Hans, we have very little definite evidence about the outcome of child psychoanalysis. We have some limited data (by the normal standards of psychotherapy research) suggesting the specific groups of children for whom intensive treatment is a necessity rather than a luxury. Paradoxically, it seems that this group is not that which analysts most frequently identify as 'good analytic cases'. However, we have to recognize that our own chart review was biased by these traditional assumptions (leading to the original selection of cases for treatment), and that cases like many of the patients who now attend our consulting rooms will not have been represented in the review in large numbers. This is why we definitely need to do prospective as well as retrospective and follow-up studies of child therapy outcomes, using both quantitative and qualitative methods.

If we fail to meet the challenge confronting us, if child analysts offer their treatment to less desperate children (with greater internal and external resources), making little attempt to demonstrate its effects in a form accessible to others, child psychoanalysis may be discredited and disappear. This would be a great loss to psychoanalysts, but a still greater one to those children who specifically need this form of help but would no longer have access to it.

References

Fonagy P, Edgcumbe R, Target M, Miller J, Moran GS (unpublished) Contemporary Psychodynamic Child Therapy: theory and technique. Unpublished manuscript, the Anna Freud Centre and UCL.

Fonagy P, Moran GS (1991a) Studies of the efficacy of child psychoanalysis. Journal of Consulting and Clinical Psychology 58: 684–95.

Fonagy P, Moran GS (1991b) Understanding psychic change in child analysis. International Journal of Psychoanalysis 78: 15–22.

Fonagy P, Moran GS, Edgcumbe R, Kennedy H, Target M (1993) The roles of mental representations and mental processes in therapeutic action. Psychoanal Study Child 48: 9–48.

Fonagy P, Moran GS (1994) Psychoanalytic formulation and treatment of chronic metabolic disturbance in insulin dependent diabetes mellitus. In: Erskine A, Judd D (eds) The Imaginative Body: Psychodynamic psychotherapy in health care. London: Whurr, pp. 60–86.

Fonagy P, Phipps-Buchan E, Target M (1993) The Hampstead Session Rating Scale. Unpublished manuscript.

Fonagy P, Target M (1996) Predictors of outcome in child psychoanalysis: a retrospective study of 763 cases at the Anna Freud Centre. J Amer Psychoanal Association 44: 27–77.

Fonagy P, Target M (1994) The efficacy of psycho-analysis for children with disruptive disorders. Journal of the American Academy of Child Psychiatry 33: 45–55.

Freud A (1965) Normality and Pathology in Childhood. Harmondsworth: Penguin Books Ltd.

Heinicke CM, Ramsey-Klee DM (1986) Outcome of child psychotherapy as a function of frequency of sessions. J Am Acad Child Psychiatry 25: 247–53.

Kantrowitz J, Katz A, Paolitto F (1990a) Follow-up of psychoanalysis five to ten years after termination: I. Stability of change. J Amer Psychoanalytic Association 38: 471–96.

Kantrowitz J, Katz A, Paolitto F (1990b) Follow-up of psychoanalysis five to ten years after termination: II. Development of the self-analytic function. J Amer Psychoanalytic Association 38: 637–54.

Kantrowitz J, Katz A, Paolitto F (1990c) Follow-up of psychoanalysis five to ten years after termination: III. The relation between the resolution of the transference and the patient-analyst match. J Amer Psychoanalytic Association 38: 655–78.

Kantrowitz J, Paolitto F, Sashin J, Solomon L (1987a) Changes in the level and quality of object relations in psychoanalysis: Follow-up of longitudinal prospective study. J Amer Psychoanalytic Association 35: 23–46.

Kantrowitz J, Paolitto F, Sashin J, Solomon L (1987b) The role of reality testing in the outcome of psychoanalysis: Follow-up of 22 cases. J Amer Psychoanalytic Association 35: 367–86.

Kennedy H, Moran G (1991) Reflections on the aims of child psychoanalysis. Psychoanaly Study of the Child 46: 181–98.

Kernberg P, Chazan SE (1991) Children with Conduct Disorders: A psychotherapy manual. New York: Basic Books.

Miller JM (1993) The Manualization of Child Psychoanalysis. Unpublished doctoral dissertation. University of London.

Sandler J, Kennedy H, Tyson R (1980) The Technique of Child Analysis: Discussions with Anna Freud. London: Hogarth Press.

Sashin J, Eldred S, Van Amerowgen ST (1975) A search for predictive factors in institute supervised cases: A retrospective study of 183 cases from 1959–1966 at the Boston Psychoanalytic Society and Institute. International J Psychoanalysis 56: 343–59.

Target M, Fonagy P (1994a) The efficacy of psycho-analysis for children with emotional disorders. J Am Acad Child Adolesc Psychiatry 33: 361–71.

Target M, Fonagy P (1994b) The efficacy of psychoanalysis for children: Developmental considerations. J Am Acad Child Adolesc Psychiatry 33: 1134–44.

Target M, Fonagy P (1996) The psychological treatment of child and adolescent psychiatric disorders. In: Roth A, Fonagy P (eds) What Works For Whom? A critical review of psychotherapy research. New York: Guilford Press.

Wallerstein RS (1989) The psychotherapy research project of the Menninger Foundation: An overview. J Consult Clin Psychology 57: 195–205.

Weber J, Bachrach H, Solomon M (1985a) Factors associated with the outcome of psychoanalysis: Report of the Columbia Psychoanalytic Center Research Project (II) International Review of Psychoanalysis 12: 127–41.

Weber J, Bachrach H, Solomon M (1985b) Factors associated with the outcome of psychoanalysis: Report of the Columbia Psychoanalytic Center Research Project (III) International Review of Psychoanalysis 12: 251–62.

CHAPTER 19

Multimodal analysis of temporal interactions in the effects of psychoanalysis and long-term psychotherapy

ROLF SANDELL[1]

In recent years, time in psychotherapy has become an issue of considerable concern for third-party payers. In Europe we hear about the devastating influence of the case management system in the US and fear that it will spread over the Atlantic. In Scandinavia as well as in Germany, the national insurance and mental health authorities signal the same message: 'Make it short!' In Germany, their message was supported by the large study by Klaus Grawe. Together with Donati and Bernauer, Grawe (1994) reviewed a number of outcome studies of various forms of psychotherapy in a *very* careful way, and in their conclusion they assert that only in very exceptional cases should psychotherapy be of longer duration than one year - and, also, that it should be of the behavioural type. If a patient does not improve significantly in 25 sessions, she or he had better sack the therapist and hire another one, according to Grawe. Buttressed by a sample of 796 studies, these conclusions have, I understand, had a strong impact on the German health insurance system.

Apart from the fact that these conclusions seriously question the kind of long-term work many of us are doing in psychoanalysis or psychotherapy, the really interesting thing about them is their empirical basis. When we analysed Grawe's sample, it turned out that just a little more than 1% of all his 796 studies had therapies of two years duration or more, and not more than another 2% were concerned with therapies of more than one year but less than two years duration. One may discuss what exactly a long term in psychotherapy is, but in Scandinavia we consider one year therapies as rather brief - although there are briefer ones, of course - and two years as, well, not very long term. So I believe we can draw this one conclusion from Grawe's study: Grawe and his associates must be clairvoyant, because they simply have not enough empirical data to draw any conclusions at all about the benefits - or the lack of benefits - of truly long-term therapies, whether psychodynamic or behavioural.

In the Stockholm Outcome of Psychotherapy and Psychoanalysis Project (STOPPP), we have the data that Grawe did not have. I shall not describe the methods of this very extensive project in detail, but our study is based on an overlapping three-wave panels design, where we have a number of panel groups overlapping each other over a very long stretch of time, including pre-treatment, during treatment, and post-treatment. To begin with, we had well over 700 persons, and after dropouts in each wave we had 452 persons left who had responded to our questionnaire, the Well-being Questionnaire, in each of three consecutive years, leaving a respectable response rate of about 60%. For each panel wave, we know whether a person was in treatment, had terminated or had not yet started, so, on the basis of that information, we may reconstruct the treatment history of all persons during these three years and sort them in relation to each other in terms of time in treatment, as in Figure 19.1.

Thus, allowing for further attrition due to missing data, there were 418 persons spread out across an ordinal time scale, where each point of time is

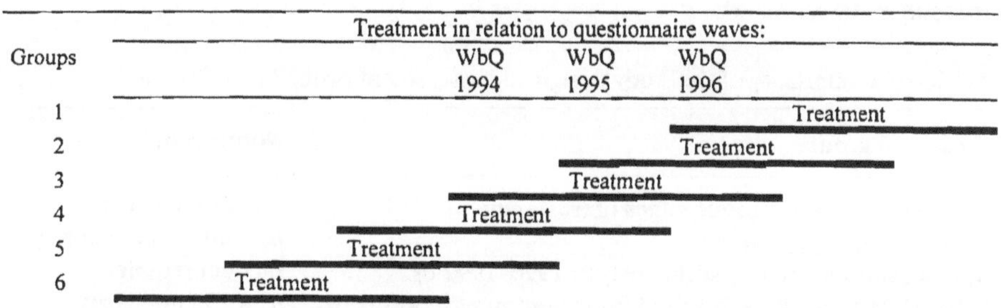

	Questionnaire waves in relation to treatment:							
Groups	Early before	Late before	Early ongoing	Ongoing	Late ongoing	Early after	After	Late after
1 $n = 4$	1994	1995	1996					
2 $n = 31$		1994	1995	1996				
3 $n = 151$			1994	1995	1996			
4 $n = 25$				1994	1995	1996		
5 $n = 51$					1994	1995	1996	
6 $n = 156$						1994	1995	1996
$N = 418$								
$N = 1254$	$n = 4$	$n = 35$	$n = 186$	$n = 207$	$n = 227$	$n = 232$	$n = 207$	$n = 156$

Figure 19.1. Groups of cases at different stages of treatment, in relation to waves of administration of the Well-being Questionnaire (WbQ) (upper panel), and in analysis design (lower panel).

relative to other points, not by any exact number of days or months but just before or after each other. However, the steps on this relative time scale correspond to intervals of *roughly* one year or more, so, in its entirety, the time scale spans a period of more than seven years.

The Well-being Questionnaire provided very elaborate information on the living conditions of each person in terms of family, work, health, economy and so forth, and also contained a number of standardized self-rating scales, the Symptom Check List-90, the Social Adjustment Scale, and the Sense of Coherence Scale. Besides the information in the Well-being Questionnaire, we also collected official data on each person for a 10-year period on healthcare utilization and national insurance utilization from the relevant authorities. Finally, we performed personal interviews twice, with a one-year interval, with about 60 persons, strategically sampled, and rated these interviews in different respects; so there is a wealth of data on a large number of persons here, as may be seen in Table 19.1. In this chapter I shall focus on some time-relevant findings in the self-ratings of symptom distress on the Symptom Check List-90, which proved to be the most sensitive of all the instruments we used.

Table 19.1. Summary of the study design and assessment procedures

Treatment groups	Norm groups
N = 700 persons at various stages of treatment (before, ongoing, or after): n_1 = 60, subsidized for psychoanalysis 1990–1992 or 1991–1993 n_2 = 140, subsidized for long-term psychotherapy 1990–1992 or 1991–1993 n_3 = 500 on waiting-list for subsidization in 1994	N = 650 persons: n_4 = 400 in community random sample n_5 = 250 university students
Pretreatment status Based on referrals: DSM-IV (American Psychiatric Association, 1994) axes I, II and V; Vocational Impairment Scale (VIS; unpublished); Severity of Psychological Disturbance Scale (SPDS; unpublished)	
Treatment conditions The Well-being Questionnaire (WbQ; unpublished): Data on previous and current psychotherapies and other treatments (type, frequency, duration, financial conditions, etc.); In referrals, complementary data on same; Therapeutic Identity (ThId; unpublished): Training and experience as therapist, therapeutic attitudes and ideals	

Table 19.1. Contd

Outcomes	*Clinical significance controls*
(a) WbQ: Sick leave and health care utilization; social and working conditions; Symptom Check List (SCL-90; Derogatis et al., 1974); Troubles Inventory (TI; unpublished); Social Adjustment Scale (SAS; Weissman, 1976); Sense of Coherence Scale (SOCS; Antonovsky, 1987)	
annually 1994–1996	1994
(b) Semi-structured interviews according to Change After Psychotherapy (CHAP; Sandell, 1987a, 1997b), annually 1994–1995: n_{11} = 20 after psychoanalysis n_{21} = 20 after long-term psychotherapy n_{31} = 20 untreated	
(c) Official records on sick leave and health care utilization from national health insurance and health care authorities, 1988–1996 (from 2 yrs before to 3 yrs after subsidization)	

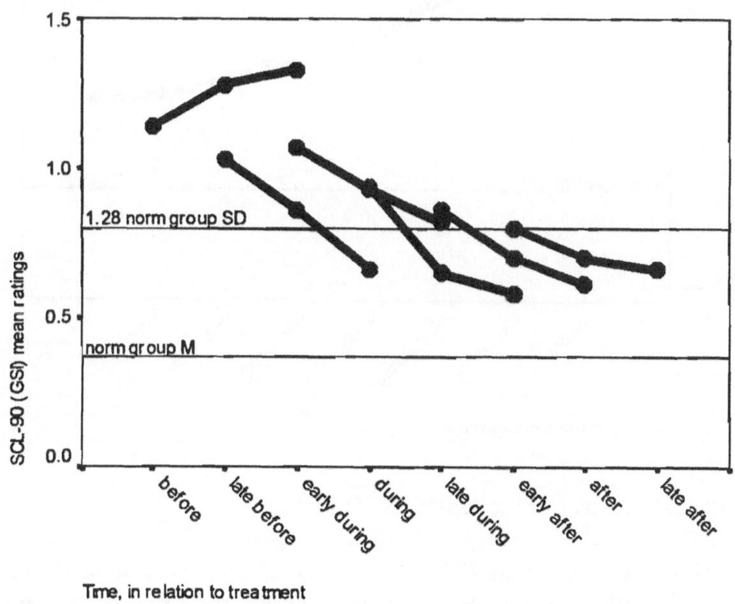

Figure 19.2. Mean trajectories across panel years for groups in different positions in the treatment process.

Figure 19.2 shows how these overlapping three-wave panels distribute themselves on a measure of symptomatic distress, the Symptom Check List-90. For comparative, or norming purposes, I have also included findings in a so-called normal sample of roughly another 400 persons. The lower straight line is the mean of this norm group, at about 0.4, and the upper straight line is 1.28 standard deviations above the mean, which is 0.8, the value that divides the 10% worst-scoring persons in the norm group from the 90% best-scoring ones. The average patient starts out quite a bit higher than this division; in fact amongst the 2% worst-scoring persons in the normal group. But you may also see that there is a downward trend in symptom distress across time, as treatment proceeds, such that at post-treatment the average patient is well within the normal range, a little below the division line - but still higher than the normal mean. In fact when you pool the panel groups in proportion to their sizes, you obtain a rather smooth curve (see Figure 19.3).

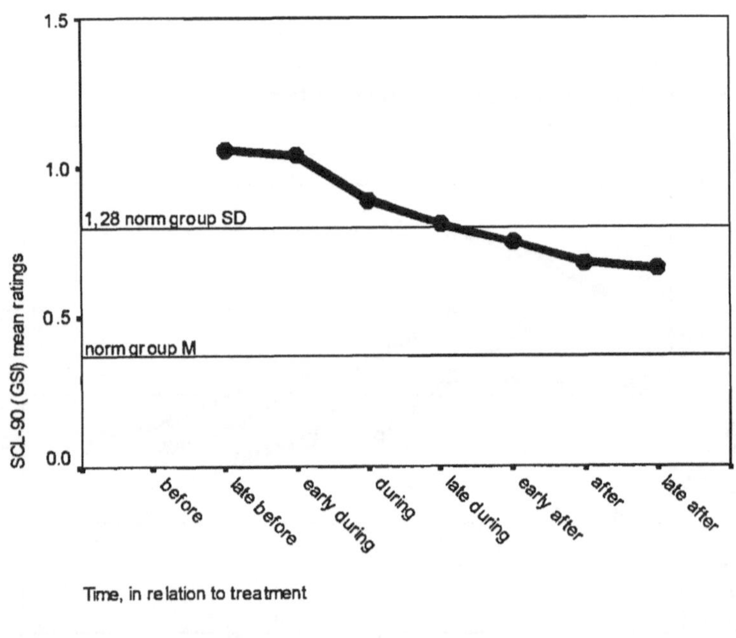

Figure 19.3. Mean trajectory across stages of treatment.

Among these more than 400 patients, about 350 were at various stages of long-term so-called psychodynamic psychotherapy, once or twice a week, and about 75 were at various stages in psychoanalysis, typically four times a week, with a member of one of the two psychoanalytic societies in

Stockholm. If we now split the group according to these two treatments, as in Figure 19.4, you see that the two treatment groups follow each other closely from pre-treatment through ongoing treatment, despite the fact that psychoanalysis had about three times the frequency of psychotherapy.

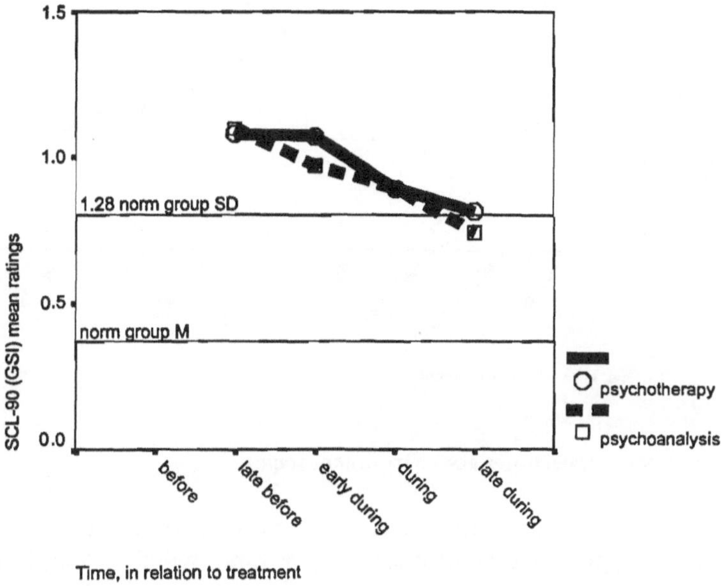

Figure 19.4. Mean trajectories across stages before and during treatment.

Obviously, there is *no simple direct* effect of frequency, such as would have been the case if the final outcome were an accumulation of the minute effects of each single session. If so, there should have been a cumulative differentiation from the very first session, and psychoanalysis would have a slope about three times that of psychotherapy from the beginning, corresponding to the ratio of frequencies. However, as can be seen from Figure 19.5, a critical differentiation sets in *as the treatments are terminated.* That implies a rather more complicated effect of frequency. We can only speculate that something is occurring during the more frequent sessions in psychoanalysis that organizes an outcome process that has to be *qualitatively* different; qualitatively because there are no further *quantitative* differences between the treatment regimes once the treatments are terminated. I believe this finding has some important implications.

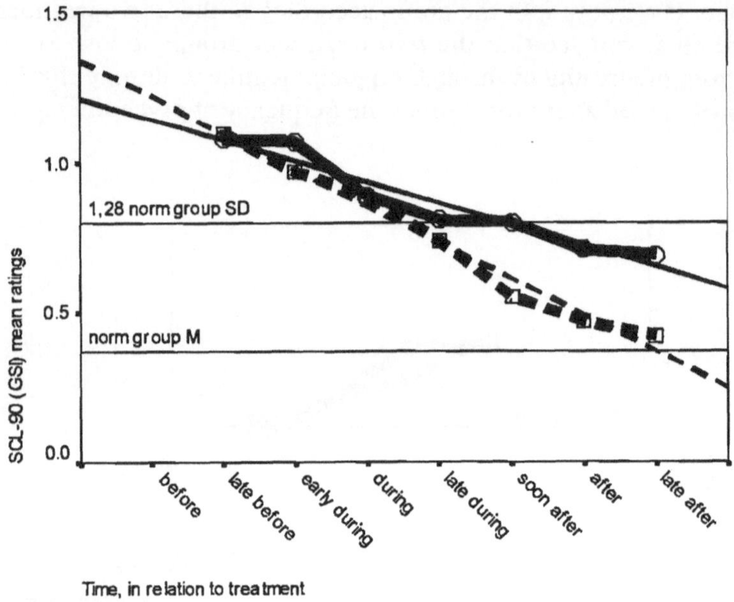

Figure 19.5. Mean trajectories across treatment stages.

For instance, the different post-treatment processes in the two treatments point to the importance of another issue of time, which is length of follow-up. It may interest you to know that long-term follow-up is almost as unusual as truly long-term psychotherapy studies, at least in Grawe's sample. If we assume what is implied in Figure 19.5, that outcome is really a process rather than a stable state, we also have to assume that this process may look different with different kinds of therapies. For instance, it is one of the explicit goals of psychoanalysis to install in the analysand a generalized capacity for self-analysis that will let the analysand continue on his or her own when new conflicts and crises occur, or old ones recur. Time-limited, focused therapies, on the other hand, by definition focus on a more specific problem that the patient presents with and, if for no other reason than the very time limit, have to rely on the hope that the solution will somehow become generalized in a more automatic way, as it were. If different therapeutic regimes produce qualitatively different post-treatment processes, we should be able to observe, given the right conditions, how one therapeutic regime will appear not particularly successful at a short range but a success at a longer range - and vice versa - both in an absolute sense and in comparison with another therapeutic regime. But if we neglect to do long-term follow-up, as have the majority of psychotherapy researchers to date, these important, and possibly differentiating, post-treatment processes will remain unnoticed. Indeed, it is my present belief that most brands of psychotherapy may have more-or-less equivalent effects at termination but widely different effects in the long run. That is, I believe, when time in therapy delivers a payoff.

What of the effects of duration? Comparing long-term psychotherapy and psychoanalysis in our data will not enlighten us in that respect because the two treatments were almost equally long, on average, between four and four-and-a-half years. So we have to look at these effects some other way, within treatments. One way to do this is to construct a causal model or – as it is now called – a structural equations model. If we consider duration as one causal variable, frequency as another, and their product, which I shall call dose, as yet another, we may see how each of these affect the state of symptoms at different lengths of follow-up. You will realize that the product of duration and session frequency, which I call dose, is the total number of sessions. This is a so-called path analysis, and, in the figures to come, the thickness of a path roughly reflects the degree of influence one variable has on another, independently of the other variables in the system, that is, keeping them constant. I have indicated negative effects with broken lines and positive effects with unbroken ones. This path diagram, in Figure 19.6, is based on

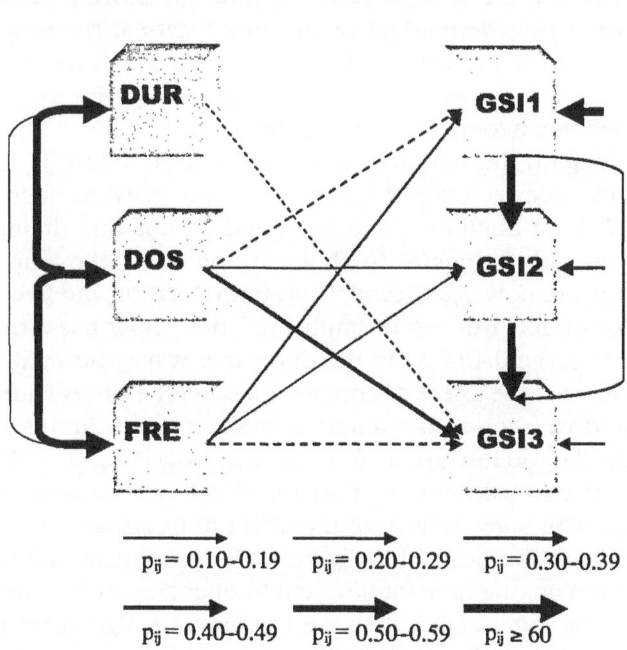

Figure 19.6. Path diagram linking outcome three annual follow-ups with duration (DUR), frequency (FRE), and their interaction (DOS).

about 150 patients after termination of treatment of psychoanalysis or psychotherapy.

As before, there are three different points of follow-up, at approximately one-year intervals. To begin with, to the left, there is a rather weak correlation between duration and frequency, as one might expect. Patients may have been in long-term low-frequency therapies as well as in brief high-frequency analyses.

Now, the interesting things start to happen when we look at the state of symptoms at the first follow-up. You'll see that there is essentially no effect of duration - it is indeed below 0.10, which is not at all significant. However, there is a somewhat stronger, positive effect of frequency (0.27), but we also have an equally strong *negative* effect of dose! This is interesting because an interaction means that the effects of duration and session frequency are conditional on each other, which in turn means that there *are* no main effects of duration or frequency. Basically, the effect of increasing duration depends on the frequency of sessions and vice versa. Briefly, and in general, because none of the effects is significant at this point of follow-up, increasing both duration and frequency may not pay off as much as would be expected on the basis of the contributions of each of them alone.

It can be seen in the second follow-up, further down Figure 19.6, that symptom state is very dependent on symptom state at the first follow-up, which means that the patients' rank order is much the same at the second follow-up as it was at the first. But neither duration, nor frequency nor dose has contributed much to the changes observed.

Concentrating on the symptom states at the third follow-up is revealing. Again, the rank order is much the same as on the previous follow-ups. But what we find about duration, frequency, and dose is that their effects are more-or-less *exactly opposite* to those at the first follow-up, although stronger, and all are now significant! Thus, both duration and frequency now have *negative* effects but, more important, dose now has a quite strong *positive* effect, in the 0.40s. As in the first panel wave, the significant interaction indicates that the effect of duration on outcome varies with frequency of sessions, and vice versa. In multiple regression terms, in this case, but in contrast to the first follow-up, as frequency increases so does the effect of duration; as duration increases, so does the effect of session frequency. One family of regression lines, reflecting the effect of frequency on outcome for different durations, can be seen in Figure 19.7, upper panel; another, for the effect of duration on outcome for different frequencies, in the lower panel.

Without going into detail, when we examine the significant interaction more closely, what we find is that increasing duration in low-frequency therapy or increasing frequency in short-term therapy would be unwise where the long-range outcome is concerned. On the other hand, increasing

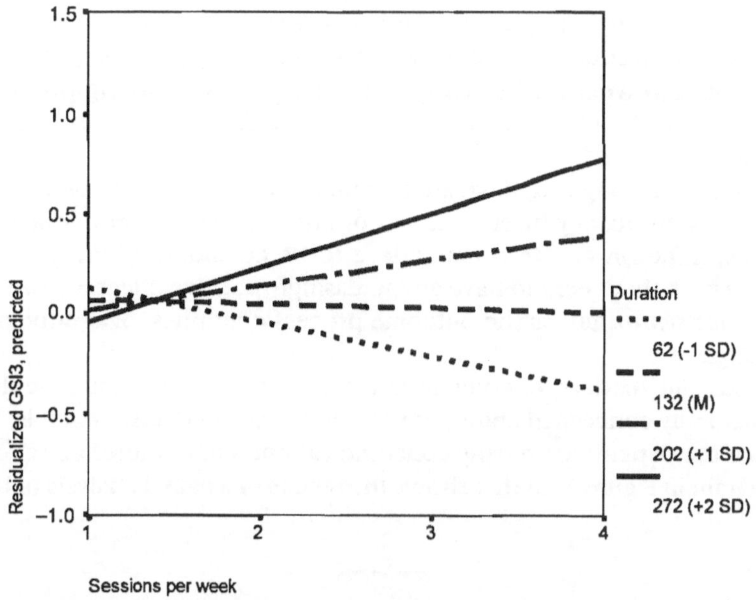

Figure 19.7a. Influence of duration (upper panel).

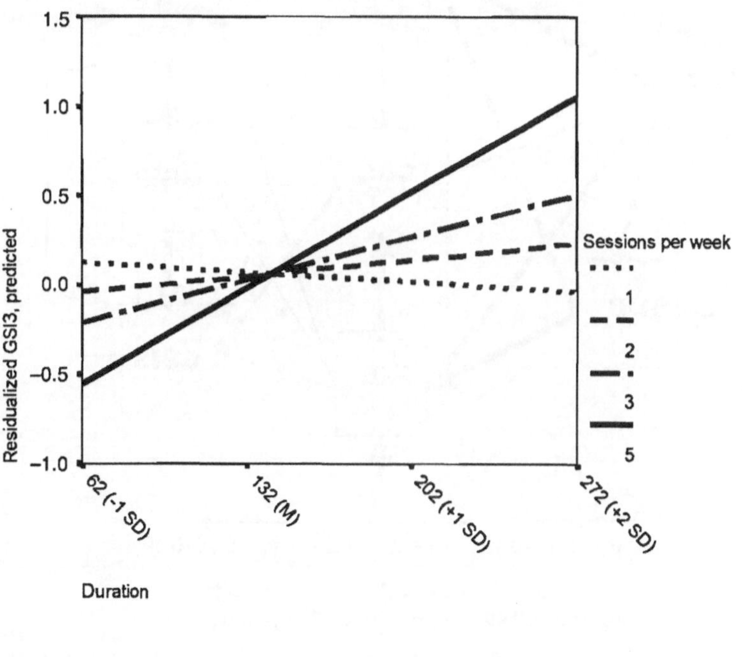

Figure 19.7b. Influence of sessions frequency (lower panel).

frequency is beneficial in long treatments, and prolonging treatments is beneficial in high-frequency treatments. The duration breaking point where increasing frequency becomes a gain, according to the present data, is around 140 weeks. Alternatively, the frequency breaking point at which increasing duration will have a positive effect is between one and two sessions per week.

So, in the long run, if we are to believe our data, we had better either stay with low-frequency brief therapies or enter high-frequency, long-term ones. Thus, duration and frequency have to be considered jointly. As they are increased, they seem to have an increasingly positive effect, *in combination but not separately,* as the outcome process continues, of producing further change.

So, time matters, not only in terms of costs, which is what the third party is naturally concerned about, but also in terms of effects, which is, I assume, what the patients are mostly concerned about. I have therefore set out a path diagram in Figure 19.8 that shows the results of a causal analysis of how costs

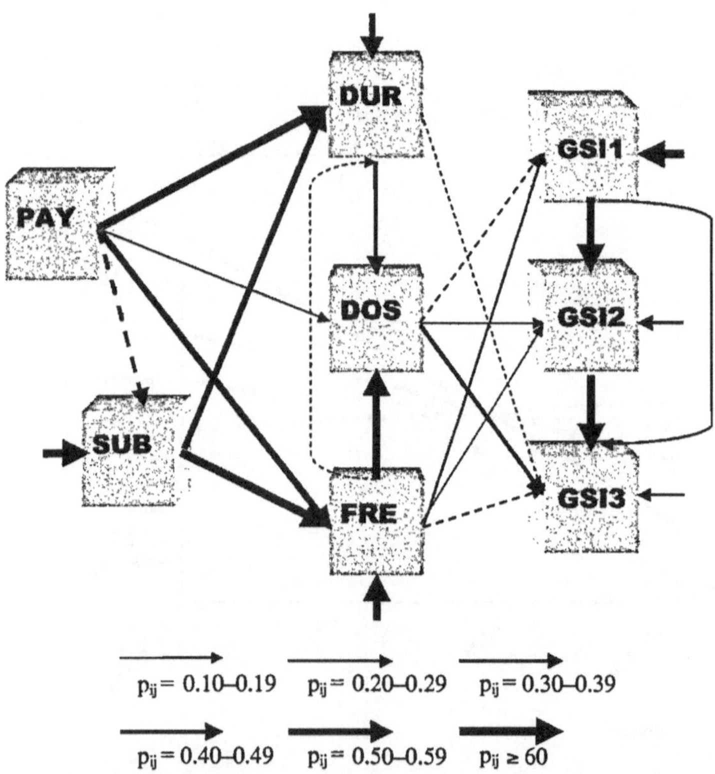

Figure 19.8. Path diagram linking outcome in three annual follow-ups with duration (DUR), frequency (FRE), their interaction (DOS), total amount paid for the treatment by the patient (PAY), and the subsidized share of the total treatment costs (SUB).

and effects are related, because all of these treatments were partly subsidized by the national insurance.

At first, it is much the same as before, that is, with the effects of duration, frequency and dose. What has been added are two variables, the amount of money paid by the patient himself or herself and the share of the total costs of treatment that was subsidized by the national insurance. What can be seen here is how very important financial factors are in helping time factors increase the effect of treatment, *indirectly.* That is, there are no *direct* effects of own payment or subsidization on outcome, as has been the assumption in psychoanalysis - that it is most effective when the patient does the paying. No signs of that. Payment factors have merely indirect effects. Therapeutic change, as we saw before, is influenced by duration, frequency, and dose in different ways at different intervals of follow-up, but increasing duration, increasing frequency, or increasing dose, are all *heavily* dependent on the money factor, either out of the patient's own pocket or in the form of subsidization from third party payers. As is well known, time costs money; but it can also be shown - a bit more persuasively than before, I hope - that time also matters in terms of therapeutic change.

Note

1. Correspondence should be addressed to Rolf Sandell, IBV, Linköping University, S-581 83 Linköping, Sweden.

References

American Psychiatric Association (1994) Diagnostic and Statistical Manual of Mental Disorders, 4th edn. (DSM-IV) Washington, DC: APA.

Antonovsky A (1987) Unraveling the Mystery of Health. San Francisco: Jossey-Bass.

Derogatis LR, Lipman RS, Rickels K, Uhlenhuth EH, Covi L (1974) The Hopkins Symptom Checklist (HSCL): A self-report symptom inventory. Behavioral Science 19: 1-15.

Grawe K, Donati R, Bernauer F (1994) Psychotherapie im Wandel. Von der Konfession zur Profession. Göttingen: Hogrefe.

Sandell R (1987a) Assessing the effects of psychotherapy II. A procedure for direct rating of psychotherapeutic change. Psychotherapy and Psychosomatics 47: 37-43.

Sandell R (1987b Assessing the effects of psychotherapy III. Reliability and validity of 'Change after Psychotherapy'. Psychotherapy and Psychosomatics 47: 44-52.

Weissman MM, Bothwell S (1976) Assessment of social adjustment by patient self-report. Archives of General Psychiatry 33: 1111-115.

CHAPTER 20

The research programme of the Institute for Psychoanalytic Training and Research (IPTAR)

NORBERT FREEDMAN

Introduction

The question of how to fathom - let alone establish the validity of - our analytic enterprise is a complex one. It is not just one question but a series of successive ones that capture our curiosity. Freud, in his advice on psychoanalytic technique, suggested the analogy of a path. He advised: start with the surface, that which is most clear and unambiguous; proceed with what can be inferred with reasonable certainty, for example resistances and defences; only much later introduce that which is most derivative, the signposts of the unconscious fantasy. That was also the approach of Ernst Kris (1951), whose teachings guided me, some 40 years ago, in my own analytic training. We might be well advised to adopt this perspective in the study of systematic analytic inquiry. It may help us to generate findings that are reliable, agreed upon consensually, and consistent with the substance and spirit of analytic thought.

It is in this fashion that we can delineate successive stages or steps of analytic research. First we start with the surface. We can ask about the patient's mode of daily living. Has treatment affected his love life, his relationships with others, his work and his sense of self-esteem? We term this the problem of the effectiveness of treatment. We proceed from the assumption that every form of analytic treatment must include a modicum of effectiveness as one of its aims. Next, we move on and ask 'what has made such change possible?' This is the problem of defining the mediating and facilitating conditions. We inquire: 'how have the events in treatment registered, what is the representation of the treatment, and how persistent is it even after termination?' In this sense we speak of the internalization of the analytic relationship and more centrally of the analytic function. (I terminated my analysis some twenty years ago, but I still continue the inner dialogue with my analyst, and will do so for the rest of my life.) Then, we also wish to know what really happened in the analytic hour. How is it possible that an unconscious memory or wish comes to life? How do transformations take place? That is the sphere of defining the attributes of analytic process itself.

The empirical pursuit of each of these problems has led us to select research methods appropriate to each. Overall, we regard our general research strategy as reflecting a reverse triangle. For the study of effectiveness, we start with the top of the triangle, the broadest representative patient sample, using, if necessary, questionnaire methods. We do so as long as we know it is just the beginning of a staging process. For the study of mediating conditions, notably of internalization, we go to the next level with a smaller, well-selected group of patients, intensively studied using methods of qualitative analysis, and observed at a point in time after termination. The passage of time - both objective and subjective - is needed so that a process of retrospective reconstruction may take place. In adopting this strategy we are implicitly affirming the view of our French colleagues (for example, Rousillon, 1998) who stress the need for the patient to appropriate the past in the present and the present in the past, so crucial experiences in treatment can be reconstructed best - *nachträglich, après coup.* Let us now add that the consolidating impact of delayed action is one way of understanding the Stockholm findings (Sandell et al., 2000). Also, the research strategy of the DPV (Leuzinger-Bohleber et al., 2000) has the same potential. That model, to our mind, is an exemplar par excellence to portray the retrospective reconstruction of treatment received. Finally, we turn to the bottom of our triangle; aiming to define analytic process, we wish to know what goes on inside the analytic hour. Here the intensive examination of a 'single case' - a series of one patient's analytic sessions - becomes the method of choice. We examine the audio recordings of an analysis of several years' duration, with a focus on crucial sessions, identified as reflecting transformation in how mental functioning is employed.

In the US, with the privatization of mental health care, and where patients do not have recourse to national health insurance, research efforts on a national scale cannot be readily undertaken. The burden falls largely upon individual psychoanalytic societies. IPTAR has mobilized its resources to pursue an integrated programme of empirical clinical research. The IPTAR research group comprises training analysts, members, candidates, and consultants, who volunteer their time freely. An important boost was a grant from the IPA Research Program, but, concurrently, additional funding has been obtained from private corporate sources. The research effort has enhanced morale and the sense of community of a small, dedicated analytic group.[2]

Much of this communal spirit has centred on the IPTAR Clinical Center (ICC). The ICC is a low-cost psychotherapy service staffed by candidates and members of the training institute. Treatment is offered to all patients until its natural completion, without regard to financial considerations. Sessions are mostly held in the therapists' private offices. Treatment is explicitly psychoanalytic in orientation. Steps have been taken so that the research effort does not intrude into the privacy of the dyadic couple.

The patient population is predominantly female, young, and middle class, with a large component of college and university students. Duration of treatment for patients on which this report is based ranged from one to over 32 months; session frequency once, twice, or three times per week.

And now, to effectiveness, to mediating conditions, and to examining the nature of analytic process.

The problem of therapeutic effectiveness and the role of duration and session frequency

We begin our inquiry with the focus on the psychological surface. One crucial guiding perspective on outcome relies on the patient's conscious report. Here we consider patients' self-appraisal as they tell us whether either during or after psychoanalytic therapy a substantial alteration in salient aspects of their life situation seems to have taken place. In part symptoms may have become less intense or pervasive; there may be more positive feelings of self-esteem or shifts in their relations to others, be it close ones or colleagues. This type of self-evaluation has been brought together under the notion of effectiveness.

This notion of effectiveness, as the criterion of treatment outcome has been introduced recently by Martin Seligman (1995). He described a study conducted by *Consumer Reports* in which over 4200 subjects, all of whom had received some form of individual psychotherapy, completed the Effectiveness Questionnaire (EQ). The findings showed not only that patients experienced a generally high level of effectiveness, but that effectiveness increased with longer duration of therapy. These observations contradicted the general practice of managed care prevalent in the US.

We were fortunate to have received from *Consumer Reports* both the method of evaluating effectiveness (in the form of the EQ) as well as statistical weighting procedures. In part, then, you will see a replication of the *Consumer Reports* study, now applied to a group of patients receiving psychoanalytic therapy conducted only by therapists with analytic training.

Within the broad frame of our international psychoanalytic community and its three regions, duration and frequency belong to 'common ground'

(Wallerstein, 1988). In our current climate of multiple models, we can use the title of the recent book by Joseph Sandler and Ursula Dreher (1996) *What Do Analysts Want?* They want many things, but they all share one common commitment: they demand time and intensity of treatment exposure. Herein we find our great unifier.

Now I would like to give you the highlights of our recently completed study on the relationship between effectiveness and varying quantitative conditions of treatment exposure (Freedman et al., 1999). Such a study is carried out on the broadest database in our hypothetical reverse triangle of inquiry. Two-hundred-and-forty-one patients who have attended the ICC were mailed the EQ and 99 patients responded - a return rate of 41%.

For each of the 99 patients we computed an Effectiveness Questionnaire score (EQ score), the primary outcome variable. It was based on three components:

- *Specific improvement,* or how much the treatment helped the respondent with 'the problems that led me to therapy';
- *Satisfaction* with his or her therapist; and
- *Global improvement,* or how respondents felt at the time of the survey compared with when they began treatment.

The three parts of the questionnaire are added together to create the EQ score, which can range from 0 to 300. For our patient sample the EQ scores ranged from 97 to 287 with a mean of 209. Here are the highlights of the findings.

Duration

It was possible to study the impact of treatment duration because patients, at the time of evaluation, had been in treatment for varying lengths of time ranging from less than one month to over two years. Analysis of variance and multiple range tests pinpointed the effect. There were significant differences between patients receiving less than six months of treatment compared to those receiving either more than 12 months or more than 25 months of treatment.

Frequency

Mean EQ scores among patients with varying levels of session frequency increased in steady increments from one to three times per week. Multiple range tests demonstrated significance between once per week ($\underline{M}$ = 195.3) and either two ($\underline{M}$ = 225.4) or three ($\underline{M}$ = 234.0) sessions weekly, but not between two and three sessions per week.

The joint effect of both duration and frequency

Using a multiple regression model the combined predictive power of frequency and duration was quite significant. Furthermore, we determined that in the sample as a whole, frequency and duration contribute to outcome in qualitatively distinct ways. This selective function of duration and frequency emerges as increasingly important as our work progresses.

The role of the therapeutic relationship

Within the talking cure probably no other process has received more convincing documentation in shaping outcome than has the patients' experience with the therapist. Recently, Luborsky (1996) in an essay on what cures in psychoanalysis, listed the alliance and its correlates as one of the principal factors leading to successful outcome. We now asked an additional question: do the parameters of duration and frequency add to outcome, apart from the quality of the connection to the therapist?

To address this question, we developed a Positive Relationship Index (PRI) that measured the degree to which patients experienced their therapists as reassuring, supportive, insightful, and so forth. As expected, this measure was a robust predictor of effectiveness in that high scorers on the PRI were those most likely to report positive outcomes.

We also noted that the specific combination of PRI and session frequency was a highly significant predictor of effectiveness. These two factors jointly accounted for over a third of the variance.

Duration, frequency, and clinical syndromes

Having shown repeatedly that our two parameters shape treatment outcome and seem to point to distinct psychological attributes, we naturally wanted to find out whether this applies selectively to different clinical constellations. In general, the preliminary observations are consistent with the view that when the clinical syndrome is one of acute disturbance, frequency of session is a forceful facilitating condition, but when the syndrome is more chronic, longer duration seems to yield a positive outcome. The role of psychoactive medication was also considered. We concluded that the findings on the impact of duration and frequency were not altered when pharmacological treatment effects were partialled out.

Now I can well imagine that as you note these affirmative results, many questions are stirring in your mind. Queries about method or inferences. To begin with, we are relying on questionnaire responses. Do the patients' responses to a set of printed questions actually reflect changes in their mode of living? Then, there is cognitive dissonance, the gnawing problem. Did the patients, consciously or unconsciously, avoid the experience of a dissonant choice and then reward the therapist or themselves with a positive answer? And finally, in the most generic sense, when change is indeed observed, how do we understand the network of correlations observed within our own framework of psychoanalytic thought? All this cries for cross-validation, for detailed description, and a deepening of inquiry. This ushers in the next phase of our work.

A mediating condition: the problem of internalization

'Tell me about anything that is on your mind for about five minutes. It could be about the therapy, your therapist, or any thing else.' This is the opening of our recorded narrative retrospective on a patient's psychotherapy. It continues . . . 'Tell me what led you to therapy . . . what was life like then . . . also tell me about your relationship to your therapist.' Then, 'I would like you to choose five words that reflect that relationship . . . and then what is your life like now.'

These questions, addressed to our patients in an extended psychoanalytically sensitive interview, formed the centrepiece of our Recall Project. The patients had terminated their treatment at the ICC at least one year earlier. At the time of this special recall visit the patients also completed objective scales evaluating internalization, attachment, and symptom levels and completed another EQ form. But the focus of this visit was the audio-recorded interview schedule. Neal Vorus, our clinical evaluator, conducted it. The interview yielded a rich portrait of, to use White's (1952) felicitous phrase, 'lives in progress'.

This programme of re-evaluation offers a broad database to tackle two research issues. First, we re-examine the issue of outcome, via continuation of our earlier study of effectiveness. Second, we explore the issue of those mediating conditions that facilitate effectiveness, that is, account for the therapeutic action of psychoanalytic psychotherapy.

Back to effectiveness

The first study relied on the EQ score – that is, a quantitative questionnaire-derived measure, as an indicator of effectiveness. Now we have the detailed interview schedule to give us a qualitative account of the progress of our patients' lives after termination, a year after the completion of the first EQ.

After three years of therapy, Josh reports that the relationship with his new wife is much better. He is more comfortable with his sexuality. 'I feel much more open, can stand up for myself, can joke; I have become more of a person.' Note that Josh's original EQ score was 265, a high rating.

Ruth found therapy useful. She still has depressive phases but less so. She feels herself less shy and awkward. 'I am still mostly interested in me, but I react with less urgency.' Ruth had an EQ score of 235, or moderate effectiveness.

Andrea opened the interview by noting, 'I was stuck in my treatment and certain things never took place. It is true I like my work better, it is true I have become more analytic. I am still depressed, but more so, still very frustrated.' Andrea had an EQ score of 202, minimal effectiveness.

These brief excerpts speak to the external validity of the EQ score. Josh, Ruth, and Andrea reflected different levels of effectiveness, both in the original scores and now also as captured in the spoken language of the interview. So far we have studied only eight cases and, for these, the trends just presented appear to be corroborated. We hope to study 30 patients and follow up with them two years later. Hence, the representation of the treatment can be traced one and three years after termination.

Towards defining internalization

Now the focus is on the ongoing, dynamic role of internalization of the therapeutic experience. To show this we look for certain markers. First, the internalized experience must be discerned at the time of recall; that is, it must be psychically active. Second, the experience must be linked to outcome that emphasizes its dynamic role. And third, the linkage between internalized experience and outcome becomes stronger with the passage of time. These conditions of presence, linkage to outcome, and persistence, as well as attenuation with time, point to a transformational process. Could they also be an empirical way of delineating *Nachträglichkeit?* Whether we can meet these conditions within our database can be questioned; but it is a frame that will guide our observations.

The notion of internalization as a force in therapeutic action has deep roots in psychoanalytic thought. We are of course aware of the diverse meanings given to the notion of internalization (for example, Loewald, 1962; Schafer, 1992; Segal, 1957). The empirical study of this concept is indeed difficult. Yet here we wish to sketch out our thrust.

Two empirically defined aspects of the notion will be examined. One, derived from a body of research by Geller (Geller and Farber, 1993), speaks of internalization *qua* interiorization of the relationship with the therapist. The second will deal with the symbolization and appropriation of dynamic conflict, that is, with the analytic function proper (Freedman and Karliner, 1999).

Internalization: taking in the therapeutic relationship

A series of phenomenologically based studies, describing the introjection of and identification with the therapist, have been developed by Geller and his associates (Geller and Farber, 1993) over the past two decades. The Therapist Involvement Scale (TIS) was developed to capture such psychic events. The scale was administered in two successive studies of patients in therapy and those who had terminated. Five highly reliable factors were extracted, and three are most pertinent to our discussion:

- *continuing the therapeutic dialogue,* including reliving difficult situations;
- *failure of benign internalization,* where the therapist is seen as scolding or who is disapproving; or
- *negative involvement,* including malevolent and persecutory images.

The first two factors, continuing the dialogue and failure in benign internalization, showed the strongest relationship to outcome and furthermore, there was a trend pointing to a stronger association among patients who were no longer in treatment, compared to those still in therapy. Although the difference in correlation was not significant, here was the first glimpse suggesting a transformational process, taking place with the passage of time.

We have begun to apply this factor scheme to the patients in our recall study. We compared two of our patients who had the highest and lowest outcome scores: Josh and Andrea. Josh has carried within himself a legacy of benign but influential representations of the therapist and their interaction. He had the highest score on 'wish to continue the dialogue' and a very low score of 'failure of benign internalization' as well as lowest on 'negative involvement'. By contrast, Andrea's transcript was highest on failure of benign internalization as well as on negative involvement. She did not wish to think about her therapist, and when she did her image was tinged with bitterness.

The five words chosen by each during the clinical interview portray the essence of internalization in these two patients. Andrea selected the words 'distant', 'awkward', 'unsatisfactory', 'educational', and 'doomed'. For various dynamic reasons, hers was a stance of 'no entry'. Josh, on the other hand, gave a word portrait of his relationship as close, tense, intense, reliable, and incomplete. In restructuring Josh's five choices we might say that Josh felt and continues to feel 'close to', 'intensely about', and 'tense with' mental representations of his therapist whom he perceives as reliable yet with whom he feels the work has been incomplete. This incompleteness may point to discontinuities within him. There were segments showing dramatic instances pointing to unintegrated anxieties over his homosexual longings. That led to notable gaps in his state of consciousness. This last observation stresses that the tracing of the internalization of the relationship is but one mediating condition.

Dynamic symbolization

This perspective focuses on the particular manner in which symbolizing emerges. Symbolization is, of course, part of life, like breathing, eating or moving about, as Suzanne Langer (1942) has made us aware; and it is part and parcel of psychoanalytic work. But what matter in the analytic process are special forms of symbolizing, often incremental in nature. Elsewhere (Freedman, Karliner and Kagan, 2000) we have delineated a Scale of Incremental Symbolization (SIS), describing varying levels of complexity of the symbolic function, from desymbolization, to incipient symbolization to discursive symbolization and then to dynamic symbolization. It is this latter aspect which is our concern here.

In dynamic symbolization we are not just dealing with linking (*Bindung*) of two experiences from distinct spheres of the mind, where one represents the other. That is so for all symbolizing activity. What matters is the linking of those diverse experiences that are conflictual and includes images or wishes previously unnamed. It may manifest itself in content, from irreverent or irrational to rational. It may show itself in the linking of diverse forms, from chaotic to cohesive; and it may also appear in the fluency of spoken language (including non-verbal aspects), notably gaps and discontinuities. In these gaps we note the intrusion of the dynamic unconscious.

Let us cite just one snippet from the transcript of Josh. 'I was troubled by my homosexual thoughts . . . I remember being naked with my father in the bathtub . . . the only occasion it ever happened . . . it was a sudden thought . . . I felt crazy . . . it was not about fucking or being fucked . . . it was also a homosexual thought about father.' He said this slowly, with long hesitation pauses, and interrupted himself in a startled tone. He held on to what he had just fathomed. It was the recognition of mental conflict that had permeated Josh's life, rooted in the past, activated in treatment, but now reconstructed in the interview and perhaps affecting his pattern of living.

Final note

This is a project *in statu nascendi*. Yet our observations so far point to a pattern of internal coherence. Our work started with the Effectiveness Questionnaire and continued with the Recall Validation Study, which provides a window on the quality of the patient's current life, and provides a view towards the nature of the continuing internal dialogue with the therapist and dynamic symbolization.

To the extent that such representations are linked to effectiveness, we obtain a portrait of the therapeutic action of psychoanalytic psychotherapy. Confidence in one's findings increases as different methods yield congruent results.

We are keenly aware of the voices of criticism. Some lend themselves to ready answers. The most salient objection to our mind deals with the fact that the very coherence that we are likely to observe may be rooted in the propensity that the patient brings to treatment, be it cognitive style or dominant defence. Yet the issue of personal continuities leaves unanswered the possibility that in spite of inner constancy, the treatment itself, for that person, has brought forth new forms of mentalization. That issue can be approached if we scrutinize changes in a single case. There we can look at shifts from moment to moment - the final stage of our research endeavour.

Moments of transformation: inside the analytic hour

We are blessed today with a rich repertoire of objective methods evaluating analytic process. Each seeks to capture bits of analytic work. The CCRT (Luborsky and Crits-Christoph, 1990) captures core conflictual relations; in the referential cycle (Bucci, 1997) not only sub-symbolic processes, but also derivatives of unconscious fantasy; in FRAMES (Dahl, 1988) aspects of the compulsion to repeat; in PERT (Gill and Hoffmann, 1982) the experienced relationship to the therapist; Jones and Winholz's (1990) Q-Sort approach; and the comprehensive process scales by Waldron (1999). Each of these is valuable in its own right. However, in the application to the study of process these methods, of necessity, have relied almost exclusively on recorded transcripts.

The issue of what is the proper database for defining psychoanalytic process even entered the debate in the House of Delegates of the IPA. I would like to share with you a dramatic episode that occurred while I was serving as representative from North America. I was a member of the Committee on Psychoanalytic Specificity. Despite wide theoretical divergences we agreed on the broad outline. Specificity involves transference, transference-regression, interpretation, the recognition of the symbolic, and the judicious use of counter-transference and so forth. When I raised the question of validation, so that these processes may be documented on a consensual basis, all hell broke loose.

The issues were as follows. 'If we rely on recordings we intrude upon the privacy of the analytic couple.' 'I know my patients' unconscious, my own counter-transference, and I can estimate the crucial events through my own subjectivity.' Also the work of prominent empirical researchers was cited as setting a dangerous precedent on the grounds that 'process' relied on recorded sessions apart from the perceptions of the engaged analyst.

At last, we reached not only a compromise but also a reasonable synthesis for what at first seemed incompatible positions. In brief, the evaluation of process should originate in the subjective and intuitive judgement of the engaged analyst; it should be corroborated by consultants, using the time-honoured methods of peer review and supervision, and then these essentially clinical procedures should receive external validity through the study of recorded texts. This ideal prescription was accepted by the house and was communicated as a news release and was sent to all IPA Societies in the three regions. Sadly, I fear most of these announcements ended in the wastepaper basket.

With some satisfaction I wish to report that these guidelines are spelled out in the project: 'What is analytic process: Can it be defined empirically?' carried out by Marvin Hurvich, Richard Lasky and myself for more than two years. (For an updated version of this procedure, see Freedman, Hurvich and Lasky, 2000.)

Clinical judgement and the objective appraisal of process

Bridging the gap between the immediacy of clinical judgement and the objective appraisal of process is the challenge facing analytic researchers. We approached this task in five successive steps.

The analyst's clinical scan

This method has been in use for some years and was developed at the SUNY Downstate Medical Center with Michael Berzofsky and Stefani Wilke (now at Heidelberg) and myself (Freedman, Berzofsky and Wilke, 2000). Following an audio-recorded session the analyst (therapist) is instructed to dictate a brief impression, about three minutes in length, depicting major transference themes, ego states, relations to the analyst, major counter-transference thoughts, and affects. A tape-splicing procedure enables us to combine these scans into a working tape. One tape can hold 20 sessions or about five weeks of analysis.

Selection of criterion sessions

The scan is our entry into the evaluation process, now carried further by three consultants, all training analysts, the authors of this work. One of us (RL) reviewed about 60 sessions so as to select 'peak' and criterion sessions to represent extreme variations in the nature of the analytic work. So, for example, an 'A' session may include a range of functions, such as explicit transference, affect communication, reflective function, interpretations received, all of which have the feel of a working session. In contrast a 'Z' criterion session might reveal a lack of these properties and has, to the analyst, the feel of a difficult hour. Both 'A' and 'Z' sessions may well be essential components of the overall analytic process. We deliberately chose terms such as 'A' and 'Z' so as not to pre-judge the specific content of the criterion session and to be open to new possibilities. The other two consultants then corroborated the choice of these criterion sessions from the scan. We observed cyclical transformations within the batch of 60. They seemed to point to regularly occurring transformation cycles in the course of an analysis.

Inside the analytic hour

The three consultants worked together to determine whether there was a match between the analyst's scan and the consultant's initial intuitive judgement. Sometimes we did not find a match and these mismatches became interesting side projects. But then we settled on those criterion sessions that allowed us to say with some confidence that what the analyst experienced and reported could also be noted by the consultants as they listened to a session.

Defining the clinical properties of an 'A' session

The three consultants listened to the session once more – listening the way a supervisor might, on the alert for new material. The aim was to describe unfolding events. It was possible to identify crucial events in the course of the hour. These were the markers signifying how mental functions were employed. Every time a new development took place a marker was named, and we did so by consensus.

In our first application of the method we studied the case of Patty, a married woman in her thirties, with one child, in a four-times-per-week 'classical' analysis. We identified session 232 from the third year of treatment as an 'A' criterion session.

The session began with a subdued comment: 'I didn't feel like coming today . . . I'm not in the right emotional state' and it ended with a strongly felt sequence: 'I am angry at you, I want to criticize you, but I wouldn't dare, but then I am angry, I don't want to torture you, but I don't want to let you off the hook easily.' The entire session can readily be highlighted under the banner 'transformation of hate in the transference'. Here is the frame of the journey. But what were the markers in between?

The markers included:

- The shifts from present to past, from the actual to the imaginary, all coming together in the relationship to the analyst, the markers of Kris's (1982) 'good hour'.

- Variations in the fluency of discourse. At critical moments there were long pauses, and then a new form of affect recognition.
- Shifts in the level of mentalization ranging from the unmentalized to incremental forms of self-reflection of affect, relationship episodes and then dynamic symbolization.
- Markers of conflict and then defence that seemed to occur in cycles.

Those looking for a clear theoretical line will feel uncomfortable. There is no line here, for within limits we seek to work within an open system. The markers are being corroborated by an independent observer, another training analyst. Session 232, the 'A' session, yielded 54 markers; session 226, the 'Z' session, yielded only 32 markers, and practically all were different. 'Z' had the properties one might find in a 'difficult' session. It is our goal to examine transformation cycles in successive years of Patty's analysis.

What is the significance of the 54 markers in an apparently productive session as it contributes to the overall task of defining analytic process? We suggest that we have identified the psychic arena, probably a more fluid one, in which transformation can take place. Clearly there may be many items contributing to a productive analysis. Which aspects are the crucial ones?

External empirical validation

The transcripts of the 'A' and 'Z' criterion sessions will of course now be studied using the range of established procedures for the evaluation of 'process'.

It is expected that each of these well-known measures will yield non-chance discrimination between 'A' and 'Z' sessions. Each of our familiar process instruments can then claim validity. But now comes the issue, which aspect is the crucial one that would point to a productive analytic process? Our prediction would be 'all and yet none' – all contributing, none sufficient. Indeed, each measure may point to different components of process as these are defined by the markers of change in mental functioning. Indeed, the chase for the crucial component of change may well be futile but the nature of what constitutes analytic process may well be within our grasp. The task of identifying the role of particular indices of process applied to a single database is at the heart of the annual CAMP meetings headed by Wallerstein.

A final note

Today, more than ever, we live in an era of multiple psychoanalytic models. While our field is often a beleaguered one, it is these models that give vitality to our discipline. The range of our markers is deliberately broad, and it is likely that adherents of each of the major models can find a ready support for their views. After all, one is likely to find observations congenial to one's own perspective. The range of our markers is broad enough to determine once more the relevance of each to multiple views of how analysis cures. And each can in turn be linked to known measures of process. All this evokes a bewildering set of possibilities. But there is a sphere of common ground, not theoretical but observational. It is inherent in our method of inquiry. It is to be found in observations within the session, within the mind of the consultants, among the items pointing to signifiers of mental change, and within the computerized analysis of text, and this common ground, captured by the five steps of evaluation, defines that arena in which transformations can arise.

Concluding remarks

The occasion was the 75th anniversary of the International Journal. It was in 1994. The place was West Point, New York and the theme 'what is a clinical fact?' A similar conference was held in London a few months later. The issue created heated debate. There was great diversity of views, and some held that the question could not be answered. That situation is not likely to be repeated in a group that is empirically minded, guided by notions of consensual validation. Nonetheless, it is worthwhile to ask that question once more and ponder it from the vantage-point of our observations and from the chapters presented here.

When patients have the opportunity to be involved in psychoanalytic therapy for more than one year and we can show that their experience of their lives is likely to be altered, be it in the quality of object relations, self-appraisal or symptom level, would that be a clinical fact?

Furthermore, if we can show that some patients fare better with more frequent sessions per week while others require long-term exposure, would that qualify as clinical fact?

We would hope of course, from the point of view of outcome, that earlier gains are sustained. But it is equally important to know whether the patient can look back upon the treatment, and finds that the memory of it is still alive, and whether changes in the patient's mental functioning are linked to outcome. These bits of knowledge surely would suggest clinical facts.

And then, if we were to look at salient sessions over successive years, in the course of an analysis, and discover the attributes of a productive treatment process, would that not be a clinical fact?

These are big issues. They will preoccupy us well into the twenty-first century. We are beginning to acquire the methodology and are grasping toward answers. It is a worthwhile effort.

Note

1. The following are members of the IPTAR Research Group: Kate Bar-Tur, Donna Bender, Norbert Freedman, Allan Frosch, Jesse Geller, Joan Hoffenberg, Marvin Hurvich, Denise Kagan, Richard Lasky, Carrie Schafer, Tracey J Strasser, and Neal Vorus.

References

Bucci W (1997) Psychoanalysis and Cognitive Science. New York: Guilford Press.

Dahl H (1988) Frames of mind. In: Dahl H, Kaechele H, Thoma H (eds) Psychoanalytic Process Research Strategies. New York: Springer-Verlag, pp. 51-66.

Freedman N, Berzofsky M, Wilke S (2000) The clinical scan method. Psychotherapy Research Unit, Downstate Medical Center, New York. Unpublished manuscript.

Freedman N, Hoffenberg J, Vorus N, Frosch A (1999) The effectiveness of psychoanalytic psychotherapy: The role of treatment duration, session frequency, and the therapeutic relationship. Journal of the American Psychoanalytic Association 47: 741-72.

Freedman N, Hurvich M, Lasky R (2000) Analytic process: Transformation cycles in the course of analytic work. Paper presented at the Annual CAMP Meeting, December 2000.

Freedman N, Karliner R (1999) On incremental symbolization: The concept and its empirical definition. Paper presented at the Annual Meeting of the American Psychological Association, Division of Psychoanalysis, April 1999.

Freedman N, Karliner R, Kagan D (2000) The Scales of Incremental Symbolization Manual. Department of Psychology, SUNY Downstate Medical Center.

Geller JD, Farber BA (1993) Factors influencing the process of internalization in psychotherapy. Psychotherapy Research 3: 166-80.

Gill MM, Hoffmann IZ (1982) A method for studying the analysis of aspects of the patient's experience of the relationship in psychoanalysis and psychotherapy. Journal of the American Psychoanalytic Association 30: 137-67.

Jones E, Winholz, M (1990) The psychoanalytic case study: Towards a method for systematic inquiry. Journal of the American Psychoanalytic Association 38: 885-909.

Kris A (1982) Free Association: Method and process. New Haven, CT: Yale University Press.

Kris E (1951) Ego psychology and interpretation in psychoanalytic therapy. Psychoanalytic Quarterly 20: 15-30.

Langer SK (1942) Philosophy in a New Key: A study in the symbolism of reason, rite and art. Cambridge, MA: Harvard University Press.

Leuziger-Bohleber M, Beutel M, Stuhr U, Rueger B (2000) How to study the quality of psychoanalytic treatment: A combination of qualitative and quantitative approaches in a represented follow-up study. Paper presented at the Joseph Sandler Research Conference, March 2000.

Loewald H (1962) On internalization. In: Loewald H (1980) Papers on Psychoanalysis. New Haven, CT: Yale University Press.

Luborsky L (1996) Theories of cure in psychoanalytic psychotherapies and the evidence for them. Psychoanalytic Inquiry 16: 257-64.

Luborsky L, Crits-Christoph P (1990) A guide to the CCRT method. In: Luborsky L, Crits-Christoph P (eds) Understanding Transference: The core conflictual relationship theme method. New York: Basic Books, pp. 15-36.

Rousillon R (1998) Historical reference, *après coup*, and the primal scene. Standing Conference on Psychoanalytical Intracutural and Interculutural Dialogue, International Psychoanalytic Association, Paris, July 1998.

Sandell R, Blomberg J, Lazar A, Carlsson J, Broberg J, Schubert J (2000) Varieties of long-term outcome among patients in psychoanalysis and long-term psychotherapy: a review of findings in the Stockholm Outcome of Psychoanalysis and Psychotherapy Project (STOPPP). International Journal of Psychoanalysis 81: 921-42.

Sandler J, Dreher AU (1996) What Do Analysts Want? London: Routledge.

Schafer R (1992) Retelling a Life: Narration and dialogue in psychoanalysis. New York: Basic Books.

Segal H (1957) Notes on symbol formation. International Journal of Psychoanalysis 37: 339-43.

Seligman MEP (1995) The effectiveness of psychotherapy: The Consumer Reports Study. American Psychologist 50: 965-74.

Waldron S (1999) Saying the right thing at the right time: Intervention quality, patient productivity, and the interdependence of analyst and patient for psychoanalytic process. Paper presented at the Research Conference of Psychoanalysis and Psychoanalytic Long Term Therapy, Hamburg University, October 1999.

Wallerstein R (1988) The assessment of structural change in psychoanalytic psychotherapy and research. Journal of the American Psychoanalytic Association 36 (Suppl.): 241-61.

White R (1952) Lives in Progress. New York: Dryden Press.

CHAPTER 21
Interaction and change in psychoanalytic long-term therapy

ENRICO E JONES

This chapter introduces the construct of *interaction structure.* Interaction structure emphasizes the presence and meaning of repetitive patterns of interaction in the therapy relationship. It is a theory about therapeutic action that attempts to address the role of psychological knowledge through uncovering meaning, and the role of interpersonal interaction in patient change. Patient and therapist interact in ways that are repetitive and mutually influencing. These patterns of interaction probably reflect the psychological structure of both patient and therapist, whether psychic structure is conceptualized in terms of object representations or compromise formations and impulse-defence configurations. It is not assumed that influence flows only in the direction of therapist to patient. Instead, the nature of the patient's influence on the therapist and on the emerging patterns of relationship are considered along with the manner in which the therapist's interventions influence patient change, providing a framework in which mutual or reciprocal influence processes between patient and therapist can be taken into account. Interaction structures allow the consideration of both the intrapsychic and interpersonal by recognizing that what is internal is an important basis for what becomes manifest in the interpersonal or interactive field. Interaction structures refer not only to how the patient's conflicts are represented in the transference, but also the characteristic manner in which the therapist reacts to these conflicts. These patterns of interaction are the observable behavioural and emotional components of the transference-counter-transference. More than one such interaction structure may occur in a therapist-patient pair, but one dominant pattern usually emerges.

This chapter describes a study of the psychotherapies of two patients diagnosed as suffering from major depressive disorder. The aim was to identify the presence of interaction structures and to determine how they might be causally linked to patient change. These cases were selected because they had contrasting outcomes: one had a successful outcome and in the second the patient reported only modest change. The research questions were threefold:

- whether there were meaningful structures of patient–therapist interaction;
- whether these differed across the two treatments and a third not reported in detail; and
- how changes in structures of interaction might be associated with patient improvement.

Interaction structures can play a mutative role through several modes. The first case, Ms A, represents a mode of therapeutic action in which repetitive, mutually influencing interactions facilitate the patient's experience and representation of certain mental states and the knowledge of her own intentionality. These slow-to-change patterns of interaction, which therapist and patient gradually came to understand, were the expressions of the transference and counter-transference. When the therapist brings unconscious counter-transference associations and reactions into awareness, this may bring them, along with the patient's transference reactions, into a mutual sphere of consciousness that the patient alone cannot accomplish. In this view of therapeutic action, insight and relationship are inseparable, because psychological knowledge of the self develops in the context of a relationship with a therapist who endeavours to understand the mind of the patient through the medium of their interaction.

In the second case, Mr B, significant repetitive patient–therapist interactions remained uninterpreted, not understood, and outside of explicit awareness. This interaction pattern, whose meaning was not sufficiently understood and interpreted, served as an impediment to Mr B's greater self-knowledge and understanding, obstructed progress in the treatment, and led to what appeared to be a therapeutic stalemate. However, interaction patterns that remain unacknowledged and not interpreted do not necessarily signal that therapy is not helpful to the patient. Uninterpreted interaction patterns can, in and of themselves, have a supportive function. For example, a patient could rely on the therapist's accepting, non-judgemental attitude to ward off harshly self-punitive introjects, relieve guilt, and bolster a threatened self-regard. Whenever the patient becomes caught up in irrational self-blame, the therapist, for example, through his attitude and interventions, repeatedly conveys that the patient is not the worthless person she feels herself to be. However, the therapist does not interpret the patient's need to rely on him for this important function, and this vital interaction and its meaning is not understood. Many such interaction structures are repeatedly enacted by both therapist and patient, at least in part unconsciously. The interaction structure construct implies that the therapist is not simply deliberately and self-consciously providing the patient with an experience that is new and contrary to the response the patient has come to expect (that is, a 'corrective emotional experience'). It implies, in addition, that the therapist is also involving him or herself in a partially unconscious transference-counter-transference interaction pattern.

Interaction structures that remain uninterpreted and outside of awareness may not necessarily serve only a defensive function. There may be a means through which unacknowledged interaction structures can promote patient change in a way that is not only supportive, but modifies psychic structure. A third case, Ms M, which is not covered in this chapter, seems to represent this mode of therapeutic action. In this mode, unconscious interaction patterns seem to be mutative by creating opportunities for the modification of the patient's problematic mental representations of self and others that had been largely outside of consciousness. Certain kinds of uninterpreted transference/counter-transference interactions, despite remaining unacknowledged, nevertheless seemed to promote this patient's capacity for self-reflection and insight into certain aspects of her mental life. In other words, in the case of Ms M, much of the work of therapy occurred, at least manifestly or explicitly, outside the transference/counter-transference matrix (see Jones, 2000).

Study design

Studying psychoanalytic constructs requires innovative research strategies, particularly new quantitative methods for the study of single cases. This study applied an innovative set of methods in intensive single case designs to identify the presence of interaction structures and to determine how they are linked to patient change. The strategy is to focus on patterns of patient-therapist interaction within and across therapy sessions and to explore the association of structure and sequence of interaction with patient change. Therapy process is considered as a sequence of actions and events that extend over time.

The two treatments I will describe were conducted as part of an investigation of longer-term psychotherapies for major depression:

- All patients meet research diagnostic criteria for major depression.
- Treatments are two years in length.
- Twice weekly.
- Experienced therapists.

- All hours video and audiotaped.
- Assessments periodically throughout treatment: Symptom Checklist, Beck Depression Inventory, MMPI, Automatic Thoughts Questionnaire, Social Adjustment Scale, IIP, SASB.
- Follow-ups at six months, one and two years post treatment.

Assessing therapy outcome

The assessment of change in psychotherapy has focused almost exclusively on the measurement of symptomatic improvement. However, for most psychoanalytically orientated clinicians, an important goal is change in *psychological structure*, that is, long-term symptom relief coupled with enduring change in the patient's mental functioning and personality. In this study, changes in patients' psychological structure were assessed using the Structural Analysis of Social Behaviour measure (SASB; Benjamin, 1993), which captures mental representations of self and other. Depressed patients tend to have high scores for self-punitive, attacking and controlling introjects on the SASB.

How we studied the therapy process

In order to use clinical data to test hypotheses it is necessary to first establish that certain kinds of observable phenomena co-occur, and then to assess the strength of their relationship. Clinical phenomena must be intersubjectively observable. That is to say, different judges can independently agree about their characteristics and whether they occur. Disagreements about the interpretation or meaning of the same case material are commonplace in clinical work and constitute important grounds for criticism of the scientific status of psychoanalytic methods for acquiring knowledge. It is crucial that any research methodology establishes the consensus, or reliability, among judges about the presence and nature of a clinical phenomenon. I thought that the study of analytic and therapeutic process would be aided by a comprehensive classification system, a method that would form the basis for observationally grounded research.

The Psychotherapy Process Q-sort (PQS) (Jones, 2000) is the product of my effort to develop such a system. It is designed to provide a basic language for the description and classification of intervention processes in a form suitable for quantitative analysis. The method is designed for application to an audiotaped or videotaped record or verbatim transcript of actual treatment hours. The PQS comprises 100 items describing patient attitudes, behaviours or experience; the therapist's actions and attitudes, and the nature of their interaction. A coding manual provides the items and their definitions along with examples to minimize varying interpretations. After studying a record of a treatment hour, clinical judges proceed to the ordering of the 100 items, each printed separately on cards to permit easy arrangement and rearrangement. The items are sorted into nine piles ranging on a continuum from 'extremely uncharacteristic' (category 1) to 'extremely characteristic' (category 9). The number of cards sorted into each pile (ranging from five at the extremes to 18 in the middle or 'neutral' category) conforms to a normal distribution. This requires judges to make multiple evaluations among items, thus avoiding either positive or negative halo effects. The special value of the Q-method is that it provides a way of quantifying the qualities of the analytic or therapeutic process, and can capture the uniqueness of each hour while also permitting the assessment of the similarities or dissimilarities between hours and patients (see Block, 1961). The PQS addresses the long-standing problem of how to achieve agreement about the nature of clinical phenomena, and judgements requiring relatively high levels of inference can be made reliably.

Videotapes of the two cases were completely randomized, and two judges who were blind to one another's ratings made independent Q-ratings. Inter-rater reliability was calculated using the Pearson product-moment correlation coefficient; average inter-rater reliability achieved $r = 0.80$ (Spearman-Brown corrected; range, 0.66 to 0.94). Q-sort composites (i.e. Q-ratings averaged across judges) were used in all subsequent analyses.

A statistical analysis called the P-technique (Luborsky, 1953, 1995) was applied to the Q-sort ratings of therapy process. The P-technique is a factor analysis of repeated measures within the same patient–therapist pair to identify potential underlying structures of interaction. In a third and final step, time series analysis (Gottman, 1981), a quantitative technique that is now gaining in popularity, was used to assess changes over time by analysing the temporal unfolding of variables. Time series analysis requires the repeated measure of a set of variables over time within the individual case and attempts to understand temporal variations or changes in the scores of certain of these variables as a function of other variables.

Ms A: An interpreted interaction structure

Ms A, a college student, was 21 years old at the beginning of treatment. She was seen twice weekly for 126 sessions over a period of 21 months. She became depressed and sought therapy after the sudden onset of an apparently serious mental disorder in an older sister with whom she had a close relationship.

Ms A: therapy outcome

Ms A's treatment was successful by all indices of patient change. Figure 21.1 plots scores on several symptom measures over the course of treatment. Her symptom scores and problem indices demonstrated clinically significant change, and she maintained these gains at six-month and one-year follow-ups. Ms A met criteria for clinically significant change both post-therapy and at one-year follow up on the BDI, the General Severity Index (GSI) of the SCL 90-R, the ATQ, and the depression scale of the MMPI, the SAS, and the IIP. There was a large correlation of the GSI with treatment session number, r = -0.82, demonstrating a significant association between patient improvement and length of treatment. Ms A's SASB sores reflected a marked decrease in her propensity for self-accusation, self-blame, and self-punishment; in short, harsh, self-critical mental representations had apparently been altered. Note that the decline in Ms A's symptoms is closely associated with a decrease in her 'self-attack' score on the SASB.

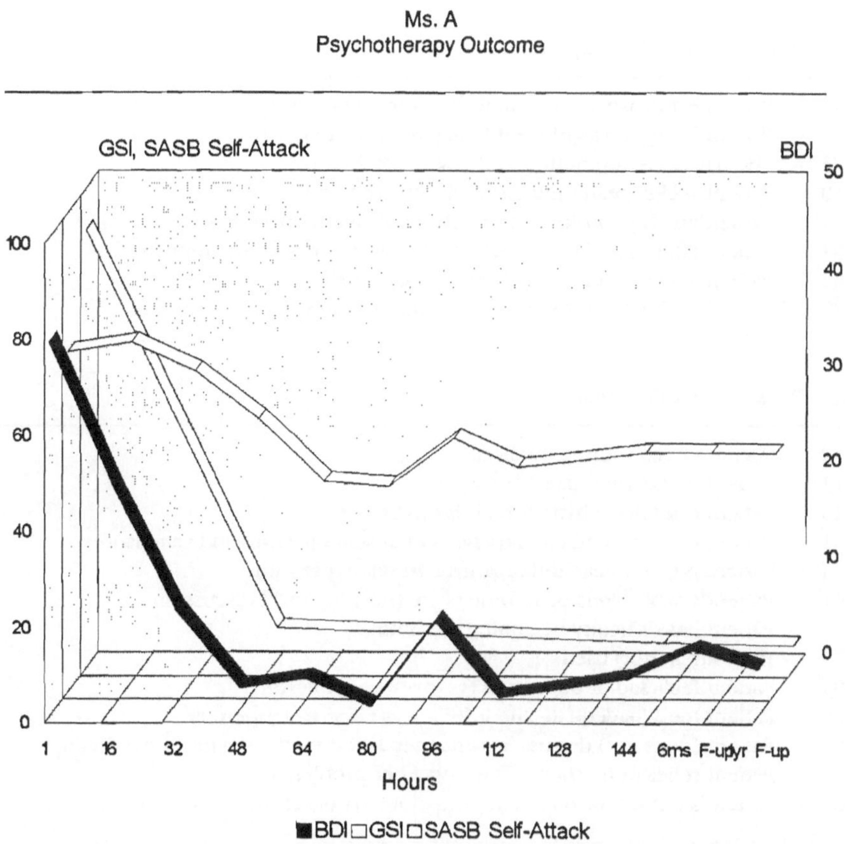

Figure 21.1. Plot of scores on Ms A's symptom measures over the 21-month treatment and at six-month, one-year and two-year follow-ups. (BDI = Beck Depression Inventory; GSI = General Severity Index of the Symptom Checklist 90 - Revised; SASB = Structural Analysis of Social Behaviour.)

Identifying interaction structures in Ms A's therapy

To determine whether structures of interaction could be identified, the Q-ratings for treatment hours (N = 63) were subjected to an exploratory factor analysis. The factor analysis yielded three interpretable clusters. Factor 1 was labelled *collaborative exploration*; factor 2, *ambivalence/compliance*; and factor 3, *provoking rescue.* Factor scales were constructed by averaging the relevant PQS items for each of the three factors. Factors 1 and 3 were not correlated with patient outcome. Only factor 3, provoking rescue, was correlated with patient improvement. The items that define factors 1 and 3 are listed in Tables 21.1 and 21.2, respectively. The appearance of the word 'not' in parentheses in the item indicates the rating of the item was reversed to simplify the presentation.

Table 21.1. Collaborative exploration

Q 97	Patient is introspective, readily explores inner thoughts and feelings.
Q 88	Patient brings up significant issues and material.
Q 73	The patient is committed to the work of therapy.
Q 10	Patient seeks greater intimacy with the therapist.
Q 55	Patient conveys positive expectations about therapy.
Q 33	Patient talks of feelings about being close to or needing someone.
Q 32	Patient achieves a new understanding or insight.
Q 72	Patient understands the nature of therapy and what is expected

Table 21.2. Provoking rescue

Q 12	Silences occur during the hour.
Q 13	Patient is (not) animated or excited.
Q 15	Patient does not initiate topics; is passive.
Q 61	Patient feels shy and embarrassed (vs unselfconscious and self-assured).
Q 54	Patient is (not) clear and organized in self-expression.
Q 41	Patient's aspirations or ambitions are (not) topics of discussion.
Q 25	Patient has difficulty beginning the hour.
Q 74	Humour is (not) used.
Q 94	Patient feels sad or depressed (vs joyous or cheerful).
Q 59	Patient feels inadequate and inferior (vs effective/superior).
Q 56	Patient (does not) discuss experiences as if distant from his or her feelings.
Q 52	Patient relies upon therapist to solve her problems.
Q 69	Patient's current or recent life situation is (not) emphasized in discussion.

We hypothesized that decline in the intensity and frequency of certain interaction structures was related to patient improvement. It is, of course, more difficult to make causal inferences from quantitative single case designs than from randomized clinical trials. However, single case designs have an advantage in affording multiple observations of the same variables taken at regular time intervals (time series data). In addition to knowing the magnitude of change in a variable, we also know *when* that change occurred relative to changes in other variables. Causality can therefore be inferred using *time series analysis*. The basic logic is as follows. If, for example, the factor labelled 'provoking rescue' influenced symptom improvement, then a score on the SCL-90-R at a given time should be predictable from past levels of 'provoking rescue' above and beyond what is predictable from knowing previous SCL-90-R scores alone. Furthermore, the influence should be unidirectional - SCL-90-R scores should not predict future 'provoking rescue' above and beyond what could be predicted from past levels of 'provoking rescue'. Time series analysis demonstrated that shifts in 'provoking rescue' indeed influenced changes on Ms A's symptom scores.

We concluded that therapeutic action, for Ms A, was located in the case-specific interaction structure, provoking rescue. This interaction structure of Ms A and her therapist was captured by the Q-items in Table 21.2. This repetitive interaction was characterized by the patient's passivity and lengthy silences accompanied by depressed affect, a strong sense of inadequacy, inferiority and humiliation, and a wish to rely on the therapist to solve her problems.

During these repetitive interactions there was a strong implicit, and often explicit, demand on the therapist to fill the painful silences and to deliver transformative explanations. The therapist, on his part, often felt ineffective, and was prompted to become more active in drawing the patient out and rescuing them both from her tortured silences. The therapist was nevertheless able to interpret this pattern as, among other meanings, a way for the patient to avoid the pain associated with talking about herself. This interaction structure also represented an unconscious effort to provoke the therapist into pursuing her, which repeated in the transference the traumatic sexual abuse the patient had experienced in childhood and early adolescence. Time series analysis demonstrated that the slow decline in frequency and intensity of this interactive pattern predicted Ms A's improvement in both her depression and her daily functioning. We attributed the eventual fading of this interaction pattern to the therapist's interpretation, and the patient's gradual understanding, of provoking rescue

Mr B: an uninterpreted interaction structure

Mr B was a 29-year-old single man who was seen for a total of 208 treatment sessions, twice weekly, over a period of two-and-a-half years. His presenting complaint was a long-standing depression and anxiety, which had recently become particularly acute.

Mr B: therapy outcome

Mr B demonstrated only modest symptom change after more than two years of twice-weekly psychotherapy. His symptom scores fluctuated considerably and at termination he was somewhat improved, although at one-year follow-up he had returned to pre-treatment levels (see Figure 21.2). Mr B met criteria for clinically significant change at post-therapy on the BDI, ATQ, and SAS, but not on the SCL-90-R, the IIP, the D-scale of the MMPI, or the 'self-attack' index of the SASB. At the one-year follow-up Mr B met criteria for clinically significant change only on the SAS. There was no correlation between session number and score on the GSI Total Score of the SCL-90-R, r = 0.00.

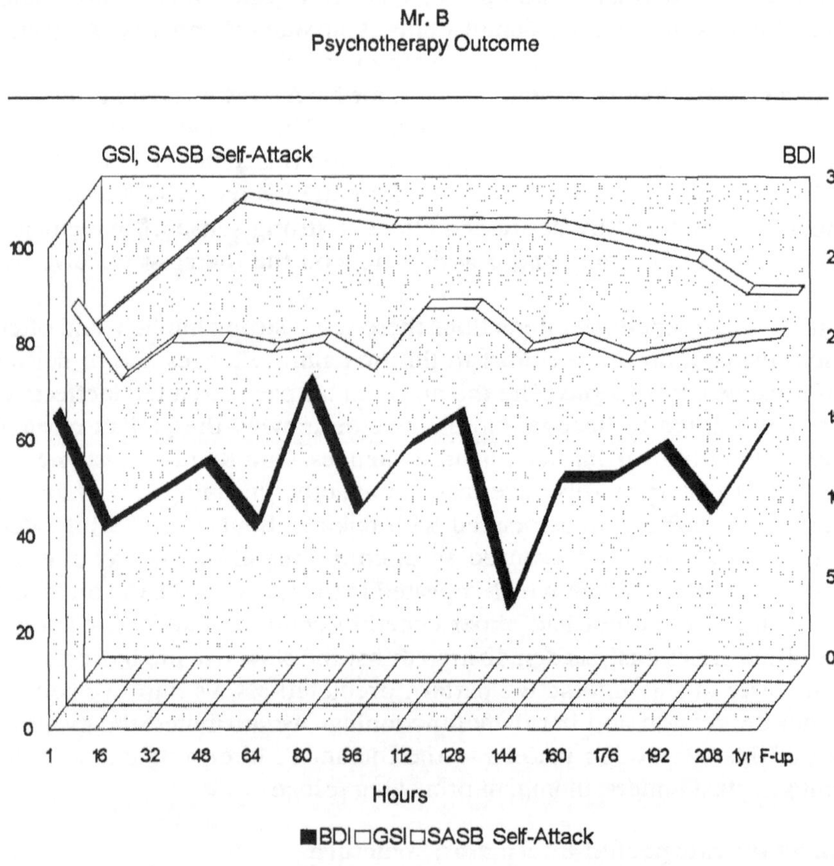

Figure 21.2. Plot of scores on Mr B's symptom measures over the 2.5-year treatment and at one-year follow-up. (BDI = Beck Depression Inventory; GSI = General Severity Index of the Symptom Checklist 90 - Revised; SASB = Structural Analysis of Social Behaviour.)

Identifying interaction structures in Mr B's therapy

As with Ms A, Q-sort ratings were made for every other treatment hour (N = 104) in completely randomized order, and subjected to a factor analysis. The factor analysis yielded three interpretable clusters: factor 1, which was similar in content to the first factor for Ms A, was identically labelled as *collaborative exploration*; factor 2 was labelled *resistant and withdrawn,* and factor 3 was labelled *angry interaction* (Table 21.3).

Table 21.3. Angry interaction

Q 14	Patient does not feel understood by therapist.
Q 9	Therapist is distant, aloof (vs responsive and affectively involved).
Q 31	Therapist does not ask for more information or elaboration.
Q 42	Patient rejects (vs accepts) therapist's comments and observations.
Q 77	Therapist is tactless.
Q 87	Patient is controlling.
Q 65	Therapist (does not) clarify, restate, or rephrase patient's communication.
Q 39	There is a competitive quality to the relationship.
Q 24	Therapist's own emotional conflicts intrude into the relationship.
Q 30	Discussion centres on cognitive themes (i.e. about ideas or belief systems).

The scores on the clusters for each rated treatment hour and the GSI of the SCL-90-R collected at regular intervals over the course of the treatment were subjected to a time series analysis to determine if one series of scores was partially predictable from another. Our data showed that symptom scores on the SCL-90-R predicted the factors 'collaborative exploration' and 'angry interaction'. In other words, changes in patient symptom level signalled changes in the nature of the interaction, rather than changes in process predicting patient symptom improvement, as with Ms A. When Mr B was more symptomatic and depressed, this signalled that he and his therapist would be less involved and collaborative, and more inclined to become caught up in angry interactions, in the next sessions. The therapist–patient interaction structure labelled 'angry interaction' was captured by the Q-items listed in Table 21.3.

These repetitive angry interactions were tense, competitive and intellectualized exchanges in which the patient attempted to control the therapist, and in which the patient did not feel understood and rejected the therapist's attempts to help. The therapist, in turn, was less tactful, and had to struggle with angry, contemptuous counter-transference reactions.

The causal direction of the relationship of interaction structures to symptom change was different from those with Ms A and her therapist, with symptom scores predicting levels and frequency of interaction patterns. In other words, with Mr B, lower levels of depression and symptom scores predicted higher levels of collaborative exploration, and higher symptom scores predicted more frequent and intense angry interaction. Mr B was more capable of working in collaboration with the therapist, and less likely to provoke tense, angry exchanges when he felt less depressed and anxious. There was no decline in the intensity and frequency of this interaction structure during the therapy (correlation between therapy session number and this factor was $r = 0.06$, n.s.) This angry interaction structure was probably insufficiently interpreted and understood, and we conclude that this unanalysed, and relatively unchanging interaction pattern was associated with the fact that the patient reported only little improvement at termination. It is an illustration of a largely unconscious pattern of interaction that may lead to a stalemate in a treatment.

Discussion

We have been able to demonstrate empirically the presence of interaction structures in all the cases we have studied. They can also, of course, be routinely observed in clinical practice. The interaction structure construct has much in common with already familiar theoretical and technical language, such as analysing the transference in the here and now, and working through. However, it provides an empirical underpinning for aspects of these concepts. Moreover, it also includes the two-person, inter-subjective component of therapeutic action. 'Interaction structure' refers to how the patient's character pathology, conflicts and symptoms express themselves in the relationship with the therapist, and how the therapist becomes involved with the patient in what might be called a symptomatic way. These patterns of interaction are the observable behavioural and emotional components of the transference–counter-transference.

Our findings also have implications for process–outcome research strategies by underscoring the complex nature of causal relations in psychotherapy. Our data suggest that although there may be similarities in interaction structures across patients, there are key differences as well. It is unlikely that a particular therapist action (transference interpretations or seemingly supportive interventions), or even certain kinds of processes invariably signify something fixed for all patients. The subjective meaning of observable processes will vary across patient–therapist dyads. The differing causal links between process and outcome, identified in just a few cases studied in depth, may indicate the impossibility of establishing subjective meaning in large sample studies. A focus on the variability within the therapy dyad is the very core of process research.

Interaction structures are the observable, enacted and emotionally experienced component of mental representations of self and other in the therapy situation. These patterns of interaction do not represent all that is dynamically unconscious. They are the manifest, behavioural aspect of the transference-counter-transference. The construct is clinically useful in a number of respects. Interaction structures capture the behavioural and emotional surface. Repetitive patterns of interaction can be observed directly by therapist and patient; they are accessible, and their presence can be confirmed consensually. They are particularly useful in providing clinical data for exploration that are alive and have a sense of immediacy. Grounding an exploration of the patient's mental life on interaction structures that can be felt and observed helps avoid an overly intellectualized consideration of what the patient is doing, and why. It also reduces the need to rely on inferences about the patient's motives and intentions that are sometimes difficult to verify.

Since these interaction patterns can be observed and mutually verified by therapist and patient, using them as a starting point for exploration reduces the problems associated with the therapist's authoritative role, such as idealizations of the therapist, patient compliance, and reliance on the therapist's authority, knowledge and wisdom. The therapist is less induced to take the role of 'the one who knows' both what is going on in the patient's mind, and the solution to the patient's problems. Recognizing interaction patterns is also helpful in clinical supervision. In fact, the clinical supervisor, who has the benefit of the perspective associated with less counter-transference, will often identify interaction structures more easily than the therapist, who may be in the grip of counter-transference feelings.

Patient change is the result of relatively specific repetitive patterns that facilitate the psychological processes that enable patients to experience and represent certain mental states, and to have knowledge of their own intentionality. Specific forms of experiences with the therapist are necessary for the patient to develop a sense of subjectivity, agency and self-knowledge. An underlying premise is that the recognition, interpretation, and understanding of the meanings of these interaction patterns are an important component of the change process.

Uninterpreted, unacknowledged interaction structures can serve a defensive function and, as with Mr B, can be the source of stalemates in therapy. However, even as they function defensively, uninterpreted interaction patterns can also serve a supportive function, and help to relieve anxiety and depressive symptoms. Uninterpreted, unacknowledged interaction structures are enacted by both therapist and patient, at least in part unconsciously. In fact, many supportive interventions, especially those that are undertaken without careful thought, mask hidden transference/counter-transference interaction patterns.

The interaction structure construct, and its associated theory of therapeutic action, is based on empirical research. In the last decades, a clinically and theoretically vigorous psychoanalysis has generated a rich and diverse set of theories about the nature of the change process. Newer self-psychological, relational and intersubjective perspectives have joined the already established drive-structural, ego-psychological and neo-Kleinian points of view. A real difficulty has been how to determine the validity, and usefulness, of these alternative, sometimes competing perspectives. The traditional methods of resolving theoretical disputes in psychoanalysis have been discussion and debate, the slow accumulation of clinical experience with certain approaches, and continued development of theory. These methods of resolving scientific problems can be very usefully augmented by empirical research. This work shows that systematic empirical inquiry is able not only to confirm psychoanalytic ideas but can also lead to new integrations.

The theoretical ferment within psychoanalysis is, of course, occurring during a time when the scientific status of psychoanalysis is being questioned by an array of critics, from areas as diverse as philosophy of science and biological psychiatry, and also from non-analytic therapists who wish to promote their own methods of intervention. In this context, the need to ground analytic theories about the change process in research has assumed real urgency. This work will hopefully fortify clinicians' convictions about the value and validity of psychoanalytic approaches to treatment. Although analytic clinicians often concede the need for research, some have not seen how the very serious difficulties in capturing empirically, and quantifying, subtle and complex clinical and theoretical constructs can be overcome. Perhaps this work will also foster the recognition that psychoanalytic research can be conducted in ways that are clinically and theoretically meaningful.

References

Benjamin L (1974/1993) Structural analysis of social behavior. Psychological Review 81(5): 392–425.

Block J (1961/1978) The Q-sort Method in Personality Assessment and Psychiatric Research. Spingfield, IL: Charles Thomas.

Gottman J (1981) Time Series Analysis. New York: Cambridge University Press.

Jones EE (2000) Therapeutic Action: A guide to psychoanalytic therapy. Northvale, NJ: Jason Aronson.

Luborsky L (1953) Intra-individual repetitive measurements (P-technique) in understanding symptom structure and psychotherapeutic change. In: Mowrer OH (ed.) Psychotherapy: Theory and research. New York: The Ronald Press, pp. 389–413.
Luborsky L (1995) The first trial of the P-technique in psychotherapy research – a still lively legacy. Journal of Consulting and Clinical Psychology 63: 6–14.

CHAPTER 22

Amalia X's psychoanalytic therapy in the light of Jones's Psychotherapy Process Q-Sort

CORNELIA ALBANI, GERD BLASER, UWE JACOBS, ENRICO JONES, HELMUT THOMÄ, HORST KÄCHELE

Introduction

This chapter describes the psychoanalytic treatment of Amalia X, a German 'specimen case', using the 'Psychotherapy Process Q-Sort' by Enrico Jones. It presents the first application of the German version of this method developed by the authors. The method proved to be a reliable and proper instrument for describing psychotherapeutic processes. Comparison of sessions from the beginning and termination phases of a psychoanalytic therapy demonstrated clinically relevant differences between the two phases of treatment.

The psychoanalytic research group at the University of Ulm, Germany, has been engaged in the systematic study of several audiotaped psychoanalytic treatments. This line of research was envisioned in the initial federal grant application that Helmut Thomä submitted to the German Research Society (DFG) in 1967, and fully developed by Horst Kächele in the following years. The Ulm research model consists of a multimodal and multimethodological investigation. We distinguish the modalities of:

- traditional clinical case presentation;
- systematic description of the treatment course through external reviewers;
- rating of clinical concepts according to manuals; and
- partly computer-aided text-analytic evaluation (Kächele and Thomä, 1993).

A description of this process as applied to a German specimen case (Kächele, submitted) is described in the third volume of Kächele and Thomä (1999) which can be viewed on the home page of the Ulm department.

The present study is an example of modality (c). Parts of the manuscript were extracted from an article describing the initial study discussed here (Albani et al., 2000).

Case description: the patient Amalia

We first would like to familiarize the reader with the patient called Amalia X.

Amalia X, a 30-year-old, well-educated woman, came to psychoanalysis because her low self-esteem had contributed to a neurotic depression in the last few years. Her entire life history since puberty and her social role as a woman had suffered from the severe strain resulting from her hirsutism. Although it had been possible for her to hide the virile growth of hair all over her body from others, the cosmetic aids she had used had not raised her self-esteem or eliminated her extreme social insecurity. Her feeling of being stigmatized and her neurotic symptoms, which had already been manifest before puberty, reinforced each other in a vicious cycle; the inhibitions of an obsessional neurosis and various symptoms of an anxiety neurosis impeded her personal relationships and, most importantly, kept the patient from forming closer heterosexual friendships. Clinical experience justified the following assumptions. A virile stigma strengthens penis envy and reactivates Oedipal conflicts. If the patient's wish to be a man had materialized, her hermaphroditic body image would have become free of conflict. The question 'am I a man or a woman?' would then have been answered; her insecurity regarding her identity, which was continuously reinforced by her stigma, would have been eliminated; and self-image and physical reality would then have been in agreement. It was impossible for her to maintain her unconscious phantasy, however, in view of the physical reality. A virile stigma does not make a man of a woman. Regressive solutions, such as reaching an inner security despite her masculine stigma by identifying herself with her mother, revitalized the old mother–daughter conflicts and led to a variety of defensive processes. All of her affective and cognitive processes were marked by ambivalence, so that she had difficulty, for example, deciding between different colours when shopping because she linked them with the qualities of masculine or feminine (Thomä and Kächele, 1992: 79).

This psychoanalytic treatment comprised a total of 517 hours and was evaluated as successful based on clinical evaluation and psychological testing. For a detailed clinical description see (Kächele et al., 1999; Thomä and Kächele, 1997). This particular patient has been the subject of quite a number of empirical studies, which qualify the case as a 'German specimen case' (Kächele, Mergenthaler and Thomä, 1998).

Data and methodology

In the present study, we applied the German version of the 'Psychotherapy Process Q-sort', PQS (Jones, 2000). Jones's method attempts to create a uniform language with a clinically relevant terminology that can describe the psychotherapeutic process in a manner independent from various theoretical models and that allows a systematic and comparable evaluation of therapeutic interactions across different therapy methods. The PQS consists of 100 items that are applied according to a rating system of nine categories (1 = extremely uncharacteristic, 9 = extremely characteristic) following the thorough study of a transcript or videotape of an entire therapy hour. The distribution of items according to the nine categories is fixed in order to approximate a normal distribution.

The database for the study was the first and last five hours of the psychoanalytic treatment of Amalia, which was conducted by an experienced analyst. The analysis according to the PQS serves to describe the characteristic elements of this treatment and to allow a comparison of the two phases in order to illustrate the relevant differences. The evaluation of the sessions was performed by two raters in randomized order and resulted in a mean inter-rater agreement of $r = 0.64$ (0.54–0.78).

Results

Characteristic and uncharacteristic items for all 10 hours

First, we will describe which items were rated as particularly characteristic and uncharacteristic for all 10 hours. A rank order of means was calculated. A further criterion for inclusion was that these items showed little or no difference in their means between the beginning and termination phases ($p < 0.10$, Wilcoxon test). These items thus provide a general description of the behaviour of the patient, the therapist, and their interaction in the beginning and termination phase of the analysis.

The attitude of the therapist is described as empathic (Q 6), neutral (Q 93), conveying acceptance (Q 18), tactful (Q 77), not condescending (Q 51) and emotionally involved (Q 9). The therapist's own emotional conflicts do not intrude into the relationship (Q 24) and the therapist does not emphasize patient feelings (Q 81). The patient has no difficulties beginning the hour (Q 25); she is active (Q 15) and brings up significant issues and material (Q 88). The patient talks of wanting to be separate (Q 29), she accepts the therapist's comments and observations (Q 42) and she feels understood by the therapist (Q 14). The interaction is characterized by a specific focus (Q 23), for example the self-image of the patient (Q 35), her interpersonal relationships (Q 63) and cognitive themes (Q 30).

Characteristic and uncharacteristic items separating the beginning and termination phases

In order to describe the differences between the beginning and termination phases of the therapy, the first and last five hours were pooled into separate blocks and the means of the ratings of the most characteristic and uncharacteristic items for both raters were calculated (Tables 22.1 and 22.2).

Jones established the practice of identifying the respective 10 highest and lowest ratings. Subsequently, the means were tested for statistical differences (Wilcoxon test, Table 22.3).

Table 22.1. Rank order for the most characteristic and uncharacteristic PQS items for the beginning phase (means across five therapy hours and two raters)

PQS items		M
10 most characteristic items		
Q 23	Dialogue has a specific focus.	7.9
Q 35	Self-image is a focus of discussion.	7.9
Q 29	Patient talks of wanting to be separate or distant.	7.8
Q 88	Patient brings up significant issues and material.	7.8
Q 30	Discussion centres on cognitive themes, i.e. about ideas or beliefs.	7.6
Q 63	Patient's interpersonal relationships are a major theme.	7.6
Q 65	Therapist clarifies, restates, or rephrases patient's communications.	7.6
Q 54	Patient is clear and organized in self-expression.	7.4
Q 3	Therapist's remarks are aimed at facilitating patient speech.	7.2
Q 18	Therapist conveys a sense of non-judgemental acceptance.	7.2
10 least characteristic items		
Q 15	Patient does not initiate topics; is passive.	1.4
Q 77	Therapist is tactless.	1.7
Q 51	Therapist condescends to, or patronizes the patient.	2.2
Q 9	Therapist is distant, aloof.	2.5
Q 14	Patient does not feel understood by therapist.	2.8
Q 25	Patient has difficulty beginning the hour.	2.9
Q 24	Therapist's own emotional conflicts intrude into the relationship.	3.1
Q 38	There is discussion of specific activities or tasks for the patient to attempt outside of session.	3.1
Q 42	Patient rejects therapist's comments and observations.	3.1
Q 85	Therapist encourages patient to try new ways of behaving with others.	3.4

Table 22.2. Rank order of the most and least characteristic PQS items in the termination phase (means across five therapy hours and two raters)

PQS items		M
10 most characteristic items		
Q 87	Patient is controlling.	8.8
Q 75	Termination of therapy is discussed.	7.8
Q 88	Patient brings up significant issues and material.	7.6
Q 6	Therapist is sensitive to the patient's feelings, attuned to the patient, empathic.	7.5
Q 35	Self-image is a focus of discussion.	7.4
Q 93	Therapist is neutral.	7.3
Q 64	Love or romantic relationships are topic of discussion.	7.2
Q 90	Patient's dreams or fantasies are discussed.	7.2
Q 18	Therapist conveys a sense of non-judgemental acceptance.	7.1
Q 13	Patient is animated or excited.	7.0
10 least characteristic items		
Q 32	Patient achieves a new understanding or insight.	1.8
Q 77	Therapist is tactless.	1.9
Q 51	Therapist condescends to, or patronizes the patient.	2.0
Q 15	Patient does not initiate topics; is passive.	2.1
Q 36	Therapist points out patient's use of defensive manoeuvres.	2.4
Q 82	The patient's behaviour during the hour is reformulated by the therapist in a way not explicitly recognized previously.	2.4
Q 17	Therapist actively exerts control over the interaction.	2.5
Q 52	Patient relies upon therapist to solve her problems.	2.5
Q 14	Patient does not feel understood by therapist.	2.6
Q 65	Therapist clarifies, restates, or rephrases patient's communication.	2.9

Description of the beginning phase using the PQS

In the beginning phase of the therapy, the patient has no difficulty beginning the hour (Q 25), initiates themes, is organized, clear and structured (Q 54) and brings up significant issues (Q 88). She accepts the therapist's comments and observations (Q 42) and feels understood by him (Q 14). The patient predominantly talks about her wish for independence (Q 29). The therapist's attitude conveys a sense of non-judgemental acceptance (Q 18) and emotional involvement (Q 9) and is characterized by tact (Q 77). The therapist's remarks are aimed at facilitating patient speech (Q 3) and he does not condescend to her (Q 51). Counter-transference reactions do not intrude into the relationship (Q 24). The therapist clarifies (Q 65) but he does not encourage the patient to try new ways of behaving with others or give her tasks (Q 85, Q 38). Dialogue has a specific focus (Q 23), the self-image of the patient (Q 35), her interpersonal relationships (Q63) and ideas or beliefs (Q 30) are central themes.

Description of the termination phase using the PQS

Several characteristics of the therapy remain the same in the termination phase. The patient brings up relevant issues (Q 88), is active (Q 15) and feels understood by the therapist (Q 14). The therapist conveys a sense of non-judgmental acceptance (Q 18), he is tactful (Q 77) and does not patronize the patient (Q 51). Self-image is still a focus (Q 35). There are differences from the beginning phase: in the termination phase the patient is animated (Q 13) and controlling (Q 87) and the therapist does not actively exert control over the interaction (Q 17), and is neutral (Q 93) and empathic (Q 6).

The patient does not achieve new insight (Q 32), but she does not rely on the therapist to solve her problems (Q 52). In the last sessions termination of therapy is discussed (Q 75), as are love relationships (Q 64) and the dreams of the patient (Q 90). The therapist does not clarify (Q 65), and does not interpret defence manoeuvres (Q 36) and the patient's behaviour during the hour (Q 82).

Items that distinguish the phases of the therapy

Table 22.3 lists the items that distinguish the two therapy phases.

Table 22.3. Comparison of the initial and termination phase of the therapy (Mean across five sessions for each time period and two raters, Wilcoxon test, sorted by size of differences)

		Session 1–5 M	Session 513–517 M
Typical items for the beginning phase			
Q 65	Therapist clarifies, restates, or rephrases patient's communication.	7.6	2.9***
Q 82	The patient's behaviour during the hour is reformulated by the therapist in a way not explicitly recognized previously.	5.9	2.4**
Q 62	Therapist identifies a recurrent theme in the patient's experience or conduct.	7.1	3.8**
Q 32	Patient achieves a new understanding or insight.	4.5	1.8***
Q 71	Patient is self-accusatory, expresses shame or guilt.	6.7	4.3**
Q 97	Patient is introspective, readily explores inner thought and feelings.	6.6	4.4**
Q 17	Therapist actively exerts control over the interaction.	4.5	2.5**
Q 61	Patient feels shy and embarrassed.	6.0	4.1**
Q 52	Patient relies upon therapist to solve her problems.	4.2	2.5**
Q 31	Therapist asks for more information or elaboration.	7.1	5.5**
Q 30	Discussion centres on cognitive themes.	7.6	6.1*
Q 59	Patient feels inadequate and inferior.	6.3	5.0*

(Contd)

Table 22.3. (Contd)

Q 3	Therapist's remarks are aimed at facilitating patient's speech.	7.2	6.3*
Q 54	Patient is clear and organized in self-expression.	7.4	6.7**
Q 22	Therapist focuses on patient's feelings of guilt.	4.2	3.6*
Typical items for the termination phase			
Q 87	Patient is controlling.	4.3	8.8**
Q 90	Patient's dreams or fantasies are discussed.	3.5	7.2***
Q 19	There is an erotic quality to the therapy relationship.	4.2	5.2**
Q 64	Love or romantic relationships are topic of discussion.	4.3	7.2**
Q 75	Termination of therapy is discussed.	5.0	7.8*
Q 84	Patient expresses angry or aggressive feelings.	4.4	6.4*
Q 39	There is a competitive quality to the relationship.	3.6	5.0**
Q 58	Patient resists examining thoughts, reactions or motivations related to problems.	3.4	5.9**
Q 20	Patient is provocative, tests limits of the therapy relationship.	3.8	5.6**
Q 74	Humour is used.	5.8	6.7*

*$p \leq 0.05$, **$p \leq 0.01$, ***$p \leq 0.001$

Typical of the beginning phase is that the therapist asks for information (Q 31), clarifies (Q 65), facilitates the patient's speech (Q 3) and identifies a recurrent theme in the patient's experience (Q 62). It is more characteristic of the termination phase that the therapist does less reformulation of the actual behaviour of the patient in the hour (Q 82), and focuses less on the patient's feelings of guilt (Q 22). He is less active in exerting control over the interaction (Q 17). In the beginning phase of the therapy, the patient has a clearer and more organized expression (Q 54), feels more shy (Q 61) and inadequate (Q 59), and expresses shame or guilt (Q 71). In the beginning phase she relies more on the therapist to solve her problems (Q 52), but is more introspective (Q 97) and achieves more new understanding (Q 32). In the termination phase the patient is controlling (Q 87), provocative (Q 20), and resists examining thoughts, reactions or motivations related to problems (Q 58). She is more able to express angry or aggressive feelings (Q 84).

In the beginning phase the discussion was more centred on cognitive themes (Q 30). In the termination phase, the termination of therapy (Q 75), the love relationship (Q 64) and the dreams of the patient (Q 90) were discussed, and more humour was used (Q 74). The beginning phase was different in that it was especially typical that there was a less erotic (Q 19), and a less competitive quality (Q 39) to the therapy relationship.

Discussion

The items that were identified as characteristic for both phases of the therapy are not items one might call 'typically psychoanalytic'. This can be accounted for by the fact that the selected hours are from the beginning and termination phases of the therapy, where the analytic work is only begun or coming to a close. The patient appears to be constructively engaged in the work and the behaviour of the analyst aims at establishing or maintaining a working alliance. Relevant themes are worked through; in particular the patient's self-image and interpersonal relationships as well as her wish for independence. The high rating of PQS item 23, 'the dialogue has a specific focus', is consistent with the assumption that the treatment was conducted according to the Ulm process model (Thomä and Kächele, 1997). This model considers psychoanalytic therapy to be an interpersonally orientated non-time-limited focal therapy in which the thematic focus changes over time. The description using the PQS items conveys the impression of intensive therapeutic, albeit not (yet) genuinely psychoanalytic, work.

Using the PQS items in comparing the beginning and termination phase yields a vivid description of the differences between these treatment phases. In the beginning phase, the therapist interacts very directly and supportively with the patient. One can surmise an interactive influence between the patient's self-accusations, her embarrassment and feelings of inadequacy and the behaviour of the therapist, who inquires and facilitates her communication. The therapeutic technique contains clarifications but also confrontations that are aimed at labelling repetitive themes and interpreting current behaviour. This corresponds to the patient's willingness to express herself clearly and to reflect on thoughts and feelings. The description of the beginning phase with the aid of the PQS supports the assumption that this treatment was successful in establishing a stable working alliance, which was most likely a decisive factor in its success.

In the termination phase, the patient is able to express angry feelings and appears less burdened by guilt, which can be considered a positive treatment result. The fact that the patient was able to engage in a love relationship during the course of treatment is another indicator for success, even though the relationship ultimately failed. Thus, in the final hours the theme of separation becomes important in the working through of that relationship and the termination of the therapy. The patient discusses dreams during the final sessions and talks about her ability to interpret them, which can be seen as an identification with the analyst's functions.

Seven items that were rated as typical for the beginning phase described the behaviour of the therapist and patient, but the items rated as typical for the termination phase were exclusively items that describe the patient and the interaction. The therapist leaves control of the hour mostly to the patient and keeps a low profile.

The description with the PQS illustrates the differences between the two treatment phases and the way in which patient and therapist influence each other's behaviour in a close interaction

The PQS does not provide complete information about the content of the therapeutic discourse. Therefore, a PQS rating does not allow the investigation of competitive treatment formulations. The description of a case by means of the PQS items has to reduce the richness of the clinical material, but provides a framework for working models concerning the patient and the therapeutic interaction. The PQS does allow the testing of hypotheses concerning therapeutic processes and their relationship to treatment success.

Jones himself discusses the PQS method as follows (Jones and Windholz, 1990): 'As a descriptive language, the Q-technique provides a set of categories shared across observers, guiding observers' attention to aspects of the clinical material that might have otherwise gone un-noted, and allowing them to emerge from the background.'

References

Albani C, Blaser G, Jacobs U, Jones E, Geyer M, Kächele H (2000) Die Methode des 'Psychotherapie-Prozeß Q-Sort'. Zeitschrift für Klinische Psychologie, Psychiatrie und Psychotherapie 48(2): 151-71.

Jones EE (2000) Therapeutic Action: A Guide to Psychoanalytic Therapy. Northvale, NJ: Jason Aronson.

Jones EE, Windholz M (1990) The psychoanalytic case study: Toward a method for systematic inquiry. Journal of the American Psychoanalytic Association 38(4): 985-1016.

Kächele H (submitted). The German specimen case of psychoanalysis. The International Journal of Psycho-Analysis.

Kächele H, Mergenthaler M, Thomä H (1998) Amalie X - the German Psychoanalytic Specimen Case. Lecture delivered at the George Klein Forum of the Midwinter Meeting of the American Psychoanalytic Association, New York, December 1998.

Kächele H, Schinkel A, Schmieder B, Leuzinger-Bohleber M, Thomä H (1999) Amalie X - Verlauf einer psychoanalytischen Therapie. Colloquium Psychoanalyse (Berlin) 4: 67-83.

Kächele H, Thomä H (1993) Psychoanalytic process research: Methods and achievements. Journal of the American Psychoanalytic Association 41: 109-29 Suppl.

Kächele H, Thomä H (eds) (1999) Lehrbuch der psychoanalytischen Therapie. Band 3. http://sip.medizin.uni-ulm.de. Ulm: Ulmer Textbank.

Thomä H, Kächele H (1992) Psychoanalytic Practice. Clinical Studies. 1 edn. Vol. 2. Berlin, Heidelberg, New York, Paris, London: Springer.

Thomä H, Kächele H (1997) Lehrbuch der Psychoanalytischen Therapie. Bd 2: Praxis (2 ed.). Berlin, Heidelberg, New York, Paris, London, Tokyo: Springer.

PART 4

CONCLUDING REFLECTIONS

Chapter 23

The psychotherapy researcher as a tightrope walker[1]

Folkert Beenen

A man has fallen from a window high in the Empire State Building. Halfway down someone shouts at him: 'How are things going?' 'So far, so good', the man is able to answer just before he smashes on the ground. The same sort of almost indestructible optimism often is also needed by the average psychotherapy researcher to go on with his work and maintain a belief in the sense of it. It is well known that the daily practice of psychotherapy and that of psychotherapy research find themselves in an ambivalent relationship. The attitude of practising clinicians to the academic wiseacres is not seldom a lightly denigrating one, and at the same time the latter will not cease to indicate that clinicians in their daily work act and treat much more on the basis of a belief system than on sound empirical scientific facts.

This ambivalence may have a lot to do with a fundamental difference in attitude. The clinician is primarily interested in clinical coherence. Questions regarding the patient material, his professional knowledge, his insight and experience are primarily guided by case studies. But the latter can be a real problem when it comes to scientific reliability and validity. Consciously or unconsciously there is a search for specific confirmation of the personal ideas and hypotheses of the author, while at the same time, material that fails to confirm, or even contradicts the author's ideas is neglected or left out.

Then there is also the problem of the uncontrollability of the material presented. Scientific scepticism concerning the value of case studies on the one hand, and the subjective search of the clinician for clinical coherence in, and with the help of, those very case studies on the other, therefore relate substantially to a difference in primary task and position. The clinician focuses on the task of following the patient as a means to increase maximally his subjective certainty in his role as the therapist of this unique patient, being convinced that this is in the best interest of his patient. As far as doubts are allowed, these should be functional and time limited instead of permanent, otherwise the therapeutic enterprise might rapidly become a ship out of control with the captain driven off course.

In the contrary case, in scientific research, it is very necessary, and by definition highly functional, to discuss and constantly put under scrutiny the pretended or supposed certainties concerning the matter under consideration. It is a matter of fact that this very attitude and position hardly fits, if at all, with a direct treatment relationship with the patient.

In a discussion I had with some colleagues, one of them formulated this problem in a concise way by stating: 'science creates paranoia'. Subjective feelings of evidence form an important and, in many situations, also a true basis for human action, whether this is in the public or the private arena. So, when the scientific approach repeatedly creates doubts, and places question marks against primary feelings of certainty, this can lead to a severe loss of hold. In this context I take it for an unnecessarily defensive attitude that clinicians feel called upon to define their work with patients as scientific research as well. Clinical work has its own different goals. As a clinician I am interested in uncovering the subjective, partly unconscious, truth of the individual patient. In such moments scientific research into general laws is not my first domain of interest, if at all. But what I would welcome very much – 'would' because it too seldom happens – is the systematic inclusion of the interpretational skills of clinicians when it comes to the understanding of outcome research. Clinical judgement would then become a factor in testing results in the research field, at the same time generating the possibility of feedback into, and integration of, research results into clinical practice. I think the way Peter Fonagy and his colleagues in London are working comes quite near to what I have in mind: individuals, and the group as a whole, are involved in a constant process of integration of clinical and research data. Another convincing example of the productivity of a collaboration like that is the extensive DPV catamnestic study in Germany by Leuzinger-Bohleber, Stuhr and Beutel. These examples make clear that, in my view, the same person can be both a practising clinician and an empirical scientist at the same time. But it is an important prerequisite that such a person can inwardly switch between these two positions.

To what extent clinical colleagues might be willing, but not able, to make this alternating switch between a clinical and a scientific attitude I do not know. But what I do know is that many of them, quite explicitly, do not seem interested. This attitude is based on a mixture of conscious rational motives and unconscious resistance and defence against everything that has to do with the abstract and the general. For the majority of these clinicians, empirical research is synonymous with big samples, statistical methods and outcomes of only trivial interest for clinical work.

I regret to say that some researchers have themselves given rise to this image, leading to the conclusion that this criticism has a certain justice. The criticism refers to the type of researcher who, in the end, makes the same mistake as some of their clinical colleagues – they confuse aims and means. Thus, they regard clinical knowledge that has not been gathered by, or tested with, the help of 'the holy scientific methods', as by definition irrelevant, or, even worse, as non-existent. This leads to the denial of a very important daily clinical reality, which this sort of researcher generally knows only from books. In the introduction to his book *Allgemeine Psychoanalytische Krankheitslehre* (Krause, 1997) Rainer Krause gives the example of a modern psychology textbook in which for that reason issues like affect, sexuality, and 'the remainder of this methodologically dirty rubbish' (p. 15) have been left out of the index of this book. He continues:

> In my opinion, this kind of model-building, outside of biology, taken together with methods aiming at an accumulation of knowledge through interpersonal aggregation of parameters in large samples, without considering the diachronic and the synchronic context of the individual, is hardly adequate to the subject of our research, namely human beings. Rarely has anything new been discovered by means of statistics. Their methods belong to the context of validation, not to the context of discovery. This is where they have their place. My own research always originates in my clinical work. This is a source of inspiration, of theoretical invention, but also of open questions. Each time there was a point at which I had to leave clinical work and procure a methodology suitable to the clinical questions, as well as other means to render the project feasible. This was really the main part of the work. The existing methods rarely suited my questions, and for financial issues, one is well advised to get accustomed to a second, non-analytical, way of thinking. This did me no harm. Analytical language is clinical, and in its richness of metaphors and its associative quality is in no way scientific.
>
> (Krause, 1997: 15)

So the circle closes even earlier than you and I possibly might have expected: some of the scientific researchers are guilty of the same unscientific, subjective defensive attitude that they blame the practising clinicians for. In Holland we call this: 'De pot verwijt de ketel dat hij zwart ziet.' (Literally: 'The pot calling the kettle black.')

Maybe this just goes to show that researchers are also human beings and that the researcher in his search for the truth needs the same security and certainty as the clinician in his work. But sad to say, in the end this can lead, for both parties, to the same unwished-for outcome: an absolute belief in one's own truth to the exclusion of free unprejudiced thinking.

There are nevertheless also moments that I think that this unexpected alikeness in human behaviour might bridge some of the gap between scientists and practising clinicians. A prerequisite would be that both groups involved should be aware of the fact that the majority of certainties are only temporary and therefore perishable, whether it concerns a research method or a clinical treatment modality. Once more I quote with approval Rainer Krause:

> 'Modern' Psychoanalysis, as well as 'modern' research, is characterised by the fact that its erroneous ways have not yet been revealed by the next generation. For this reason I do not want to write with the authority of someone who has knowledge in a certain historical period. Part of this clarity is to also regard psychoanalytical theories, whether in the tradition of Freud, Klein or Schultz-Henke, as outflows of the unconscious psychic reality of their authors. One should not believe in them any more than one takes the literal messages of our patients at face value. Understanding and empathy are called for, not believing. Our theories are phases in the creational history of our science and convincing only during certain periods of time. Then they lose their integrative and heuristic potential, and as far as one has to 'believe' in them, they come to be dead and anti-enlightening texts.
>
> (Krause, 1997: 14)

So I arrive at a first conclusion: relevant scientific psychoanalytic research absolutely needs the clinician and his clinical skills as a source of inspiration and renewing ideas, and for this it needs the integration of research results in clinical practice. Equally indispensable, that very clinical work needs empirical scientific research for the constant testing and validation of clinical knowledge. So the question is no longer whether it is *possible* for both parties to have a fruitful collaboration; no, we can determine that this collaboration is absolutely *necessary*. I think it is in the spirit of current discussions to conclude that only in this way can we ensure that psychoanalysis as a science and as a clinical treatment modality does not cease to exist within a decade.

This brings me to the second aspect of my theme: *the psychotherapy researcher as a tightrope walker*. The tightrope-walking capacity for the researcher is not only essential for keeping balance in the relationship with the clinicians, but also in dealing with the constant pressure of the general forces in society, and with the specific influences also of the dynamics in the organization of psychoanalysis.

In the administrative and organizational power structures within the IPA and its component societies, a great majority of psychoanalysts minimize or neglect the importance of empirical scientific research in our field. A minority even strongly distrust it, and show a hostile, rejecting attitude. I am still undecided over whether, after all these years, the tide is on the turn, but I do want in any case to express my appreciation for the strong efforts of the very active IPA Research Committee since the beginning of the 1990s. They never cease to make clear that the real danger for psychoanalysis lies in a defensive, ignorant attitude towards systematic empirical research in our field, as well as in spectacular scientific progress in neighbouring academic disciplines like neurology, cognitive psychology and so forth.

To stand still is to decline and, already, historical scientific sociological deliberations lead to the conclusion that it is completely unrealistic to expect that current psychoanalytical knowledge will have eternal proof and value. I would imagine that Freud, if he were still alive, would today have been one of the first of those wanting to renew his inheritance day by day, and he would surely appreciate using modern scientific capacities and research results to guide this constant renewal process.

Next, I want to cast a glance outside psychoanalysis at 'the real world'. It may be true that the dynamics within our psychoanalytical community make the life of the researcher quite complicated. At the moment this applies *a fortiori* to the demands and inferences coming from outside our profession. Not to lose balance here, as a researcher, demands a delicate equilibrium between scientific integrity and an opportunist business attitude.

Administrators, financiers, and consumers of care, all of them representing interested groups of society, in general want, as rapidly as possible, a subjective certainty regarding questions like: does therapy help anyway? Does therapy A help better than therapy B? How can the whole enterprise be cheaper, shorter and better? Questions, by the way, which are also in the mind of the average patient coming into treatment.

Apart from the fact that these questions, as such, are justified, they nevertheless put quite a lot of pressure on researchers to furnish the third party funders and the public as quickly as possible with strong and unequivocal answers to this type of question. In my opinion this can be a real threat to the scientific quality of psychotherapy research.

Value-free scientific inquiry, has, some decades ago, rightly been shown up as a naive academic myth. But the other extreme is as big a danger as well. It puts in danger an unprejudiced search for scientific knowledge and insight in our field. As soon as research questions, methodologies and outcomes are directly linked up to concrete values (read: money), an inevitable breeding ground for manipulative scientific research has been created. When I say this, I do not primarily think of deliberately organized manipulation of scientific data. The pity of it is that this kind of manipulation also takes place without the societal pressure I referred to, as the history of science has taught us.

No, the danger consists in the emergence of a would-be scientific objectivity that relates only partially, or not at all, to verified and validated knowledge in our field. And then again we find our scientific researchers in exactly the same position they blame the practising clinicians for. Researchers who nowadays suggest that they can answer those basic questions regarding psychotherapy I referred to in a reliable and valid way are scientifically no less suspect than clinicians who build their subjective knowledge on case material. Before they realize it, these researchers become jammed between scientific integrity, self-interest and the interest of the commissioners, who are mostly also the financiers.

Behind the scenes, in most countries, collective spending and supplies for mental health care continue to be systematically reduced and limited. Free market principles, and so-called healthy rivalry are expected to have a beneficial effect on reorganizing the mental health market - a market that is said to have created an increasing need through a constantly enlarging, but not transparent, offer of treatments. This seems to be the conviction of most administrators and politicians.

There are not many of us who can withstand the force and power of money. This results in a predicable reaction in therapy land to the 'divide and rule' policy of the administrators - a reaction that is, most of the time, not as elegant as it should be. In effect, this leads to an egocentric dance around the golden calf of the money available in the mental health field. A golden calf, by the way, that in the meantime has been reduced to critical proportions: before we know it, we may be dancing around a skeleton.

So we have to wait and see if this competition, seemingly deliberately created by society, between different therapeutic theories and modalities really works out in the interests of the consumer as well as of the public treasury, as the initiators of this line seem to believe. One outcome, for sure, will be that a label of scientifically proved superiority for one method against another will become a powerful and eagerly used weapon in the combat for a place in the market.

We have only to look at the way things are going in the related area of psychopharmaceuticals, long since our commercial competitor, to get an idea of what possibly awaits us. The pharmacological industry sponsors heavily one scientific congress after the other, one research project after another and one psychiatrist after another. It is evident and accepted that with the power of money, the laurels in the field are won for specific products, and heavily sponsored scientific research projects constantly prove how excellent, desirable and so on the new product is.

A Dutch colleague, from the University of Leiden, recently came up with some quite discomforting data (Vandenbroucke, 1999). He analysed a number of studies on the side effects of the so-called third generation contraceptive pill in comparison to the second generation one in current use. The new pill is suspected of causing significantly more venous thromboses than the older one, based on a difference in certain progestagene hormones. And now an interesting phenomenon occurs: all but one of the non-sponsored studies found at least a twofold increase of the risk for venous thrombosis, whereas all the sponsored authors came to the conclusion that there is no increase at all of risks when using the new pill. And the story is not over yet.

The large database of one of the non-sponsored studies was acquired by one of the authors of the sponsored studies. You can probably guess what happened. This author, using slightly different classes and criteria, reanalysed the data. He found that there is no reason for worry, because these data also justify the conclusion of all the other sponsored studies, that the risks are the same for both types of pills.

And in the field of smoking and health risks, to give one more example, Barnes and Bero (1998) showed, in comparing a number of meta-studies regarding the danger of so-called 'passive smoking', that authors who regularly visited meetings of the tobacco industry or had been sponsored by them in the past, systematically found no harm in passive smoking. Other meta-studies, based on the same publications, nevertheless did find clear negative effects.

So it is all too easy to imagine that in the battlefield of the free market, care insurance companies, and care suppliers of mental health, will increasingly use the research weapon to promote a unique and superior product, just like in the field of pharmacology. The members of different and rival psychotherapeutic schools will expect their professional societies to warrant and strengthen their position in the market. Modern management tools and measures present themselves for achieving these goals, just as they have proved their effectiveness in the commercial field. Nowadays you can't even buy a dog biscuit that has not been scientifically tested and proven to be top of the bill, condemning all other products to a second choice position.

In the Netherlands two behaviour therapy researchers recently launched a promising scientific commercial argument by bluntly stating that symptom-orientated behaviour therapy is in effect the only psychotherapeutic treatment of scientifically proven effectiveness. Therefore society should finance this type of psychotherapy alone. Even the unimaginative can picture these researchers dressed in the same white medical coats and looking with the same slightly compassionate superior glance we recognize from the dog biscuit researchers presenting their conclusions in a TV advertising spot.

These colleagues also state that other, old-fashioned, no longer relevant and unscientific schools of therapy, amongst which, of course, are person-orientated psychoanalytic psychotherapies, should be completely removed from the market. Or, more subtly, should die an easy death by not being financed.

But if we have a closer look at the arguments, the statement in the article that: 'sometimes, in case of some specific problems or combinations of problems, even science has to be silent and cannot give a judgement on which therapies might help' suffices to conclude that the authors suffer an unjustified overestimation of the scientific state of the art in our field and profession. This leads to the improper use of scientific research as a means to come to categorical statements that can have a far-reaching impact on societal and financial administrative measures.

Fortunately we do not have to despair completely because there is a bright spot in the article. The authors make a generous gesture by stating that from the point of view of civilization, for the time being those few treatments for which a definite scientific judgement is not yet available should retain their finance. But, in that case, therapists at least have to do their very best . . ..

Back to the possible contribution of psychotherapy research to administrative and financial decisions in our field. It seems to me that the power of scientific arguments also has a strong correlation with the level of acceptance or non-acceptance of the phenomenon of psychotherapy as such. I think it is still true that the person-orientated schools of psychotherapy, especially psychoanalysis, with their strong focus on individual freedom, autonomy and so on, are experienced as a substantial threat to 'official' values, norms and rules of certain proven structures in our society. What I am saying is that the rational link between public financing and the scientifically proven effectiveness of psychotherapy also keeps out of sight and discussion the broadly present ambivalence and underlying irrational objections against psychoanalysis as such.

In this connection it is interesting to observe that official somatic medicine seems to puts itself in a smarter and less controversial position. Every doctor knows that, in the doctor–patient relationship, phenomena like setting at ease, reassurance, advice and confrontation, comfort and support – in short a multitude of curative factors clinically known from the therapeutic transference relationship, are of substantial importance for the success of the treatment. Nevertheless, in the official medical somatic scientific models, most of these patient–doctor variables are left out of consideration because they are difficult to operationalize and objectify, and therefore are a potential threat to the scientific status of medicine. So they are banished to the domain of the charlatan. Ironically enough, just to give an example, the number of diagnostic laboratory tests generated by general medical practice, 'just for certainty, to reassure and comfort the patient', in the Netherlands alone, amounts to several hundred thousand a year, not to speak of the enormous number of other strictly scientifically judged questionable or unnecessary treatments, operations and so on, that as we all know, take place. But as long as these irrational decisions and activities are not part of officially recognized medical science, and at the same time are executed under the standards of official medicine, the financing is much less under discussion than it is in the irrational psychotherapeutic enterprise.

I started this chapter with a man falling out of the window of the Empire State Building. Was this a psychotherapy researcher who had lost his balance? Or, even worse, one who jumped out of despair? Let us hope those statements are just fantasy. But let us also hope that it won't get that far. Psychoanalysis and psychoanalytic psychotherapy are two precious goods, and of such great value, that they do not deserve to be ruined in unnecessary and unproductive internal battles and *Prinzipienreiterei* (fundamentalism). In the end all parties need each other very badly: clinicians, researchers, psychoanalytic organizations and societies, the administrative entities and persons who have the societal responsibility for mental health supplies and, last but not least, the people who need our skills, our fellow human beings in psychic trouble.

We need to use every collaborative effort to make sure that, in the twenty-first century, psychoanalysis can assert its important curative, cultural and societal position and influence, and that it will be able to extend the scientific foundation of our body of knowledge. If psychotherapy research is able to build a solid empirical scientific basis for our profession and, at the same time, can avoid becoming entangled in opportunistic justification procedures, then it can realize an important and balanced scientific contribution to achieving this goal.

Note

1. This chapter is a revision and extension of an earlier one published under the title 'De toekomst van de psychotherapie research. Over het toenemend reclame gehalte van wetenschappelijk psychotherapie onderzoek', in the *Tijdschrift voor Psychotherapie* (1995) 21: 6.

References

Barnes DE, Bero LA (1998) Why review articles on the health effects of passive smoking reach different conclusions. JAMA 279: 1566–70.

Krause R (1997) Allgemeine Psychoanalytische Krankheitslehre. Grundlagen. Köln: Kohlhammer, vol. 1.

Vandenbroucke JP (1999) Hoe wordt medische kennis gemaakt? Gezondheidsraadlezing (30 September).

CHAPTER 24

Long-term psychoanalytical treatment – a challenge for clinical and empirical research

DIETER BÜRGIN

A book was recently published with the title *The Death of Psychoanalysis: Murder, suicide or rumour greatly exaggerated?* (Prince, 1998). Its main thesis is: 'Psychoanalysis is in danger of becoming marginalized, if not extinct . . . will it survive? Will it locate itself in medicine, in social science, in philosophy or in something *sui generis?*'

If Winnicott said that the process of analysis was about beginning it, continuing it, surviving it and ending it, we can modify this appropriately; as a movement, analysis began and has persisted, but is now fighting for its life. In recent decades it has largely lost contact with important related sciences and has become inward looking and defensive. This isolation, for which it has only itself to blame, allows it to continue navel gazing but rarely permits fruitful dialogue with other scientific disciplines. Analysis has thus increasingly acquired a bad reputation. An analyst hardly ever fills a university chair these days. An analytical training may even be deliberately undisclosed in interviews for a job because it is beginning to appear as a distinct handicap.

Whether psychoanalysis is a form of psychotherapy, or whether it is rather a form of character development with possible therapeutic side effects, is a question that has not been extensively debated in recent years. It is generally assumed that health insurance companies in many European countries will pay for psychoanalysis as a matter of course. Most of the other forms of psychotherapy have developed means to evaluate their efficacy, but not psychoanalysis. But today, and for the foreseeable future, those who pay are demanding evidence of efficacy that fulfil today's scientific criteria (validity, reliability, verifiability) for every psychotherapeutic methodology.

In many places, psychoanalysis has failed to establish a research culture that enables the psychoanalytical process to be objectified using techniques acceptable to psychoanalysts. In many psychoanalytical associations it is also taboo to talk about the issue of research, or to make it clear that not every psychoanalyst is automatically a researcher as well.

Over almost a decade's activity on the research council of the Swiss National Science Foundation, I found that barely one in a hundred grant applications used a thorough psychoanalytical methodology. Thus, all the research money flowed into other forms of psychotherapy. Only in the past five to 10 years has the idea of research become more common in Europe. The Hamburg International Congress was therefore a milestone, and supplements the activities of the IPA Research Committee and the research seminars in London.

What might be the subject of psychoanalytical research? Which methods should be applied? Can the psychoanalytical process be studied per se, or must it have a shadowy existence only within the intimacy of an analytical relationship? Can the efficacy of a psychoanalytical process be investigated at all? Our French colleagues have considerable qualms about this last question. What, then, does research into psychoanalysis mean? What is the psychoanalytical research arena? Which are the appropriate methods?

Clinical research must not be taken simply to mean presenting cases in the conventional sense. Wallerstein (1989, 1990) has said that, at the moment, there exist a multitude of psychoanalytical methods and thus numerous types of psychoanalysis, which in many respects have little in common other than their metaphors. Although we can consider clinical case presentations from different psychoanalytical perspectives, and perhaps reach views that are not too far from one another, this fact does not help in terms of research.

It is certainly legitimate to deduce theoretical concepts from case material. Concepts uncovered in this way, however, must then be verified or disproved using other methods. In the subjective original form, they can at best help the analyst to cope somewhat better in similar situations. Thus the formulation of subjective concepts, in the sense of helpful constructs, may facilitate a better clinical understanding within the psychoanalytical community. When in contact with other sciences, on the other hand, external verification of concepts elaborated in this way is unavoidable if psychoanalysis is not to be dismissed as no more than pseudoscientific, and the analysts as sect adherents, believers, devotees and obfuscators.

Psychoanalysis does not have much of a tradition of systematic and objective research methodology. It has closer links with hermeneutic scientific methods (history, sociology or linguistics) than with those of biology, neuroscience or psychology. To ensure a connection with the other sciences and to avoid becoming a science adrift between sciences, psychoanalysis must define itself afresh at a general and theoretical level as well as in terms in which theory is formed and data acquired.

Freud's definition of psychoanalysis includes three points. First, it is a 'technique of investigating mental processes'; second, a 'method of treatment for neurotic disturbances' and third, the sum of psychological insights that together form a 'new scientific discipline' (Freud, 1923: 211).

According to the IPA, psychoanalysis represents, first, a theory of the structure and function of personality, second, a particular psychotherapeutic method, and third, the application of this theory to other branches of science.

Freud conceived of psychoanalysis as a 'continuation of biology' ('the piece of knowledge that borders on biology' Freud, 1920: 31) and as a 'natural-scientific psychology' (Freud, 1895: 387) - as an empirical science. He gave at least the same significance to experiences from outside the analytical setting as to those that were gained within it. Thus, in the foreword to the 'Three Essays on the Theory of Sexuality' he wrote: 'If people understood how to learn from directly observing children, these three essays would not have needed to be written' (Freud, 1920: 32).

Science is a process of recognition orientated towards the connection between things; it orders, justifies, explains and evaluates, and thus researches methodically. Although science aims to be a process of pure discovery, it is always - consciously or unconsciously - part of a higher-level world picture and historically determined value system, and can never be without preconceptions. One of its chief characteristics is the constant examination of its preconditions, methods and results, i.e. a continuing capacity for revision. It must therefore also clarify its relationship to belief, revelation and common sense. As a process of human discovery it uses research methods which attempt to approach its subjects through particular theoretical constructs using either inductive-experimental-empirical methods (natural science) or more descriptive and interpretative procedures (humanities).

Freud identified similarities between progress in scientific work and in psychoanalysis:

> Progress in scientific study is carried out similarly to analysis. One comes to the study with expectations, but has to suppress them. Through observation, one soon finds out something new here and there, but the pieces do not at first fit together. One makes assumptions, builds helpful constructions that one withdraws if they do not prove themselves, one needs patience, a readiness for all possibilities, one renounces former convictions so as not to miss new, unexpected moments, and in the end the whole effort is worth it, the disparate findings grow together, one gains insight into a whole piece of mental working, one has achieved the task and is now free for the next one. But in analysis one has to manage without the help that experiment gives to research.
>
> (Freud, 1933: 188)

Freud also resisted describing science as an illusion: 'Scientific research, however, is for us the only way that can lead to the understanding of external reality. It is on the other hand nothing but self-deception to expect something from intuition and contemplation; they can give us nothing more than barely discernible information about our own inner life' (Freud, 1927: 354). 'A law, that at first we held to be unconditionally valid, proves instead to be a special case of a more wide-ranging legitimacy, or is limited by another law that we reveal only later; a crude approach towards truth is replaced by a more carefully tailored one, that anticipates further modification' (Freud, 1927: 379).

Freud considered the fact that psychoanalysis uses its object of research as its research tool as well, as one of its peculiarities: 'All sciences rest on observations and experiences, which are transmitted by our psychological apparatus. But since our science has this apparatus itself as an object of enquiry, the analogy stops here. We make our observations . . . in that we supplement what is omitted with the conclusions that suggest themselves, and translate it into conscious material' (Freud, 1949: 81).

Statements like these bring psychoanalysis into the area of semiotics and communication sciences, albeit while considering a specific subjectivity (transference), a special context (dyadic setting) and a hermeneutic that bridges the gaps in consciousness with particular assumptions.

Freud's scientific position on the 'present state of error', as we might also describe science, is shown in his relationship to the empiricism, reflection and knowledge of constant change in the recognition of the moment. 'Psychoanalysis . . . seeks to solve the next problem of observation, feels its way through the experience, is always unfinished, always ready to adjust or modify what it has learnt. Psychoanalysis tolerates the fact that its main terminology is unclear, its conditions temporary, to the same extent as physics or chemistry, and expects future study to define these more clearly' (Freud, 1923: 229).

Freud knew from his own experience how openness to new directions in science is necessary, as well as scepticism. He knew only too well the fate of a new scientific theory:

> At first it meets with harsh rejection, is disputed intensely over decades, but no more than a generation is required for it to be recognised as a great step forward towards the truth . . . the new truth has awakened affective resistance . . . from the beginning there are adherents and opponents, and the number and importance of the former increases until they have the upper hand.
>
> (Freud, 1937: 170)

Psychoanalysis is also a member of the ranks of psychotherapeutic treatment methods, despite its specificity. Although its potential for change is more than clear from countless case histories, the need to produce detailed proof of efficacy is unavoidable if it is to hold fast to the psychotherapeutic claim - even if it defines itself as an art. It will have to develop and present selected methods to evaluate and prove its specific therapeutic effect and efficiency, so long as payment by the State or health insurance companies continues to be expected.

In Freud's time, the situation was rather different. 'From the beginning, healing and research have been interdependent in psychoanalysis, discovery brought therapeutic success, one was unable to treat without finding out something new' (Freud, 1926b: 293).

The reality today, however, is that research and treatment no longer occur together, unless research is viewed as a completely personal activity removed from the demands of objectivity.

In 1926 Freud was still able to formulate his therapeutic optimism: 'As a therapeutic technique, psychoanalysis is gaining ever more adherents, because it helps the patients more than any other treatment method' (Freud, 1926c: 500).

Nevertheless, he immediately placed reservations on his statement: 'The use of analysis to treat neuroses is only one of its applications; perhaps the future will show that it is not the most important' (Freud, 1926a: 283). 'The future will probably judge that the meaning of psychoanalysis as a science of the unconscious far outweighs its therapeutic significance' (Freud, 1926c: 501).

We know today that psychoanalysis is not the therapy of choice for all mental disturbances, that other techniques exist that work more quickly and efficiently. But we have not yet developed a valid and generally recognized method to enable us to identify the specific changes occurring in psychoanalysis with an accepted and reliable definition for claims of 'structural change': a method that removes it from the field of unverified evidence, and allows it to be examined in a way that is both scientific and understandable by others. I do not think we need to be afraid of such activities. On the contrary, I am convinced that psychoanalysis has weighty specifics to show, that it should take up this challenge, and the challenge of understanding why, and perhaps how, other therapeutic processes work, without losing heart, and that it has not a little to contribute as a science of relationships.

Freud was concerned that the therapeutic aspects of psychoanalysis, whether of a more medical or more psychological form, could unintentionally overgrow the scientific aspects: 'I want to ensure that the scientific side is not overwhelmed by therapy' (Freud, 1925: 291).

Psychoanalysis sees the person as a being who creates meanings and inner worlds. Irrational behaviour is ubiquitous and merits understanding. Fundamentally, psychoanalysis assumes that perceptions and needs are furnished with conscious, unconscious and sometimes symbolic meanings.

Naturally, psychoanalysis cannot fulfil the standards of providing evidence in the same way as the natural sciences. And thus Bohleber (1996) is right when he questions the value of empiricism. But how can a connection between unconscious motives and their visible manifestations be proven? Either we start from assumptions that we have previously established (a fixed, generally recognized metapsychology), form hypotheses from the patient's 'material', and strengthen or negate these using further statements by the patient. Or we abstract from the interactional events what appear to us to be rules, which we then use as further aids to orientation, and attempt to apply them to other patients as well. In most cases it is probably a mixture of the two approaches. Thus, in psychoanalysis we find ourselves mostly in an area of conflict between hermeneutics and empirical science. Psychoanalytical theory resists being investigated simply within the usual type of empirical research design because so much is not directly observable but can only be deduced. It is apparent that an individual life history and relationships are not reproducible and thus also not operationalizable. Nevertheless, validation of psychoanalytical theory may be viewed as a task of our times. In tackling this task, we must protect ourselves from going astray, from reducing the definition so as to be able to describe it, and also from mystification simply to avoid having to validate it. Should the effects of psychoanalysis be demonstrated by a reduction in visits to the doctor, a lower rate of absenteeism from analysis, or small shifts in transference? Should analysis primarily convince and transmit conviction, or should it surprise and stimulate? Do we die for the truth, or for something we believe to be true? Giordano Bruno was martyred; Galileo Galilei recanted, because he knew that truth can be denied but not changed, and that it requires no human sacrifices.

If psychoanalysis represents a method of character development that also has therapeutic effects, can it demand payment from health insurance companies? Or must the therapeutic demand be satisfied primarily by psychoanalytical psychotherapy? If so, how is this to be differentiated from psychoanalysis in a strict sense? Can we demand unequivocal specificity of psychoanalysis at all?

Can findings and data from other sciences, such as cognitive psychology, neuroscience, linguistics, chaos theory, ethology, ethnology, paediatrics, and so forth, be used to validate or further develop psychoanalytical theory? Can new metaphors be gained from these fields, which expand the spectrum of meanings of psychoanalytical theory? In any case, it appears to make sense to keep the distinction between different discourses, for example, the discourse about efficacy, or the one about psychoanalysis as an art, or about research, or about how scientific psychoanalysis is.

The economic situation is compelling reactive research everywhere, particularly research on the efficacy of psychotherapeutic procedures. We should not neglect active research, which is characterized not only by activity, but also by originality. This, however, requires research teams, large amounts of funding, know how and time, and can be carried out in the clinical sector only by specialized centres – if possible in collaboration with colleagues in psychoanalytic practice. As there is not just one but several analyses, and each approach contains a different bias, the situation is complicated even further.

We need to know not only to whom the planned research is addressed but we must also manage to link prevention, cure and rehabilitation, in addition to considering the questions of differential indicators and the duration of follow-up studies. There are many disadvantages to follow-up studies, although these can produce very exciting results, as we (Sandell, Heinzel, Keller and especially the Anna Freud Centre in London and Professor Leuzinger-Bohleber's DPV study) have found.

Nevertheless, one should aim at prospective studies, both for the evaluation of efficacy and for basic research. But here we will have to manage without strict randomization, and no pseudo-objectivity can be achieved. We will have to detach ourselves from the ideal of complete resolution of conflict or transference, and to be content with problems diminishing over the course of analysis and, at best, new forms of conflict management coming to the fore. The use of audio or video recording will be unavoidable for any scientific or research activity. Finally, on the basis of an explicit theoretical understanding, it will be possible to make predictions and verify or negate hypotheses.

In this highly complex field with so many variables we must also find appropriate methods of reducing data, so that in the empirical furore we do not simply create data cemeteries, and curiosity and enthusiasm do not die out in the passage between clinical work and empirical research. Therapeutic aspects based on existing capacities and skills will have to supplement those of psychopathology in a dialectical fashion. Empirical points of view and manuals for the procedures of psychoanalytical psychotherapy will probably be unavoidable for research purposes. But is there not also a danger of standardization and rigidity? How will we protect ourselves so that these procedures will not just be used defensively? Or is it only with their help that we will be able to approach manifestly aggressive transference at all scientifically? Where, in the end, is the place for the creative, artistic, unmistakably individual part of our profession?

Since the treatment goal as such does not exist, nobody has a monopoly on its definition; and since the psychoanalytical process is a course that includes at least two real persons and two virtual protagonists, interaction research (which is able to record intrapsychic processes and unconscious determinants as well as examining behaviour) will come to the fore methodologically. I am assuming that the analytical process can not only be recorded interpersonally and intrapsychically for both protagonists, but can also allow emotional relationships and the flexibility of the cathexes to be researched in an intersubjective context. In the research setting we will continue to be confronted, in the transformation of clinical to statistical data, with the simplification of the almost endlessly variable clinical material. But it may be possible to extract a creative objectification, which touches deeply within the analytical dialogue. A mismatch of analyst and patient may require - as the diverse narratives in the DPV study show - conscious triangulation in order to become an opportunity for opening out (anew) into a dialogical exchange.

Perhaps we need to ask new and different questions in order to elucidate how an intersubjective process proceeds together with inter-emotionality and inter-intentionality; how the changing faces of social referencing and affect attunement are played out, and how the asymmetric but joint creation of a subsidiary third party takes place.

The fundamental dichotomies of libido and aggression, of relationship to the self or to the object, of construction and destruction and so forth, also include the questions of clinical treatment and the empirical research of process and result. Long-term psychoanalytical treatment would be a hollow thing without an explicit theory, without a theory of technique, without reflection and at the same time involvement, and without an attempt at empirical research.

Psychoanalysis can develop either in the direction of an increasing educational function and application of theory, or in the field of empirical research, in the same way that in Escher's famous picture fish become birds and birds become fish. Why do we need research in psychoanalysis? To examine therapeutic efficacy; to examine the theory; to examine practical applications; to make connections with other sciences; to avoid becoming esoteric or isolated.

The Hambury International Congress, with its many exciting research results, has shown us that the title of the book I mentioned at the beginning of my talk is false. It should not be called *the death of psychoanalysis*, but *the rebirth of psychoanalysis*. This means we should concern ourselves particularly with the questions of how something, especially a third party, comes into being as in Escher's picture. Solving such triadic puzzles and conflict situations still requires - even after a century of gestation - a great deal more time.

References

Bohleber W (1996) Krieg um Freud. Zur Verschiebung der Freud-Ausstellung in der Library of Congress in Washington DC. Psyche 50(7): 589-98.

Freud S (written 1895; first pub. 1950) Entwurf einer Psychologie. GW, Nachtragsband: 387.

Freud S (1920) Vorwort zur vierten Auflage der 'Drei Abhandlungen zur Sexualtheorie'. GW, Vol. V: 31, 32.

Freud S (1923) Psychoanalyse und Libidotheorie. GW, Vol. XI: 211, 229.

Freud S (1925) Die Widerstände gegen die Psychoanalyse. GW, Vol. XIV: 291.

Freud S (1926a) Die Frage der Laienanalyse. GW, Vol. XIV: 218, 283.

Freud S (1926b) Nachwort zur 'Frage der Laienanalyse'. GW, Vol. XIV: 293.

Freud S (1926c) Psycho-Analysis. GW, Vol. XIV: 500, 501.

Freud S (1927) Die Zukunft einer Illusion. GW, Vol. XIV: 354, 379, 380.

Freud S (1933) Neue Folgen der Vorlesungen zur Einführung in die Psychoanalyse. GW, Vol. XV: 188.

Freud S (1937) Der Mann Moses und die monotheistische Religion. GW, Vol. XVI: 170.

Freud S (1949) Abriß der Psychoanalyse. Schriften aus dem Nachlaß. GW, Vol. XVII: 81.

Prince RM (ed.) (1998) The Death of Psychoanalysis. Paperback. London: Aronson.

Wallerstein RS (1989) Eine Psychoanalyse - oder viele? Zeitschrift für Psychanalyse. Theorie und Praxis 4: 126-53.

Wallerstein RS (1990) Psychoanalysis, the common ground. International Journal of Psychoanalysis 71: 3-19.

CHAPTER 25
Present challenges to psychoanalysis

OTTO F KERNBERG

Two recent publications illustrate the kind of challenges psychoanalysis faces today. One of them, the article 'How to read Freud' by Colin McGinn, in the New York Review of Books of 4 November 1999 raised the usual critical questions regarding psychoanalysis that are quite fashionable in intellectual circles in the US, and not only the US, at this time. In a critical, highly selective, and partly out-of-context reading of Freud, the author points to Freud's basic theories of unconscious motivation, unconscious repression, infantile sexuality, and the death drive, to conclude that there is no evidence for any of these hypotheses. McGinn uses 'common sense' criteria and his personal experience to assert these points. This article amounts to a radical critique and rejection of psychoanalysis, without any reference to the development of psychoanalytic formulations over the past hundred years, nor any reference to any research dealing with these issues, not to speak of overwhelming contrary evidence from massive accumulated clinical and research experience. It would be easy to dismiss this superficial and arbitrary critique as irrelevant to psychoanalytic science and practice, if it were not such a typical example of the kind of statements one finds in the media at this time.

The second article is Erik Kandel's paper 'Biology and the future of psychoanalysis' in the *American Journal of Psychiatry,* of April 1999. Kandel, one of leading neuroscientists in the US, explores the present day problems of, and challenges to, psychoanalysis. He refers to recent research regarding declarative and procedural memory, relating it to preconscious and unconscious motivation. He reviews the influence of normal and pathological attachment on the HPA system, including the evidence that chronic stress may induce biochemical and hormonal alterations that, in turn, influence the structure of the hippocampus. He cites the evidence for central nervous system structures involved in cognitive control and emotional loss of control, and the influence of psychotherapeutic interventions on modifications in these cerebral functions and structures. He is sharply critical of the lack of empirical research to test psychoanalytic hypotheses, in the face of growing evidence of the relationship between neurobiological and psychodynamic functions. Kandel conveys the impression that he sees psychoanalysis at a crossroads: it may evolve into a basic science of human behaviour, or else it may eliminate itself, as a psychological system isolated from the development of neurosciences and other scientific fields at the boundary of psychoanalysis.

I believe these two articles point to the two poles of the contemporary critique of psychoanalysis: at one extreme, we find a popular culture that has abandoned its concern with individuality and subjectivity in a search for pragmatic adaptation, a culture where a combination of 'Freud bashing' and playing into the simplest layers of conventional wisdom are used to belittle psychoanalysis. This cultural development is indirectly supported by the critique of psychoanalysis derived from academic developments in cognitive-behavioural psychology, on the one hand, and the advances of psychopharmacological approaches to mental illness on the other. The financial constraints on long-term psychotherapeutic interventions, throughout the most advanced countries where psychoanalysis has flourished, provide an important motivation for those critiques.

At the other extreme, the most advanced developments in the neurosciences, the recognition of the importance of matching sophisticated research on brain structure and functions with equally sophisticated research on psychological motivation and structures poses urgent questions and challenges to psychoanalysis. Addressing these questions may significantly strengthen its position, together with neurobiology, as a fundamental pillar of our knowledge of the human mind.

We are thus faced with urgent challenges that, I believe, may either help to assure the future of psychoanalysis as a science, a profession, and a treatment method, or else, should we fail to live up to those challenges, limit psychoanalysis to remaining a fundamental contribution to the cultural and philosophical heritage of the twentieth century. Freud's contributions, I am certain, will survive as a most important contribution to our understanding of the human being, regardless of the future developments of psychoanalysis as a science. However, the future developments of psychoanalytic science itself and its applications, both clinical and as an instrument of research on the social and cultural conflicts of mankind, are not yet assured.

In our efforts to develop psychoanalysis as a science, a profession, and a treatment method, we are faced by both external constraints and constraints within the psychoanalytic community. Constraints external to the field of psychoanalysis are scientific, cultural and political, and financial. Within the scientific realm, biological psychiatry has posed important challenges to psychoanalytic theories of psychopathology. For example, the evidence for biological determinants of depression, the pathology of neurochemical systems that trigger abnormal depressive affect with corresponding neurobiological and psychophysiological consequences, demands an integration of those findings with psychodynamic theories of depression. In fact, the findings regarding normal and pathological attachment and the neurochemical consequences of prolonged object loss create a potential bridge between biological and psychodynamic determinants of depression. The infant's objective behaviour in insecure attachment, the subjectively experienced loss of an object or loss of love by an external object, the internalized loss of the love by the object represented by severe superego pressures, all constitute a potential continuum of aetiological factors. We need to explore this continuum in our theory development, and in research, as well as in our clinical approach to patients. The effects of antidepressant medication in the context of psychoanalysis and psychoanalytic psychotherapy need to be re-examined in the light of such theory and hypothesis building.

A second example is obsessive-compulsive neurosis, an area where psychoanalysis made pioneering contributions many years ago, but has more recently left the field to the biological sciences. There is abundant clinical evidence of the effectiveness of psychoanalysis in treating obsessive-compulsive personality structure, but not for severe obsessive-compulsive symptomatology that seriously affects free associations. This is an area that demands our renewed attention, particularly in the light of the effectiveness of SSRI medication in some cases. Psychoanalysis has made significant advances in the treatment of personality disorders and in reducing neurotic symptoms secondary to such disorders. At the same time, the neurobiological advances and psychopharmacological treatment of anxiety states and depressive reactions point to the mutual influences of affective disturbances and personality disorders that may be clarified by complementary psychoanalytic and neurobiological research.

Psychoanalytic research on infant development and affective communication have established other bridges with neurobiology, particularly regarding cognitive development, symbolization, and communication on the one hand, and the nature of clinical interactions, the psychology of empathy, projective identification, and psychotherapeutic change, on the other.

Regarding the challenges to psychoanalysis as a treatment method, the effectiveness of psychoanalysis – or rather, the specificity of psychoanalytic treatment in bringing about fundamental personality change – needs to be related to the changes obtained by psychopharmacological means, cognitive-behaviour therapies, and relatively non-specific psychosocial interventions. It may seem trivial to state this at a time when psychoanalysis is under strong pressure from insurance companies and governmental agencies to provide empirical evidence of effectiveness and is being questioned because of its high cost and long duration. Thanks to the work of a relatively small number of researchers, mostly concentrated in the US, Germany, the UK, and the Scandinavian countries, we have advanced significantly in demonstrating the effectiveness of psychoanalytic treatment and psychoanalytic psychotherapy, and the relationship between psychoanalytic process and outcome. But, still much remains to be done in this field. A concerted international effort in carrying out systematic research on the relationship between process and outcome, and on empirically validated comparative outcome studies, I believe, is an urgent task for the psychoanalytic community. Major constraints, in this regard, are the relative slowness with which we have been able to develop appropriate research methodology, and the length of psychoanalytic treatment that allows for unaccounted-for variables to complicate our evaluation of process and outcome. This contrasts with the relative ease with which shorter, non-analytic therapeutic methods with relatively simple, quantifiable interventions have shown effectiveness, and thus expanded their influence.

Constraints in the cultural and political field include not only the culturally dominant anti-subjective mood referred to earlier, but also the negative reactions that wild psychotherapies supposedly based on psychoanalytic principles have caused in many countries. The chaotic nature of the psychotherapeutic field, particularly in countries where poorly trained psychotherapists use idiosyncratic modifications or applications of psychoanalytic theory - coupled with a relative isolation of psychoanalytic institutions from the universities - has created massive scepticism within academic circles, the media, the public at large. This poses a real threat to psychoanalytic practice. The recent efforts of psychoanalytic societies and institutes to increase their contacts with their academic and cultural environment have partially counteracted these negative tendencies. In the long run, however, it is scientific progress in psychoanalysis and derived psychotherapies, such that their scientific strength is recognized by the related disciplines in university settings, which I believe will influence culture at large and assure the position of psychoanalysis, while protecting the public from questionable therapeutic practices.

One could argue that a most important, underlying, latent yet permanent external constraint and challenge to psychoanalysis is derived from the revolutionary contributions of psychoanalysis to our understanding of the individual as well as culture and society. I am referring to the very points ironically dismissed in the article by McGinn: the culture shock derived from the psychoanalytic discovery of the importance of unconscious motivation and unconscious repression; the shocked indignation that the discovery of infantile sexuality produces to this day; the resistance to acknowledging the fundamental nature of what Freud described as the death drive - the profoundly destructive and self-destructive tendencies of mankind that were so abundantly evident in the historical developments of the twentieth century.

Undoubtedly, the permanent difficulty in accepting fundamental psychoanalytic truths has something to do with the perennial attacks on psychoanalysis. However, it would be self-defeating to dismiss the objective nature of the challenges that I referred to before, by pointing to cultural resistances and their unconscious motivation. If psychoanalysis does not live up to the challenges referred to before, it will be because of its lack of objective response to them, thus leaving profoundly motivated prejudices and biases untouched.

There are also important internal obstacles to psychoanalysis confronting the external challenges mentioned. To begin with, the very private, intimate and subjective nature of psychoanalytic treatment, and the private, isolated way in which this treatment is carried out produce powerful resistances against systematic research and the demonstration of psychoanalytic results. It has taken many years to convince only a limited segment of the psychoanalytic community that ongoing recording of psychoanalytic sessions may be carried out without fundamentally disturbing the psychoanalytic process. Even to test the hypothesis that observation of the psychoanalytic process is possible without destroying that process itself has been hard to achieve.

The resistance to psychoanalytic research within the psychoanalytic community has many sources: the lack of training in scientific methodology within psychoanalytic institutes and some of the professions from which future psychoanalysts are recruited; the relative slowness of advances in appropriate research methodology; the difficulties in matching observable behaviour with fundamental hypotheses regarding the psychoanalytic process; the dramatic discrepancy between the slow and relatively modest progress in knowledge acquired through systematic research, on the one hand, and the extraordinary breakthroughs in psychoanalytic theory and practice achieved by our most gifted theoreticians and clinicians, on the other.

The ironical question: 'what has research done to influence psychoanalytic method and practice?' can only be answered honestly by stating 'so far, very little'. At the same time, the progress in the sophistication of research methods, and the breakthrough in studying significant psychoanalytic hypotheses - such as projective identification - outside the clinical situation proper, promise an acceleration of the development of knowledge derived from research, and a future where systematic research will, indeed, contribute to psychoanalytic practice.

To the constraints derived from the private, intimate, isolated, and subjective ambience of the psychoanalytic situation is added the important contribution of the culture of psychoanalytic education. Psychoanalytic institutes focus, in practice, on the transmission of knowledge, not on the generation of new knowledge; they have as yet not only neglected to attempt to develop new psychoanalytic knowledge as part of the educational process but implicitly have often also discouraged psychoanalytic research. Sometimes the very interest in psychoanalytic research has been interpreted as implicit doubt about psychoanalytic truth. Psychoanalytic institutes, in order to protect their autonomy, have also isolated themselves from departments of psychiatry and clinical psychology, and even marginalized those psychoanalytic educators and researchers whose prominence in university settings might have provided important bridges between psychoanalytic institutes and departments of psychiatry and psychology.

A few psychoanalytic institutes have developed departments of research, and have made a research focus a consistent aspect of psychoanalytic education. In most institutes, however, research methodology is just one subject among many others, and research does not represent a fundamental mission of the educational institution. The Research Committee and the Research Advisory Board of the International Psychoanalytic Association are carrying out the very important mission of educating and stimulating a network of psychoanalytic researchers throughout our international community, and several large psychoanalytic societies have independently undertaken to develop a strong research arm. It is essential that our efforts in this regard be intensified, co-ordinated, and become an essential part of the life of the psychoanalytic community.

An additional internal constraint has been the reluctance to develop therapeutic methods derived from psychoanalysis proper. While recognizing that psychoanalysis is not a universal treatment for all types of psychopathology, and recognizing that certain severe psychopathologies require psychoanalytic psychotherapy rather than psychoanalysis proper (or a combination of psychotherapeutic and psychopharmacological treatments, or the combination of individual with a family or group therapeutic process), a prevalent attitude has been not to investigate these fields within the realm of psychoanalytic institutes and societies. The fear has been that focused attention on such related and derivative fields might dilute the nature of psychoanalytic practice, threaten the identity of the psychoanalytic practitioner, and tend to confuse the work of psychoanalysts with that of less well, or idiosyncratically, trained practitioners in the sociocultural environment.

One consequence of this institutional attitude has been the abandonment of the psychotherapeutic field to psychotherapy groups that have entered into competition with psychoanalysis. A paradoxical development has evolved in many countries, where psychoanalysts have trained professionals from other fields outside the psychoanalytic institutions, eventually leading to the development of new groups and organizations of professionals who felt excluded from the psychoanalytic community, and motivated to develop their own, competing institutions.

One unfortunate consequence of the polarization between a small minority of committed psychoanalytic researchers, on the one hand, and a majority of committed clinicians, educators, and theoreticians on the other has been mutual ignorance and even hostility, which has damaged developments on both sides of this divide. Important developments have taken place in psychoanalytic theory and practice: for example, the reformulations of psychoanalytic theory derived from psychoanalytic object relations theory, and new developments in transference and counter-transference diagnosis and management. In contrast, empirical researchers operate at times within the framework of a psychoanalytic theory that is already dated and does not correspond to the latest developments in the clinical field. The 'monolithic' attitude of some empirical researchers, questioning the importance of non-empirical, clinical and hermeneutic research has led to a sense in large segments of the psychoanalytic community that their work is being ignored, that 'qualitative' research, in contrast to 'quantitative' forms, is not valued. The potential split between the clinical and the research community within psychoanalysis urgently needs to be overcome, because we need each other, and the future of psychoanalysis requires genuine collaboration.

Perhaps the most important internal constraint the psychoanalytic community faces at this time has been the tendency to 'circle the wagons', to focus defensively on our internal difficulties, on the differences between alternative psychoanalytic theories, on the political struggles within psychoanalytic institutions themselves, rather than focusing on the external reality that surrounds us. It is difficult to put this point very precisely, but there is a lack of systematic discussion about where psychoanalysis is going at this point, or how to respond to our external challenges, while, at the same time, an inordinate amount of energy is devoted to problems of internal organization, which indicates, I believe, this self-defeating defensive posture. As an illustration, much of the energy in the institutional efforts of the American Psychoanalytic Association is dedicated to the institutional relationship between the Board of Professional Standards and the Executive Council of the Association; or else, at the level of the International Psychoanalytic Association, a similar tendency exists to focus excessively on the vicissitudes of its internal structures and functioning, and not sufficiently on the relationship with our external world. It has happened that, when the International Psychoanalytical Association has taken initiatives regarding scientific activities in one or another region, such initiatives have been experienced as in competition with those of the same region. In short, with respect to psychoanalytic organizations, I believe that it is crucial that we direct our attention outward: the argument that we should clarify, first of all, our psychoanalytic identity, is questionable. I believe that it is in a constructive interaction with our environment that our identity is shaped and consolidated, both at the level of individual practitioners and at the level of psychoanalytic institutions.

One additional internal constraint has been the institutionally somewhat dismissive attitude toward applied psychoanalysis. Freud's creative awareness of the applicability of psychoanalytic discoveries of the unconscious world of the individual to the manifestations of the Unconscious at the level of culture and society has not received sufficient attention within the practical reality of our institutional functioning. Applied psychoanalysis has often been delegated to psychoanalytic societies rather than explored by psychoanalytic institutes (in countries where these are organizationally separate). While the most prestigious psychoanalytic function is that of the training analyst, the psychoanalysts working in the field of psychoanalysis applied to social issues, community mental health, history, religion, anthropology, art and literature, tend to occupy peripheral institutional positions.

Fundamental contributions within psychoanalysis to the psychology of small and large groups, to the understanding of ideology formation, urban violence, international conflict, the changing nature of artistic styles, religion, have often been neglected by our psychoanalytic institutions. Applied psychoanalysis has been left in the hands of a few specialists, rather isolated from the mainstream of psychoanalytic education and practice; and research in that area has not been enthusiastically supported by the psychoanalytic community. Here again, it is probably psychoanalytic institutes that should be able to channel significant interests, human resources, and even research support to psychoanalysts pioneering in all these areas. Or else, in those countries where psychoanalytic societies themselves carry a major burden of psychoanalytic education, they may take on this task.

Throughout this discussion, I have focused repeatedly on the responsibility of psychoanalytic institutes to take on the task of developing new knowledge and fostering psychoanalytic science. This university function of psychoanalytic institutes is, I believe, essential for the future of psychoanalysis as a science, a profession, and a method of treatment. Obviously psychoanalytic institutes do not have the resources for carrying out systematic research alone, and will need to establish inter-institutional and inter-disciplinary efforts, reaching out to local universities and academia, as well as engaging the psychoanalytic community itself in active efforts in this regard. We cannot expect all psychoanalysts to be simultaneously clinicians, educators, researchers, and theoreticians but our educational efforts may increase the number of those professionals who are willing and enthusiastically engaged in pursuing these efforts. Such an approach is in radical contrast to the traditional tendency, in many places, to look with some suspicion at psychoanalysts dedicated to pursuits other than psychoanalytic practice proper.

It is eminently reasonable on the part of many dedicated, experienced, profoundly committed psychoanalytic practitioners and teachers to be concerned over the possibility that much research undertaken outside the psychoanalytic situation may lose touch with the deepest levels of unconscious conflict and motivation, and dilute the observable manifestations of the Unconscious while attempting to research them. There is much premature, reductionist, even superficial reaching of conclusions on the basis of some limited empirical research on infant development, affect communication, psychotherapy, and observations outside the clinical psychoanalytic situation in general. All of this may be true, but does not invalidate the importance of advancing along the road of systematic research: qualitative and quantitative, clinical and hermeneutic, naturalistic and empirical. After all, there is also much idiosyncratic speculation and unfounded assertion reached on the basis of unsystematic clinical thinking.

In conclusion, we must unite our efforts, reconcile the implicit divide between practitioners and researchers, and explore the boundaries between psychoanalysis and neurobiology, thus strengthening the role of psychoanalysis as a fundamental science, and work across the boundaries with the social sciences as well. Continuation of our qualitative evaluation of individual cases and systematic research on process and outcome must go hand in hand. If we fail, psychoanalysis will have made its contribution to culture, and that, I believe, cannot be questioned. If we succeed, we will have assured the future of psychoanalysis as a science, a profession, and a method of treatment.

Index

  patient evaluation 161–3